PROGRESS WITH
CHEMISTRY 2

PROGRESS WITH
CHEMISTRY 2

Brian Stewart

Head of Science,
Matthew Humberstone Comprehensive School,
Cleethorpes

CASSELL

CASSELL LTD
1 St Anne's Road, Eastbourne
East Sussex BN21 3UN

First published 1985

ISBN 0 304 31223 1

Consultant Editor: David Browning
Editor: Christine King

Designed and typeset by DP Press
Sevenoaks, Kent

Colour reproduction by Hong Kong Graphic Arts Ltd

Printed in Italy by Tipolitografia G. Canale & C. SpA, Turin

Preface

There are many chemistry texts available to schools. One of the features that distinguishes the *Progress with Chemistry* series is its two-book structure. Book 1 contains those topics that are most basic and are needed by all GCSE candidates. The present volume, Book 2, contains topics which are found by students to be more difficult, and those which may not be required by all GCSE candidates. I believe this two-book structure will appeal to students with the wide range of abilities found in comprehensive schools, and it will allow teachers the greatest flexibility in designing courses.

The book is in three sections. Within each section, and throughout the book as a whole, the topic Units are arranged into a sequence that I feel is one logical way to organize the material outlined in syllabuses. However, this should not seem to suggest the only logical order of teaching the material: there will be as many different ways of using this book as there are teachers using it. Section I deals with atomic structure, the relationship between the properties of substances and their structures, chemical bonding, and the fundamentals of periodicity. Section II deals with important aspects of inorganic chemistry (in the context of the periodic table), with reactivity series, electrolysis, redox, reversibility, chemical calculations and energy changes, and with organic chemistry and radioactivity. Section III is concerned with industrial chemistry such as the uses of minerals, the manufacture of sulphuric acid and ammonia, and the petroleum and steel industries. There is a separate chapter on the social implications of industrial chemistry, its control and development.

With flexibility in mind, Units have been kept as short as possible. Summaries, extensions and revision questions have been included throughout the text. With the final examination in mind, a comprehensive set of questions from recent national and regional examinations is included (Unit 48). A major consideration (and constraint) in writing this series has been my awareness of the reading skills of pupils: great care has been taken to control sentence structure and limit vocabulary. I hope this sympathetic approach will facilitate comprehension and increase the appeal of the series to young readers.

Throughout this lengthy project I have benefited from the advice and practical help given by the editors Christine King and David Browning and I would like to express my thanks to them. I am also grateful to my wife for typing the manuscript and compiling the index, and for all other less tangible forms of assistance she has given me.

Contents

Acknowledgements

The Publishers wish to thank the following for provision of and permission to reproduce illustrations:

Accrington Tile and Brick Company (p. 196 *tr*)
Ardea London (p. 89 *br*)
D. Alan Beaumont (pp. 140, 150 *br*)
Blue Circle Industries PLC (p 198 *b*)
British Alcan Aluminium Ltd (p. 223)
British Museum (Natural History)/Geological Museum (pp. 14, 27 *l*, 96, 100, 190 *bl*, *br*, 195, 197 *b*) Crown Copyright p. 196 *bl*)
British Petroleum (p. 151)
British Steel Corporation (pp. 220, 226)
British Tourist Authority (Britain On View) (pp. 190 *tr*, 197 *t*)
Cavendish Laboratory, Cambridge University (C.E. Wynn-Williams) (p. 177 *t*, 177 *r*)
Bruce Coleman/Werner Stoy (p. 190 *tl*)
Colorific (Terence Spencer p. 194 *t*, Douglas Kirkland/Contact p. 194 *br*)
Crafts Council (A. Holloway p. 93 *l*, P. Harrison p. 93 *r*, P. Solven 194 *l*)
The Distillers Company PLC (pp. 169, 172)
Dunlop Ltd (p. 193 *r*)
Duracell UK (p. 101)
Esso (p. 213)
Gibbs Oral Hygiene Service (p. 89 *bl*)
Hadfield Ltd (p. 221)
Robert Harding Picture Library (pp. 31, 93 *c*, 150 *bl*, 182, 198 *t*, 223)
Imperial Chemical Industries PLC (pp. 132 *bl*, 202, 245 *br*)
ITT Semiconductors (p. 193 *l*)
Johnson Wax (p. 14)
National Coal Board (pp. 132 *tl*, 246)
Price's Patent Candle Company Ltd (p. 27 *r*)
Ann Ronan Picture Library (pp. 2, 47, 116, 132 *tr*, 133, 177 *l*, 240)
Royal Doulton Ltd (p. 196 *br*)
Bernard Salt/Environmental Science (p. 245 *tr*)
Science Photo Library (p. 91) (Dr Tony Brain p. 14, Dr G.J. Hills, p. 19 *l*, Dr G. Cranstoun p. 19 *r*, Martin Dohrn pp. 35, 89 *tl*, *tr*, Science Source p. 79 *l*, Dr H. Edgerton p. 132 *br*, John Walsh p. 245 *l*)
Shell Photo Library (pp. 79 *c*, *r*, 156, 162, 164, 171, 211, 214, 215)
Tate and Lyle PLC (p. 150 *b*)
Thorn EMI Lighting Ltd (p. 84 *l*)
Tioxide UK Ltd (p. 243)
Topham Picture Library (pp. 196 *tl*, 217)
United Kingdom Atomic Energy Commission (pp. 84 *r*, 231, 233, 234, 236, 237, 238)
Zinc Development Corporation (p. 103)

Thanks are also due to the following examinations boards for permission to reproduce questions from past papers. The origin of questions is also acknowledged separately in the text.

Joint Matriculation Board (JMB)
Northern Ireland General Certificate of Education Examination Board (NI)
Southern Regional Examinations Board (SREB)
Southern Universities Joint Board (SUJB)
The Associated Examining Board (AEB) (from Chemistry Syllabus I Nov. 1982 (paper 2, Q2, Q9), 1983 (paper 2, Q8, Q12), 1984 (paper 2, Q7, Q9); Syllabus II 1981 (paper 3, Q3, Q8) (paper 2, Q5, Q8), 1983 (paper 2, Q5), 1984 (paper 3, Q4); Integrated Science 1980 (paper 1, Q6)
The West Yorkshire and Lindsey Regional Examining Board (TWYLREB)
University of Cambridge Local Examinations Syndicate (CAMB)
University of London School Examinations Board (LOND)
Welsh Joint Education Committee (WJEC)

SECTION I

STRUCTURE, BONDING AND THE PERIODIC TABLE

John Dalton (1766–1844) laid the foundations of the atomic theory

Unit 1
Atoms and electrons

Atomic theory

Dalton's ideas about atoms allowed chemists to explain experimental observations and scientific laws.

For example, it was suggested that matter is conserved in chemical change (i.e. no mass is lost or gained) *because* atoms are indestructible (except in very special circumstances). Therefore, elements cannot be decomposed *because* the atoms they are made up of are indestructible; also in any one element all the atoms are chemically identical. Compounds have constant compositions *because* atoms join together in fixed ratios, and so on.

Of course, the atomic theory has been improved and changed to fit new facts from time to time. For example, Avogadro's ideas about molecules in elements were included very early in the history of the theory. We have been forced to change our ideas about atoms in the light of discoveries about the nucleus of the atom. However, we still find the basic ideas of the atomic theory very useful in helping us to understand chemical change.

- *Atomic theory is used to explain observations about elements, compounds and chemical change.*

Ionic theory

The ideas of ionic theory were put forward in the last century to explain the behaviour of electrolytes (see Revision Q2). Ions are considered to be atom-sized particles that have positive or negative electrical charge. In the simplest cases, the ions are single atoms with electrical charge. In other cases, the charge is shared by two or more atoms joined together.

- *Ions are atom-sized particles that have positive or negative charge.*

The question that we must try to answer at the start of this book is: *how do atoms get electrical charges*? We can answer this question with the idea of *electrons*.

A synthesis reaction: $\mathbf{H_2(g) + I_2(g) \rightarrow 2HI(g)}$

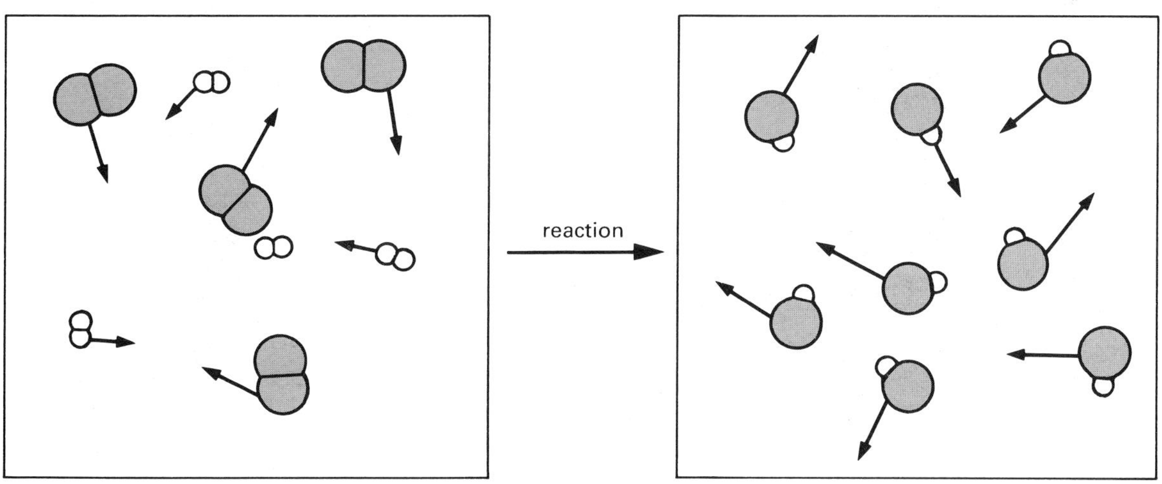

No atoms are lost or gained, therefore there is no overall mass change.
The compound formed has constant composition because all its molecules are chemically the same.

Atomic theory and chemical change

What are electrons?

Our ideas about electrons are something like this:

1. All atoms contain small particles called electrons.
2. Electrons are much smaller than even the smallest atom.
3. All electrons are exactly alike and they have negative charge.

● *Electrons are negatively charged particles found in all atoms.*

If all atoms contain negative particles, why aren't all atoms negatively charged? In fact, atoms are *neutral*. So, there must be a quantity of *positive* charge in each atom, as well as the negative charge of the electrons. In a neutral atom the positive charge must be just enough to balance (cancel out) the negative charge.

● *Atoms are normally neutral because the negative charge of the electrons is balanced by a positive charge in the atom.*

The positive charge is thought to be found in a central part (called the *nucleus*) of the atom. The electrons are thought to be found nearer the outside of the atom.

You will learn more about the structure of atoms in Unit 2. At this stage we will concentrate on the electrons.

Adding extra electrons to atoms

Suppose an atom has a certain number of electrons when it is neutral. What would be the result of adding one or two extra electrons?

The most obvious result would be that the positive and negative charges in the atom would no longer cancel out. There wouldn't be enough positive charge to balance the negative charge of the extra electrons. The atom as a whole would no longer be neutral. It would become a *negatively charged atom*. In other words, it would become a *negative ion*. So this is how we think negative ions are formed.

● *Atoms are converted into negative ions if they gain extra electrons.*

Removing electrons from atoms

Positive ions are formed in the opposite way to negative ions. If an atom *loses* one or two electrons, there will be 'too much' positive charge in the atom; the positive charge will no longer be balanced by the negative charge of the electrons. So the atom will become positively charged: a positive ion will be formed.

● *Positive ions are formed when atoms lose electrons.*

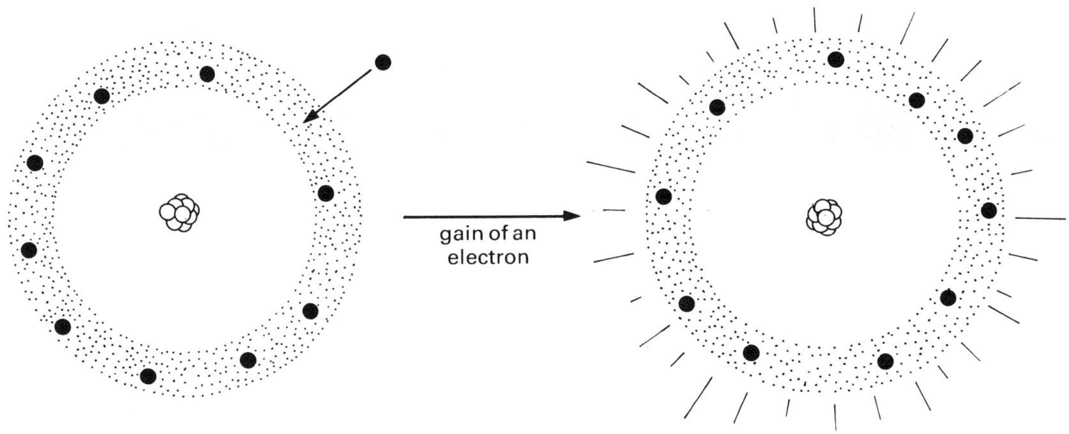

Neutral atom:
negative charge of electrons balanced by positive charge in centre of atom.

Negative ion:
too much negative charge for the amount of positive charge.

Changing an atom into a negative ion

Summary

1. Atomic theory is used to explain observations about elements, compounds and chemical change.
2. Ions are atom-sized particles that have positive or negative charge.
3. Electrons are negatively charged particles found in all atoms.
4. Atoms are normally neutral because the negative charge of the electrons is balanced by a positive charge in the atom.
5. Atoms are converted into negative ions if they gain electrons.
6. Positive ions are formed when atoms lose electrons.

Extension

1. Suppose atoms of an element X usually form *negative* ions. Would this happen by *loss* or *gain* of electrons?
2. Suppose atoms of element Y usually form *positive* ions. Would this happen by *loss* or *gain* of electrons?
3. Imagine what might happen if an atom of X bumped into an atom of Y! Complete the following word equation to show a possible result of such a collision:

   atom of X + atom of Y → negative ion of ____ + ______ ______.

4. Explain what has happened to the electrons that are involved in the above change.

Revision

1. The illustration on p. 3 shows an artist's impression of the molecules changing in a reaction. Draw similar pictures to show the molecules changing in the following reactions:

   i $2H_2(g) + O_2(g) \rightarrow 2H_2O(g)$

   ii $2CO(g) + O_2(g) \rightarrow 2CO_2(g)$

   iii $N_2(g) + 3H_2(g) \rightarrow 2NH_3(g)$

2. The ideas of the ionic theory were put forward in Book 1 (Unit 19) to explain the behaviour of electrolytes. How do electrolytes behave? You will recall that:

   i electrolytes only conduct electricity when in *liquid* form;
   ii metals are generally formed at the negative electrode, and non-metals at the positive electrode, during electrolysis.

   a Which part of the ionic theory explains i above?
   b Which part of the ionic theory explains ii above?
   c Which element is usually the exception to ii above?

   (Note: ionic bonding is the subject of Unit 8 in this book.)

3. Look at 'Changing an atom into a negative ion' (p. 4). Draw a similar picture to show what happens when an atom is changed into a positive ion.

Unit 2
Nuclear atoms

The nucleus of the atom

In the last Unit we learned that the negative charge of electrons in atoms is balanced by a positive charge. Experiments have shown that the positive charge is contained in a tiny solid mass in the centre of the atom. This centre of the atom is called the *nucleus*.

- *The positive charge of an atom is contained in the atomic nucleus.*

The rest of the atom is mainly empty space. The electrons fly about in the empty space round the nucleus. They cannot easily escape from it (because they are attracted by the oppositely charged nucleus). This idea is illustrated in the next diagram.

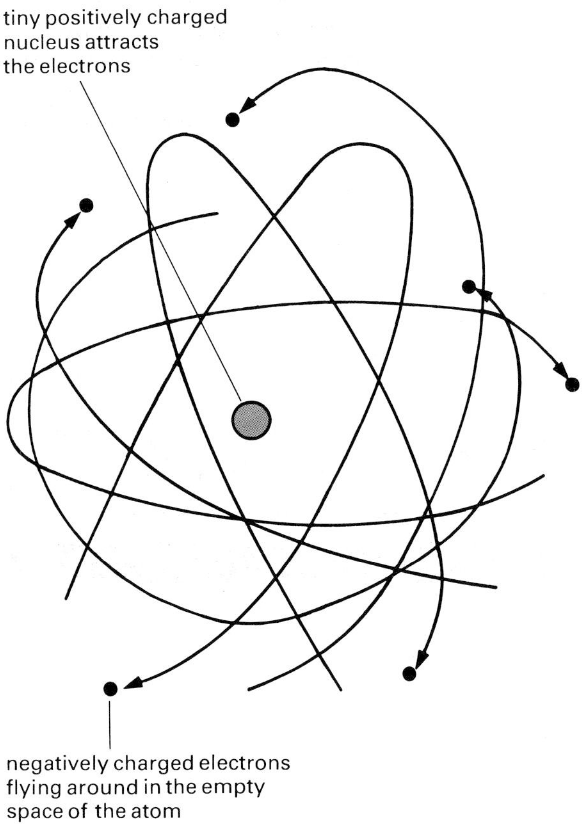

The nucleus and electrons in an atom

Protons and neutrons

We also believe that the nucleus has two different kinds of particles. Firstly there are positively charged particles called *protons*. One proton has enough positive charge to balance the negative charge of one electron. (The electron's charge may be expressed as -1 'atomic charge units'. In these units the proton's charge is $+1$.) So, a neutral atom has the same number of protons as electrons.

- *The nuclei of atoms contain positively charged particles called protons.*

Secondly, there are also some neutral particles in the nucleus. These are called *neutrons*. The neutrons act as a kind of 'glue' to hold the nucleus together. (You wouldn't expect protons, all with positive charge, to stick together in a nucleus, would you? Why not?) Usually there are slightly more neutrons than protons in a nucleus.

Neutrons and protons have almost the same mass, about one atomic mass unit (that is, roughly the same mass as one atom of hydrogen). They are much more massive than electrons. So, most of the mass of an atom is in the nucleus. The mass of the electrons in an atom hardly counts towards the total mass.

- *Neutral particles with the same mass as protons are also found in atomic nuclei. These particles are called neutrons.*

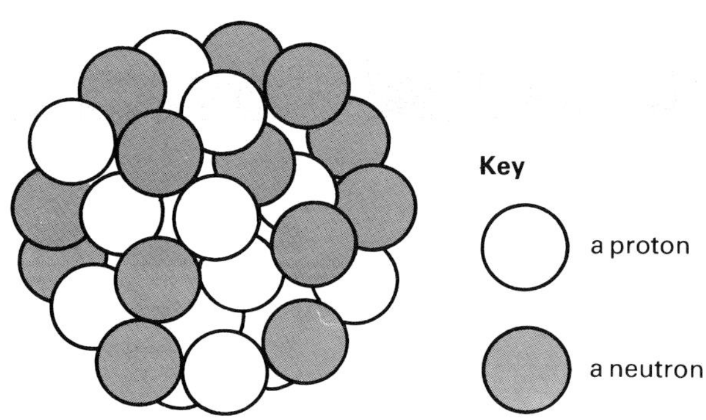

Protons and neutrons in a nucleus

Summary

1. The positive charge of an atom is contained in its nucleus.
2. The nucleus of an atom is made of particles called protons and neutrons.
3. A proton has a positive charge which is just sufficient to balance the negative charge of an electron.
4. A neutron has no charge but has the same mass as a proton.
5. The mass of an electron is very small compared with the mass of a proton or neutron, so most of the mass of an atom is contained in its nucleus.
6.

Particle found in atoms	*Mass (atomic mass units)*	*Charge (atomic charge units)*
electron	very small	−1
neutron	1	0
proton	1	+1

Extension

The three particles found in atoms are sometimes called *sub-atomic* particles.

1. Name two sub-atomic particles that may be found in the nucleus of an atom.
2. Name the sub-atomic particle that travels in orbit round the nucleus.
3. Name a positively charged sub-atomic particle.
4. Name a neutral sub-atomic particle.
5. Name a negatively charged sub-atomic particle.
6. Name the two sub-atomic particles that have almost equal mass.
7. In your own words, explain the meaning of 'sub-atomic'.

Revision

1. i What force holds electrons close to the nucleus of the atom and stops them flying off on their own?
   ii Why would protons not be expected to stick together in a nucleus of an atom?
   iii The nucleus of an ordinary hydrogen atom has only one proton and no neutrons. But every other kind of nucleus has more than one proton and some neutrons.
   Why are neutrons important in a nucleus with more than one proton?
2. You will remember having learned about John Dalton's atomic theory earlier on in chemistry. Dalton would probably have been surprised by our modern ideas about the nucleus and electrons in atoms. He imagined atoms to be much simpler than we now think they are.
   i Give a list of the main ideas that Dalton had about atoms.
   ii Describe how our ideas about atoms have changed since Dalton's day.
3. Copy out and finish off the following table.

Particle found in atoms	*Mass (atomic mass units)*	*Charge (atomic charge units)*
		−1
neutron		
	1	

Unit 3
More about ions

Here are the most important ideas we have learned about ions so far:

a ions are positively and negatively charged particles found in electrolytes;
b metal atoms (and hydrogen atoms) generally form positive ions: non-metal atoms generally form negative ions;
c positive ions are formed when atoms lose electrons: negative ions are formed when atoms gain electrons.

In this section, we shall learn more about ions, starting with the words *cation* and *anion*.

Cations and anions

The word 'cation' is the name given to a positive ion, and 'anion' is that given to a negative ion.

● *Cations are positively charged ions: anions are negatively charged ions.*

You may be wondering why ions have special names? The reason is easy to understand; the names of the ions come from the names of the electrodes in electrolysis cells. The positive electrode is commonly called the *anode*, and the negative electrode is called the *cathode*. During electrolysis, positive ions move to the negative electrode: negative ions move to the positive electrode.

● *Ions that move to the cathode are called cations. Ions that move to the anode are called anions.*

The electrical charge on ions

Ions are formed when atoms lose or gain electrons. Here are some questions you might have been asking yourself about atoms losing and gaining electrons:

1. What is the maximum number of electrons that an atom can lose or gain?
2. Is the same number always lost or gained for a particular kind of atom?
3. Are there any atoms that can form both positive ions *and* negative ions?

The answers to questions like these were worked out by studying the results of electrolysis experiments. Here are some answers:

1. Some atoms gain *one* electron when they form negative ions. Some gain *two*. A few atoms can gain *three* electrons. (The ions formed are called uninegative, dinegative and trinegative ions respectively.) But there are no ions formed by the gain of more than three electrons.

   The same applies to loss of electrons to form positive ions. Loss of one, two or three electrons is possible, but not more than three. (The ions formed are called unipositive, dipositive and tripositive ions respectively.)

● *Ions may be formed from atoms by the loss or gain of up to three electrons.*

2. All the cations in sodium chloride are sodium atoms that have each lost *one* electron. All the anions in sodium chloride are chlorine atoms that have each gained one electron. In other words, all the cations in sodium chloride are alike. And all the anions in sodium chloride are alike. The same usually applies to other electrolytes. (However, see Extension.)

● *Usually, all the cations in an electrolyte are alike, and all the anions in an electrolyte are alike.*

3. You might think from this that a particular atom can form only one kind of ion. This is often true; for example, sodium atoms can form ions only by losing one electron. But some atoms can form ions with different charges, depending on the compound they are in. For example, iron atoms can form cations by losing either *two* or *three* electrons. Some iron compounds contain iron

cations with two electrons-worth of charge, and other compounds contain iron cations with three electrons-worth of charge.

Most elements tend to form only positive ions or only negative ions. You will remember that:

- *Metal atoms generally form cations and non-metal atoms generally form anions.*

But there are exceptions. For instance, hydrogen atoms can form both cations and anions by either loss or gain of electrons.

Signs and symbols

We have already learned the symbols for *atoms* of some of the elements, for example:

Na for an atom of sodium
Cl for an atom of chlorine
Fe for an atom of iron
O for an atom of oxygen.

We can use the same symbols for ions formed from single atoms if we *add a charge sign*. This is how it is done:

Cations	Number of electrons lost per atom	*Anions*	Number of electrons gained per atom
Na^+	1	Cl^-	1
Fe^{2+}	2	Br^-	1
Fe^{3+}	3	O^{2-}	2
H^+	1	H^-	1

Ions formed from single atoms are called *simple* ions.

The names of simple ions

Cations and anions are named differently. These examples show the methods used to name them:

1. *Cations:*
Na^+ is simply called the sodium ion.
H^+ is simply called the hydrogen ion.

But, as we have seen, some atoms can form more than one kind of cation. The Fe^{2+} ion and Fe^{3+} ion are shown as examples in the table above.

Fe^{2+} is called the iron(II) ion (said as 'iron-two ion').
Fe^{3+} is called the iron(III) ion (said as 'iron-three ion').

(The numbers used in these names are called 'oxidation numbers', or 'valency numbers'. You will notice that, for these simple cations, the oxidation number is the same as the charge on the cation.)

2. *Anions:*
Cl^- is called the chloride ion.
Br^- is called the bromide ion.
O^{2-} is called the oxide ion.
H^- is called the hydride ion.
S^{2-} is called the sulphide ion.

- *For simple anions, the name ending of the atom is often changed to '-ide'.*

Discharge of ions

'Discharge' means 'loss of positive or negative charge'; in other words, discharge of an ion makes a neutral particle. A simple ion would be changed back into an atom if it was discharged. This process takes place at the electrodes in electrolysis.

- *Discharge of ions happens at the electrodes during electrolysis.*

How does this happen?

We know that ions move to the oppositely charged electrode during electrolysis. The cations go to the cathode and anions to the anode. What happens when they get there? The answer is, electrons are transferred to the cations from the cathode, and electrons are removed from the anions by the anode. So, two processes that happen during electrolysis are:

a migration of ions to the electrodes;
b discharge of ions at the electrodes.

These processes are illustrated in the diagram overleaf.

Migration and discharge of ions during electrolysis

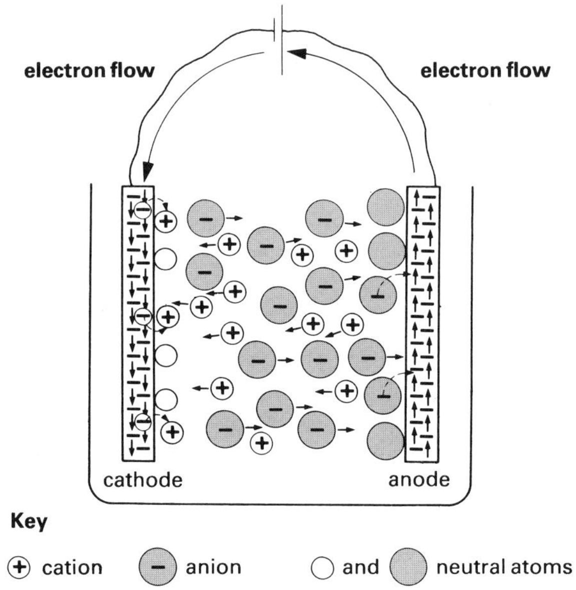

Note: Of course, the ions are not drawn to scale here. There should really be millions of millions of ions in the picture.

Summary

1. Cations are positively charged ions, and anions are negatively charged ions.
2. Ions may be formed from atoms by the loss or gain of up to three electrons.
3. Usually in an electrolyte all the cations are alike, and all the anions are alike.
4. Symbols for simple ions are made by using the symbol for an atom of the element, and a charge sign.
5. For simple anions, the name ending of the atom is often changed to -ide.
6. Discharge of ions happens at the electrodes during electrolysis; neutral particles are formed.

Extension

1. Salts can be prepared that contain more than one cation or more than one anion. For example, the salt $Cu(NH_4)_2(SO_4)_2.6H_2O$ contains the cations Cu^{2+} and NH_4^+. (You can see that the total positive charge of one Cu^{2+} ion and two NH_4^+ ions is balanced by the negative charge of two SO_4^{2-} ions.)

   Make a table to show the *names* and *formulas* of the cations and anions in the following salts:

   i $CrK(SO_4)_2.12H_2O$
   ii $KMgCl_3.6H_2O$
   iii $FeNH_4(SO_4)_2.12H_2O$
   iv $Fe(NH_4)_2(SO_4)_2.6H_2O$

2. **Complex ions**
   So far in this section, ions have been described as 'simple' ions. This question introduces the idea of 'complex' ions.

   Note that the words simple and complex do not mean the same as 'easy' and 'difficult'. So, what are *simple ions* and *complex ions*?

   A simple ion is one made from only one atom (e.g. Na^+ or O^{2-}). All the ions we have met so far have been of this type. But some ions are made from more than one atom. The atoms of the ion are stuck together, and the charge of the ion is shared by all the atoms in it. Ions like this are called complex ions. Some examples are shown in the chart on the right. Study it carefully.

   Now copy and complete the following table. (Use it as a reference table until you have learned the information in it.)

Name	*Atoms in the ion*	*Charge of the ion*	*Formula*
ammonium	1 nitrogen 4 hydrogen	1+	NH_4^+
carbonate			CO_3^{2-}
dichromate(VI)			$Cr_2O_7^{2-}$
hydrogen-carbonate			HCO_3^-
nitrate (or nitrate(V))	1 nitrogen 3 oxygen	1−	
nitrite (or nitrate(III))	1 nitrogen 2 oxygen	1−	
sulphate (or sulphate(VI))			SO_4^{2-}
sulphite (or sulphate(IV))	1 sulphur 3 oxygen	2−	

(**Note:** Oxidation numbers used in the names of complex ions do *not* normally correspond to the charge of the ion.)

Some complex ions

Shape of ion	*Atoms present in the ion*	*Charge of the ion*	*Formula of the ion*
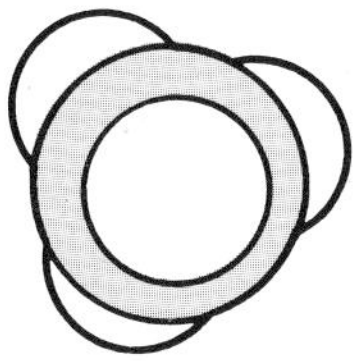	4 hydrogen atoms 1 nitrogen atom	1+	NH_4^+
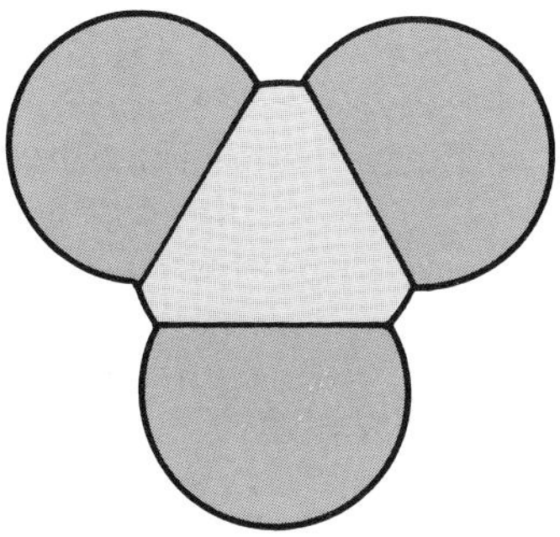	1 nitrogen atom 3 oxygen atoms	1–	NO_3^-
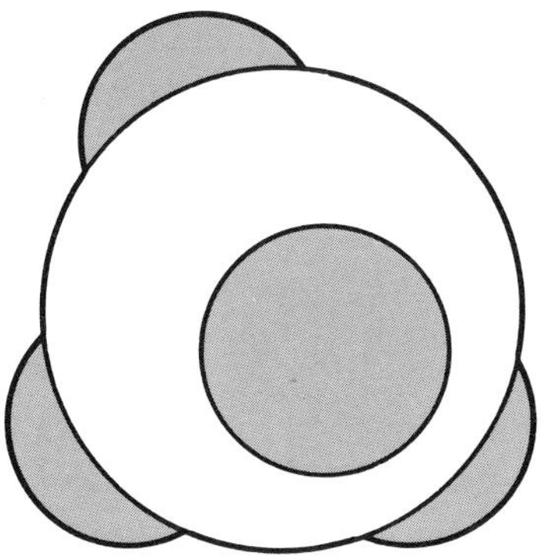	1 sulphur atom 4 oxygen atoms	2–	SO_4^{2-}
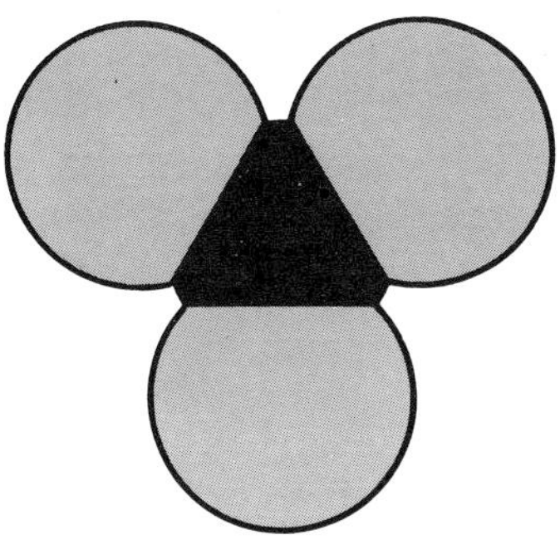	1 carbon atom 3 oxygen atoms	2–	CO_3^{2-}

Revision

1. What name is used for each of the following:
   - i the positive electrode in electrolysis cells
   - ii the negative electrode in electrolysis cells
   - iii positive ions
   - iv negative ions
   - v particles lost or gained by atoms when ions are formed
   - vi particles lost or gained by ions during their discharge
2. In each of the following cases, say whether a *cation* or an *anion* would be the most likely product:
   - i the ion formed from a non-metal atom
   - ii the ion formed from a sulphur atom
   - iii the ion formed from an atom by loss of one electron
   - iv the ion formed from a metal atom
   - v the ion formed from a phosphorus atom
   - vi the ion formed from an atom by gain of two electrons
3. This question is about the following ions:
   - *A* Fe^{2+}
   - *B* Fe^{3+}
   - *C* H^{+}
   - *D* O^{2-}
   - *E* Na^{+}

   Choose from the above:
   - i the ion formed from a sodium atom
   - ii the ion formed from an oxygen atom
   - iii the ion formed from an iron atom by loss of three electrons
   - iv an anion
   - v a cation formed from a non-metal atom
4. This question is about ions with positive charge.
   - i What name is used for *ions with positive charge*?
   - ii Copy and complete the table below. It shows the names and formulas of some common positive ions. (You can use this table as a reference table until you have learned the information in it.)
5. This question is about simple anions.
   Make a table (like the one below) to show the *names* and *formulas* of common anions. (Use it as a reference table until you have learned the information in it.)
   Include the following ions:
   - i Br^{-}
   - ii chloride
   - iii F^{-}
   - iv hydride
   - v I^{-}
   - vi nitride (N^{3-})
   - vii O^{2-}
   - viii phosphide (P^{3-})
   - ix sulphide (S^{2-})

Unipositive cations		*Dipositive cations*				*Tripositive cations*	
Name	*Formula*	*Name*	*Formula*	*Name*	*Formula*	*Name*	*Formula*
hydrogen	H^{+}	barium	Ba^{2+}		Mg^{2+}		Al^{3+}
lithium		calcium		tin(II)		iron(III)	
	K^{+}	cobalt(II)			Zn^{2+}		Cr^{3+}
	Ag^{+}		Fe^{2+}				
sodium		lead(II)					

Unit 4
Structure, volatility and forces of attraction

Crystalline solids

You will have found out about crystals earlier on in chemistry. Here are some observations about crystals:

a Crystals have straight edges and flat sides.

b Most solid substances can be made in the form of crystals.

c When crystals of a substance are prepared, they generally all have the same kind of shape: the crystals of the substance all have the same angles even when the shapes seem different.

d Generally, the crystal angles are a fixed property of a substance.

e Sometimes a substance can have more than one type of crystal shape. This depends on how the crystals are formed.

We should now ask some questions about these observations. Why do the crystals of a substance have fixed shapes? Why are the faces smooth and the edges straight? Can we explain why crystal angles are usually a fixed property of a substance? How is it that a substance can sometimes be crystallized in different crystalline forms? In other words, *how can we explain the facts about crystals*?

Organized structures in solids

There is a theory to explain the observations about crystals. It has to do with the arrangement of particles in solids. The facts point to this conclusion:

- *The particles in crystalline solids are arranged in regular patterns.*

We have met this idea before in the Kinetic Theory (Book 1). It was suggested then that the particles in solids are stuck to their neighbours and arranged in a pattern. (But liquids and gases have no regular arrangement of particles.) The pattern is called the *structure* of the solid.

- *The arrangement of the particles in a solid is called the structure of the solid.*

How does the idea of structure explain the facts about crystals? The illustration below shows how it would be possible to build up a smooth-faced, straight-edged crystal by keeping to a regular arrangement of particles. You can see that if every crystal were built up according to the same pattern, then the angles would be the same in different crystals. And if the same substance shows different crystalline forms then it must be because the pattern (structure) has changed.

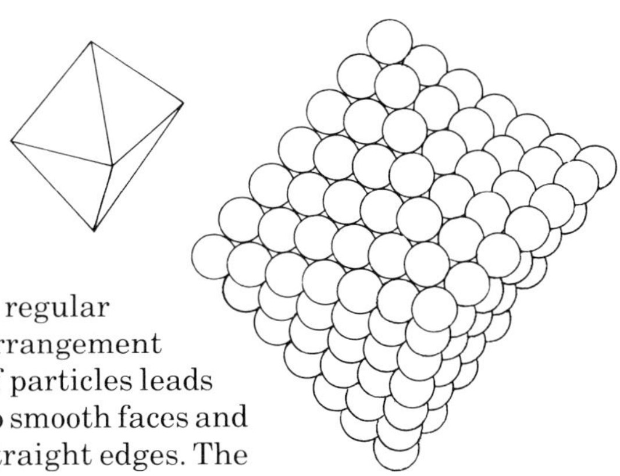

A regular arrangement of particles leads to smooth faces and straight edges. The angles will be the same in different crystals of a substance.

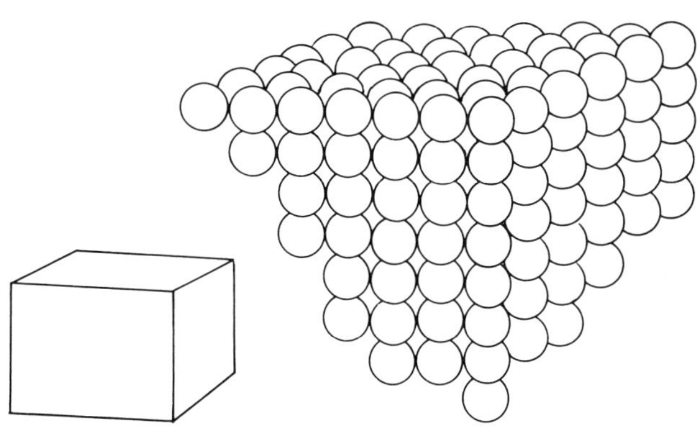

If the structure changes, different shapes are formed.

The idea of structure explains the facts about the shapes of crystals

Crystals of alum (left), galena (centre), and cerrusite (right) show characteristic crystal properties

Volatile substances and involatile substances

A substance that is easily turned into a vapour is said to be *volatile*. An *involatile* substance is one that evaporates only slightly at ordinary temperatures. As a rule, volatile substances have low boiling temperatures (and melting temperatures). Involatile substances have high boiling temperatures (and melting temperatures).

● *A volatile substance is one that evaporates quickly and has a low boiling temperature.*

It is interesting to compare the volatilities of different substances. Boiling temperatures can vary a great deal from substance to substance, as the next chart shows (p. 15).

Even substances that look similar on the surface can have quite different properties. The experiment described next is a simple one to compare the volatilities of two substances. The substances chosen look similar: both are shiny black solids. They are graphite and iodine.

You may be wondering what volatility has got to do with structure. What do experiments like the one on p. 15 tell us? Let us look at the ideas we have talked about so far in this section.

Air fresheners contain volatile substances

A tungsten light bulb filament (x 160) is very involatile

Elements				*Compounds*	
aluminium	2450	magnesium	1120	aluminium oxide	2980
argon	−186	mercury	357	ammonia	−33
beryllium	2450	neon	−246	calcium chloride	1600
boron	3900	nitrogen	−196	calcium oxide	2850
bromine	59	oxygen	−183	carbon dioxide	−78
carbon	4800	phosphorus	281	carbon monoxide	−191
chlorine	−33	platinum	4000	ethanol	78
copper	2580	potassium	766	lead(II) bromide	914
fluorine	−188	silicon	2700	methane	−161
iodine	183	silver	2200	silicon oxide	2200
iron	2900	sodium	890	sodium chloride	1465
lithium	1331	sulphur	444	tetrachloromethane	77

Boiling temperatures of some elements and compounds (°C)

Comparing the volatilities of graphite and iodine

Method

Heat small samples of each element in pyrex test-tubes.

Watch for signs of evaporation.

Result

Iodine

Melts easily at moderate temperature. A lot of evaporation to form a purple vapour.

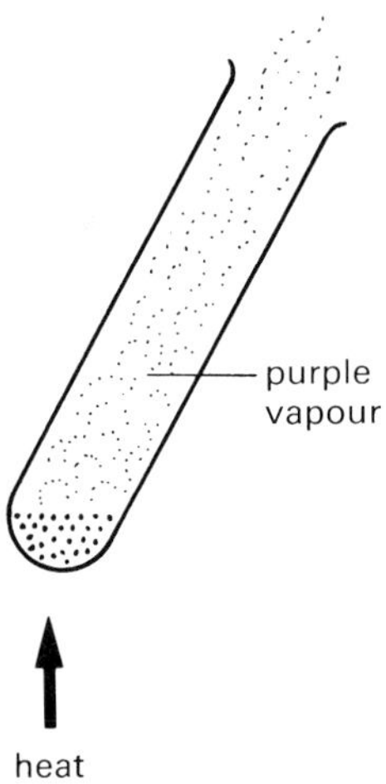

Graphite

No change even at high temperature

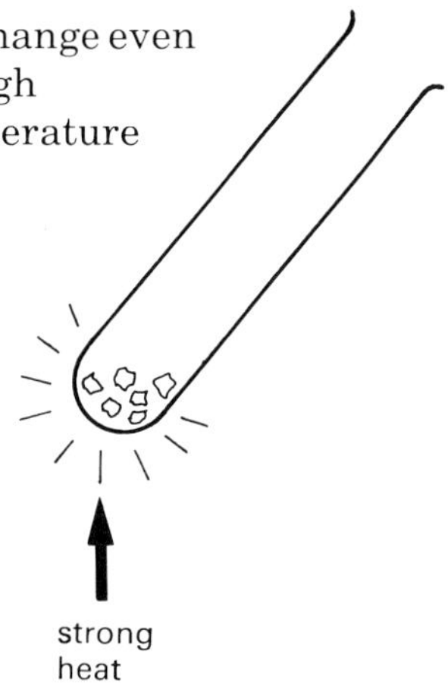

Conclusion

Iodine is quite volatile. Graphite is very involatile.

Note: You can check the boiling temperatures of iodine and graphite (carbon) in the table above.

Safety note

Iodine vapour should not be inhaled.

a Crystalline solids (like graphite and iodine) are considered to be regular arrangements of particles, that is, they are said to have structures.

b Some solids evaporate very easily. Others evaporate only with the greatest difficulty, that is, at very high temperatures.

So, here is an obvious question: *why are some structures easily broken down, while others are stable even at high temperatures?*

The forces holding structures together

To answer the question above we should think back to earlier work on the Kinetic Theory (Book 1, Unit 2.) Remember what was said about evaporation and melting then?

The Kinetic Theory picture of melting and evaporation is like this: as the temperature rises, particles in a solid 'rattle about' more and more. Eventually they can escape from their positions in the solid structure. When this happens we call the process 'melting', and a liquid is formed. As temperature rises still further, a liquid evaporates because some particles have enough energy to escape from its surface. More and more evaporation happens as the temperature rises because more and more particles have enough energy to escape.

But why do the particles need energy to escape? Why don't they just fly apart? The evidence suggests that the particles in the solid (or liquid) state are held together by *forces of attraction*. In other words, faster motion of the particles (caused by heat energy) is needed to overcome the forces holding the particles together.

So, to return to the question above 'why are some structures easily broken down, while others are stable?', an answer is:

- *Particles in volatile substances are held together by weak forces. Particles in involatile substances are held by strong forces.*

Although you can't really draw a picture of a force, the diagram below illustrates the idea of volatile and involatile solids.

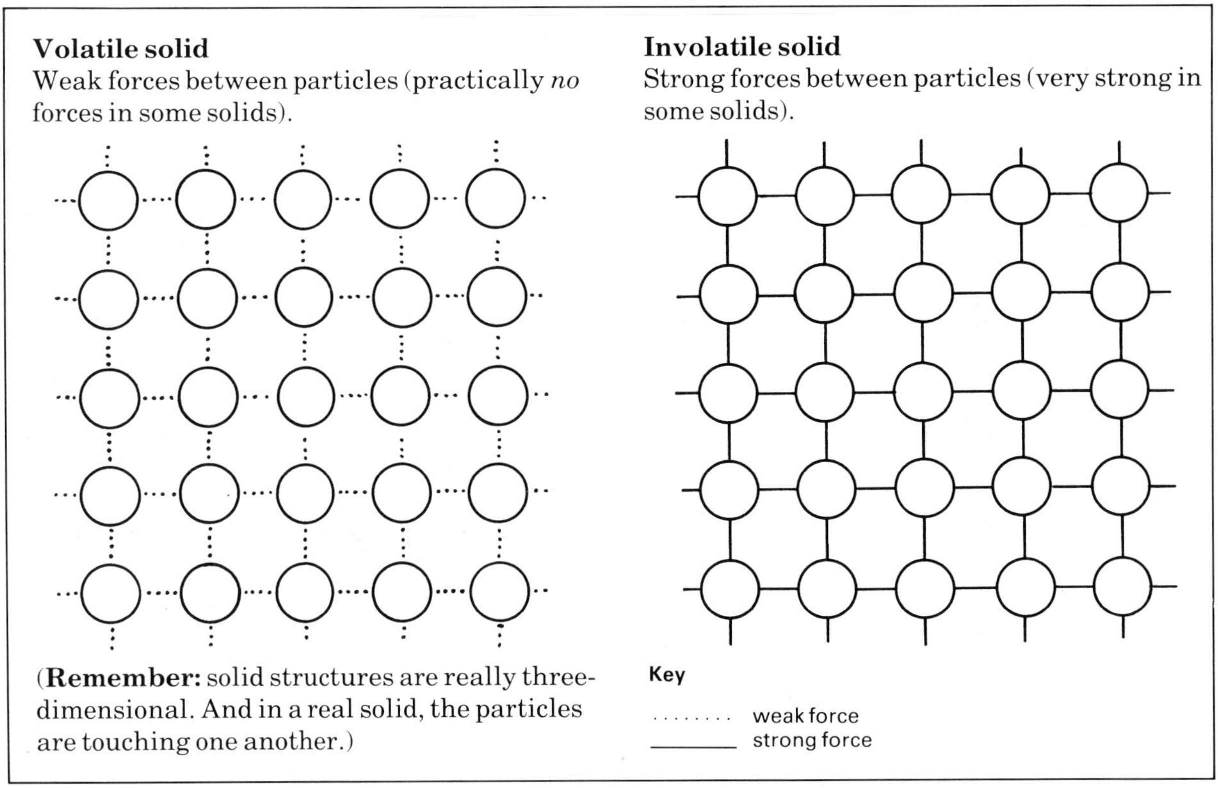

Volatile and involatile solids

Summary

1. Many solids are crystalline.
2. The particles in crystalline solids are arranged in regular patterns.
3. The arrangement of the particles in a solid is called the structure of the solid.
4. The idea of structure explains the facts about the shapes of crystals.
5. A volatile substance is one that evaporates easily and has a low boiling temperature. The opposite of volatile is involatile.
6. Particles in volatile substances are held together by weak forces. Particles in involatile substances are held by strong forces.

Extension

1. This question is about the volatilities of the following *metals*:

   lithium, iron, mercury, platinum, potassium, silver

   i Use a ruler to make a vertical scale similar to the one shown in the diagram. Mark temperatures on it from 200 °C to 4000 °C. Now mark the boiling temperatures of each of the six metals, and label each point.

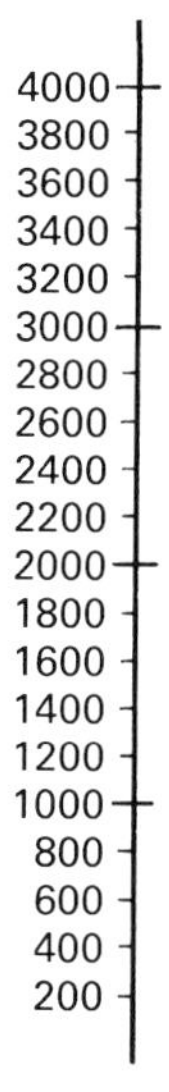

A temperature scale (°C)

   ii What is the *range* of the boiling temperatures of the metals on the scale, i.e. the gap between the highest and the lowest?

   iii Which of the metals on the scale is the most volatile?

   iv Which of the metals on the scale belong to the alkali metal family?

   v Name another member of the alkali metal family that is included in the chart on p. 15.

   vi Put the boiling temperatures of these additional alkali metals on the scale. What do you notice about the order of boiling temperatures of these three alkali metals?

2. This question is about the volatilities of the following non-metallic elements:

   carbon, chlorine, hydrogen, iodine, silicon, sulphur

   i Make another vertical scale similar to the one shown above. Mark the boiling temperatures of the six non-metals.

   ii What is the range of the boiling temperatures?

   iii Which of the non-metals on the scale is most volatile?

   iv Which of them is most likely to have the crystal structure with the strongest forces between the particles?

   v Which of the named elements is one of the halogens?

   vi Name the other halogens that are included in the chart on p. 15.

   vii Put the boiling temperatures of these additional halogen elements on the scale. What do you notice about the order of boiling temperatures of these halogen elements? (think about their atomic masses).

Revision

1. Arrange the following substances in order of volatility (with the most volatile first): carbon, copper, ethanol, iodine, oxygen, sodium, water.
2. In this section we have learned about the forces that hold particles together in a crystal. We have seen that you can work out

how strong the forces are from observations about volatility. In each of the following cases, i, ii, iii and iv, say which of the pair of substances has strong forces between the particles and which has weak forces:

i bromine and lead(II) bromide
ii neon and iron
iii sodium chloride and methane
iv carbon monoxide and silicon

3. We have tried to sort substances out into two classes: volatile substances and involatile substances. But sometimes it is difficult to distinguish between substances. There is no sharp dividing line between volatile and involatile.

Here are 10 substances. Sort them into *three* groups: (i) volatile, (ii) involatile, and (iii) intermediate volatility:

aluminium, argon, ethanol, iodine, iron, methane, phosphorus, tetrachloromethane, silicon oxide, sodium chloride.

4. This question is about the volatilities of the following compounds. (Most of their boiling temperatures are given in the chart on p. 15 in this section):

aluminium oxide, ammonia, calcium chloride, calcium oxide, carbon monoxide, lead(II) bromide, silicon oxide, sodium chloride, tetrachloromethane, water.

i Use a ruler to make a vertical scale like the one in the diagram above. Now show the positions of the boiling temperatures of the ten compounds named above (don't forget to label each point).
ii Underline the names of all the compounds on the scale that are 'metal + non-metal compounds'.
iii What do you notice about the volatilities of 'metal + non-metal compounds', compared with most of the 'non-metal + non-metal compounds'?
iv What do you conclude about the forces between the particles in 'metal + non-metal compounds'?
v Which 'non-metal + non-metal compound' is different from the others named?
vi What do you conclude about the forces between the particles in this compound compared with the other 'non-metal + non-metal compounds'?

Unit 5

Structures of elements (I): metals and the carbon allotropes

In the last Unit we started to learn about *structures.* You will remember that the particles in crystalline solids are arranged in patterns. They are held together by forces. In some cases the forces are weak, and in others the forces are strong. In the case of involatile substances the forces are strong. In this section we are going to concentrate on involatile *elements*, that is, elements with 'strong-force structures'.

Giant structures

'Strong-force structures in which all the particles are joined tightly to their neighbours' are called '*giant structures*' since in a substance with a 'strong-force structure' the whole of a crystal is joined up by a network of strong forces. Countless millions of particles may be joined together. So 'giant' structure is a good name for this kind of structure.

- *Giant structures are structures in which all the particles in a crystal are joined to their neighbours.*

Giant structure elements

There are two different types of giant structure element. It depends on what type of particle is joined up in the network. Nearly all the *metals* have giant structures. The particles in metal structures are *positive ions* (cations). A few *non-metals* have giant structures, for example, boron, silicon and carbon. The particles in these non-metal structures are *atoms*. (You will find out about what holds the cations or atoms together in Unit 10.)

Let us start with the metals.

Metallic giant structures

Most metal structures are based on a simple pattern. Each cation has 12 neighbours, that is, 12 other cations touching it. In fact, it is impossible to have more than 12 neighbours, if all the cations are the same size. This type of arrangement is called *close packing*. About 40 of the metals, that is, more than half of all the metallic elements, have close-packed structures.

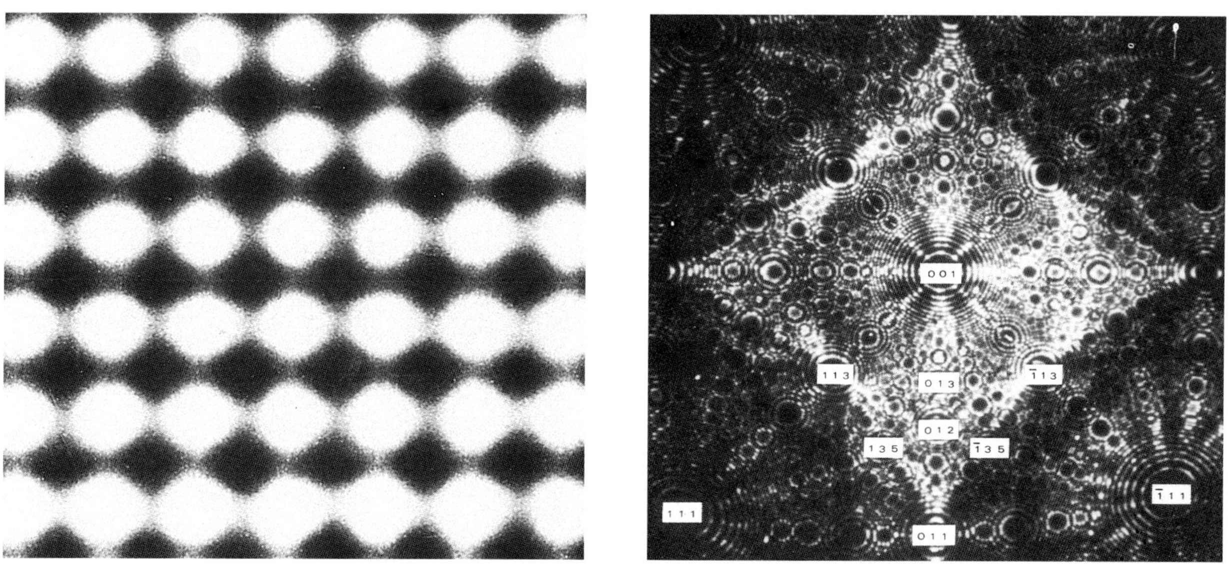

Metals have regular structures: gold lattice (left); iridium crystal lattice (right) (magnifications are approximately 50 million times and 5 million times respectively)

- *Structures in which a particle has 12 neighbours are called close-packed structures.*

The diagram below illustrates the idea of close packing.

The other giant structure for metals is one in which each cation has eight neighbours. The neighbours are arranged in a cubic pattern round the central cation. This is called the *body-centred cubic structure* (diagram right).

The alkali metals and iron are examples of metals with the body-centred cubic structure.

1. Every cation has six cations around it in one plane. (Try this yourself with marbles of the same size on a flat surface.)

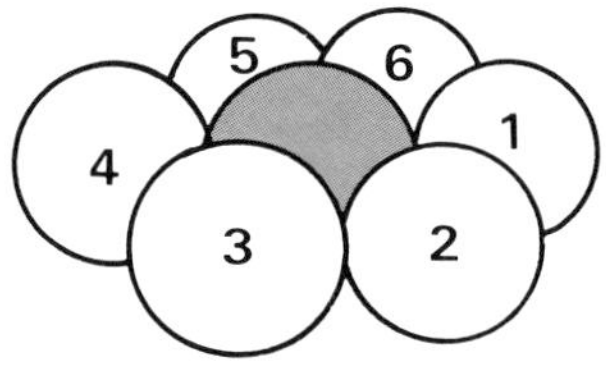

2. Added to this are three more neighbours on top, and three underneath. This makes a total of 12 neighbours.

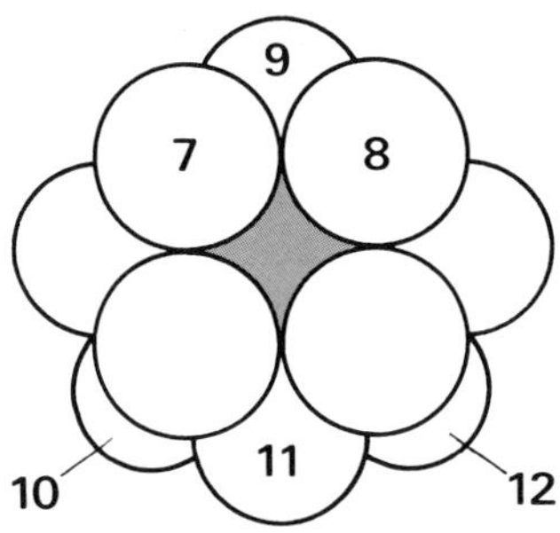

3. If this pattern is continued, the giant structure is formed.

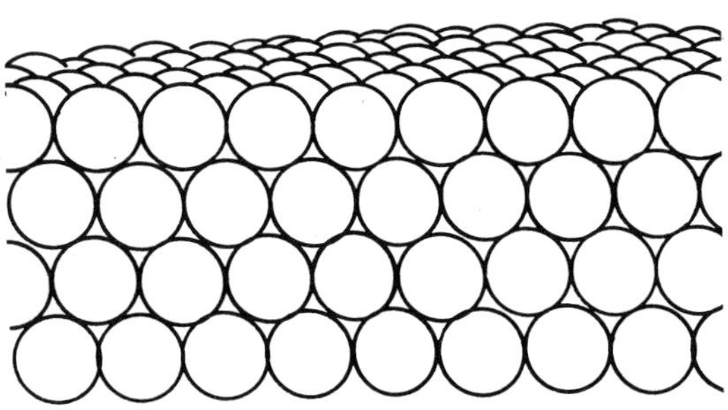

The cations are arranged in flat layers (planes). The layers are stacked on top of each other.

Close packing of cations in metals

Eight neighbours are arranged in a cubic pattern round the central cation ('C').

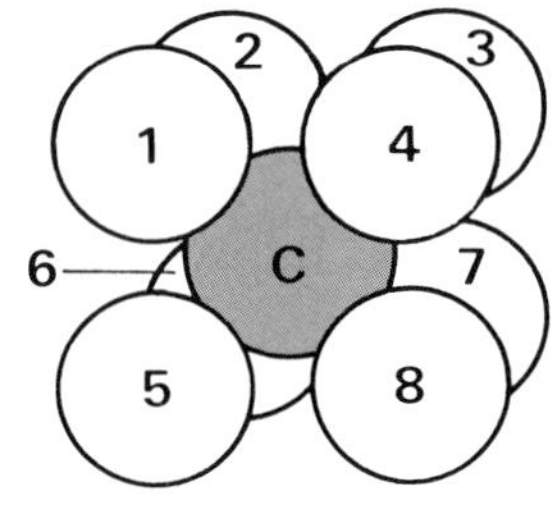

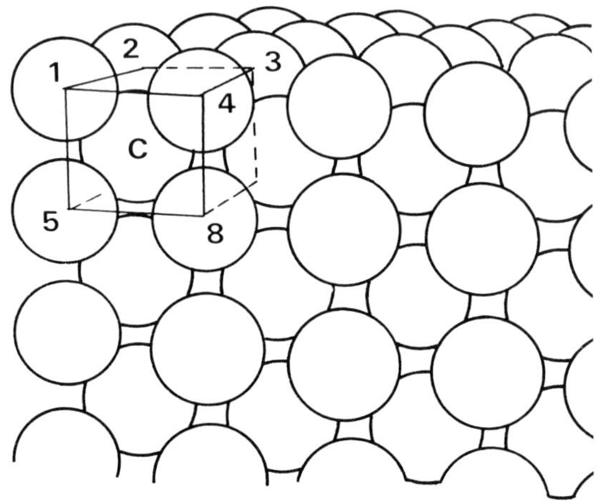

The body-centred cubic structure

Each atom has four neighbours in a tetrahedral arrangement.

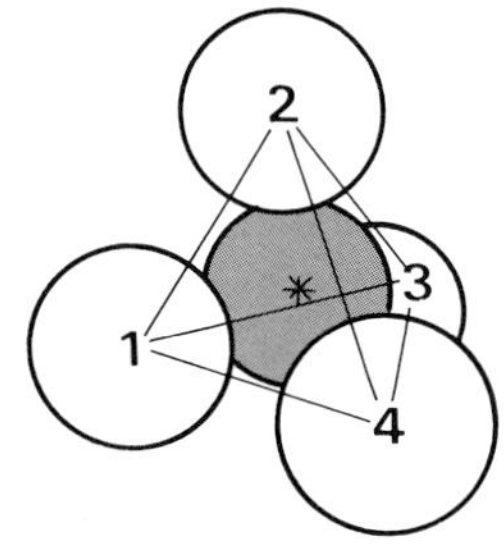

The pattern is continued to build up a three-dimensional structure like this:

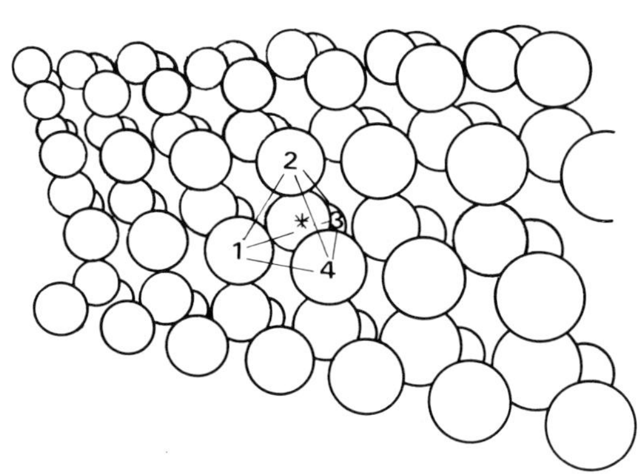

The giant structure of diamond

Non-metals with giant structures

Carbon is the most interesting of the involatile non-metals as far as structure is concerned. This is because it has the property of *allotropy*. We have met allotropy before (see Book 1, Unit 15):

- *When an element has more than one form (in the same state) the element is said to have the property of allotropy.*

The two allotropes of carbon are called *diamond* and *graphite*.

The atoms are arranged in planes in a hexagonal pattern. Each atom has three neighbours. The diagram shows a plane viewed from above.

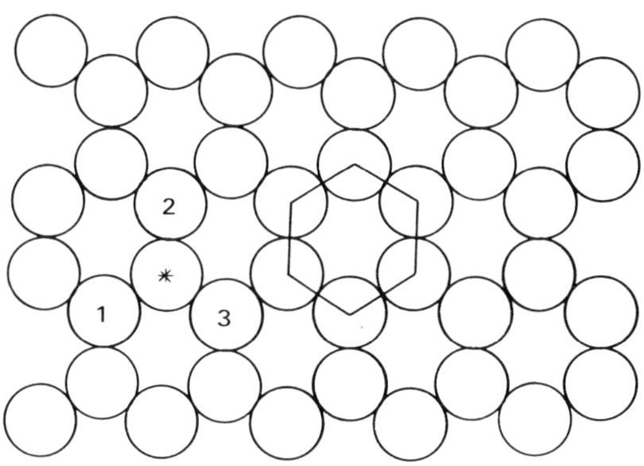

Each plane is a two-dimensional giant structure. Millions of these planes of atoms are stacked on top of one another. Only weak forces hold neighbouring planes together (but forces within each plane are strong).

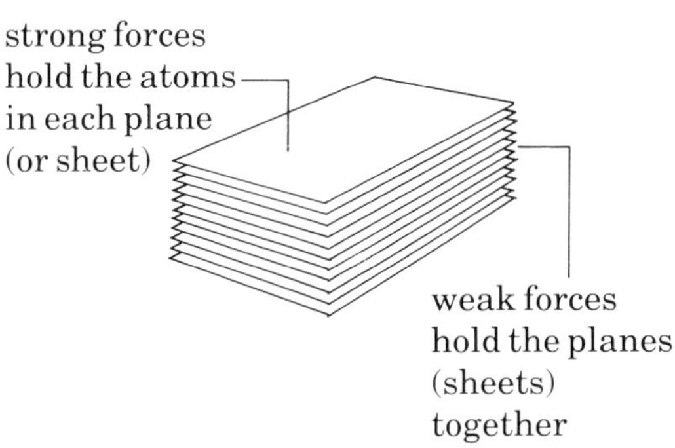

The giant structure of graphite

Why are the allotropes of an element different? After all, allotropes of an element are made of the same type of atoms. For example, diamond and graphite are both composed of only carbon atoms. In spite of this, diamond and graphite have very different properties. Why?

The answer to the question has to do with the structures of the allotropes. Both diamond and graphite have giant structures. But they are *different* giant structures. The same atoms are used, but they are arranged differently.

- *The allotropes of carbon (diamond and graphite) have different properties because the carbon atoms are arranged differently in each allotrope.*

A similar reason explains the differences between properties of allotropes of other elements.

Structures have been worked out for diamond and graphite. They are illustrated in the diagrams on p. 20 and on the left of this page.

The giant structures of non-metallic elements, for example those of carbon and silicon, are sometimes described as *macromolecular structures* (some *compounds* also have macromolecular structures).

We have met quite a few new terms in this section, terms like 'giant structure' and 'macromolecular structure'. The following chart should help you to get these terms sorted out.

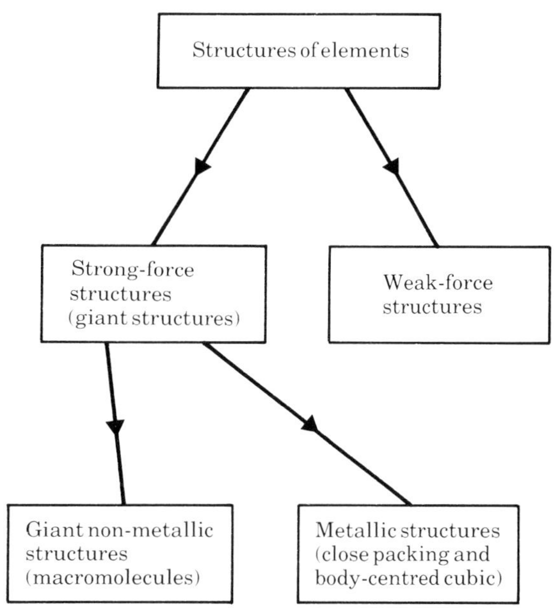

Summary

1. Particles in crystals are held to their neighbours by forces that may be either weak or strong.
2. Strong-force structures are called giant structures.
3. Most metals and several non-metals have giant structures.
4. The giant structures for metals are the close-packed structure (12 neighbours) and the body-centred cubic structure (eight neighbours).
5. The allotropes of carbon (graphite and diamond) have different properties because their atoms are arranged in different giant structures.
6. Diamond's structure is based on the tetrahedral arrangement of atoms (four neighbours).
7. Graphite has a structure in which carbon atoms are arranged in planes. Each atom has three neighbours.
8. The giant structures of diamond and graphite are examples of macromolecules.

Extension

This extension is about the properties and uses of carbon's allotropes, and how the properties of the allotropes are related to their structures.

1. If you scrape a piece of graphite across a white surface it leaves a black line. This is because traces of graphite flake off onto the white surface. How is this property used?
2. Diamond is very hard and scratches other surfaces. How is this property used?
3. What are the main differences between the structures of diamond and graphite?
4. Use the idea of graphite's structure to explain why it is soft and 'flaky'.
5. Use the idea of diamond's structure to explain why it is hard and 'scratchy'.

Revision

1. In each of the following cases, say whether the forces involved are weak or strong:
   - i forces between particles in a volatile substance
   - ii forces between particles in an involatile substance
   - iii forces between atoms in the diamond structure
   - iv forces between atoms in a graphite plane
   - v forces between planes of atoms in the graphite structure
2. A giant structure is a type of structure that:
   - *A* all involatile substances have
   - *B* only involatile metals have
   - *C* all volatile substances have
   - *D* only volatile non-metals have
   - *E* volatile and involatile substances have

   Choose one of A to E to complete the statement.
3. This question is about the following numbers:

   A 1   *B* 3   *C* 4
   D 8   *E* 12

   Choose the number that is the number of neighbours round a:
   - i particle in a close-packed structure
   - ii particle in a body-centred cubic structure
   - iii carbon atom in graphite
   - iv carbon atom in diamond
4. i What does the word 'allotrope' mean?
   - ii What are the allotropes of carbon called?
   - iii One of the main differences between the allotropes of carbon is that one of them is hard, and the other is soft. Which allotrope is hard?
   - iv What are the other differences between the properties of these allotropes?
   - v Name another element that shows allotropy.
5. Choose the ending that best completes the sentence:

   A macromolecular structure is a type of structure found in:
   - *A* metallic elements only
   - *B* non-metallic elements only
   - *C* compounds only
   - *D* some non-metallic elements and some compounds
   - *E* some metals, some non-metals and some compounds

Unit 6
Structures of elements (II): the volatile elements

In the last Unit we learned about the structures of the metals and involatile non-metals such as carbon, but what about iodine, sulphur, bromine and all the gaseous elements? What kind of structures have these volatile elements got?

Weak-force structures

The volatile elements have not got giant structures; the particles in the structures of volatile elements must attract one another only weakly. There is another important difference between these 'weak-force structures' and giant structures: the particles are not atoms or ions. Instead, the particles in 'weak-force structures' are molecules.

- *Volatile substances have molecular structures.*

Perhaps we should refresh our memories about molecules (see Book 1, Unit 4). You should know that the word molecule means 'a group of atoms joined together to form a particle'.

- *A molecule is a particle made from two or more atoms joined together.*

The molecular elements

Most compounds are made of molecules. In compounds the atoms making up the molecule are atoms of different elements. But many elements are also made of molecules; these 'molecular elements' have molecules made of only one kind of atom. Some examples are shown on p.24. Have a look at the examples given. There are several things you will notice:

a *several of the molecular elements are gases*
Hydrogen, nitrogen, oxygen and chlorine are gases. (Can you think of any other gaseous elements?) If you think about it, you will realize that a gaseous substance could never have a giant structure. Giant structures are features of involatile solids. In fact, we can make the following statement about gaseous substances:

- *Gaseous substances must be composed of free particles, that is, molecules or isolated atoms.*

Of course, the reverse does not have to be true: not all molecular substances are gases. Iodine and sulphur are molecular solids; bromine is a molecular liquid.

b *several of the molecules of the elements have two atoms*
All the examples given, apart from sulphur, have molecules with two atoms. Molecules with two atoms are called *diatomic molecules*. Bromine is a liquid element with diatomic molecules.

- *Elements with diatomic molecules are common.*

Sulphur has molecules with eight atoms joined together in a ring.

c *molecules can be given a formula*
A shorthand way of writing 'a molecule containing eight atoms of sulphur' is 'S_8'. This is called the *formula* of a sulphur molecule. Other molecules can be shown by a formula in a similar way. For example, hydrogen molecules have the formula H_2. This shows that hydrogen molecules are diatomic.

- *The formula of a molecular element shows the number of atoms in the molecule.*

Let us now return to the structures of the solid elements.

Solid structures of the molecular elements

Let us take iodine as a first example. As we have seen above, iodine is made of diatomic molecules. Iodine crystals have a structure in which the diatomic molecules are arranged in a

Element	*Molecule*	*Formula*
hydrogen		H_2
nitrogen	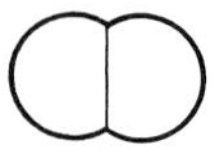	N_2
oxygen		O_2
sulphur	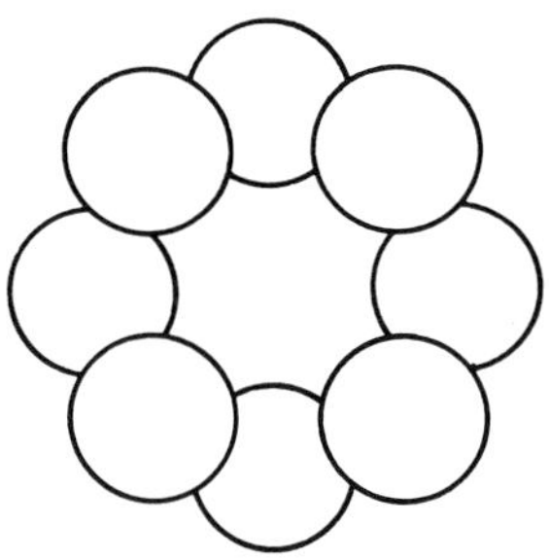	S_8
chlorine		Cl_2
iodine	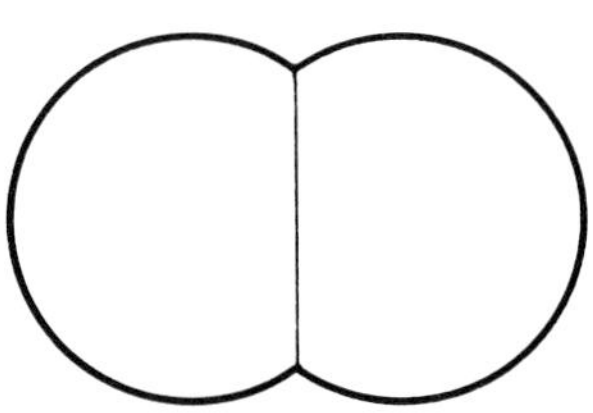	I_2

Molecules of some of the elements

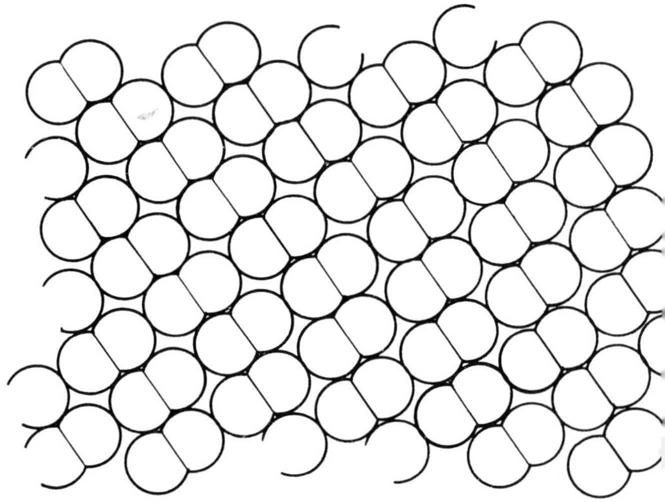

The crystal structure of an element with diatomic molecules

pattern. An idea of what this structure is like is given in the illustration above.

If the diatomic gases were cooled and crystallized, they would have structures similar to that of iodine.

What is special about molecular structures? We should make sure that our ideas are properly sorted out before going any further. This is the basic idea:

- *Molecular structures are 'weak-force structures', that is, the forces holding neighbouring molecules together are weak.*

So when a molecular solid or liquid is heated, the neighbouring molecules (particles) can be separated from one another easily. (Remember, this was not possible with giant structures. Particles in giant structures are not easily separated.)

The next picture illustrates the idea of a molecular substance evaporating.

The liquid in the illustration might be the element bromine. Bromine has diatomic molecules. The molecules fly apart easily; *but* the atoms in the molecules do *not* come apart. It is important to keep this in mind. The forces between the molecules may be weak, but *the forces holding the atoms together in the molecules are strong*. So the atoms in the molecules do not come apart easily.

- *The atoms in molecules are not separated during physical changes such as evaporation.*

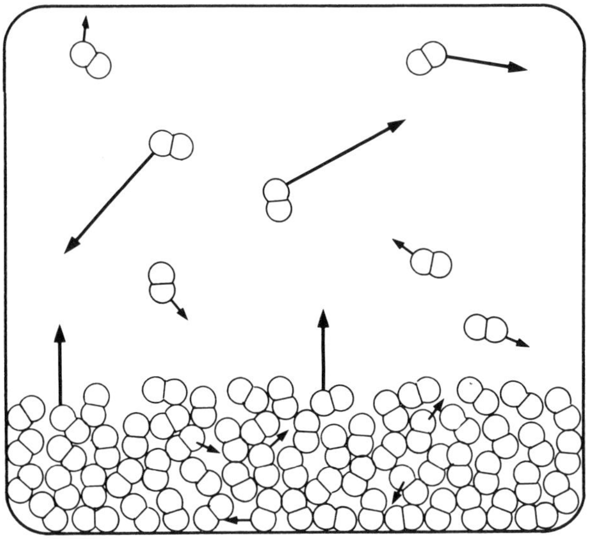

A molecular substance evaporating

Allotropes of sulphur

We have learned about the allotropes of sulphur earlier (see Book 1, Unit 15). Sulphur has two allotropes called *rhombic* sulphur and *monoclinic* sulphur. Unlike carbon's allotropes, sulphur's allotropes have similar properties. For example, the densities and melting temperatures of rhombic sulphur and monoclinic sulphur are only slightly different. Also, one sulphur allotrope is easily changed into the other. (Do you remember the idea of a 'transition' temperature? see Book 1, p. 68.) Again, this is very different from the behaviour of graphite and diamond. It is very difficult to change graphite into diamond.

We explained the fact that carbon's allotropes have very different properties by comparing their structures. We say that diamond and graphite have very different properties because their structures are very different. So, why are the allotropes of sulphur similar? This question can be answered using the idea of structure once again. The theory is that the sulphur allotropes have similar structures. Both monoclinic and rhombic sulphur have S_8 ring molecules (see p. 24). The only difference between them is the way the molecules are arranged. The patterns are slightly different above and below the transition temperature.

● *Crystals of monoclinic sulphur and rhombic sulphur both contain S_8 ring molecules.*

Summary

1. Volatile substances are made of molecules, that is, they have molecular structures.
2. Molecular structures are 'weak-force structures', that is, the forces holding neighbouring molecules together are weak.
3. A molecule is a particle made from two or more atoms joined together.
4. All gaseous substances are molecular.
5. The formula of a molecular element shows the number of atoms in the molecule, for example S_8 molecules have eight sulphur atoms.
6. Elements with diatomic molecules are common, for example H_2, N_2, O_2, F_2, Cl_2, Br_2, I_2.
7. The atoms in molecules are not separated during physical change.
8. Crystals of monoclinic and rhombic sulphur both contain S_8 molecules.

Extension

Whereas most gaseous elements exist as diatomic molecules under normal conditions, the noble gases occur as single unattached atoms. These unattached atoms are sometimes referred to as *monatomic* molecules.

1. The monatomic nature of the noble gases fits in with their unreactiveness with other elements. Explain.
2. The idea of monatomic molecules does not fit in with the definition of a molecule given in this Unit. Explain.
3. Write a definition of 'molecule' that can be applied to noble gases as well as to other molecular substances.

Revision

1. This question is about the following substances:

   A bromine *B* helium *C* methane
   D silicon *E* sulphur

   Which of them is;

   i not an element
   ii an element that forms no compounds
   iii an element that usually exists as diatomic molecules
   iv an element with a giant structure
   v an element with eight atoms per molecule
   vi a liquid element
   vii an involatile element
   viii a colourless gaseous element

2. i Substance X has a molecular structure. Substance Y has a giant structure. Describe how you would expect the physical properties of substances X and Y to differ from one another.
   ii Give two examples of elements with molecular structures.
   iii Give two examples of elements with giant structures.

3. This question is about the allotropes of sulphur.
   i What are the names of the allotropes?
   ii Explain why the properties of the allotropes are similar.
   iii What is a 'transition temperature'?

Unit 7
Properties and structures of compounds

Two types of compound

Compounds may be sorted out (classified) into two sorts (or classes); these are *electrolytes* and *non-electrolytes*.

● *Compounds can be sorted out into electrolytes and non-electrolytes.*

a *Electrolytes* are substances that conduct electricity when molten or when dissolved in water, but not when solid (see Unit 3). These facts about electrolytes are explained by the *ionic theory*. This theory says that electrolytes contain charged particles called ions. The ions are free to move about when the electrolyte is dissolved or melted.

Examples of electrolytes include salts such as sodium chloride, copper(II) sulphate, potassium iodide and lead(II) bromide. Bases such as sodium hydroxide and calcium oxide are also electrolytes. These are *involatile* substances. So we could deduce that solid electrolytes have giant structures.

● *Solid electrolytes have giant structures consisting of ions.*

b *Non-electrolytes* are compounds that do *not* conduct electricity, whether solid or liquid. So we would not expect them to be made of ions. Most non-electrolytes are *volatile* substances. Volatile non-electrolytes may be either solids that melt at low temperature, or liquids or gases at room temperature. Some examples are given in the next table.

low-melting-temperature solids	naphthalene, other hydrocarbons (like those in candle wax), sulphur trioxide
volatile liquids	silicon tetrachloride, tetrachloromethane, hydrocarbons (such as benzene and octane)
gases	ammonia, carbon monoxide, carbon dioxide, sulphur dioxide, hydrogen chloride, hydrocarbons (such as methane, propane)

It should be clear that compounds such as those in the table have *molecular structures*.

The molecules in low-melting-temperature solids are packed together to form a pattern. The forces holding the molecules to their neighbours are weak. We met this idea in the Unit on volatile *elements* (Unit 6). The basic idea is the same with volatile *compounds*.

● *The structures of volatile solids are made up by molecules packing together in a pattern.*

Salt is an electrolyte and is involatile

Candle wax consists of volatile non-electrolytes

Patterns of ions in solid electrolytes

Sodium chloride crystals

These crystals are made up of equal numbers of sodium ions (Na^+) and chloride ions (Cl^-). The ions are arranged in a pattern in the crystals. Each sodium ion has *six* neighbouring chloride ions, that is, six Cl^- ions are touching each Na^+ ion. Also, each Cl^- ion has six Na^+ ions in contact with it. The next illustration shows the *sodium chloride structure.*

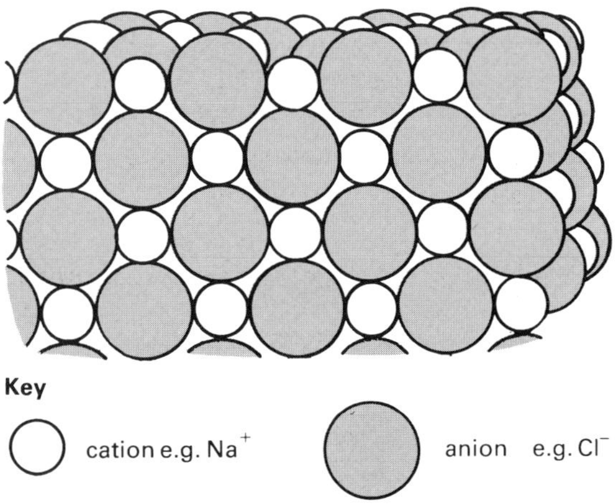

The pattern of ions in the sodium chloride structure

Other electrolytes may also have a sodium chloride type of structure. For example, calcium oxide has ions arranged in the same pattern. Each Ca^{2+} ion has six neighbours, and each O^{2-} ion also has six neighbours.

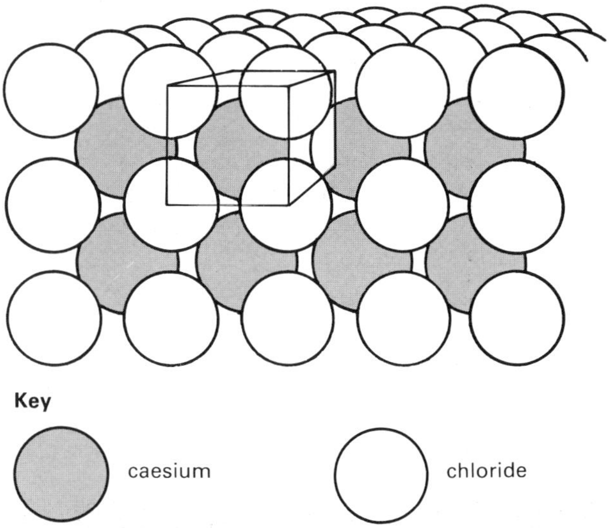

The caesium chloride structure

Caesium chloride crystals

The sodium chloride pattern is not the only way equal numbers of cations and anions can be arranged. The diagram below shows another arrangement. This is called the *caesium chloride structure*. Each ion has *eight* neighbours in this structure. The basic unit is a body-centred cube, that is, eight anions surrounding a cation, and eight cations surrounding an anion (see Unit 5).

Summary

1. Compounds can be classified into electrolytes and non-electrolytes.
2. Solid electrolytes have giant structures of ions.
3. Most non-electrolytes are volatile substances.
4. The structures of volatile solids are made up by the packing together of molecules in a pattern.
5. The sodium chloride structure and the caesium chloride structure are two common patterns for solid electrolytes.

Extension

1. Two simple structures for solid electrolytes are the sodium chloride structure and the caesium chloride structure. They are both structures of compounds of the AX type (where A is a cation and X is an anion) – in other words, compounds in which there are equal numbers of cations and anions.
   i Name the electrolytes A, B, C, D and E below:

   A CaF_2 *B* KCl
   C KI *D* MgO
   E NaH

   ii One of the above electrolytes could not have either the sodium chloride structure or the caesium chloride structure. Which one is it?
   iii Explain your answer to part ii.
2. Why do some AX compounds have the sodium chloride structure while others have the caesium chloride structure?

The answer is, the cations in some AX compounds are too big to fit in the holes between the anions. For example, Na^+ ions are smaller than Cs^+ ions. The Na^+ ion can fit into the hole between six Cl^- ions, but the Cs^+ ion needs a bigger hole. The hole between eight Cl^- ions is big enough. So, sodium chloride has one structure and caesium chloride has another.

The following table gives information about the relative sizes of some ions.

Ion	*Relative radius*
Na^+	9.5
Ba^{2+}	13.5
O^{2-}	14.0
Cs^+	17.0
Cl^-	18.0

i Draw circles (to scale) to represent the following pairs of ions side by side:

A Na^+ and Cl^-
B Cs^+ and Cl^-
C Ba^{2+} and O^{2-}

ii Would you expect barium oxide to have the sodium chloride structure or the caesium chloride structure? Give a reason for your answer.

Revision

1. Which of the following is *not* true?

A Electrolytes have giant structures of ions
B Most electrolytes are volatile solids
C Molecular substances may be solids, liquids or gases at room temperature
D Crystalline solids consist of ions or molecules arranged in a pattern
E Many non-electrolytes are molecular solids

2. This question is about the following numbers:

A 1   *B* 4
C 6   *D* 8
E 12

Which of the above numbers is the number of:

i anions touching each cation in the sodium chloride structure
ii cations touching each anion in the sodium chloride structure
iii cations touching each anion in the caesium chloride structure
iv atoms touching each carbon atom in the diamond structure
v cations touching each cation in the close-packed structure of a metal

3. In this section we have seen that most compounds can be classified under two main headings. The two headings are:

a electrolytes, e.g. sodium chloride
b volatile non-electrolytes, e.g. naphthalene.

i The following table gives data about some compounds:

Compound	*Conductivity of the molten compound*	*Melting temperature*
A	poor	low
B	good	high
C	poor	low
D	poor	high
E	poor	low

Which of the compounds in the table has the properties of an electrolyte?
Which of the compounds in the table could not be classified under either of the two main headings mentioned above?

ii Silicon(IV) oxide is an example of a compound that is not an electrolyte and is not volatile. It has a giant structure of atoms. It closely resembles one of the non-metallic elements, both in its structure and in its properties. Which one of the following elements is most likely to resemble silicon(IV) oxide?

A carbon (diamond)
B iodine
C oxygen
D sulphur (rhombic)
E zinc.

Unit 8
Ionic bonding

In this Unit we shall find out more about how ionic compounds are formed, and what holds them together.

Electrons in atoms

All atoms contain one or more electrons. All the atoms of a particular element have the same number of electrons. Different elements have atoms with different numbers of electrons. The number of electrons in a neutral atom of an element is called the *atomic number* of the element, and is characteristic for each element. The atomic number is given the symbol Z. The atomic numbers of some elements are shown in the next table, and a complete list is given in Appendix II.

The electrons in atoms are arranged in patterns. The pattern of the electrons is called the *electronic structure* of the atom. The electrons are arranged in groups called *shells*. The shells of electrons are at different distances from the nucleus.

- *The electronic structure of an atom is made up of shells of electrons.*

The electronic structures of some atoms are shown in the next figure. You can see that lithium atoms have three electrons arranged in two shells. The shell nearest the nucleus has two electrons. Potassium atoms have 19 electrons arranged in four shells.

Electronic structures can be given in a shorthand form, as shown in the next table. For instance, in the case of sodium (Na) the electronic structure is given as 2.8.1, which means that Na has two electrons in the innermost shell, eight electrons in the next shell, and one electron in the outer shell.

Atom	*Z*	*Electronic structure*
Li	3	2.1
O	8	2.6
F	9	2.7
Na	11	2.8.1
Mg	12	2.8.2
Cl	17	2.8.7
K	19	2.8.8.1

Stable electron patterns

'Stable' means 'difficult to change'. Particular numbers of electrons, arranged in certain ways, are found to be 'stable'. Elements with stable electron arrangements are unreactive because their atoms need a lot of energy (compared with other atoms) before their electron patterns can be disturbed.

The least reactive of the elements are the *noble gases*. The electron arrangements (electronic structures) in atoms of four of the noble gases are:

He	2	Ar	2.8.8
Ne	2.8	Kr	2.8.18.8

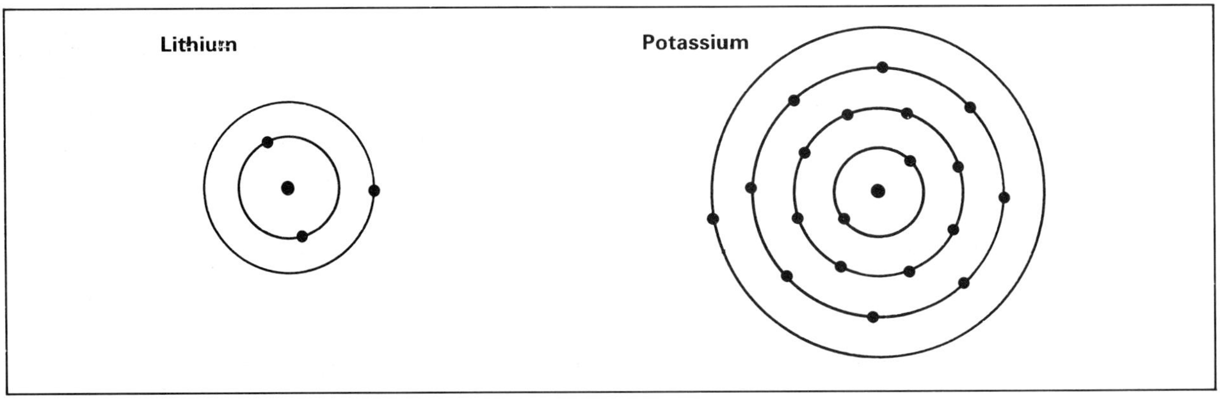

The electronic structures of Li and K

The noble gas neon is used in coloured lights, like those at Piccadilly Circus

You will notice that the outer shells of these atoms have *two* electrons (in the case of He) or *eight* electrons (in the case of Ne, Ar and Kr). These numbers of electrons are considered to be stable numbers for the outer shells of atoms. Noble gas atoms will not readily lose electrons or gain extra electrons, and this explains why noble gases are unreactive.

- *Noble gases are unreactive because they have stable electronic structures.*

Atoms of other elements can increase the stability of their electronic structures by chemical reaction. This can result in ion formation.

Ion formation

One way that atoms can get noble gas stability is by losing or gaining electrons. One or more electrons may be given to or taken from another atom in a reaction. The two atoms would have to bump into one another to transfer electrons in this way.

After the reaction, the atoms end up with either more or less than their normal numbers of electrons. In other words, they are electrically charged. As you know, electrically charged atoms are called *ions*.

- *Transfer of one or more electrons from one atom to another results in ion formation.*

The idea of ion formation is illustrated in the next figure.

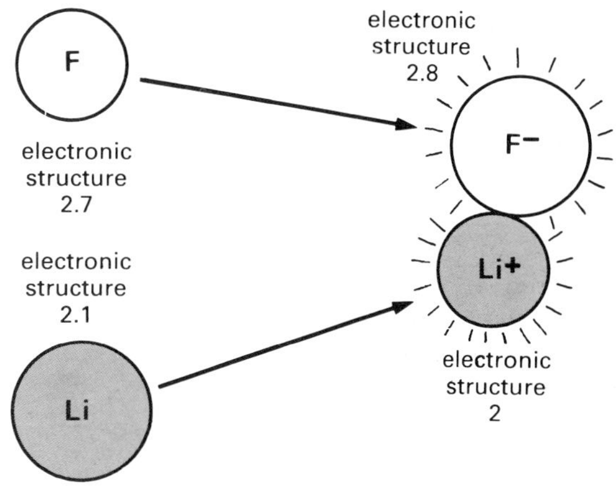

Ion formation when reactive atoms collide

You will notice that the F^- ion has the same electronic structure as a neon atom. And the Li^+ has the same electronic structure as a helium atom. When other ion pairs are formed, the same sort of thing happens. The table below gives two more examples.

Oppositely charged ions are attractive

Once ions are formed in a reaction, they stick together. They have *opposite* charges from one another, and are attracted to one another. The force of attraction between opposite charges is called *electrostatic attraction*. (Ions with charge

Atoms	*Electronic structures of the atoms*	*Ions formed*	*Electronic structures of the ions*	*Corresponding noble gas atoms*
Cl Na	2.8.7 2.8.1	Cl^- Na^+	2.8.8 2.8	Ar Ne
O Mg	2.6 2.8.2	O^{2-} Mg^{2+}	2.8 2.8	Ne Ne

of the same sign repel each other.) The force of attraction between ions explains why electrolytes are so involatile. Electrostatic attraction between ions is often called *electrovalent bonding*, or simply *ionic bonding*.

● *An ionic bond (electrovalent bond) is the result of an electrostatic force of attraction between oppositely charged ions.*

Formulas of ionic compounds

We know that cations and anions are formed in simple ratios to one another. It makes sense that there must be equal numbers of sodium ions and chloride ions in sodium chloride crystals. One Na^+ ion is formed for every Cl^- ion, so the ratio of cations to anions in sodium chloride is 1 : 1.

The same is true in, for instance, magnesium oxide. There is one Mg^{2+} ion for every O^{2-} ion. But in magnesium fluoride the ratio of cations to anions is 1 : 2. For every Mg^{2+} ion formed, there must be *two* F^- ions. In other ionic compounds, the ratio might be 2 : 1, or 1 : 3, or 2 : 3, but it is always a *simple ratio*, that is, a ratio composed of small whole numbers.

The table on the right summarizes the general situation.

Cation's charge	*Anion's charge*	*Ratio of cations to anions*	*Example*
+1	−1	1 : 1	NaCl
+1	−2	2 : 1	Na_2Cl_2
+2	−1	1 : 2	$CaCl_2$
+2	−2	1 : 1	MgO
+3	−1	1 : 3	AlF_3
+3	−2	2 : 3	Al_2O_3

If you know the charges of a few common ions, you can work out the formulas of many ionic compounds. The rule is: *the total charge of the cations in the formula is the same as the total charge of the anions in the formula.*

Look at the reference table below giving formulas of common ions. You could work out the formulas of hundreds of ionic compounds by using combinations of cations and anions from the table. For example, taking Ba^{2+} and Br^-, you get $BaBr_2$; or using K^+ and $Cr_2O_7^{2-}$ you get $K_2Cr_2O_7$. Just make sure you have the right ratio of cations and anions to balance their charges. (But beware! Just because you can work a formula out doesn't prove that a compound of that formula will exist.)

Can you work out the formulas of potassium bromide, copper(II) iodide, lithium oxide, and iron(III) oxide?

● *You can work out the formulas of many ionic compounds if you know the formulas of common ions: just make sure you have the correct ratio of cations to anions.*

	Cations			*Anions*		
	+1	+2	+3	−1	−2	−3
Simple ions	H^+ Li^+ Na^+ K^+ Cs^+ Ag^+	Mg^{2+} Ca^{2+} Ba^{2+} Co^{2+} Cu^{2+} Zn^{2+} Fe^{2+} Pb^{2+}	Al^{3+} Fe^{3+}	F^- Cl^- Br^- I^-	O^{2-} S^{2-}	P^{3-} N^{3-}
Complex ions	NH_4^+			NO_3^- OH^- HCO_3^- HSO_4^- MnO_4^-	SO_4^{2-} CO_3^{2-} $Cr_2O_7^{2-}$	PO_4^{3-}

Reference table of formulas of common ions

Summary

1. The pattern of electrons in an atom is called the electronic structure of the atom.
2. Atoms often end up with noble gas electronic structures when they react together.
3. If one or more electrons are completely transferred from one atom to another, ions are formed.
4. Ionic bonding (electrovalent bonding) is electrostatic attraction between oppositely charged ions.
5. The total positive charge of all the cations in a compound is balanced by the total negative charge of all the anions.
6. You can write the formulas of many ionic compounds if you learn the formulas of common ions.

Revision

1. This question is about the following words:

A atoms
B electrons
C elements
D ions
E shells

Choose one of the words to complete the following sentences:

i All atoms contain one or more particles called ________.
ii Different ________ have atoms with different numbers of electrons.
iii The number of ________ in a neutral atom of an element is the same as its atomic number.
iv All the ________ of a particular element have the same number of electrons.
v Electrons in atoms are arranged in groups called ________.
vi Transfer of electrons between atoms results in the formation of ________.

2. We can draw pictures to show the electronic structures of atoms (see diagram p. 30). Draw pictures to show the following electronic structures:

i 2.6 (O)
ii 2.8.1 (Na)
iii 2.8.7 (Cl)

3. Draw pictures to show the electronic structures of the *ions* that make up the following compounds:

i LiCl
ii NaF
iii Li_2O

4. This question is about the following electronic structures:

A 2.6
B 2.7
C 2.8
D 2.8.1
E 2.8.2

Which is the electronic structure of:

i a noble gas atom
ii an atom that could form ions with charge 2+
iii an atom that would not be likely to form ions
iv an atom of an element with atomic number 8
v an atom that could form ions with charge 2−
vi an ion that could be formed from Na (2.8.1)

5. Copy the following table and finish it:

Atom	*Z*	*Electronic structure of atom*	*Ion formed*	*Electronic structure of ion*	*Corresponding noble gas*
Li	3	2.1	Li^+	2	He
O	8	2.6	O^{2-}		Ne
F	9	2.7			
Na	11				
Mg	12				
S	16				
Cl	17				
K	19				
Ca	20				

6. Look at the reference table of common ions on p. 32. Write the formulas of the following ions:

   i copper(II)
   ii iron(II)
   iii iron(III)
   iv ammonium
   v dichromate(VI)
   vi hydrogencarbonate

7. A compound is formed from ions X^{2+} and Y^-. Which of the following is its formula?

   A XY
   B YX
   C XY_2
   D X_2Y
   E X_2Y_2

8. Look at the reference table of common ions on p. 32. Write the formulas of the following ionic compounds:

   i potassium oxide
   ii calcium chloride
   iii barium oxide
   iv potassium sulphide
   v caesium fluoride

9. Look at the reference table of common ions on p. 32. Write the formulas of the following ionic compounds:

   i cobalt(II) oxide
   ii zinc iodide
   iii sulphur dioxide
   iv ammonium chloride
   v sodium dichromate(VI)
   vi iron(III) oxide

10. This question is about the following noble gas electronic structures.

   A (He) 2
   B (Ne) 2.8
   C (Ar) 2.8.8
   D (Kr) 2.8.18.8
   E (Xe) 2.8.18.18.8

   Choose the noble gas structure formed when the following atoms ionize:

   i Li ($Z = 3$)
   ii S ($Z = 16$)
   iii Ba ($Z = 56$)
   iv Ca ($Z = 20$)
   v Cl ($Z = 17$)
   vi F ($Z = 9$)

Unit 9
Covalent bonding

We know that ionic bonding (electrovalent bonding) results in giant structures held together by strong forces of attraction. So, ionic solids are involatile. We also know that the forces between molecules in molecular substances are weak. So, molecular substances are volatile. Many are gases or liquids at room temperature.

Water is a molecular substance. Its molecules can be separated from one another quite easily. So water *evaporates* quite quickly at room temperature.

$$H_2O(l) \rightarrow H_2O(g)$$

But how can you *decompose* the water molecules, or, in other words, separate the atoms that make up the water molecules? This change is much more difficult. Water molecules can be decomposed only at very high temperatures, for example above 1000 °C.

$$H_2O(g) \rightarrow 2H(g) + O(g)$$

Water is a molecular substance: it evaporates easily

Before we go any further it is important to be clear about the fact that molecular substances have weak forces *between* the molecules, but strong forces *inside* the molecules.

● *The atoms within molecules are held together by strong forces.*

What holds atoms together in molecules?

Are atoms sticky? Is there a kind of 'glue' holding atoms in molecules?

In a way, the answer is, 'yes', the 'glue' is *electrons*. When certain atoms are put together, we know that transfer of electrons can happen. This results in ion formation. But when other atoms are put together, electrons from the two atoms may pair up and form a type of bond called a *covalent bond* between the atoms. The pair of electrons has the same effect as a spot of glue between the atoms: it holds the nucleus of one atom close to the nucleus of the other.

● *A pair of electrons holding two atoms together is called a covalent bond.*

Let us look at an example: the covalent bond in a hydrogen chloride molecule, HCl.

The covalent bond in a hydrogen chloride molecule, HCl

The easiest way to understand the covalent bond is to look at a 'dot and cross picture'. In this kind of picture, the electrons from one of the atoms are shown by dots, and the electrons from the other atom are shown by crosses. Usually only the outer shell electrons are included in the picture. A hydrogen atom might be shown like this:

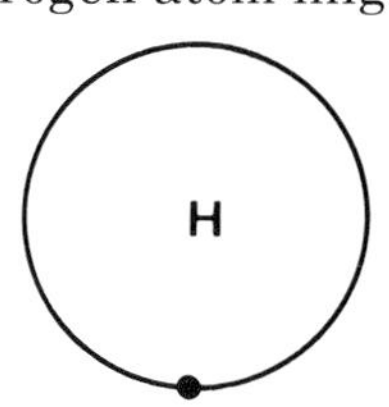

A chlorine atom might be shown like this:

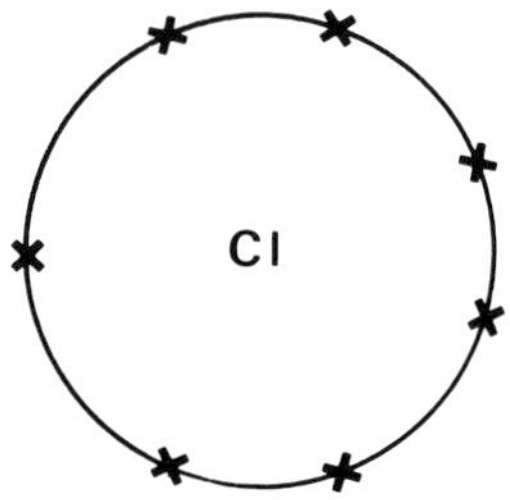

When the HCl molecule is formed, one of the chlorine atom's electrons pairs up with the hydrogen atom's electrons to form the covalent bond. The picture looks like this:

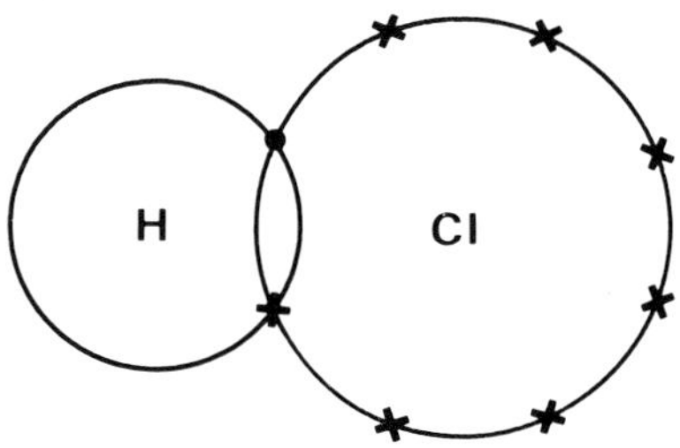

The positively charged nuclei are held together because of their attraction for the paired-up electrons. Covalent bonding in other molecules also involves pairs of electrons. Usually, just as in hydrogen chloride, the two atoms each provide one electron to make up a pair. Sharing of electrons by atoms is a feature of all covalent bonds. The figure on p.37 shows some more examples.

Noble gas stability in molecules

Look at the dot and cross pictures again. How many electrons are there in the *outer* shell of each atom in the molecules? Look at the ammonia molecule, for example. After the electrons have been paired up, this is the situation:

a each hydrogen atom has a share of *two* electrons;
b the nitrogen atom has *eight* electrons, including three pairs shared with the hydrogen atoms.

If you look at the other molecules mentioned above, you will find that there seems to be a pattern. This is shown in the following table.

Molecule	*Atoms in the molecule*	*Original number of outer shell electrons*	*Number of outer shell electrons after pairing up*
hydrogen chloride	H Cl	1 7	2 8
ammonia	N H H H	5 1 1 1	8 2 2 2
water	O H H	6 1 1	8 2 2
tetrachloro-methane	C Cl Cl Cl Cl	4 7 7 7 7	8 8 8 8 8

The pattern is quite obvious: by sharing electrons, the atoms in a molecule end up with either two or eight electrons in their outer shells, that is, a stable electronic structure. You will remember that these are the numbers of electrons in the outer shells of the noble gases (helium has two electrons, while neon, argon and the other noble gases have eight electrons in their outer shells).

● *Sharing of electrons in a covalent bond generally leads to noble gas numbers of electrons in the outer shells of atoms in a molecule.*

Summary

1. The atoms in molecules are held together by strong forces.
2. The strong forces between atoms in molecules are called covalent bonds.
3. A covalent bond is formed between two atoms when two electrons pair up, one from each atom.
4. The joining together of atoms by the sharing of electron pairs is called covalency.
5. Covalency generally leads to noble gas numbers of electrons for atoms in molecules.

Ammonia molecule 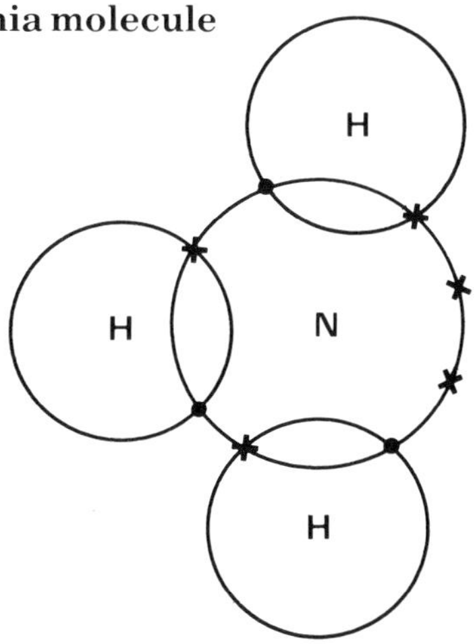	There are *three* covalent bonds in this molecule. The nitrogen atom has five electrons in its outer shell. It uses three of them to form electron pairs with electrons from hydrogen atoms. The formula of the molecule is NH_3.
Water molecule 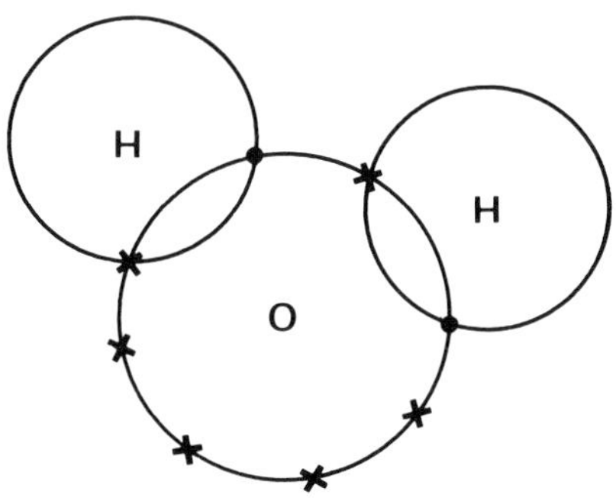	There are *two* covalent bonds in this molecule. The oxygen atom uses two of its six outer shell electrons. The hydrogen atoms each provide one electron. The formula of the molecule is H_2O.
Tetrachloromethane molecule 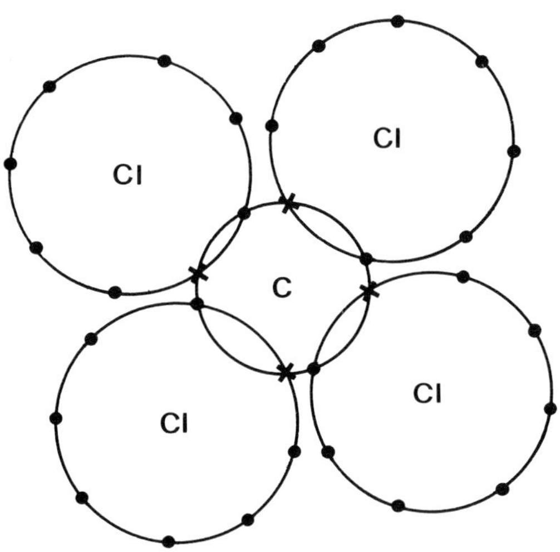	There are *four* covalent bonds in this molecule. The chlorine atoms use one of their seven outer shell electrons. The carbon atom uses all its four outer shell electrons. The formula of the molecule is CCl_4.

Covalency: joining atoms together by the sharing of electron pairs

Revision

1. Complete the statement below by using the words in the following list:

decomposed, separated, strong, volatile, weak.

'The forces between molecules in a molecular substance are ________. These forces are easily overcome and the molecules are therefore easily ________. This explains why molecular substances are generally ________.

However, the forces between the atoms in a molecule are ________. So most molecular substances can be ________ only with difficulty.'

2. Atoms X and Y each have *one* electron in their outer shells. Atom W has *seven* electrons in its outer shell.

The compound with formula XW is formed by *covalency*, but the compound YW is formed by *electrovalency*. Draw dot and cross pictures to show the electron arrangements in the compounds:

i XW
ii YW

3. This question is about atoms with the following atomic numbers:

A 7
B 10
C 11
D 17
E 20

Which atom could have:

i one electron in its outer shell
ii two electrons in its outer shell
iii five electrons in its outer shell
iv seven electrons in its outer shell
v eight electrons in its outer shell

4. i What is the number of electrons in the outer shell of each of the following atoms? (their atomic numbers are given in brackets).

a B $(Z = 5)$
b C $(Z = 6)$
c Cl $(Z = 17)$
d P $(Z = 15)$
e Si $(Z = 16)$

ii Work out dot and cross pictures to show electron arrangements in the following molecules (show outer shell electrons only):

a BCl_3 (boron trichloride molecule)
b CH_4 (methane molecule)
c PH_3 (phosphine molecule)
d $SiCl_4$ (silicon tetrachloride molecule)
e Cl_2O (chlorine monoxide molecule)

5. This question is about the following molecular chlorides:

A ACl
B BCl_2
C CCl_3
D DCl_4
E ECl_5

i Which chloride could be a chloride of an element with:

a one electron in the outer shell of its atoms
b two electrons in the outer shell of its atoms

ii Which chloride could be a chloride of the element with atomic number:

a 4
b 6

Unit 10
More about electrons and bonding

In the last Unit we learned that atoms can be joined together by a pair of shared electrons. This is called covalency. We also learned how to show the electron arrangements in molecules by drawing dot and cross pictures. However, dot and cross pictures can take a long time to draw, especially when a molecule has a lot of atoms, for example $C_{10}H_{22}$. So, usually when we draw the structures of molecules, we use *lines* to show the covalent bonds. One line is used for each pair of shared electrons.

For example, the structure of methane's molecule would be drawn like this:

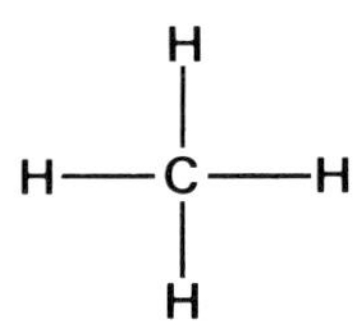

Instead of:

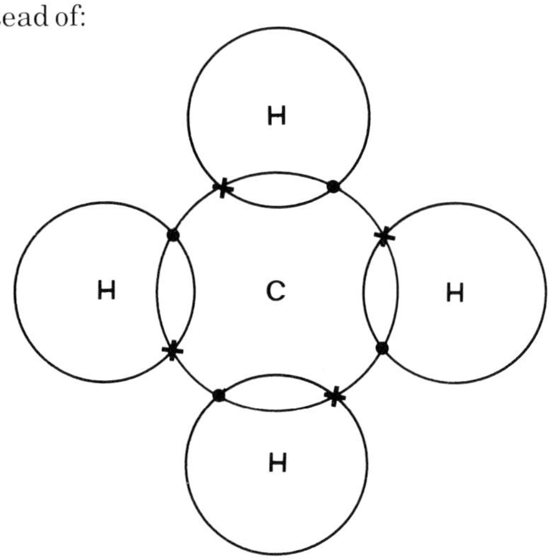

Electrons that are not shared are ignored. So, the structure of an ammonia molecule would be drawn like this:

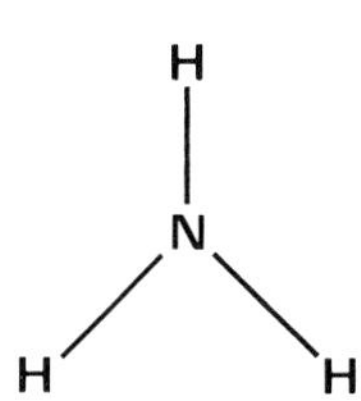

Instead of:

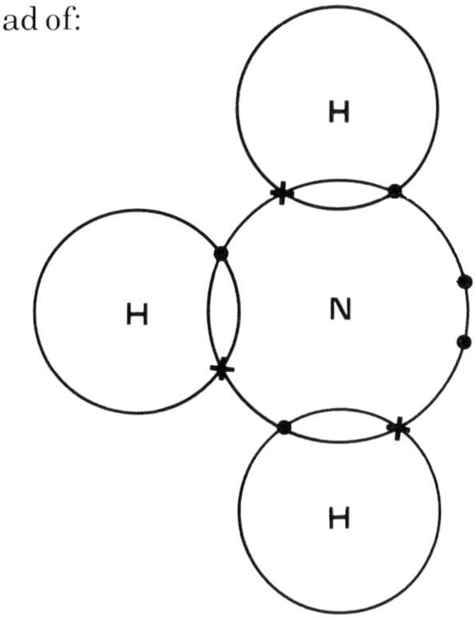

● *Covalent structures can be drawn using lines for pairs of electrons.*

Double bonds and triple bonds

All the covalent bonds we have met so far have had two electrons. Is it possible for atoms to share more than two electrons? The answer to this question is 'yes'.

Double covalent bonds have twice as many electrons as ordinary covalent bonds. In other words, they have four electrons instead of two. Two electrons are provided by each of the joined atoms to form the double bond. (Would you expect a double bond to be stronger or weaker than a single bond? The greater number of electrons paired will result in an increased negative charge in the space between the nuclei, so the nuclei will be held together more strongly.)

Examples of molecules containing double bonds are CO_2 (carbon dioxide molecule), O_2 (oxygen molecule) and C_2H_4 (ethene molecule). Their electron arrangements are shown in the next figure.

Triple covalent bonds have six shared electrons, three from each atom. But molecules with triple bonds are not very common. And six electrons in a bond is the most you can have (there are no quadruple bonds).

Molecular formula	*Dot and cross picture*	*Line picture*
O_2	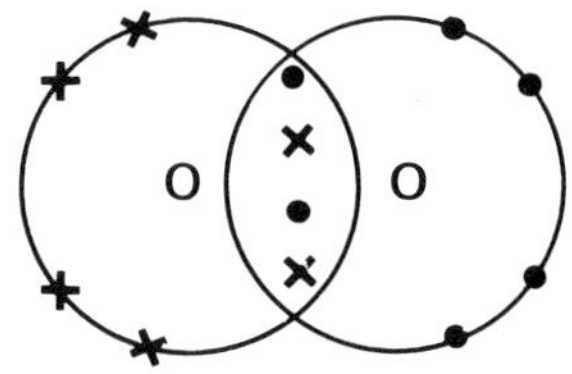	O=O
CO_2	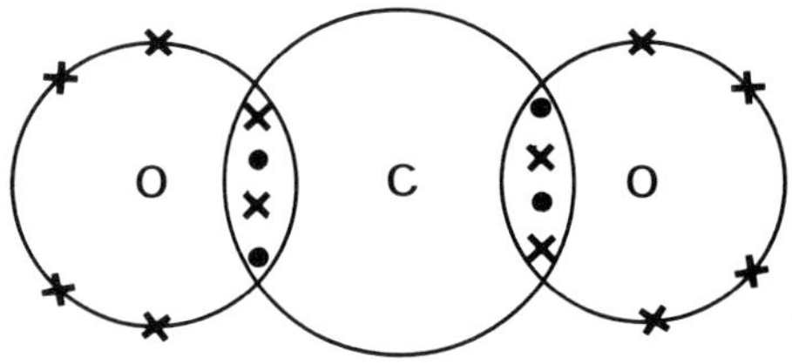	O=C=O
C_2H_4	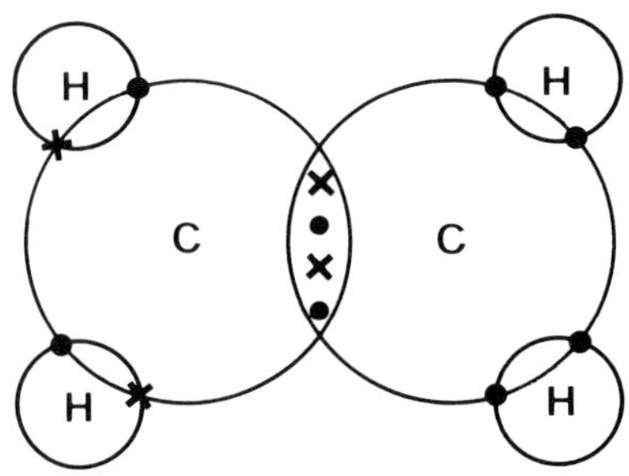	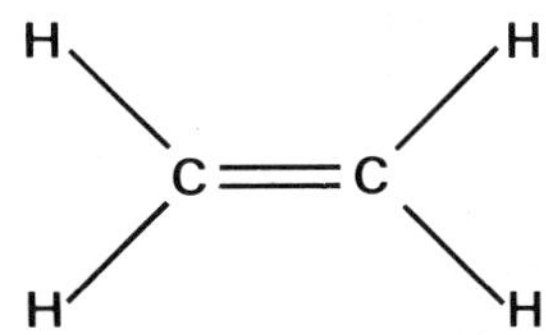

Structures of some molecules containing double bonds

N_2 (nitrogen molecule) and C_2H_2 (ethyne molecule) are examples of molecules with triple bonds.

● *Double bonds have four shared electrons and triple bonds have six shared electrons.*

Covalent giant structures

Most of the giant structures we have met have been ionic structures or metallic structures. But do you remember the giant structure of diamond? It was neither ionic nor metallic. We called it a *macromolecular structure* (Unit 5). The atoms in this type of structure are held together by covalent bonds.

Using the line method to show covalent bonds we could draw the diamond structure as in the next figure (right).

You should compare this structure with the picture of the diamond structure on p. 20.

● *Macromolecular structures such as diamond are held together by covalent bonds.*

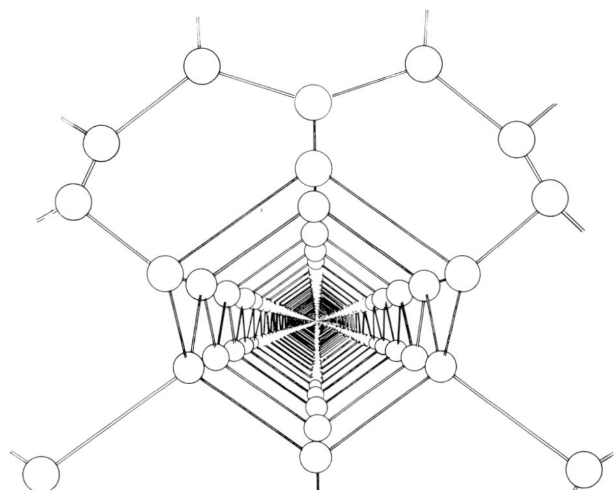

Covalent bonding in the macro-molecular structure of diamond

Delocalized electrons

In an earlier Unit we learned how the graphite structure differs from the diamond structure (see Unit 5). One difference between the two structures is the number of atoms joined to each carbon atom. In diamond the number is *four* (as we have just seen above). But in graphite the number of neighbouring atoms is *three*. This suggests that only three electrons are used by the carbon atoms for bonding in graphite. In fact all four electrons are used, but the fourth electron is used in a special way. It is free to wander about in the layers of atoms, that is, it isn't restricted to the space between two atoms. An electron that isn't attached to particular atoms is said to be *delocalized*. Each of the carbon atoms in the graphite structure provides one of these delocalized electrons. So there are a great many of them in a graphite crystal. It is these 'free' or delocalized electrons that give graphite its electrical conductivity.

The *metallic giant structures* also contain delocalized electrons. As you know, this type of structure is a regular arrangement of cations and is common to the majority of metals (see Unit 5). Delocalized electrons migrate throughout the structure. It is as though the cations were sunk in a 'sea of electrons'. There is an attractive force between the 'sea of electrons' and the cations. The force is called the *metallic bond*. The metallic bond is responsible for holding the metallic giant structure together. The presence of delocalized electrons in metal structures also explains why all metals are good conductors.

The next illustration shows a (two-dimensional) view of delocalized electrons in a close-packed arrangement of cations.

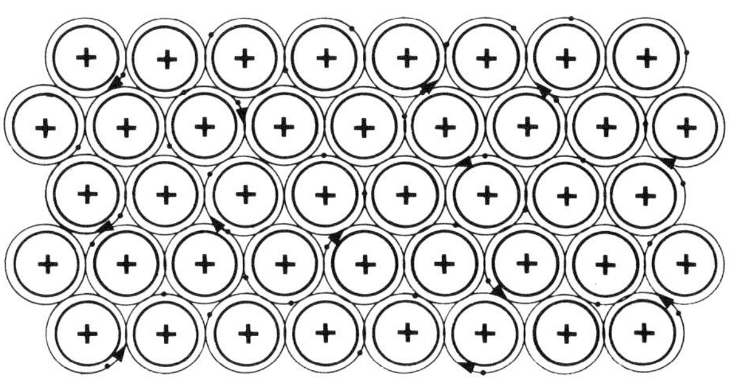

Delocalized electrons in a close-packed structure

- *Metals and graphite are good conductors of electricity because their structures have delocalized electrons.*

The co-ordinate bond

In most covalent bonds between atoms, half the shared electrons are provided by one atom and half by the other. This has been the case in all the examples we have looked at so far. For example in boron trifluoride molecules, each covalent bond has an electron from a fluorine atom and an electron from a boron atom:

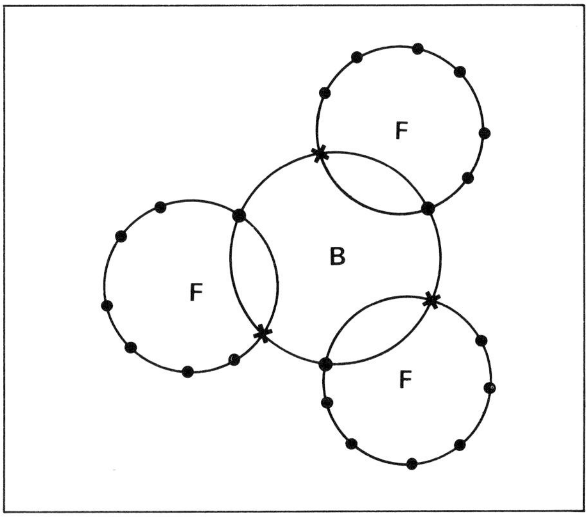

Covalent bonds in BF_3

However, in some molecules, *both* the shared electrons are provided by one of the bonded atoms. This type of covalent bond is called a *co-ordinate bond.* (It is important to realize that a co-ordinate bond has exactly the same effect as an ordinary covalent bond: it holds the nuclei of the atoms close together. The only difference between a co-ordinate bond and an ordinary covalent bond is the source of the shared electrons.

The particles in the diagram on p. 42 contain atoms joined by co-ordinate bonds.

As the examples in the diagram show, arrows are used in line pictures to show co-ordinate bonds. The direction of the arrow indicates which atom is accepting the pair of electrons.

- *When both electrons of a covalent bond are provided by one atom, the bond is called a co-ordinate bond.*

Particle	*Dot and cross picture*	*Line picture*
ammonium ion NH_4^+	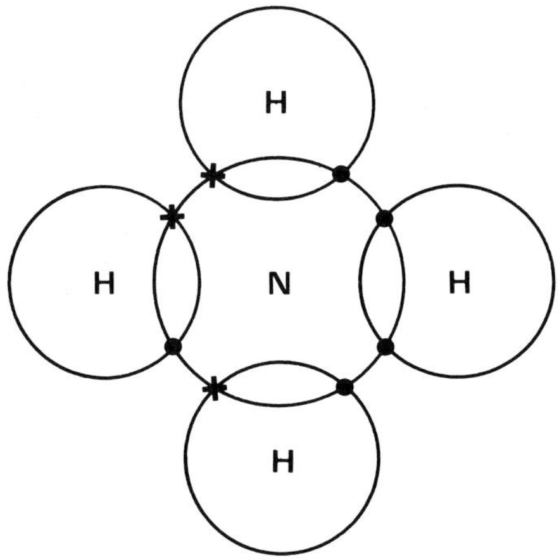	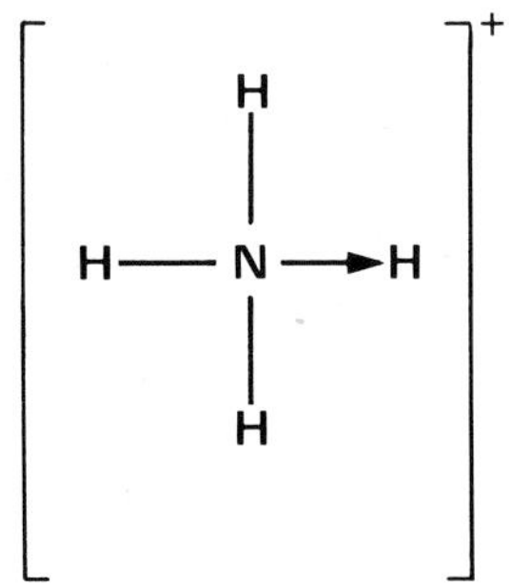
oxonium ion H_3O^+	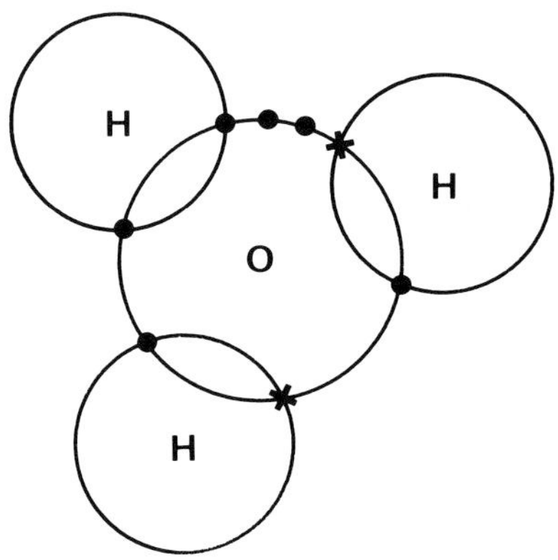	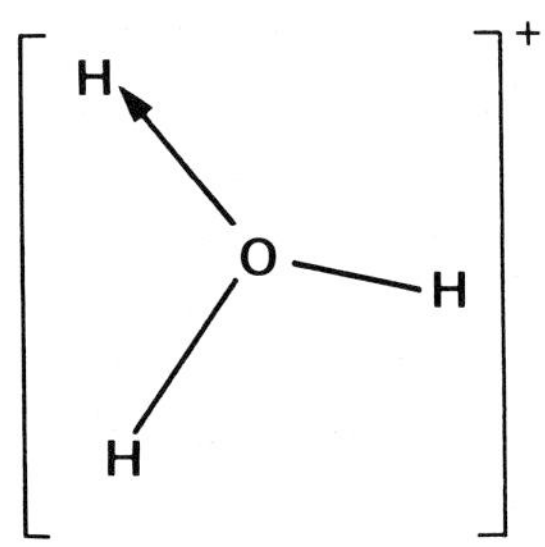
BF_3NH_3 molecule	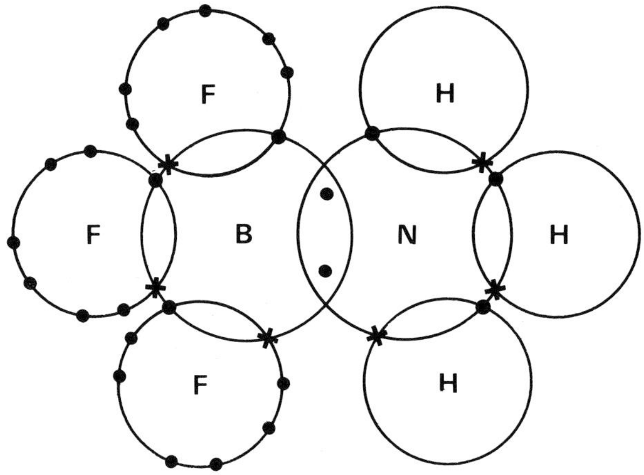	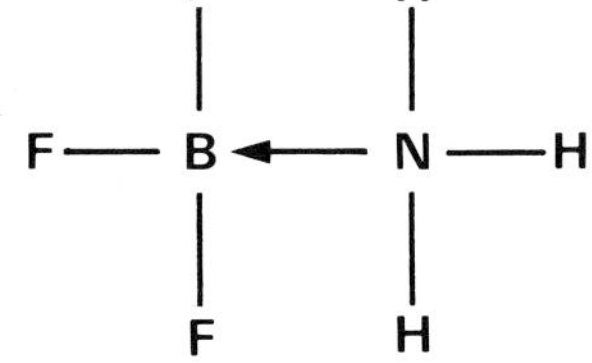

Particles with co-ordinate bonds

Summary

1. Covalent structures can be drawn using lines for pairs of electrons.
2. Double bonds have four shared electrons, and triple bonds have six shared electrons.
3. Macromolecular structures such as diamond are held together by covalent bonds.
4. Metals and graphite are good conductors because their structures have delocalized electrons.
5. When both electrons of a covalent bond are provided by one atom, the bond is called a co-ordinate bond.

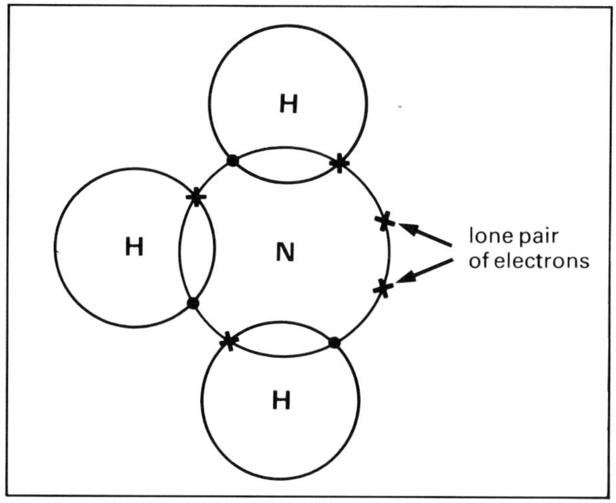

Ammonia

Extension

1. Most of the structures of molecules that we have looked at seem to have outer shells with two or eight electrons. But these 'noble gas numbers' are not the only possible numbers for electron shells in molecules. Many stable molecules have outer shells with more or less than a noble gas number of electrons.
   i Work out dot and cross pictures for the following molecules (use outer shell electrons only):
   a BF_3
   b SO_3
   c SF_6
   d PF_5
   ii How many electrons are there round the central atom in each of the above molecules?
2. Pairs of electrons that are *not* used in bonding are called *lone pairs*. For example, the ammonia molecule (above) has three bonding pairs and one lone pair.
   Which of the following molecules (A–E) has:
   i no lone pairs
   ii one lone pair
   iii two lone pairs
   iv three lone pairs
   v four lone pairs

A	H_2O	*B*	HCl
C	CO_2	*D*	CH_4
E	PH_3		

Revision

1. Draw dot and cross pictures to show the electron arrangements in the following molecules. (Show outer shell electrons only.)
   i Cl_2 (chlorine):
   Cl——Cl
   ii CF_4 (tetrafluoromethane):
   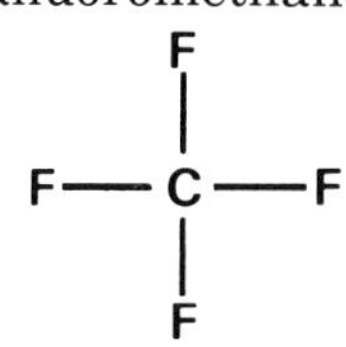

   iii H_2S (hydrogen sulphide):
   H—S—H
   iv Cl_2O (chlorine monoxide):
   Cl—O—Cl
   v PH_3 (phosphine):
   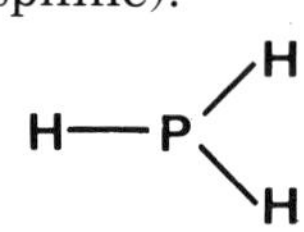

2. Use the line method to show the covalent bonds in the following molecules.
   i sulphur dioxide:
   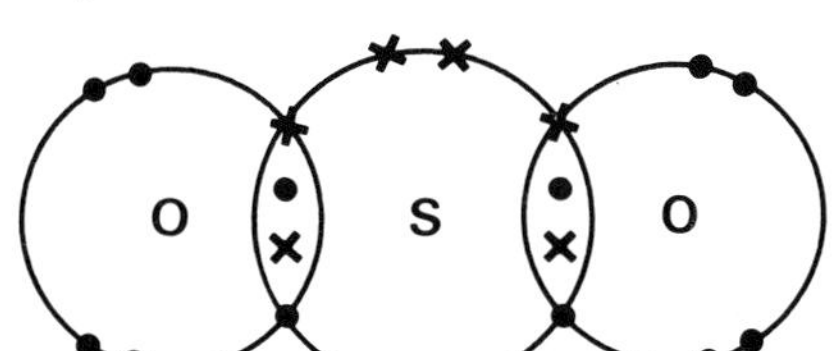

ii hydrogen cyanide:

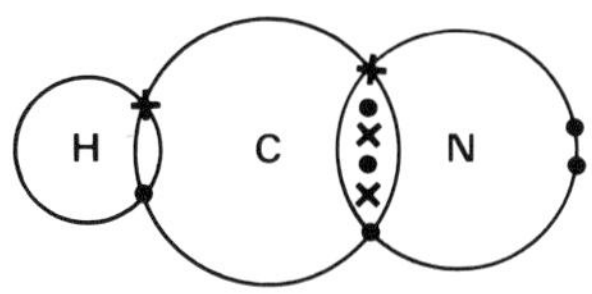

iii ethane:

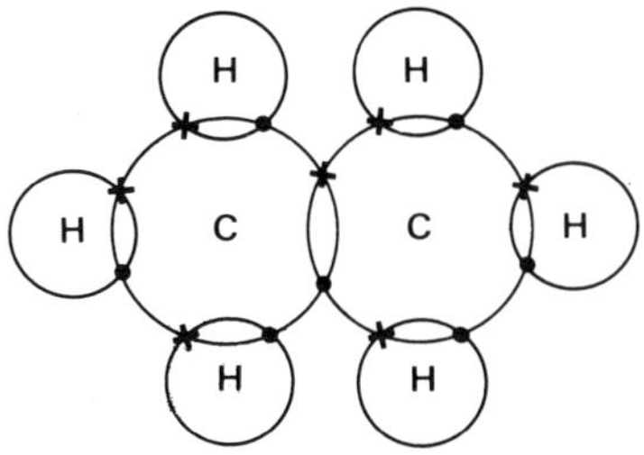

iv carbonic acid:

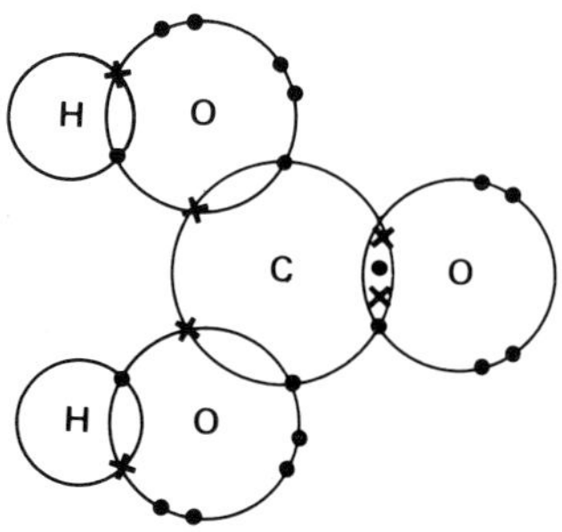

v silicon tetrachloride:

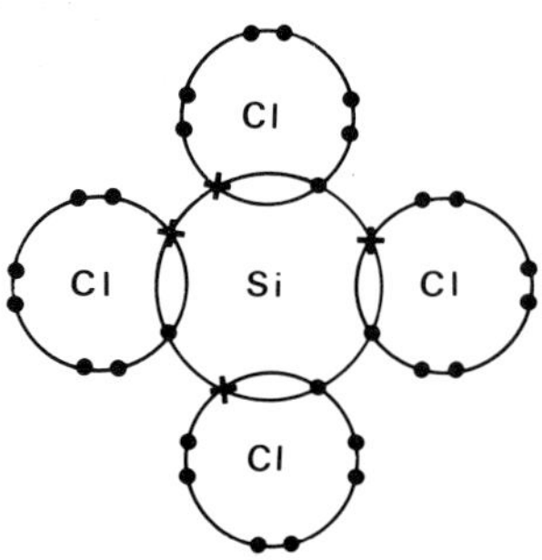

3. Give the *molecular formula* of each of the compounds mentioned in question 2.

4. This question is about the structures of the following solids:

A diamond
B graphite
C magnesium
D sulphur
E sodium chloride

Which of the solids has a:

i low melting temperature
ii giant structure of cations and anions
iii molecular structure
iv macromolecular structure with no free electrons
v giant structure of cations with delocalized electrons
vi layer structure with delocalized electrons

5. This question is about the following formulas:

A CH_4
B C_2H_4
C C_2H_2
D NH_3
E CO_2

Which is the formula of:

i ammonia
ii carbon dioxide
iii ethene
iv ethyne
v methane

6. This question is about the covalent bonds in the following molecules:

A O_2
B N_2
C CH_4
D C_2H_4
E HCl

Which molecule has:

i one single bond only
ii one triple bond only
iii one double bond only
iv four single bonds only
v one double bond and four single bonds

7. The structures of nitrogen and ethyne molecules can be represented like this:

nitrogen: $N \equiv N$
ethyne: $H - C \equiv C - H$

Draw dot and cross pictures to show the electron arrangements in each of the above molecules.

Unit 11
The periodic table

There is a good deal of variety amongst the elements. We know examples of reactive gases and unreactive gases, reactive solids and unreactive solids. Just think of the contrast between elements like fluorine and carbon, or sodium and argon, for example.

However, some elements do show resemblances to one another. These similarities were noticed early in the history of chemistry.

Triads

One of the first people to draw attention to these 'family resemblances' amongst the elements was a German chemist called Johann Döbereiner. In 1829 he pointed out that many of the elements could be grouped together in threes. He called these groups of three 'triads'. The metals lithium, sodium and potassium are an example of such a triad. The elements chlorine, bromine and iodine form another.

Döbereiner also noticed that there was often a pattern in the relative atomic masses of the elements in the triads. If the three elements were arranged in relative atomic mass order, the relative atomic mass (A_r) value of the one in the middle was close to the average of the other two. For example, 79.9 (Br) is close to the average of 35.5 (Cl) and 126.9 (I). (Is the same true for Li, Na and K? Test your arithmetic on these A_r values: 6.9, 23.0 and 39.1.)

● *Döbereiner suggested that many of the elements could be grouped in threes.*

Octaves

Nearly 40 years later, in 1866, the English chemist John Newlands went a step further. He suggested that a pattern could be seen when the elements were written out in order of atomic mass. Similar elements seemed to crop up at regular intervals. So, according to Newlands, starting with any element in the list a related element was to be found seven places further on. He called this relationship the 'Law of Octaves'. Some examples are shown in the next figure.

The noble gases are not shown because they had not been discovered at the time of Newlands' work. The fact that there were other elements as well as the noble gases waiting to be discovered resulted in the pattern breaking down: Newlands did not realize that he might have to leave spaces in the list of the elements.

● *Newlands tried to show that elements with similar properties were linked by a simple law of numbers.*

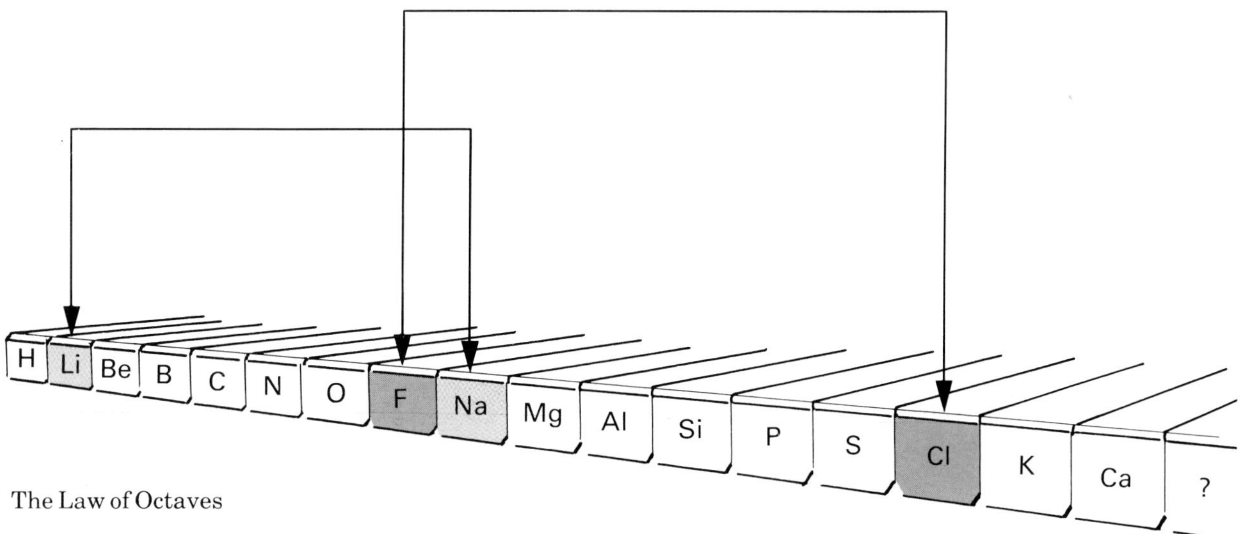

The Law of Octaves

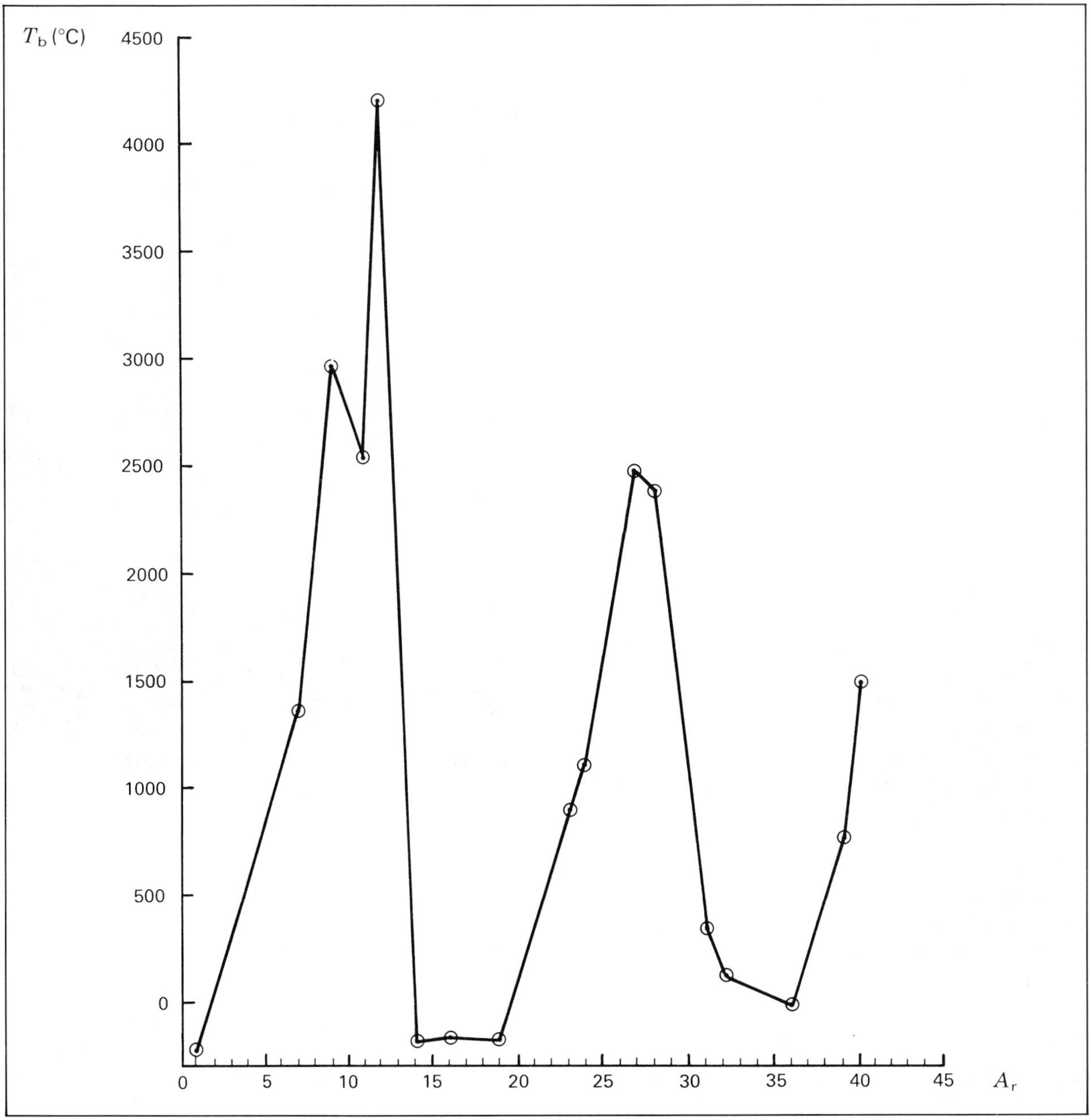

A graph to show how boiling temperature (T_b) varies with relative atomic mass (A_r)

Lothar Meyer

Although Newlands' idea was not accepted immediately, it did start other chemists thinking. It suggested that the properties of the elements were somehow related to their atomic masses. Further evidence along these lines was put forward by the German chemist Lothar Meyer in 1869. He showed that when physical properties (like melting temperature, density, etc.) were plotted against relative atomic mass values the graphs showed a pattern. An example is illustrated in the figure above for the elements with atomic masses up to 40. (The noble gases are not shown on the graph.)

If you look at the graph, you will see that it has crests and troughs that follow one another like a series of waves. The 'wave' pattern continues if values for all the elements are plotted. Lothar Meyer found that graphs for other properties of the elements also had regular crests and troughs (see Questions 2 and 3).

● *Lothar Meyer showed that the physical properties of the elements varied regularly with relative atomic mass.*

Dmitri Mendeleev

In the same year as Lothar Meyer published his results, a Russian chemist called Dmitri Mendeleev (1834–1907) published a paper that finally solved the problem. The paper had the title 'The Relations between the Properties of the Elements and their Atomic Weights'. In it, Mendeleev considered chemical properties of the elements (and their compounds) as well as their physical properties. He showed that the elements grouped themselves into families when they were tabulated in relative atomic mass order. However, the pattern of families in the table only made sense if gaps were left in the list in a few places. Mendeleev realised that these gaps corresponded to elements which had yet to be discovered. For example, places were left for the elements Ga, Sc and Ge. Mendeleev was able to make accurate predictions about the properties of these undiscovered elements. He did this by looking at the properties of their close relatives in the table. The importance of Mendeleev's classification was later confirmed by the discovery of elements with the properties that he had predicted for them.

Mendeleev's classification is the basis of modern forms of the periodic table.

● *Mendeleev did the most to establish the idea of the periodic classification of the elements.*

Modern periodic tables

There is more than one way to arrange the elements in order so that similar elements are close together. A common form of the periodic table is shown in Appendix IV (p.271). If you look at a modern periodic table, you will notice that the elements are no longer listed in atomic mass order. Instead, atomic numbers (see Unit 8) are used. The reason for this will become clear when you have studied Unit 12.

Dmitri Ivanovich Mendeleev (1834–1907)

● *Modern forms of the periodic table are based on the atomic number order of the elements.*

Divisions in the periodic table

Groups

This is the name given to the vertical families of elements. The main groups are usually numbered from the left, as shown in the figure at the top of p.48.

Group I contains the alkali metals and group VII contains the halogens. You will notice that the noble gas family has the group number 0. This is because the noble gases were discovered after the numbering system of the groups was worked out.

● *In the periodic table, families of elements are arranged in vertical columns called groups. The groups are numbered I to VII, and 0.*

The only element not in a group is the first element in the list, hydrogen.

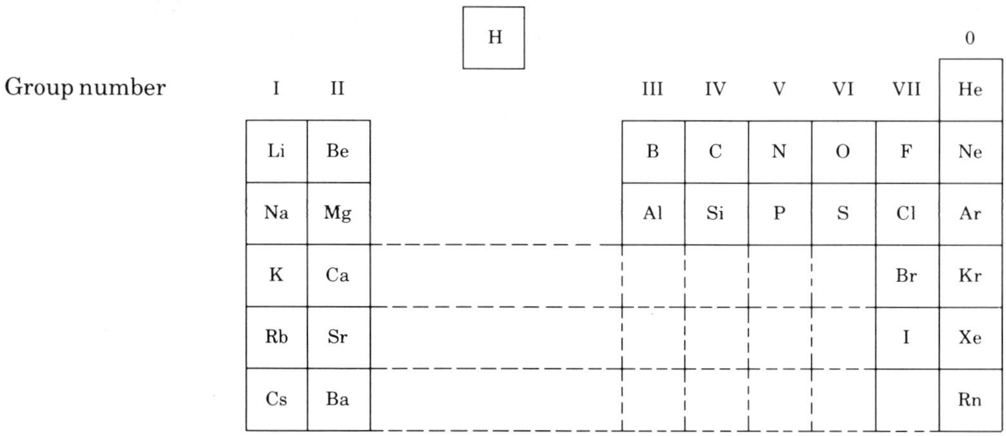

Groups in the periodic table

Periods

Horizontal rows in the periodic table are called *periods*. The periods are also numbered. Period 1 contains the elements H and He, period 2 contains the elements from Li to Ne, and so on.

● *Rows of elements going across the periodic table are called periods.*

The elements in a period are not similar to one another. Instead, you can see steady changes in their properties as you look across the period. In general, the elements on the left of a period are metals. Those on the right are non-metals. Look at period 3, for example:

Period 3	Na	Mg	Al	Si	P	S	Cl	Ar

Sodium and magnesium are reactive metals. Aluminium is a less reactive metal. Silicon, phosphorus, sulphur and chlorine are non-metals.

Diagonal division of the periodic table

This brings us to one last point concerning divisions in the periodic table: the line that divides the metals from the non-metals in the periodic table is a *diagonal*. It runs from top left to bottom right, as shown in the next figure.

● *Metals are found on the left, and non-metals on the right, of the periodic table.*

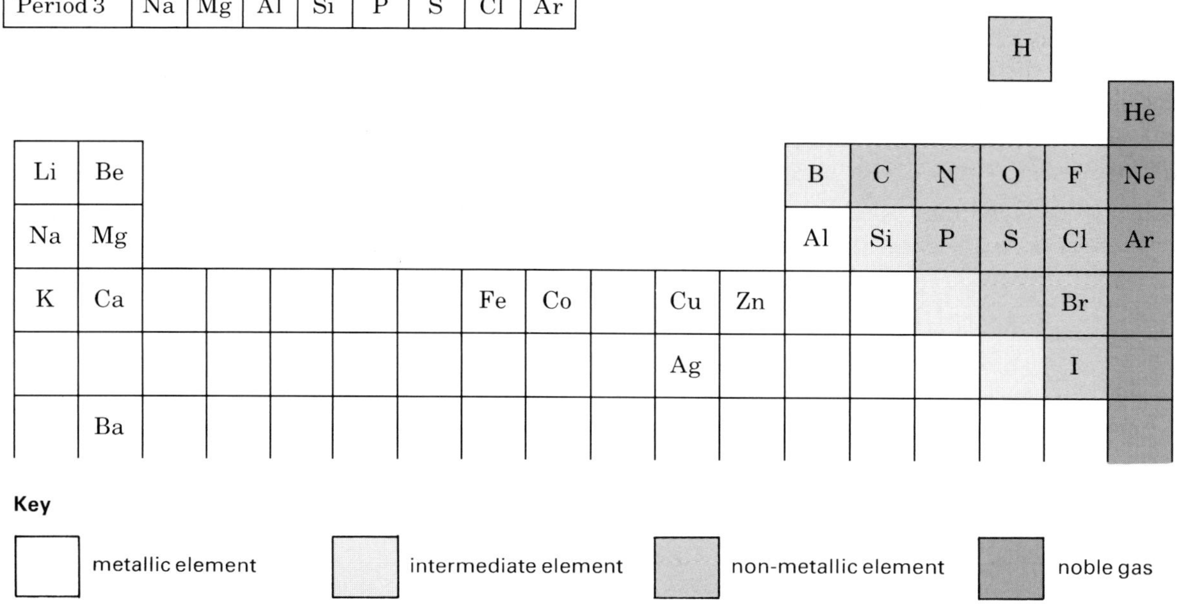

Diagonal division of the periodic table into non-metals and metals

Summary

1. Döbereiner suggested that many of the elements could be grouped into threes.
2. Newlands tried to show that elements with similar properties were linked by a 'Law of Octaves'.
3. Lothar Meyer showed that the physical properties of the elements varied regularly with relative atomic mass.
4. Mendeleev established the periodic classification of the elements.
5. Modern forms of the periodic table are based on the atomic number order of the elements.
6. Families of elements in the periodic table are arranged in vertical groups. The groups are numbered I to VII, and 0.
7. Horizontal rows of elements in the periodic table are called periods.
8. A diagonal line divides metals (on the left) from non-metals (on the right) in the periodic classification.

Extension

If Newlands had written his law 30 years later, it would not have been a law of 'octaves'. This is because of discoveries made by William Ramsay between 1894 and 1898.

1. Find out more about William Ramsay. What did he discover?
2. Explain why Newlands' law would not have mentioned octaves in 1898.

Revision

1. This question is about the following elements, which are in sets of three:

A	Ca,	Sr,	Ba
B	Cl,	Br,	I
C	Cu,	Ag,	Au
D	Li,	Na,	K
E	S,	Cl,	Ar

   i Which of the sets would not have been one of Döbereiner's 'triads'?

   ii Explain why the set you have chosen could not have been a 'triad'.

   iii Choose one of the other sets and write down the A_r values for the elements in it.

   iv Take the highest and lowest of the three A_r values and work out their mean (average) value.

   v Compare the mean value with the A_r value of the middle element in the 'triad'. What do you notice?

2. The graph given in the figure on p.50 shows how the densities of the first 20 elements vary with A_r. The noble gases He, Ne and Ar are not included in the graph. Their densities (when liquid) are:

He	0.15 g cm^{-3}
Ne	1.20 g cm^{-3}
Ar	1.40 g cm^{-3}

   i A_r and Ar are two different symbols. What do they stand for?

   ii Make a sketch of the graph and indicate on it the positions of He, Ne and Ar.

   iii On your sketch graph, show the positions of:

   a two members of group III

   b three alkali metals

   Comment on their positions.

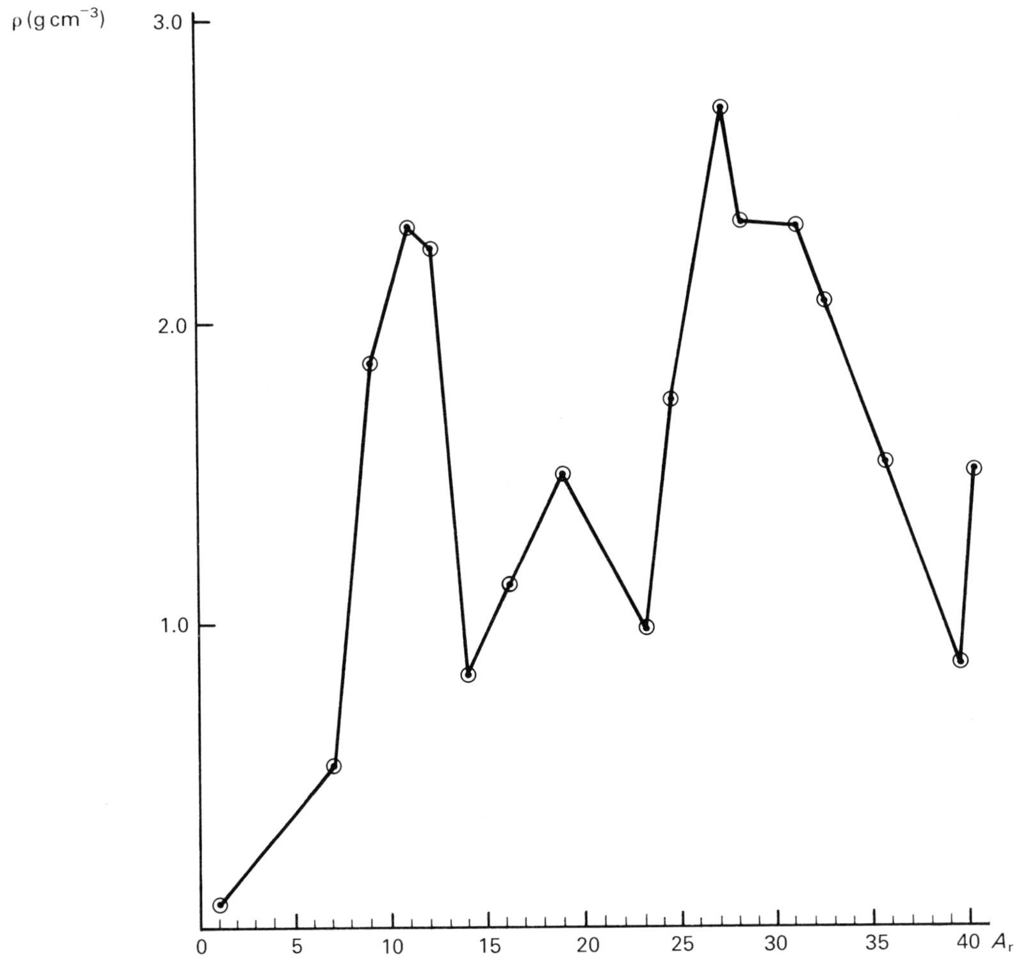

Note: Density shown for elements which are gases at room temperature is the value of the liquid state

A graph to show how density (ρ) varies with relative atomic mass (A_r) for the first 20 elements

3. The graph given in the figure on p.51 shows how melting temperature (T_m) values vary with the atomic number (Z).

   i What does the value of Z tell you about atoms of an element?

   ii What relationship between T_m and Z does the graph show?

   iii Pick out elements that clearly illustrate the relationship, indicate their positions on a sketch of the graph of T_m against Z and explain the relationship.

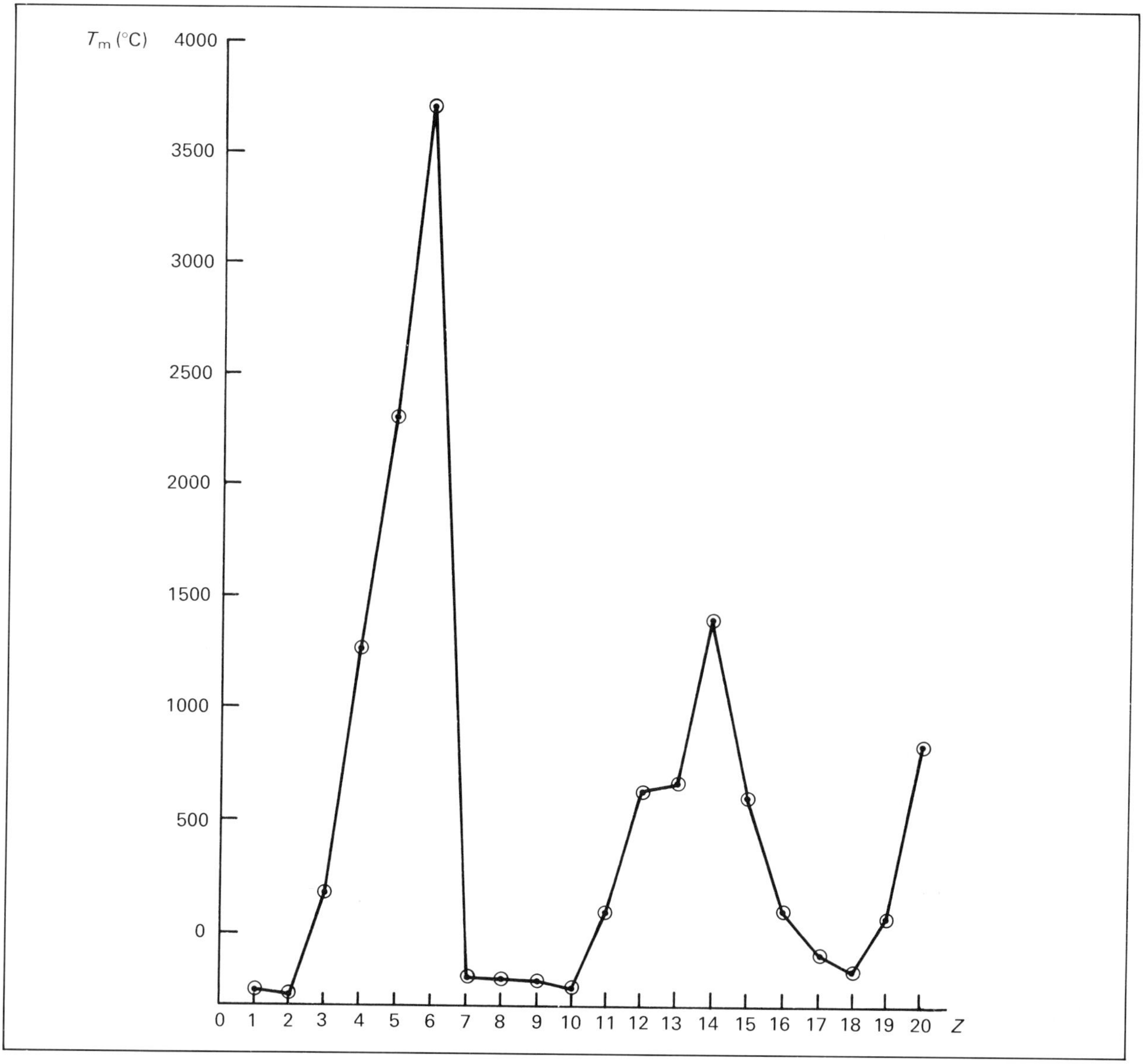

A graph to show how melting temperature varies with atomic number (Z) for the first 20 elements

Unit 12
Protons and periodicity

Mendeleev's periodic table was worked out by looking for resemblances between the elements when they were arranged in relative atomic mass (A_r) order. However, there were a few places in the table where the elements had to be taken out of order to make a logical pattern of chemical families. This will become clear if you look at the next table. It shows part of the list of elements in relative atomic mass order.

Relative atomic mass	*Element*
28.086	silicon
30.974	phosphorus
32.064	sulphur
35.453	chlorine
39.102	potassium
39.984	argon
40.080	calcium

If you look back to the periodic table on p. 48 in the previous Unit you can see immediately what is wrong. Potassium and argon are the wrong way round in the table above. If you listed elements strictly according to atomic mass, these two elements would end up in the wrong groups. Potassium would be included in the noble gases, and argon in the alkali metals. That wouldn't be a very sensible arrangement, would it? So:

- *Atomic mass order is not a very reliable way of listing the elements to show periodicity.*

Atomic number

All atoms contain one or more protons in their nuclei (see Unit 2). All the atoms of a particular element have the same number of protons. Different elements have different 'atomic proton numbers'. If the elements are listed in order of 'atomic proton numbers' (instead of A_r values) all the elements get into their correct family groups. In other words, 'atomic proton number' gives the position of an element in the periodic table. The 'atomic proton number' is called the *atomic number* of the element (which is equal to the 'atomic electron number', as we saw in Unit 8).

- *The atomic number of an element gives its position in the periodic table as well as the number of protons in its atoms.*

The atomic number of an element is given by the symbol Z, for example for hydrogen $Z = 1$, for sodium $Z = 11$, for chlorine $Z = 17$.

Neutrons

Why do elements sometimes get in the wrong place if you use atomic mass instead of atomic number to put them in order? The answer has to do with the number of *neutrons* in the nucleus. You will remember that neutrons are particles found in the nucleus alongside protons. A neutron has no charge, but has the same mass as a proton.

Obviously, the overall mass of an atom depends on the mass of the neutrons in the nucleus, as well as the protons. (Electrons also contribute to the mass of the atom, but not much.) The neutron and proton numbers go up roughly in proportion to one another. In most cases, as the next table shows, the number of neutrons is slightly more than the number of protons.

Atom	*Neutron number*	*Proton number*
Be	5	4
Na	12	11
P	16	15
Mn	30	25
I	74	53
Au	118	79

There isn't a fixed ratio of neutrons to protons, so we can see why the atomic mass is only *roughly* proportional to atomic number. This explains why atomic mass order is not a reliable way of listing the elements.

In the case of potassium and argon, K has one more proton than Ar, so K comes after Ar in the periodic table. But Ar has enough extra neutrons to put it after K in the atomic mass list. (There is more about the 'potassium–argon question' in Extension 2.)

Isotopes

One definite thing we can say about atoms of a particular element is this: they all have the same number of protons in the nucleus. In other words:

- *All atoms with a particular proton number (atomic number) are atoms of the same element.*

After all, it is the atomic number that fixes the electron number in the neutral atom. And it is the electron number and arrangement that fix the properties of the atom.

However, the neutron number doesn't have much importance when it comes to the properties of the atom. In fact, the *chemical* behaviour of atoms with different neutron numbers is identical, providing they all have the same proton numbers. We now know that most elements are mixtures of atoms with different neutron numbers. The different varieties of the element are called *isotopes*.

- *Varieties of an element with atoms containing different numbers of neutrons are called isotopes of the element.*

Dalton's original idea, that all atoms of a particular element are identical, has therefore turned out to be wrong. The idea of isotopes is illustrated in the next figure.

A shorthand way of describing isotopes

The isotopes are described using the following formula:

$^{A}_{Z}X$

X is the symbol for an atom of the element
Z is the atomic number of the element
A is the 'mass number' of the isotope (i.e. the number of protons and neutrons in the nucleus.

The best way to understand this system is to look at a few examples.

Isotope	*Proton number (atomic number)*	*Neutron number*	*Mass number*
$^{6}_{3}Li$	3	3	6
$^{7}_{3}Li$	3	4	7
$^{35}_{17}Cl$	17	18	35
$^{37}_{17}Cl$	17	20	37

Abundance of isotopes

Some elements are almost entirely made of one variety of atom. But most elements have at least two isotopes, and many elements have several. Examples are given in the chart on p.54, which also shows the percentage of each isotope.

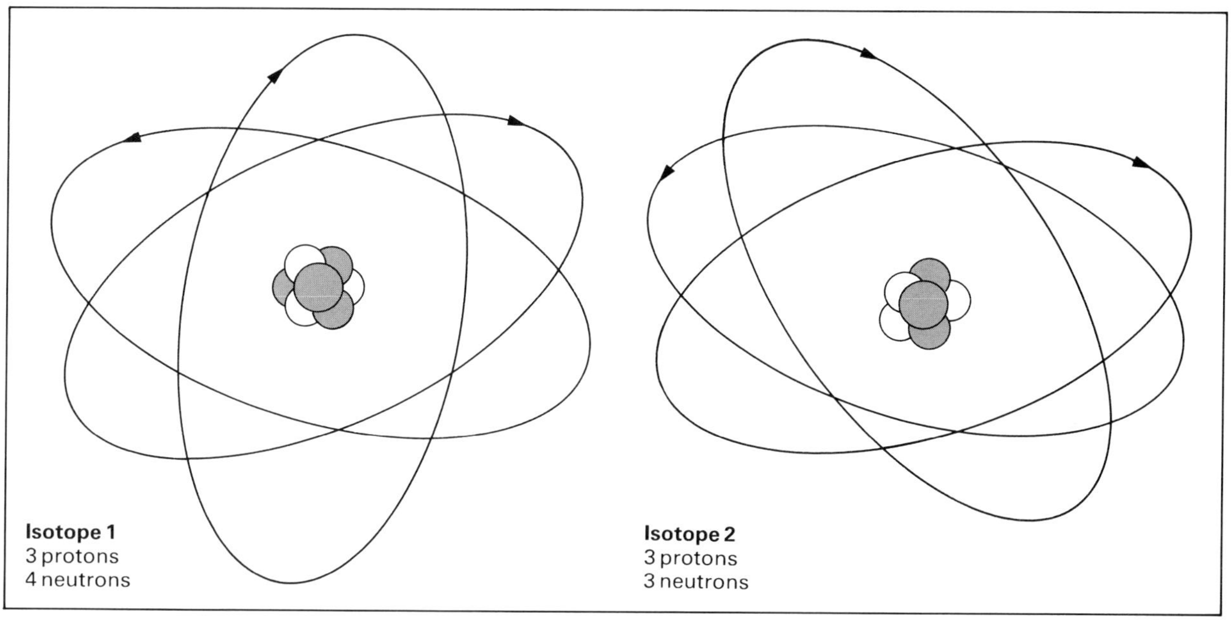

Isotopes of the element lithium

Element	*Atomic number*	*Isotope*	*Abundance (%)*
hydrogen	1	$^{1}_{1}H$	99.985
		$^{2}_{1}H$	0.015
lithium	3	$^{6}_{3}Li$	7.4
		$^{7}_{3}Li$	92.6
beryllium	4	$^{9}_{4}Be$	100
carbon	6	$^{12}_{6}C$	98.9
		$^{13}_{6}C$	1.1
chlorine	17	$^{35}_{17}Cl$	75.5
		$^{37}_{17}Cl$	24.5
iodine	53	$^{127}_{53}I$	100
uranium	92	$^{234}_{92}U$	0.006
		$^{235}_{92}U$	0.720
		$^{238}_{92}U$	99.274

Definition of atomic mass unit

Two isotopes of carbon are given in the table in the last section; the most abundant is ^{12}C. This is the atom that is taken as the standard for the *relative atomic mass scale.* On this scale, one atom of ^{12}C is said to have 12 *mass units.* The masses of all other atoms are expressed in this unit. An atom of ^{1}H has a mass of almost exactly one unit on the relative atomic mass scale.

Summary

1. The atomic number of an element is the number of protons in the nucleus of any atom of the element. All atoms with a particular atomic number are atoms of the same element.
2. The relative atomic mass of an element is a measure of the mass of a number of atoms of the element compared with the same number of atoms of a standard, for example hydrogen.
3. The number of neutrons in the nucleus of an atom does not affect the chemical properties of the atom.
4. Varieties of an element with atoms containing different numbers of neutrons are called isotopes of the element.
5. Most elements consist of at least two isotopes and many have several.
6. A shorthand way of describing isotopes is to use the $^{A}_{Z}X$ system.
7. The mass number (symbol '*A*') of an atom gives the total number of protons and neutrons in the nucleus of the atom.

Extension

1. The *relative atomic mass* of an element is the average mass of the atoms in a sample of the element, compared with a standard atom. We have seen in this section that an element may be made up of several isotopes. The mass numbers of the isotopes of an element are different. You can work out the approximate relative atomic mass of the element from the mass numbers of the isotopes, if you know the percentage abundance of each isotope.

   Here are two examples to illustrate the method:

Element	*Isotopes*	*Approximate abundance (%)*	*Approximate relative atomic mass*
chlorine	^{35}Cl	75	$(\frac{75}{100} \times 35) + (\frac{25}{100} \times 37) = 35.5$
	^{37}Cl	25	
copper	^{63}Cu	70	$(\frac{70}{100} \times 63) + (\frac{30}{100} \times 65) = 63.6$
	^{65}Cu	30	

Use the following information to work out A_r values of the elements gallium, bromine and silver.

Element	*Isotopes*	*Approximate abundance (%)*
gallium	^{69}Ga ^{71}Ga	60 40
bromine	^{79}Br ^{81}Br	50 50
silver	^{107}Ag ^{109}Ag	51 49

2. **The potassium–argon question**
Argon consists entirely of the atom $^{40}_{18}Ar$, so its relative atomic mass is approximately 40. But potassium has two isotopes with the following abundances:

^{39}K 93%
^{41}K 7%

Use this information to determine the A_r value of potassium. What is unusual about the result? Can you explain what has happened?

Revision

1. This question is about the following terms:
A atomic number
B group number
C mass number
D neutron number
E relative atomic mass

Choose the one that is:
i the average mass of atoms of an element compared with a standard
ii the number of protons in the nucleus of an atom
iii the sum of the numbers of protons and neutrons in the nucleus
iv usually given the symbol *Z*
v usually given the symbol *A*
vi equal to *A* minus *Z*

2. Draw pictures to show the nucleus in each of the following atoms. Use different colours or shading to show protons and neutrons.
i $^{1}_{1}H$
ii $^{2}_{1}H$
iii $^{3}_{2}He$
iv $^{4}_{2}He$
v $^{9}_{4}Be$

3. The letters A, B, C, D and E have been used instead of the proper chemical symbols for the elements in the following cases:
A $^{6}_{3}A$
B $^{12}_{6}B$
C $^{32}_{16}C$
D $^{60}_{28}D$
E $^{70}_{32}E$

Choose from the above an isotope:
i of the element carbon
ii of the element sulphur
iii with mass number 32
iv with atomic number 32
v with neutron number 32

4. This question is about the following numbers:
A 8
B 16
C 24
D 32
E 48

Choose the one that is:
i the atomic number of the element sulphur
ii the approximate relative atomic mass of the element oxygen
iii the number of neutrons in $^{16}_{8}O$
iv the number of neutrons in $^{86}_{38}Sr$
v the atomic number of the atom $^{32}_{16}S$
vi the mass number of the atom $^{32}_{16}S$

Unit 13
Valency patterns

Covalent or ionic compounds?

Just knowing the formula of a compound will not tell you whether the compound has covalent or ionic bonding. For example, here are the formulas of some chlorides:

HCl, ICl, KCl, NaCl.

The formulas are all of the 'XCl' type, but two of the compounds are ionic and two of them are covalent. Here are the formulas of some oxides:

BaO, CO, CaO, NO.

These formulas are all of the 'XO' type, but, once again, two of the compounds are ionic and two are covalent.

So, how can you tell which compounds are likely to be covalent and which are likely to be ionic? The obvious answer is, check their properties. See if they are *electrolytes*. Find out if they are *volatile or involatile*. The chlorides KCl and NaCl are involatile electrolytes, so they must have ionic structures. The same applies to the oxides BaO and CaO. But the chlorides HCl and ICl, and the oxides CO and NO, are volatile; they are non-electrolytes, so they must be molecular substances with covalent bonding.

● *You can tell what kind of structure a compound has if you know its properties.*

Now, we want to know about the structures of compounds we meet. Does this mean we have to learn the facts about all the compounds we are likely to come across? That would be a very big job! Fortunately, the facts about ionic and covalent compounds fall into a pattern. Looking at the periodic table of the elements will help you to see the pattern. You will remember that:

● *Metals are found on the left side of the periodic table. Non-metals are found on the right.*

How does this help us to work out the facts about the structures of compounds? Well, look back at the formulas of the compounds that were mentioned at the beginning of this section: HCl, ICl, KCl, NaCl, BaO, CO, CaO and NO. The covalent ones are HCl, ICl, CO and NO. Where are their elements in the periodic table? The ionic ones are KCl, NaCl, BaO and CaO. Where are their elements in the periodic table? See if you agree with the following conclusions.

1. A compound formed by two elements that are both on the right of the periodic table is likely to be covalent.
2. A compound formed by an element on the left and an element on the right of the periodic table is likely to be ionic.

We can label these 'R–R' compounds and 'L–R' compounds respectively. So, HCl, ICl, CO and NO are 'R–R' compounds, and KCl, NaCl, BaO and CaO are 'L–R' compounds.

● *R–R compounds are generally covalent; L–R compounds are generally ionic.*

Now we can make predictions about other compounds we meet. For example, what kind of structures would you expect for the compounds BN, CoO, KF, LiI, PBr_3, SF_6?

Valency numbers

In previous sections we have learned how electrons are used to bind atoms together (see Units 8 and 9). The electrons may be either *transferred* or *shared*. Ions are formed when electrons are transferred (this is called *electrovalency*). Molecules are formed when electrons are shared (this is called *covalency*).

However, in both kinds of valency, definite numbers of electrons are used for binding atoms, and the number of electrons used fixes the combining power of an atom with other atoms. For example, carbon atoms have four electrons that can be used in bonding. The electrons used in bonding can be called the 'valency electrons'. (Valency electrons are nearly always the outer shell electrons of the atom.) Because carbon has four valency electrons it forms compounds with formulas CH_4, CF_4, CCl_4, CO_2, CS_2, etc.

● *The combining power of an atom is fixed by the number of electrons it uses in valency.*

You can often work out the number of valency electrons in an atom if you know its electron structure. Then you can work out possible formulas for many compounds of the atom. But it is usually quicker to learn 'valency numbers' for the common elements. The following table shows the usual valency numbers of some common elements.

+1	*+2*	*+3*	*+4*	*−3*	*−2*	*−1*
Li Na K Ag Cu H	Mg Ca Ba Zn Cu Pb Co Fe	Al Fe	C Si Pb	N P	O S	F Cl Br I H

Notes

1. A few metals have more than one valency number. These are shown in more than one column above, for example Cu, Fe, Pb.
2. Most of the non-metals have additional valency numbers (not shown above), for example:
   P: + 3, +5
   S: + 4, +6
   Cl: + 1, +3, +5, +7
3. Positive and negative numbers are used to indicate possible combinations of atoms: those with numbers of opposite sign can combine.

Using valency numbers

You should learn the valency numbers of the common elements. You will then find that you can work out probable formulas for many of the compounds that you meet in chemistry.

All you have to do is add together the right numbers of atoms so that the valency numbers cancel out. For example, when zinc (+2) and iodine (−1) combine together the formula ZnI_2 is expected (+2 is cancelled out by 2 × (−1)).

● *The valency numbers of the atoms in most formulas cancel out if the correct ratio of atoms is used. (In a few cases formulas cannot be predicted from valency numbers: see Extension 1.)*

The other examples given in the next table should help to make the method clear.

Atoms and their valency numbers		*Formula of the compound*
Li (+1)	F (−1)	LiF
Mg (+2)	Cl (−1)	$MgCl_2$
H (+1)	S (−2)	H_2S
Al (+3)	O (−2)	Al_2O_3
P (+3 or −5)	O (−2)	P_2O_3 or P_2O_5

Summary

1. You can tell whether the structure of a compound is ionic or covalent if you know the properties of the compound.
2. However, there is a 'rule' about the type of structure that a compound is likely to have:
   R–R compounds are generally covalent;
   L–R compounds are generally ionic.
3. Elements on the left side of the periodic table are metals: elements on the right side are non-metals.
4. The combining power of an atom is fixed by the number of electrons that it uses in valency.
5. Valency numbers of the elements can be used to work out probable formulas for compounds.
6. The valency numbers of the atoms in most formulas cancel out if the correct ratio of atoms is used.

Extension

1. Carbon's valency number is 4 in all its common compounds except in one of its oxides.
   i Give the formula of the oxide in which carbon does not have valency 4.
   ii What is the valency number of carbon in this oxide?
   iii Give the name and formula of the oxide of carbon in which its valency number is 4.
   iv List the main differences between the properties of these two oxides of carbon.

2. When a metal has more than one valency number, the numbers are included in the names of the compounds. Work out the formulas of the following compounds:

   i copper(I) chloride
   ii copper(II) oxide
   iii iron(II) chloride
   iv iron(III) oxide
   v lead(IV) oxide

3. i For many elements the valency number is the same as the group number in the periodic table. Which of the following have valency numbers the same as the group number of the element?

   A Ca
   B F
   C Fe
   D Li
   E Na

   ii In other cases, the valency number and group number are not the same. Which of the elements listed below have valency numbers that are related to the group number of the element like this:

   Valency number = group number − 8

   A Al
   B Ba
   C F
   D Na
   E O

Revision

1 This question is about the following substances:

   A a gas
   B a solid that dissolves in water to form a conducting solution
   C an involatile solid that is an insulator even when molten
   D a solid that can be decomposed by electrolysis when molten
   E a volatile liquid

   Which of the five substances could be:

   i covalent compounds
   ii ionic compounds

2. This question is about the following formulas:

   A HCl
   B KCl
   C BaO
   D CO
   E CO_2

   i Which of them are formulas of:

      a covalent compounds
      b ionic compounds

   ii Which formula would not be predicted using valency numbers?

3. In each of the following cases say whether the formula is that of a covalent compound or an ionic compound:

   i BF_3
   ii CaH_2
   iii Cl_2O
   iv H_2S
   v MgI_2

4. This question is about the following valency numbers:

   A +5
   B +2
   C +1
   D −1
   E −2

   Choose one that is the valency number of:

   i an alkali metal
   ii phosphorus
   iii oxygen
   iv a halogen
   v calcium

5. Use the table of valency numbers given in this Unit to work out formulas for the following compounds:

   i potassium sulphide
   ii aluminium bromide
   iii silver oxide
   iv hydrogen iodide
   v aluminium sulphide
   vi sodium hydride
   vii zinc bromide
   viii sodium nitride
   ix silicon bromide
   x lithium fluoride

6. Hydrogen can have valency number +1 or −1. Work out its valency number in each of the following compounds:

i NaH
ii HCl
iii H_2O
iv BaH_2
v HI

7. Some additional valency numbers for non-metals are shown below:

Non-metal	P	S	Cl
Valency numbers	+3, +5	+4, +6	+1, +3, +5, +7

i Use these numbers to work out the formulas of oxides of:

a phosphorus
b sulphur
c chlorine

ii Nitrogen forms several oxides. Work out the valency numbers of nitrogen in the following:

a N_2O
b NO
c NO_2

Unit 14
Electronic structures and the periodic table

Some questions about the periodic table

We shall start this Unit by asking some questions about the periodic arrangement of the elements.

First of all, *why* are some elements similar to others? Secondly, how do families of elements come to be arranged regularly in the atomic number list of the elements? In other words, *why are the properties of the elements linked to their atomic numbers?*

Ion formation

The type of ion formed is one of the most obvious resemblances shown by elements in groups. Look at the next figure.

Some ions of elements in groups

				$_1H$			0*
I	II	III	IV	V	VI	VII	He
Li^+	Be^{2+}					F^-	Ne
Na^+	Mg^{2+}					Cl^-	Ar
K^+	Ca^{2+}					Br^-	Kr
Rb^+	Sr^{2+}					I^-	Xe
Cs^+	Ba^{2+}						

*Group 0 elements never form compounds containing simple ions.

This chart shows that elements in a particular group form ions with the same charge. In other words, families of elements have atoms with the same ability to lose or gain electrons. For example, all the elements in group I have atoms that can lose one electron. Ions with one unit of positive charge are formed, that is, unipositive ions. Why should this be? Why is there always *loss* of an electron, never gain? Why is it only *one* electron, never two or three?

Similar questions could be asked about the group II or group VII or group 0 elements. Why are the charges on group II ions always 2+? Why do group 0 atoms form no ions?

Stable numbers of electrons

The noble gases, group 0, have electron numbers as follows:

He: 2
Ne: 10
Ar: 18
Kr: 32
Xe: 54

As we have seen, these atoms form no simple ions. In other words, they will neither gain nor lose electrons easily. Here is an explanation:

- *Noble gas atoms have stable numbers of electrons.*

('Stable' simply means 'not easily changed'. So, the statement above means: the numbers of electrons in noble gas atoms are difficult to alter.)

How does this idea about stable numbers of electrons fit in with ion formation of other elements? Look at these elements lined up in atomic number order:

$_1H$	$_2He$	$_3Li$	$_4Be$

We know that the atom H can *gain* an electron to form the ion H^-. So it ends up with two electrons. On the other hand, the atom Li can *lose* an electron to form the ion Li^+. So it also ends up with two electrons. These are both stable ions. It seems that:

- *Two electrons is a stable number of electrons in other atoms besides He.*

Now look at this line of elements:

$_9F$	$_{10}Ne$	$_{11}Na$	$_{12}Mg$

We know that the atom F gains an electron to form F^-. And the atom Na loses an electron to form Na^+. In each case, the ions end up with 10 electrons, like the Ne atom (what about the Mg^{2+} ion?). It seems that:

- *Ten is another stable number of electrons for an atom to have.*

If you consider the line of elements Cl, Ar, K and Ca you will find that *18 is another stable number of electrons.*

Patterns of electrons in atoms

It is reasonable to accept that certain numbers of electrons in atoms are specially stable. This has led to the following ideas about the way electrons are arranged in atoms:

1. When there are more than two electrons in an atom, they are divided up into sets called 'shells of electrons'.
2. The first shell has an orbit close to the nucleus. The second shell has an orbit further away from the nucleus, and so on.
3. Each shell has room for only a certain number of electrons: 2 in the first shell, 8 in the second, 18 in the third (although 8 is a stable number for the third shell of some atoms).

The way the electrons in an atom are grouped together is called the *electronic structure* or the *electronic configuration* of the atom. The electronic structures of some atoms are illustrated in the figure on p.62.

Conclusions

Look at the electronic structures for a family of elements, for example group I:

Li: 2.1
Na: 2.8.1
K: 2.8.8.1

or group VII:

F: 2.7
Cl: 2.8.7
Br: 2.8.18.7

You can see that *different elements in a family of elements have atoms with similar electronic structures.* They have the same number of outer shell electrons. This is how the theory of electronic structures explains the family resemblances of certain elements. We believe that:

- *Atoms with similar electronic structures have similar properties.*

A table showing the electronic structures of the first 20 elements is given in Appendix 1 at the back of the book (p. 267).

Summary

1. Noble gas atoms have stable numbers of electrons, and the numbers 2, 10, and 18 are especially stable numbers of electrons in any atom.
2. Electrons in atoms are arranged in shells at different distances from the nucleus. Full shells can contain only a certain number of electrons (2, 8 or 18) depending on the distance from the nucleus.
3. Different atoms in a family of elements have similar electronic structures, that is, the same number of outer shell electrons.
4. Atoms with similar electronic structures have similar properties.

Electronic structures of some atoms

Atom	*Atomic number*	*Picture of the electronic structure*	*Electronic structure 'shorthand'*
H	1	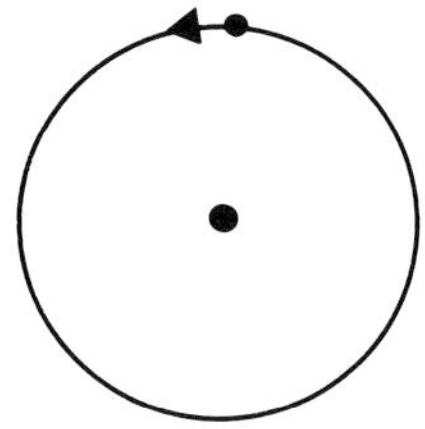	1
He	2	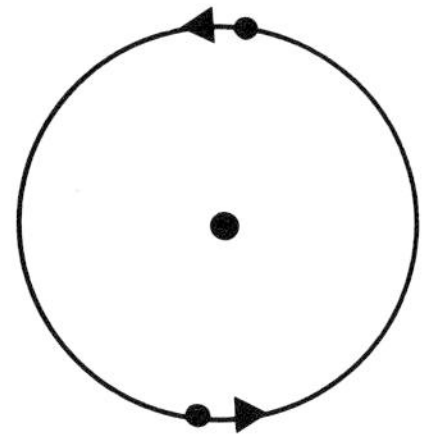	2
Li	3	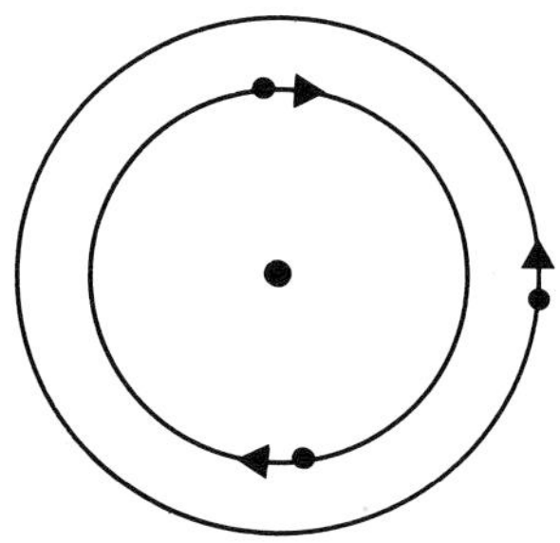	2.1
Ne	10	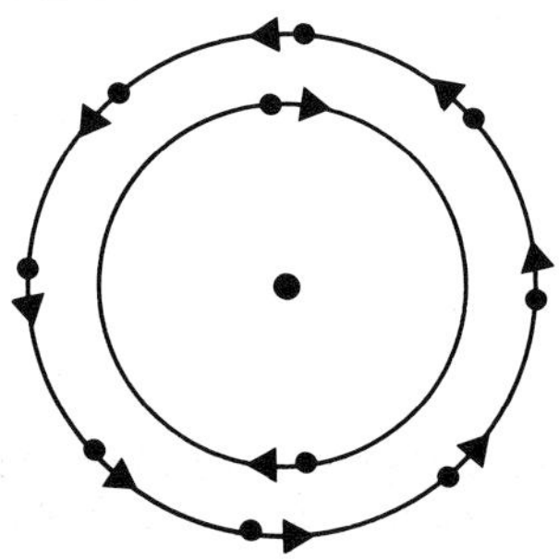	2.8
Na	11	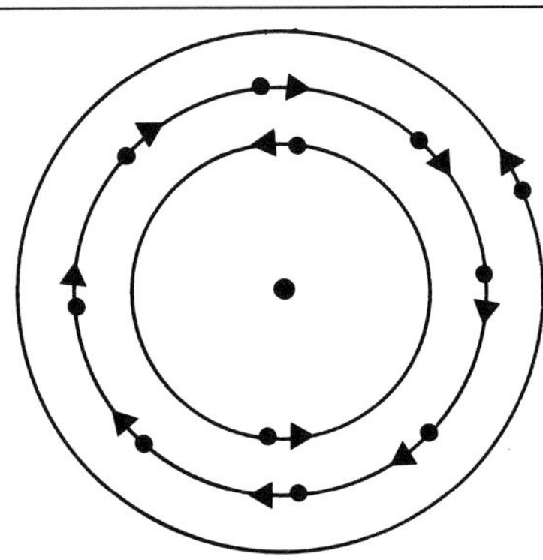	2.8.1

Revision

1. This question is about the following atoms:

   A Br
   B Ca
   C Na
   D Ne
   E O

   Choose the atom that will usually form:

   i unipositive ions
   ii dipositive ions
   iii uninegative ions
   iv dinegative ions
   v no simple ions

2. Choose from the following the atom or ion that does not have a stable number of electrons.

   A K^+
   B O^{2-}
   C S^-
   D Ca^{2+}
   E Ar

3. i Name the elements that have the following atomic numbers:

   a 4 *b* 12 *c* 20 *d* 38 *e* 56

   ii To which group in the periodic table do the above elements belong?
   iii Give the electronic structures for the first three elements in the group.
   iv Name the element in this group that has the electronic structure 2.8.18.8.2.
   v What will be the electronic structure and formula of the stable ion formed by this element?

4. Draw pictures to illustrate the electronic structure:

   i 2.7
   ii of the element with atomic number 13
   iii of the atom K
   iv of the ion K^+

5. The following atoms are lined up in atomic number order:

$_{17}Cl$	$_{18}Ar$	$_{19}K$	$_{20}Ca$	

   i What is the number of electrons in *a* Cl *b* Ar?
   ii What is the number of electrons in *a* Cl^- *b* K^+?
   iii Give the formula of the stable ion formed by Ca.
   iv How many electrons are there in this calcium ion?
   v What conclusion can you draw about the numbers of electrons in stable ions and in noble gas atoms?

6. The number of *outer shell* electrons for various atoms is given below:

   A 1
   B 3
   C 4
   D 7
   E 8

   From your knowledge of the way atoms behave, which of the above belongs to an atom which is most:

   i likely to form unipositive ions
   ii stable
   iii likely to form negative ions

SECTION II

ELEMENTS, COMPOUNDS AND CHEMICAL CHANGE

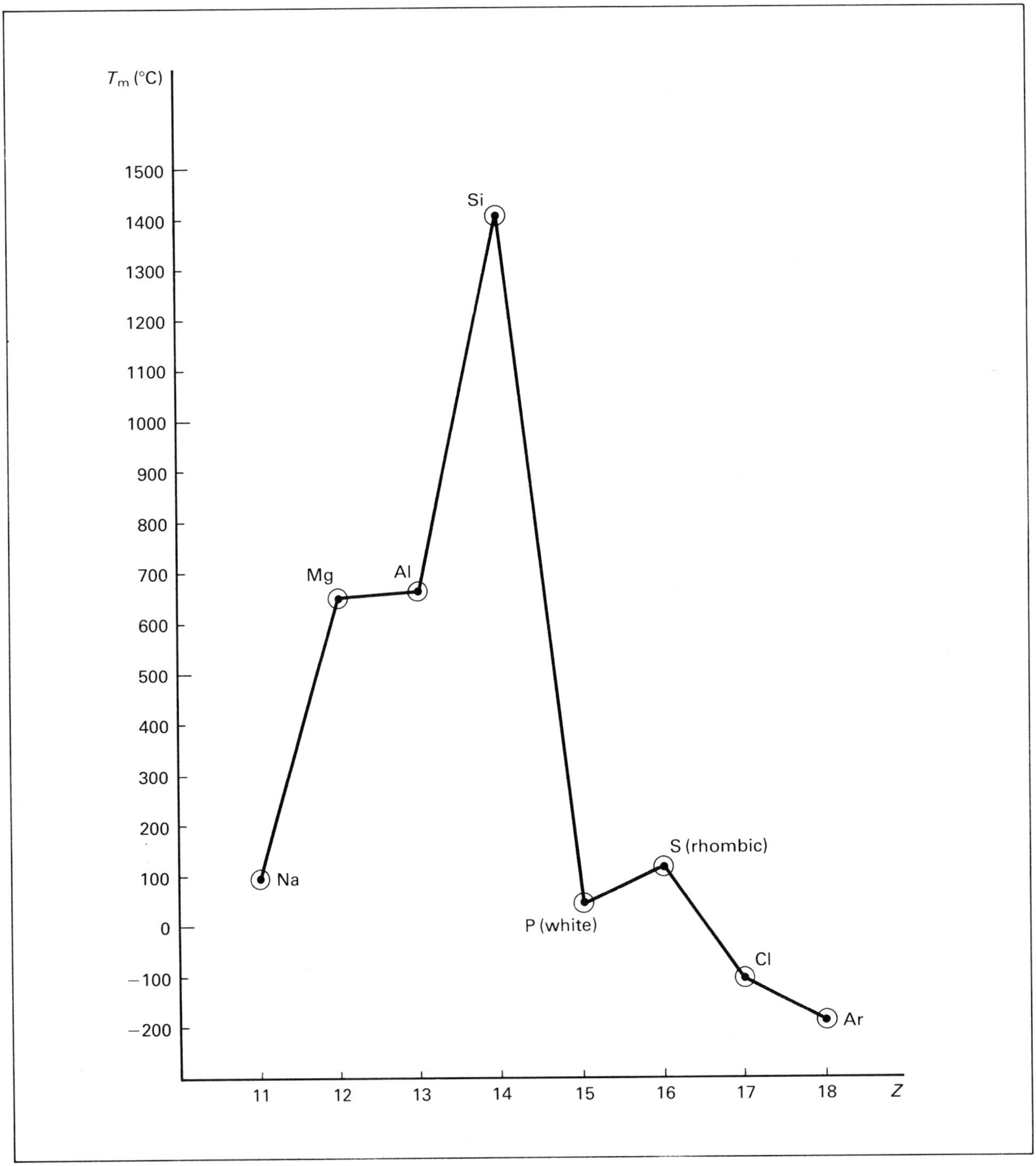

Melting temperatures of the elements in period 3

Unit 15
Elements in a period: physical properties in period 3

The properties of the elements change as you cross the periodic table. Period 3 has been chosen to illustrate the changes. You would see similar changes if you looked at other periods, for example period 2.

In this Unit, the *physical properties* of the elements will be considered. Their *chemical properties* will be considered in the next one.

The elements in period 3

The elements in period 3 have atomic numbers from 11 to 18. Here they are in atomic number order:

$_{11}$Na	$_{12}$Mg	$_{13}$Al	$_{14}$Si	$_{15}$P	$_{16}$S	$_{17}$Cl	$_{18}$Ar

As you can see, the period includes metals, non-metals, and the noble gas argon. The metals are found on the left of the period, and the non-metals on the right.

- *Elements with metallic character are found on the left side of period 3, and non-metals on the right.*

Physical properties of the elements in period 3

The division of period 3 into metals and non-metals becomes clear when you begin to examine the properties of the elements. We shall look at two important physical properties: melting temperature and electrical conductivity.

The melting temperatures of the elements are given in the graph on p.66.

You can see that the T_m values increase from Na to Si. After Si, there is a sudden drop to P. This observation links Si with the metals Na, Mg and Al. Looking at this property, you might conclude that Si is a metal like Na, Mg and Al; however, the picture changes slightly when you look at the next property: electrical conductivity.

The figure below shows electrical conductivity data. (The size of the spot represents the conductivity of equal amounts of the solid element.) Note that P, S, Cl and Ar have conductivity values that are practically zero. Si is a *semiconductor* (see Unit 39).

The first three values increase steadily from left to right again. These high values confirm the metallic character of Na, Mg and Al. But this time, there is a drop between Al and Si, although the value for Si is still much higher than those for the elements P to Ar. This suggests *weak* metallic character for Si.

- *Silicon has physical properties that suggest that it has weak metallic character.*

Structures of the elements

What about the structures of elements in period 3? How are their atoms arranged?

Ideas about the structures have been suggested which fit in with the observed properties. For example, melting temperature data suggests that the element Si has a *giant structure*. Melting temperature and conductivity data taken together suggest that Na, Mg and Al have *metallic giant structures*. *The elements on the right of the period have*

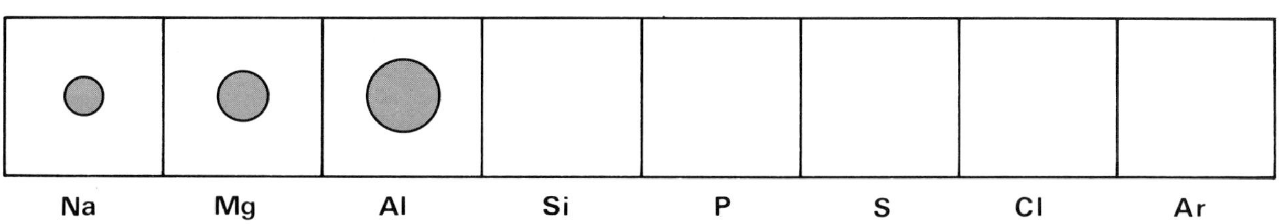

Electrical conductivities of the solid elements (values for P, S, Cl and Ar are invisibly small)

molecular structures. Other evidence supports this conclusion.

The arrangements of atoms in the giant structures have been worked out. They are given in the next table.

Element	*Structure*	*Number of neighbours joined to each atom*
Na	body-centred cubic	8
Mg	close packed	12
Al	close packed	12
Si	diamond structure	4

You can find pictures of these giant structures in Unit 5.

The molecular shapes of the remaining elements are shown in the figure on the right.

- *Structures of the elements in period 3 vary from giant structures on the left to molecular structures on the right.*

Bonding in the elements of period 3

Clearly, the forces between Ar atoms are practically non-existent. But what kinds of bond hold the atoms together in the other structures described above?

The good conductors (Na, Mg, Al) have 'free electrons'. In other words their properties are best explained by the idea of the *metallic bond*. This has been dealt with in Unit 10. You will recall that metallic structures are considered to be regular arrangements of cations. The cations are held together by a cloud of free ('delocalized') electrons within the structure. Each atom contributes one or more electrons to the cloud. The metallic bond is the attractive force between the positive cations and the negatively charged electron cloud.

Let us now leave the true metals on the left of the period, and look at the molecular elements on the right.

The bonding in molecules has been described in a previous Unit (Unit 9, p.35). The force that holds the atoms together in the molecule is called the *covalent bond*. It is the result of the sharing of electron pairs between pairs of atoms. The electrons are generally not free to move away from the two atoms that are joined by the bond. In other words, they are localized electrons. The diagrams on p.69 show the

Molecule	*Shape*	*Number of neighbouring atoms joined to each atom*
P_4 (white phosphorus)		3
S_8 (rhombic and monoclinic sulphur)	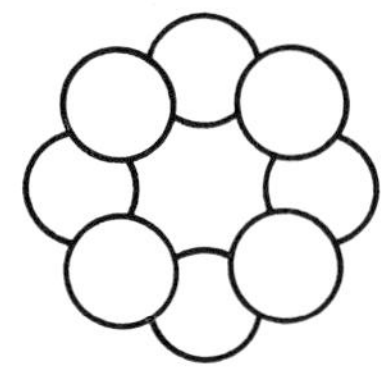	2
Cl_2		1
Ar	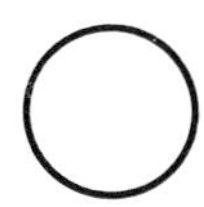	0

Molecules of period 3 elements

electron arrangements in the molecules Cl_2 and S_8. (Only outer shell electrons are considered.)

The bonding in silicon seems to be part-way between metallic and covalent (judging from its poor conductivity). It is usually described as having a giant covalent structure. This suggests the electrons are largely localized between pairs of atoms.

So, the bonding in elements of period 3 may be summarized like this:

Metallic bonding				*Covalent bonding*		
$_{11}Na$	$_{12}Mg$	$_{13}Al$	$_{14}Si$	$_{15}P$	$_{16}S$	$_{17}Cl$

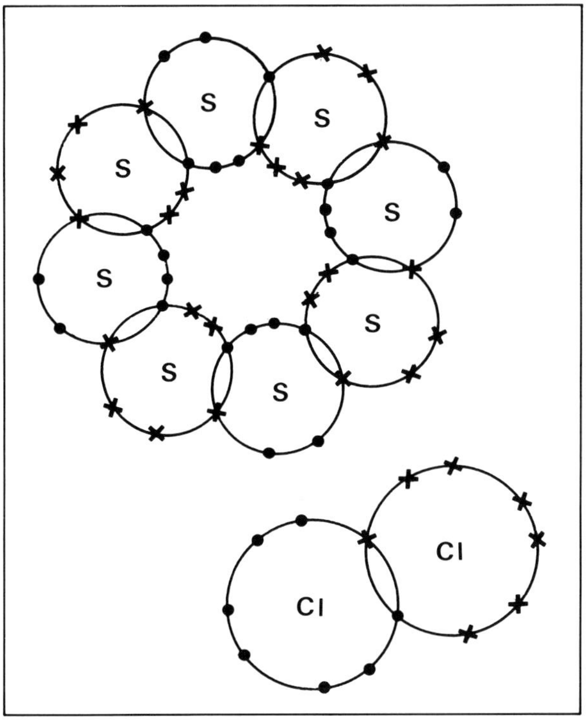

Electron arrangements in Cl_2 and S_8 molecules (only outer electrons shown)

Summary

1. There is a change from metal on the left to non-metal on the right of period 3. (The element on the extreme right is a noble gas.)
2. Silicon has physical properties that suggest that it has weak metallic character.
3. Structures of the elements in period 3 vary from giant structures on the left to molecular structures on the right.
4. Elements on the left have atoms joined by metallic bonds. Those on the right have atoms joined by covalent bonds.
5. Structures and bonding can be summarized as follows:

$_{11}$Na	$_{12}$Mg	$_{13}$Al	$_{14}$Si	$_{15}$P	$_{16}$S	$_{17}$Cl	$_{18}$Ar
Giant structures				Molecular structures			
Metallic bonding			Covalent bonding				

Extension

1. Data giving the melting temperatures and atomic numbers of the period 2 elements is shown below:
   - i Draw a graph of T_m(°C) (vertical axis) against Z (horizontal axis).
   - ii Look at the shape of the graph. How does it compare with the graph for period 3 elements?
2. i Use the data given in Extension 1 to help you answer the following questions about period 2 elements:
   - *a* Which elements have giant structures?
   - *b* Which elements have molecular structures?

   ii Use your knowledge of period 3 to predict where in period 2 we are likely to find:
   - *a* metallic conductors
   - *b* non-conductors
   - *c* intermediate conductors

Element	*Li*	*Be*	*B*	*C*	*N*	*O*	*F*	*Ne*
Z	3	4	5	6	7	8	9	10
T_m(°C)	180	1280	2300	3730	−210	−218	−220	−249

Revision

1. Draw 'dot and cross' pictures to show the electron arrangements in the following molecules:
   - i F_2
   - ii O_2
   - iii N_2
2. Explain the following facts using the ideas of structure and bonding:
   - i silicon has a very high melting temperature compared with chlorine
   - ii aluminium conducts electricity, but sulphur is an insulator
3. Summarize the trends in physical properties of the elements that are observed in crossing a period of the periodic table from left to right.

Unit 16
Elements in a period : chemical properties in period 3

Looking for patterns in reactions

In this Unit we shall look at the reactions of the period 3 elements with water, acids and oxygen. Studies of this sort show patterns in the chemical behaviour of the elements. For example, certain reactions are typical of metallic elements, but non-metals react differently. Also, the metals are not all equally reactive, and there is a regular trend in their reactivity.

See if you can sort out the patterns as we go along.

Reactions of the period 3 elements with water

Sodium reacts vigorously with cold water (and even with water vapour in the air):

$$2Na(s) + H_2O(l) \rightarrow 2NaOH(aq) + H_2(g)$$

Magnesium reacts very slowly with cold water but reacts rapidly when heated in steam:

$$Mg(s) + H_2O(g) \rightarrow MgO(s) + H_2(g)$$

Aluminium reacts in steam, but not in cold water. Hydrogen is formed once again. Silicon, phosphorus and sulphur give no reaction with water or steam.

Chlorine reacts with water in the following way:

$$Cl_2(g) + H_2O(l) \rightarrow HClO(aq) + HCl(aq)$$

You will notice that no hydrogen is formed in the reaction of chlorine with water.

● *The only elements that form hydrogen when they react with water are the reactive metals.*

Reactions of the period 3 elements with acids

Sodium's reaction with dilute acids is dangerously violent and should not be investigated!

Magnesium reacts vigorously with dilute acids to produce hydrogen:

$$Mg(s) + H_2SO_4(aq) \rightarrow MgSO_4(aq) + H_2(g)$$

$$Mg(s) + 2HCl(aq) \rightarrow MgCl_2(aq) + H_2(g)$$

(Some nitrogen oxide is formed in addition to hydrogen if nitric acid is used.)

Aluminium's surface is covered with a thin film of oxide. This protects it from attack by acids at first. Once a reaction gets going, it is quite brisk.

$$2Al(s) + 6HCl(aq) \rightarrow 2AlCl_3(aq) + 3H_2(g)$$

Silicon, phosphorus, sulphur, chlorine (and of course, argon) give no reaction with dilute acids.

● *Non-metals in period 3 show no reactivity towards dilute acids.*

Patterns start to show

Metals and non-metals clearly react differently under the same conditions. We have seen that the metals in period 3 give hydrogen when reacted with water and dilute acids: non-metals don't. Producing hydrogen like this can be thought of as a guide to chemical reactivity of metals. The most reactive metal is therefore sodium, and the least reactive is aluminium. It seems that the strength of metallic reactivity drops from Na to Al. Elements to the right of aluminium show no metallic reactivity.

● *Chemical reactivity of metals in period 3 drops as the period is crossed from left to right.*

Formation of ions

The reactions of metals with water and dilute acids involve the formation of ions from metal atoms. For example, when Na reacts with water, the cation Na^+ is formed, and when Mg reacts with acid, the cation Mg^{2+} is formed.

Can we use the idea of ion formation to explain the observed reactivity pattern in period 3? The answer to this question is, yes, if we extend the idea of ion formation as follows:

a energy is needed to remove an electron from an atom, that is, to form a cation;
b some metal atoms need less energy to form cations than do other metal atoms;
c the metals that need the least energy to form cations will be the most reactive.

Thinking along these lines, we reach the following conclusion:

● *Elements further to the left in a period form cations more easily than do those on the right.*

This statement fits in with the idea of metal atoms forming cations, while non-metal atoms form anions (see Unit 3).

Reactions of period 3 elements with oxygen

Oxygen is a very reactive element and reacts with most other elements. In other words, oxides of most elements can be formed by synthesis. In period 3, all the elements apart from chlorine and argon react with oxygen. (Oxides of chlorine do exist, but they are prepared by indirect methods.) Silicon reacts well only at high temperatures. Sodium, magnesium, phosphorus and sulphur burn vigorously.

The oxides that may be formed by synthesis are: Na_2O, Na_2O_2, MgO, Al_2O_3, SiO_2, P_2O_3, P_2O_5, SO_2 and SO_3. Here is an equation for the synthesis of one of them:

$$2Mg(s) + O_2(g) \rightarrow 2MgO(s)$$

Can you write balanced equations for the other synthesis reactions?

● *Oxygen reacts with all the elements in period 3 except chlorine and argon.*

Valency patterns in period 3

Valency numbers have been introduced in a previous Unit (see Unit 13). When we look at the valency numbers for elements in period 3, this is what we find:

Na	*Mg*	*Al*	*Si*	*P*	*S*	*Cl*	*Ar*
+1	+2	+3	+4	±3 +5	−2 +4 +6	±1 +3 +5 +7	0

Note: Na can be shown to have valency number +1 in both its oxides, Na_2O and Na_2O_2.

You will recall that formulas of many compounds can be predicted using the valency numbers. For example, using the elements in period 3 we could suggest the formulas:

$NaCl$ $(+1-1=0)$
Na_2S $(2\times(+1)-2=0)$
$SiCl_4$ $(+4-4\times(-1)=0)$

But remember: not all predicted compounds actually exist.

Summary

1. The only elements that form hydrogen when they react with water are the reactive metals.
2. Non-metals in period 3 show no reactivity towards dilute acids.
3. Metallic reactivity in period 3 drops as the period is crossed from left to right.
4. Elements further to the left in a period form cations more easily than those on their right.
5. Oxygen reacts with all the elements in period 3 except chlorine and argon.
6. The elements in period 3 show a pattern in their valency numbers.

Extension

This question is about valency patterns and electron structures.

1. Copy the following table and finish it to show the electron structures of the period 2 elements.

2. Explain how the maximum valency number of an element is connected with the electron structure of its atoms. Give examples to illustrate your answer.

Element	*Li*	*Be*	*B*					*Ne*
Z	3	4						
Electron structure	2.1							
Number of outer shell electrons	1						7	8
Valency numbers		+2	+3					

Revision

1. When aluminium reacts in steam, the aluminium is converted into aluminium oxide. This reaction is a reduction–oxidation reaction.
   - i Write the formula of aluminium oxide.
   - ii Name the other product of the reaction of aluminium with steam.
   - iii Write a balanced equation for the reaction.
   - iv Which reactant is oxidized in the reaction?
   - v Which reactant is the oxidizing agent?
2. Write balanced equations to show the synthesis of each of the following oxides:
   - i Na_2O
   - ii MgO
   - iii Al_2O_3
   - iv P_2O_5
   - v SO_2
3. The oxides of chlorine are:

   Cl_2O
   ClO_2
   Cl_2O_6
   Cl_2O_7
   - i Which of their formulas could have been predicted using the valency number idea?
   - ii Which of their formulas could not have been predicted using valency numbers? (Oxygen's valency number is -2.)
4. Elements that react with hydrogen usually achieve only their lowest valency number. Write down the formulas of all the hydrides of the period 3 elements. (Hydrogen's valency numbers are ± 1.)

Unit 17
Compounds of the period 3 elements

In this Unit we shall be looking at physical and chemical properties of two important groups of compounds: *chlorides* and *oxides*. For comparison purposes we have again chosen the period 3 elements.

Let us start with chlorides.

Chlorides of elements in period 3

Here are the formulas of the period 3 chlorides:

$NaCl$	$MgCl_2$	$AlCl_3$	$SiCl_4$	PCl_3 PCl_5	S_2Cl_2

(How many of these formulas could be predicted using the usual valency numbers of the elements?)

Physical properties of the period 3 chlorides

The melting temperatures and electrical conductivities of the period 3 chlorides are shown in the figure (right). (The size of the spot represents the conductivity of equal amounts of the liquid chlorides.)

The chlorides on the left of the period are clearly much less volatile than those on the right. There is also a change in electrical conductivity as you cross the period. The chlorides on the left are much better conductors (when molten) than those on the right.

● *Chlorides of elements on the left of period 3 are involatile electrolytes. Those on the right are volatile non-electrolytes.*

Structures and bonding of period 3 chlorides

What do physical properties of the chlorides tell us about their structures? The answer is, quite a lot (if you remember work done in Unit 7).

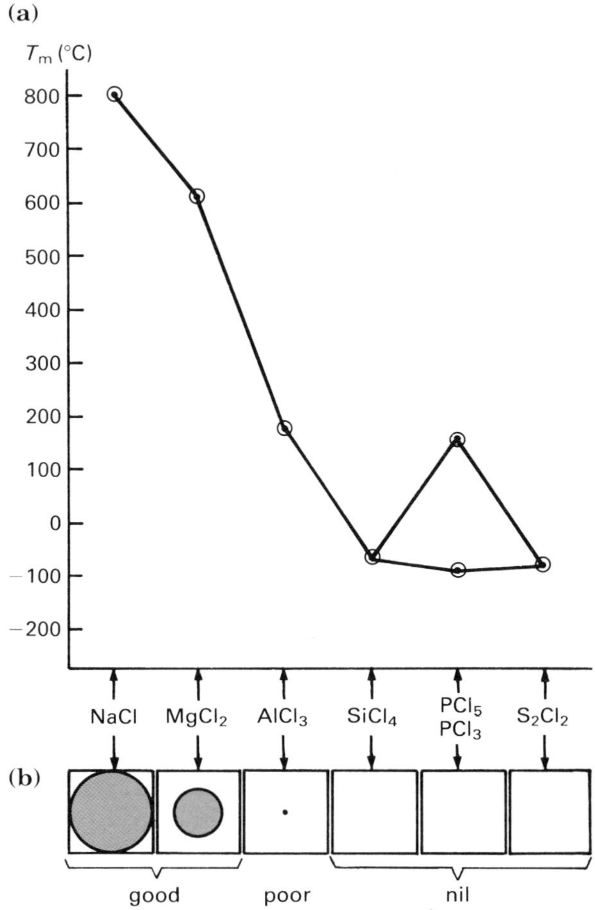

Melting temperature data for chlorides (a); conductivities of the liquid chlorides (b)

The physical properties of the chlorides suggest that those on the left of the period have *ionic giant structures*. Those on the right have *molecular covalent structures*. Examples are shown in the figure on p. 75 (top).

The dividing line in the period seems to be between $MgCl_2$ and $AlCl_3$. So, the overall picture looks like the figure below.

	NaCl	*$MgCl_2$*	*$AlCl_3$*	*$SiCl_4$*	*PCl_3/PCl_5*	*S_2Cl_2*
Structure	GIANT		MOLECULAR			
Bonding	IONIC		COVALENT			

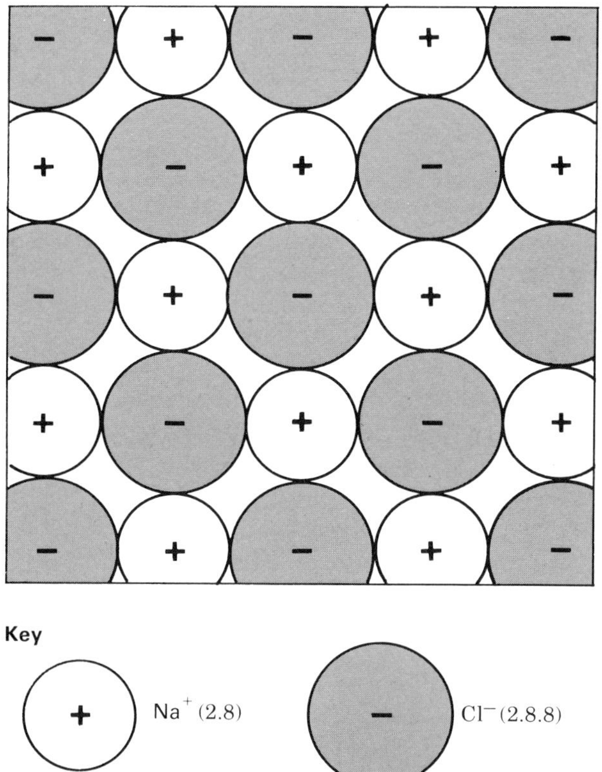

Structures of two chlorides in period 3

◀ **(i) Giant ionic structure of Na^+Cl^-:** each ion is attracted by all oppositely charged neighbours
(ii) Molecular structure of PCl_3: molecules show little attraction for their neighbours

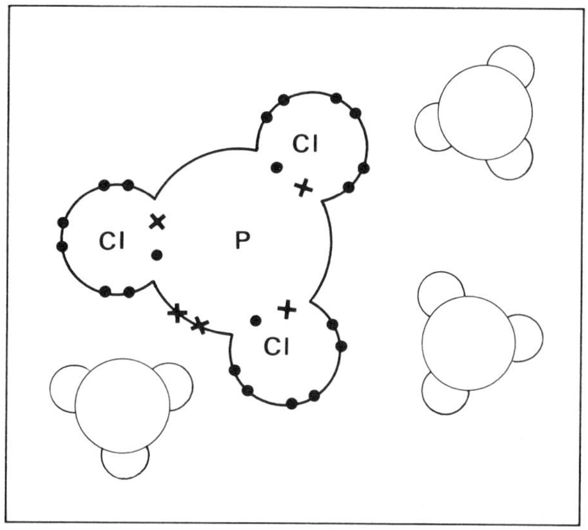

Chemical properties of period 3 chlorides

Chemical behaviour also illustrates the division between the left and right sides of the period, for example, the reactions of the chlorides with water: NaCl and $MgCl_2$ simply dissolve. The ions become 'hydrated' as they enter the solution. Hydration does not involve the destruction of ions and is easily reversed (i.e. no chemical reaction happens). We may picture a hydrated ion as in the figure (right). (The oxygen part of the water molecule is slightly negatively charged. This causes it to be attracted to the cations in solution.)

$AlCl_3$, $SiCl_4$, PCl_3, PCl_5, and S_2Cl_2 react with water. Water molecules are destroyed and new molecules are formed. This kind of chemical change is called a *hydrolysis* reaction, for example:

$$AlCl_3(s) + 3H_2O(l) \rightarrow Al(OH)_3(s) + 3HCl(aq)$$

$$2S_2Cl_2(l) + 2H_2O(l) \rightarrow SO_2(aq) + 4HCl(aq) + 3S(s)$$

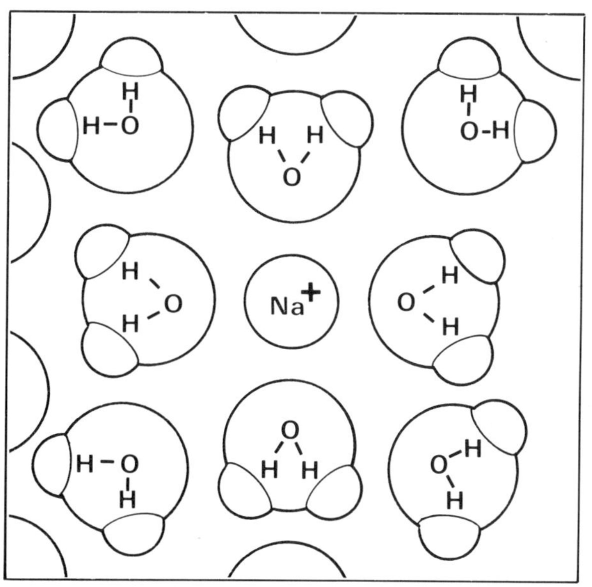

A hydrated Na$^+$ ion

● *Chlorides on the left of the period are hydrated by dissolving in water. Those on the right are hydrolysed.*

Oxides of elements in period 3

Here are the formulas of the period 3 oxides:

Na_2O Na_2O_2	MgO	Al_2O_3	SiO_2	P_4O_6 P_4O_{10}	SO_2 SO_3	Cl_2O ClO_2 Cl_2O_7

You should compare this table with the earlier one showing formulas of chlorides. Can you see any patterns or similarities in the tables?

Physical properties of the oxides

Melting temperatures and electrical conductivities of some of the oxides are compared in the table below. (Where more than one oxide of an element exists, the one that best illustrates the trend across the period has been chosen.)

Once again, the left and right sides of the period are different. On the left, the oxides are involatile electrolytes. On the right they are volatile non-electrolytes. This is the same pattern as we found for chlorides. This time, however, the division of the period seems to come between Al_2O_3 and SiO_2. (Where was it for the chlorides?)

- *The oxides of Na, Mg and Al are involatile electrolytes. Those of P, S and Cl are volatile non-electrolytes.*

Structures and bonding of the oxides

The physical properties of the oxides suggest ideas about their structures. The involatile electrolytes must have *giant structures* with *ionic bonding*. The volatile non-electrolytes must be *molecular* substances. The oxide in the middle (SiO_2) has a high melting temperature, so it must have a giant structure. However, SiO_2 is not an electrolyte so it cannot be ionic. It is usually described as having a *giant covalent* structure.

The overall picture for the period looks like the figure at the bottom of the page.

Chemical properties of the oxides

It is not just physical properties that are different at opposite ends of the period: the oxides also have chemical differences. The best way to illustrate this is to look at the behaviour with water (as we did for chlorides).

Several of the oxides react with water and dissolve in it. Here are some equations:

$$\mathbf{Na_2O(s) + H_2O(l) \rightarrow 2NaOH(aq)}$$

$$\mathbf{MgO(s) + H_2O(l) \rightarrow Mg(OH)_2(aq)}$$

$$\mathbf{P_4O_{10}(s) + 6H_2O(l) \rightarrow 4H_3PO_4(aq)}$$

$$\mathbf{SO_3(s) + H_2O(l) \rightarrow H_2SO_4(aq)}$$

In the case of the metal oxides, the solutions formed are alkaline. For the non-metal oxides, acids are formed. This is a familiar pattern that we have come across before: *metal oxides are often basic; non-metal oxides are often acidic.*

	Na_2O	*MgO*	*Al_2O_3*	*SiO_2*	*P_4O_{10}*	*SO_3*	*Cl_2O*
T_m(°C)	920	2900	2040	1610	580	17	−20
Electrical conductivity of liquid	high	high	high	low	nil	nil	nil

Melting temperatures and electrical conductivities of period 3 oxides

<table>
<tr><td></td><td>NaNa_2O</td><td>MgO</td><td>Al_2O_3</td><td>SiO_2</td><td>P_4O_{10}</td><td>SO_3</td><td>Cl_2O</td></tr>
<tr><td>Structure</td><td colspan="4">GIANT</td><td colspan="3">MOLECULAR</td></tr>
<tr><td>Bonding</td><td colspan="3">IONIC</td><td colspan="4">COVALENT</td></tr>
</table>

Structure and bonding of period 3 oxides

	Na_2O	MgO	Al_2O_3	SiO_2	P_4O_{10}	SO_3	Cl_2O
Product with water	alkali	alkali	–	–	acid	acid	acid
Acidic–basic character	BASIC		AMPHOTERIC	ACIDIC			

For those oxides which are insoluble in water (Al_2O_3, SiO_2), or only slightly soluble (MgO), the best way to investigate acidic or basic nature is to try reacting them with laboratory acids and alkalis. As you would expect, MgO dissolves well in acids to form salts. This confirms its basic properties. On the other hand, SiO_2 is insoluble in acids but tends to dissolve in concentrated alkalis. This suggests that it has an acidic nature.

What happens with Al_2O_3? This oxide behaves like MgO (dissolves in acids) and like SiO_2 (dissolves in alkalis). So Al_2O_3 has both basic and acidic characteristics. A substance with properties of both acids and bases is said to be *amphoteric*.

The situation can be summarized as in the figure above.

Summary

1. The chlorides and oxides of the period 3 elements have formulas that show a pattern.
2. Chlorides and oxides on the left of period 3 are involatile electrolytes. They have giant ionic structures.
3. Chlorides and oxides on the right of period 3 are volatile non-electrolytes. They have molecular covalent structures.
4. Chlorides on the right of the period are hydrolysed by water.
5. Oxides on the left of the period are basic: those on the right are acidic.
6. Compounds near the middle of the period often have intermediate properties; for example, aluminium oxide is *amphoteric*.

Extension

1. This question is about the melting temperatures of the following chlorides and oxides:
   chlorides: NaCl $MgCl_2$ $AlCl_3$ $SiCl_3$ PCl_5 S_2Cl_2
   oxides: Na_2O MgO Al_2O_3 SiO_2 P_4O_{10} SO_3 Cl_2O
   i Draw a sketch graph to show the melting temperature trend for the *chlorides* across period 3.
   ii Use the information on p. 76 to draw another sketch graph showing the melting temperature trend for *oxides* in period 3.
   iii Comment on the two graphs, point out *one* similarity and one difference between the trends for chlorides and oxides.

2. i Draw 'dot and cross' pictures to show the electron structures of ions in Na_2O. (Include outer shell electrons only.)
   ii Na_2O_2 contains the *peroxide ion*, O_2^{2-} i.e. an anion consisting of two oxygen atoms joined together covalently. Draw a 'dot and cross' picture to show a possible electron structure for the peroxide ion.
   iii Na_2O_2 reacts with cold water to form hydrogen peroxide and sodium hydroxide. Write a balanced equation to represent this reaction.

Revision

1. This question is about the following compounds:

A CO_2 *B* Na_2O *C* PCl_3
D SiO_2 *E* SO_3

i Which is a compound of a group V element?
ii Which has an ionic structure?
iii Which has a giant structure but is a non-electrolyte?
iv Which does not react with water?
v Which is not a period 3 compound?

2. This question is about the following oxides:

A Na_2O *B* MgO *C* Al_2O_3
D SiO_2 *E* P_4O_{10}

Choose one that:

i is amphoteric
ii is a basic oxide that is sparingly soluble in water
iii reacts with water to form a common laboratory alkali
iv forms acidic solutions when it reacts with water
v has a giant covalent structure

3. This question is about the following compounds:

A NaCl *B* Na_2O *C* S_2Cl_2
D SO_2 *E* SO_3

Which of them:

i does not react with water
ii reacts with water to form HCl and other products
iii reacts with water to form an alkali
iv reacts with water to form sulphuric acid
v is a gas that reacts with water to form an acid

4. Several chlorides of the period 3 elements can be represented by the general formula XCl_n. For example, $n = 4$ when X is Si.

i Give the formulas of all the other period 3 chlorides of the type XCl_n.
ii Explain how the group number of the elements is related to the value of n in the formulas.
iii Which of the period 3 elements have chlorides that do not fit into the pattern?

5. i Is MgO ionic or molecular?
ii What evidence is there to support your answer?
iii Is $SiCl_4$ ionic or molecular?
iv What evidence is there to support your answer to (iii)?
v Draw 'dot and cross' pictures to show the electronic structures of each compound. (Show outer shell electrons only.)

6. Many of the chlorides and oxides of the period 3 elements are of similar appearance. For example, all the following are white solids: NaCl, $MgCl_2$, $AlCl_3$, PCl_5, Na_2O, Na_2O_2, Al_2O_3, SiO_2, P_4O_6, P_4O_{10}.

i If you had samples of SiO_2 and P_4O_{10} that were unlabelled, what *physical* test could you do in the laboratory to sort them out?
ii What *chemical* test could you do to sort out $AlCl_3$ and $MgCl_2$?

(In each case, describe the test and state the results you would expect for both compounds.)

7. i What do you understand by *hydrolysis*?
ii Give an example of a chloride that can be hydrolysed.
iii Write an equation for the hydrolysis reaction.
iv As a rule, what type of chloride (ionic or covalent) is hydrolysed?
v Which of the following is an exception to the rule:

A $AlCl_3$ *B* CCl_4 *C* $SiCl_4$
D PCl_3 *E* S_2Cl_2

8. 'Compounds of elements near the middle of period 3 have properties that are intermediate between those of the extreme left and right.'

Make a list of examples that support this statement.

Unit 18
Elements in group VII: the halogens

The group in the periodic table

The elements in group VII are fluorine, chlorine, bromine, iodine and astatine. They appear in the periodic table like this:

VII
$_{9}F$
$_{17}Cl$
$_{35}Br$
$_{53}I$
$_{85}At$

(Make sure you know what the numbers represent.)

Astatine is a rare, radioactive element. Fluorine is a dangerously reactive element that is difficult to prepare in the laboratory. In this Unit we shall concentrate on Cl, Br and I.

● *Chlorine, bromine and iodine are the most important halogens for school chemistry.*

Safety note: The halogens are hazardous chemicals. Chlorine and bromine are especially dangerous because of their corrosive properties. They should be confined to a fume cupboard and used only by the teacher. Iodine discolours the skin and its vapour has similar properties to those of chlorine.

Physical properties of the halogens

The halogens look very different from one another. First impressions would not suggest a family connection between the elements.

Chlorine is a pale green gas, bromine is a dark red liquid and iodine is a black crystalline solid. *The halogens are not similar to one another in physical appearance.* However, there are some similarities in physical properties. For example, their electrical conductivities are very poor; *they are typical non-metals.*

Structure and bonding in halogens

The halogens have diatomic molecules with formulas of the type X_2. The atoms in these molecules are held together by a single covalent bond. The illustration on p.80 shows a diatomic

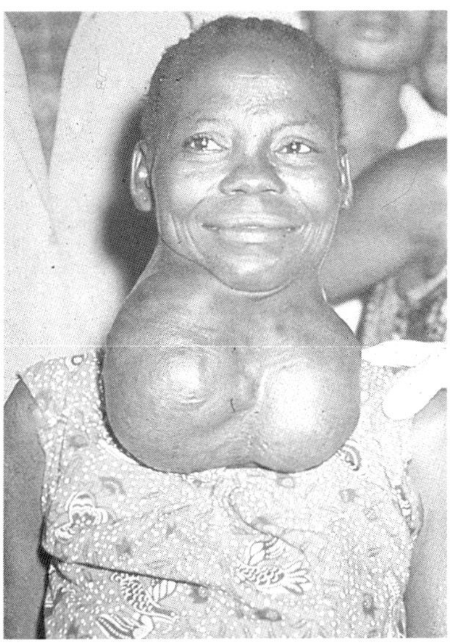

The body needs iodine to keep the thyroid gland working properly; a shortage in the diet causes goitre . . .

. . . chlorine is needed to make PVC plastics, it is used for products such as these drink bottles and electrical cable covering

halogen molecule. Only outer electrons ('valency electrons') are shown. You will recall that different elements within a group of the periodic table have atoms with the same number of outer shell electrons (see Unit 14). In the case of the halogens, the number of outer shell electrons is seven. So the picture of the diatomic molecule shown in the figure could be Cl_2, Br_2 or I_2.

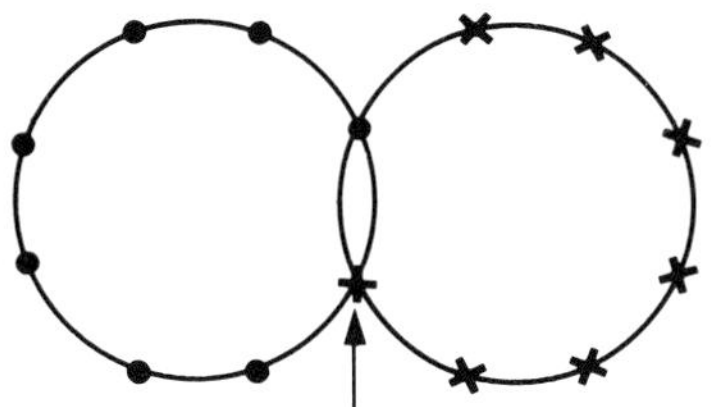

Bonding in a halogen molecule

● *In the halogens, pairs of atoms are held together by single covalent bonds to form diatomic molecules.*

Chemical properties of the halogens

Halogens may not be closely similar in their physical appearance. However, we have seen that their atoms and molecules have similar electron patterns. And when we look at chemical properties the family resemblances become more and more obvious.

We shall look at their reactions with metals, hydrogen, water and alkalis.

Reactions with metals

Most metals react with the halogens. In many cases the reactions are vigorous.

Of the three halogens chlorine, bromine and iodine, chlorine tends to be most reactive and iodine the least. But in spite of differences in reactivity, the elements show a clear group pattern. Equations for their reactions with aluminium illustrate this:

$$2Al(s) + 3Cl_2(g) \rightarrow 2AlCl_3(s)$$

$$2Al(s) + 3Br_2(l) \rightarrow 2AlBr_3(s)$$

$$2Al(s) + 3I_2(s) \rightarrow 2AlI_3(s)$$

Reactions with hydrogen

There is a clear group pattern here too:

$$H_2(g) + Cl_2(g) \rightarrow 2HCl(g)$$

$$H_2(g) + Br_2(g) \rightarrow 2HBr(g)$$

$$H_2(g) + I_2(g) \rightarrow 2HI(g)$$

Once again, reactivity decreases down the group. Chlorine and hydrogen react explosively in sunlight, or when heated. Bromine and hydrogen react smoothly when heated with a catalyst. Iodine and hydrogen react together incompletely at high temperatures.

Reactions with water

Chlorine and bromine are slightly soluble in water. In both cases, the solutions formed have bleaching properties. This is because some of the dissolved halogen molecules react as follows:

$$Cl_2(aq) + H_2O(l) \rightarrow HCl(aq) + HClO(aq)$$

$$Br_2(aq) + H_2O(l) \rightarrow HBr(aq) + HBrO(aq)$$

The acids HClO and HBrO are responsible for the bleaching properties of the solutions.

Iodine is practically insoluble in water and has no bleaching properties.

Reactions with alkalis

Halogens dissolve well in alkalis. Colourless solutions of salts are formed. For example, when chlorine dissolves in sodium hydroxide solution, the ions $Cl^-(aq)$, $ClO^-(aq)$ and $ClO_3^-(aq)$ are formed.

The first products are Cl^- and ClO^-:

$$Cl_2(aq) + 2OH^-(aq) \rightarrow H_2O(l) + Cl^-(aq) + ClO^-(aq)$$

On warming, ClO_3^- is formed:

$$3ClO^-(aq) \rightarrow 2Cl^-(aq) + ClO_3^-(aq)$$

The reactions of Br_2 and I_2 with alkali produce BrO_3^- and IO_3^- even in cold conditions.

Chlorine gas also reacts with solid alkalis. The mixture of NaOH and CaO called 'soda lime' may be used for the absorption of chlorine gas.

● *Reactions of halogens with metals, hydrogen, water and alkalis point to clear family resemblances within the group.*

Compounds of the halogens

We have seen how the halogen elements are similar to one another in the way they react with other substances. Their compounds (e.g. with a particular element) also have close family resemblances to one another. This is illustrated with two examples below: the *hydrides* and the *sodium salts*.

Hydrides of the halogens

HCl, HBr and HI are remarkably similar in several ways. They are all colourless gases. They all dissolve well in water. Their solutions are all strongly acidic. The acidity is the result of the following reactions:

$$\mathbf{HCl(g) + aq \rightarrow H^+(aq) + Cl^-(aq)}$$

$$\mathbf{HBr(g) + aq \rightarrow H^+(aq) + Br^-(aq)}$$

$$\mathbf{HI(g) + aq \rightarrow H^+(aq) + I^-(aq)}$$

The main difference between HCl, HBr and HI is ease of oxidation. HCl may be oxidized only by strong oxidizing agents. Potassium manganate(VII) is the oxidizing agent used in the usual laboratory preparation of chlorine:

$$\mathbf{2HCl(aq) + \underset{\text{from manganate (VII)}}{[O]} \longrightarrow H_2O(l) + Cl_2(g)}$$

HBr is easier to oxidize and HI is easier still. For example, a solution of HI will oxidize slowly on standing in air. The solution slowly goes brown as iodine is formed:

$$\mathbf{2HI(aq) + \underset{\text{from air}}{[O]} \longrightarrow H_2O(l) + I_2(aq)}$$

Sodium salts of the halogens

These are ionic compounds with formulas NaCl, NaBr and NaI. They are all colourless (white) solids. They dissolve well in water to form conducting solutions. They form cubic crystals.

● *Families of halogen compounds such as hydrides (and salts) show closely similar properties to one another.*

Displacement reactions

In general, the ease of oxidation of chlorides, bromides and iodides varies as follows:

chloride – – – – –	**bromide** – – – – –	**iodide**
(most difficult to oxidize		(most easily oxidized)

If a halogen is added to a solution containing a dissolved halide, a reaction may happen. For example, when chlorine is bubbled into a solution containing a dissolved iodide, this reaction happens:

$$\mathbf{Cl_2(aq) + 2I^-(aq) \rightarrow 2Cl^-(aq) + I_2(aq)}$$

In effect, the halogen atoms are competing with one another for electrons. Removal of electrons is a form of oxidation. So, the chlorine has oxidized the iodide. This observation agrees with the observed trend in the ease of oxidation of the hydrides.

Competition reactions of this sort are called *displacement reactions*. We say that the iodine in the reaction above has been displaced by the chlorine.

Summary

1. The important halogens for school chemistry are chlorine, bromine and iodine.
2. The halogen elements form diatomic molecules, for example Cl_2, Br_2, I_2.
3. The bonding in halogen molecules is single covalent bonding. All the halogens have atoms with seven outer shell electrons.
4. The halogens are not closely similar in their physical appearance, but have many chemical properties in common.
5. The halogens show group resemblances in their reactions with metals, hydrogen, water and alkalis.
6. Families of halogen compounds like hydrides (and sodium salts) show group resemblances.

Extension

1.

Element	*Z*	*State (at room temperature)*	*Density (g cm^{-3})*	*Boiling temperature (°C)*
F	9	g	1.1*	−188
Cl	17	g	1.6*	−35
Br	35	l	—	59
I	53	s	4.9	184
At	85	s	—	380

*Liquid state.

The table gives information about some physical properties of the halogen elements:

i Look at the boiling temperature data. There is a trend in boiling temperature (T_b) as Z increases. What is the trend?

ii Show the relationship by drawing a graph of T_b (vertical axis) against Z (horizontal axis).

iii The density data for Br and At are not given. Use a graphical method to predict approximate values for their densities.

2. The element at the bottom of group VII is astatine, At.

i Write probable formulas for:

a the hydride of At

b the sodium salt of At

ii List the properties you would expect for each of the compounds mentioned in (i) above.

Revision

1. This question is about the following equations:

A $X + Cl \rightarrow XCl$

B $2X + Cl_2 \rightarrow 2XCl$

C $X + Cl_2 \rightarrow XCl_2$

D $2X + 3Cl_2 \rightarrow 2XCl_3$

E $X + 2Cl_2 \rightarrow XCl_4$

Which equation best represents the synthesis of:

i aluminium chloride (i.e. X = Al)

ii magnesium chloride (i.e. X = Mg)

iii phosphorus(III) chloride (i.e. X = P)

iv silicon chloride (i.e. X = Si)

v sodium chloride (i.e. X = Na)

2. This question is about the laboratory preparation of aluminium chloride. The method is synthesis carried out by heating aluminium in a stream of dry chlorine.

The pieces of apparatus provided are shown in the figure on p.83.

i The following chemicals are also provided:

A aluminium

B anhydrous calcium chloride

C concentrated hydrochloric acid

D potassium manganate(VII) crystals

E soda-lime

Which of the chemicals would be placed in:

a the absorption tube

b the U-tube

c the tap-funnel

d the combustion tube

e the flask

ii Which of the following is the best sequence of connections for the apparatus?

A I – II – V – IV – III

B II – IV – V – III – I

C III – V – II – IV – I

D IV – V – III – II – I

E V – I – II – III – IV

3. Draw pictures to show the electronic structures of:

i a chlorine atom

ii a chlorine molecule

iii ions in the compound NaF

iv molecules in the compound ClF

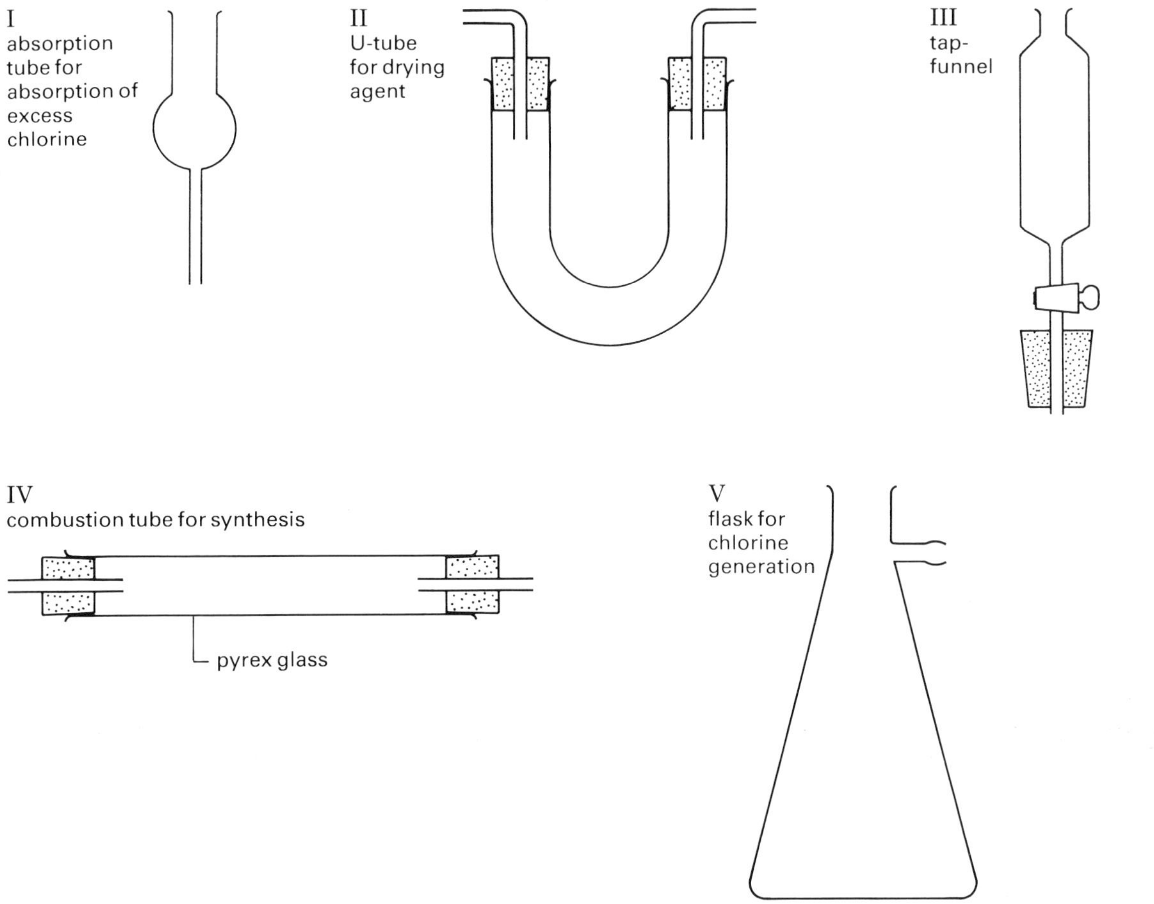

4. Hydrides of the halogens dissolve in water to form acidic solutions. Write equations to show probable reactions between the following pairs of substances:
   - i aqueous hydrogen chloride and sodium hydroxide
   - ii aqueous hydrogen chloride and potassium hydroxide
   - iii aqueous hydrogen bromide and sodium hydroxide
   - iv aqueous hydrogen iodide and sodium hydroxide
   - v aqueous hydrogen iodide and ammonium hydroxide

5. i Name a halogen that would displace bromine from a solution of a bromide.
   - ii Would you expect bromine to displace chlorine? Explain your answer.
   - iii Write equations showing displacement reactions involving:
     - *a* Cl_2 and Br^-
     - *b* the elements bromine and iodine
   - iv Chlorine was bubbled into three solutions: A, B, and C.

     Solution A showed no effect.
     Solution B became orange-red.
     Solution C became dark brown.

     Which of the solutions A, B or C contained:
     - *a* a bromide
     - *b* a chloride
     - *c* an iodide

Unit 19
Elements in group I: the alkali metals

The group in the periodic table

The group I metals are often called the alkali metals. They are found on the left of the periodic table, like this:

I	
$_{3}Li$	
$_{11}Na$	
$_{19}K$	
$_{37}Rb$	
$_{55}Cs$	
$_{87}Fr$	

In this Unit we shall deal mainly with lithium, sodium and potassium. (Rubidium and caesium are less common. Francium is a rare radioactive element.)

● *The group I elements include Li, Na and K.*

Safety note: The group I metals (alkali metals) are very reactive. Lithium is less dangerous than the others, but should only be used under the close supervision of the teacher. Sodium and potassium must not be used by pupils. Potassium is especially dangerous. (Old stocks of potassium which have turned yellowish on the surface must be discarded and must not be cut up.)

Physical properties of the elements

All the elements in this group are metals. They are good conductors. Unlike most metals, the alkali metals are very light, that is, they have low densities. Li, Na and K will float on water. They are much softer than familiar metals like iron, aluminium and copper; the alkali metals can be easily cut with a knife. Melting

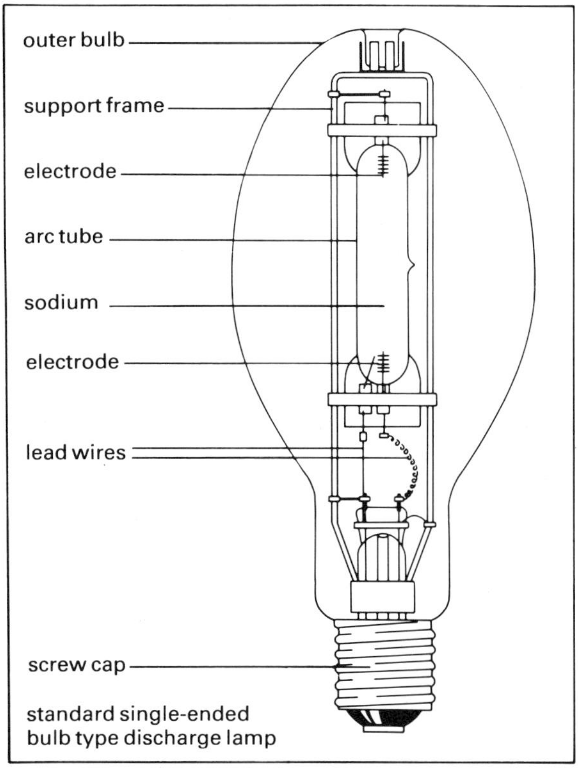

Sodium vapour is used in some light bulbs

Liquid sodium is used as a coolant in nuclear reactors (p. 231); it circulates through large cooling coils

	Electrical conductivity	*Hardness*	*Density* $(g\,cm^{-3})$	T_m (°C)
$_{3}Li$	good	quite soft	0.53	181
$_{11}Na$	good	soft	0.97	98
$_{19}K$	good	soft	0.86	63
$_{37}Rb$	good	soft	1.53	39
$_{55}Cs$	good	soft	1.87	29

Physical properties of group I elements

temperatures are also much lower than those of everyday metals.

Some physical properties are given in the table above.

A study of physical properties such as density, softness and melting temperature shows the close family resemblances of the metals in group I.

● *The elements in group I have closely similar physical properties.*

Structures and bonding of the group I metals

You may remember work done previously on the giant structure of metals (see Unit 5).

Of all the elements, about 70 are metals (many of them very rare). More than half of these metals have *close-packed* structures. A smaller group of metals (about 15) have another metallic structure called *body-centred cubic.* The group I metals all have this less common type of structure.

In body-centred cubic structures, each atom has eight neighbours in contact with it (see Unit 5).

The force that holds metallic giant structures together is called the *metallic bond*. This type of bonding results from the presence of delocalized electron ('free electrons') in the structure (see Unit 10).

● *The group I metals have body-centred cubic structures held together by the metallic bond.*

Chemical properties of group I metals

The group I metals are found near the top of the reactivity series. They all react vigorously with water, oxygen and most other non-metals. As a rule, the elements in the group react along similar lines. In other words, their chemical properties show a *group pattern*.

This is illustrated by their reactions with water.

Reactions with water

$$2Li(s) + 2H_2O(l) \rightarrow 2LiOH(aq) + H_2(g)$$

$$2Na(s) + 2H_2O(l) \rightarrow 2NaOH(aq) + H_2(g)$$

$$2K(s) + 2H_2O(l) \rightarrow 2KOH(aq) + H_2(g)$$

Lithium reacts briskly with water, but not as energetically as does sodium. Potassium's reaction releases enough heat to ignite the hydrogen that is formed. Alkaline solutions are formed in each case.

● *The chemical properties of the alkali metals show a group pattern.*

Their reactions with water also lead to another conclusion: generally, reactivity is higher for elements nearer the bottom of group I.

This observation is further illustrated by other reactions of the elements.

Reactions with oxygen

Lithium forms lithium oxide, Li_2O, only:

$$4Li(s) + O_2(g) \rightarrow 2Li_2O(s)$$

Sodium reacts similarly to form sodium oxide, Na_2O, but sodium peroxide (Na_2O_2) is formed as well. Potassium reacts with oxygen to form yellow potassium superoxide, KO_2.

Reactions with other non-metals

You may have seen the reaction of sodium and chlorine:

$$2Na(s) + Cl_2(g) \rightarrow 2NaCl(s)$$

This is a vigorous synthesis reaction. Lithium reacts less vigorously and potassium more vigorously than does sodium.

Sulphides, hydrides and nitrides may also be formed in synthesis reactions with the group I metals. The trend in reactivity can usually be seen in these reactions too. Li is less reactive than Na, which in turn is less reactive than K.

● *Reactivity is higher for elements nearer the bottom of group I.*

Compounds of group I metals

In general, compounds of the group I metals have properties that are typical of ionic compounds, for example high melting temperatures and high electrolytic conductivity.

Oxides and hydroxides

Oxides such as Li_2O and Na_2O have high melting temperatures and are good conductors when molten. These properties suggest ionic structures. The simple oxides contain the ions Li^+ or Na^+ together with the oxide ion, O^{2-}.

The oxides react vigorously with water and dissolve to form alkaline solutions:

$$\mathbf{Na_2O(s) + H_2O(l) \rightarrow 2NaOH(aq)}$$

Chlorides

The chlorides LiCl, NaCl and KCl are colourless crystalline solids. They have high melting temperatures and are electrolytes. These properties suggest ionic structures. For example, sodium chloride contains the ions Na^+ and Cl^-.

Unlike many covalent chlorides (which are hydrolysed by water) these ionic chlorides simply dissolve when mixed with water.

Other salts

The chlorides mentioned above could be formed by synthesis reactions. However, they are normally prepared by neutralization of hydrochloric acid with the appropriate alkali. Chlorides are salts of hydrochloric acid.

There are salts of many other acids and the alkali metals. Most are colourless and soluble in water. Here are some examples:

Na_2SO_4, K_2SO_4, $NaNO_3$, K_2CO_3, $KMnO_4$, Na_3PO_4.

(Which one is *not* colourless?)

● *Many compounds of the group I metals are colourless, ionic solids.*

Summary

1. The group I elements (alkali metals) include Li, Na and K.
2. The group I elements have closely similar physical properties, for example low melting temperatures, low densities, etc.
3. They all have body-centred cubic structures held together by metallic bonding.
4. Their chemical properties show a group pattern, for example all the metals react in a similar way with water.
5. There is a trend towards higher reactivity for the elements nearer the bottom of group I.
6. Many of the compounds of group I elements are colourless, ionic solids.

Extension

1. The group properties of the alkali metals include softness, low density, low melting temperature, high reactivity. This question is about other metals with some of the same properties. In each case, choose one metal from the list that is the best example of:

   i a soft metal (Al, Ca, Fe, Pb, Zn)
   ii a low density metal (Al, Cu, Fe, Hg, Pb)
   iii a low melting metal (Al, Cu, Fe, Hg, Mg)
   iv a highly reactive metal (Ag, Ca, Cu, Hg, Pb)

2. Use the data for the alkali metals given on p. 85 in this Unit to draw graphs of:

   i density against Z
   ii T_m against Z

   Comment on the group trends that the graphs show.

3. Write equations for the reactions, and describe what you would expect to see, when Rb reacts with:

   i water
   ii chlorine

4. Both sodium and caesium form chlorides of the type X^+Cl^-. However, they have different structures.
   - i Use your knowledge of the electronic structures of atoms to explain why the two formulas are similar.
   - ii What is the number of Cl^- ions in contact with each cation in:
     - *a* CsCl
     - *b* NaCl
   - iii The Na^+ ion is smaller than the Cs^+ ion. How could the sizes of group I cations account for the fact that the chlorides have different structures?

Revision

1. This question is about the following group I metals:
   - *A* caesium
   - *B* lithium
   - *C* potassium
   - *D* rubidium
   - *E* sodium

   Which of them has the:
   - i symbol K
   - ii highest position in the group
   - iii largest atom
   - iv lowest density
   - v highest melting temperature
   - vi least vigorous reaction with water
2. Write a brief summary of chemical properties of the group I elements, giving examples of:
   - i typical reactions
   - ii trends in the group
3. i Describe a laboratory procedure for the preparation of potassium chloride crystals starting from KOH(aq).
   - ii How would you attempt to prepare potassium carbonate starting from CO_2(g)?

4 This question is about the following substances:
   - *A* Na
   - *B* Na_2O
   - *C* NaOH
   - *D* H_2
   - *E* H_2O
   - i Which of them does not appear in the equation for the reaction of sodium with water?
   - ii Which substance is oxidized in the reaction of sodium with water?
   - iii Which substance is reduced in the reaction?
   - iv Which substance is the reducing agent?
   - v Which substance is the oxidizing agent?

Unit 20
Elements in group II

The group in the periodic table

The group II elements are found on the left of the periodic table, like this:

I	II	
	$_4$Be	
	$_{12}$**Mg**	
	$_{20}$**Ca**	
	$_{38}$Sr	
	$_{56}$**Ba**	
	$_{88}$Ra	

The commonest members of the group are magnesium, calcium and barium. Beryllium and strontium are rarer elements. (Radium is a very rare radioactive element.)

● *The group II elements include Mg, Ca and Ba.*

Safety note: All soluble barium compounds are poisonous.

Physical properties of the elements

All the elements in the group are good conductors: they are all metals. They have relatively low densities, although not as low as those of group I metals. Melting temperatures are also higher than those of group I metals.

Both densities and melting temperature values can be used to show the trends in properties in the group. On the whole, as you go down the group, the trends are towards higher density values and towards lower melting temperatures. These trends are similar to those found in group I. The graphs on the right illustrate the trends in group II.

● *The group II elements are harder, more dense and have higher melting temperature than those in group I.*

Structure and bonding of the group II elements

The dominant structure in group II is the metallic giant structure called close packing (see Unit 5). The force holding the structures together is called the metallic bond (see Unit 10).

● *The group II metals have typical metallic structures and bonding.*

Chemical properties of the group II metals

The metals are found near the top of the reactivity series. However, taken as a whole, group II metals are less reactive than those in

(i) Densities

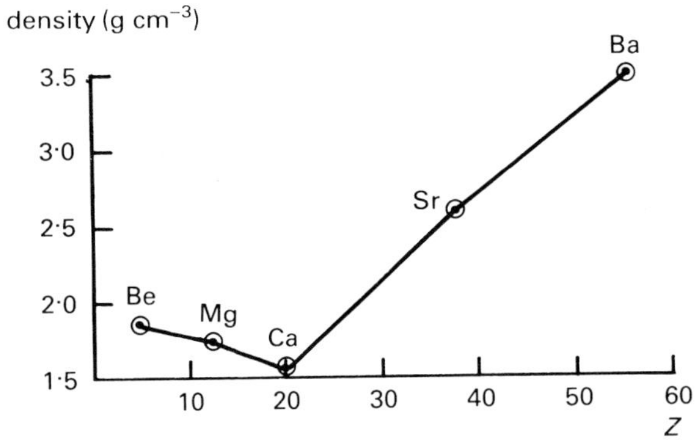

(ii) Melting temperatures

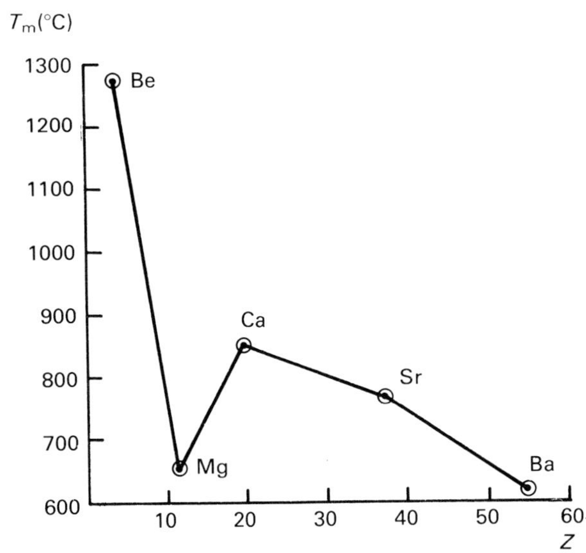

Trends in group II

Fireworks contain salts of group II metals to produce bright colours

Calcium is needed by living things to make bones, teeth, and shells

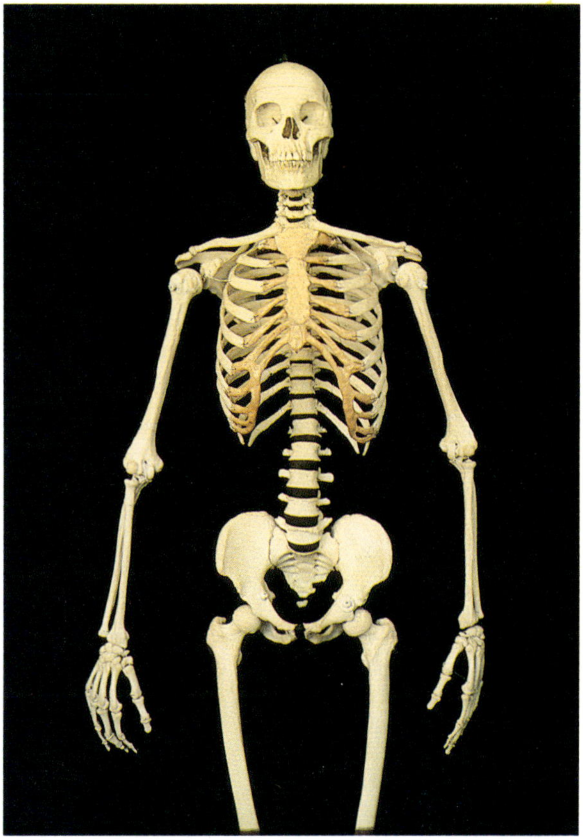

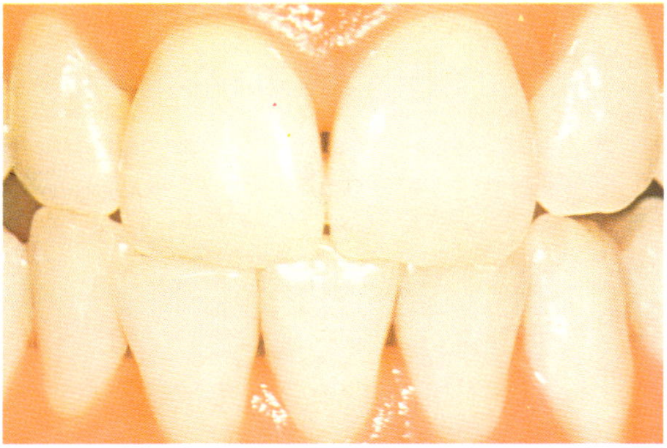

group I. This is seen clearly if neighbours in the periodic table are compared with one another. For example, compare Na with Mg, or K with Ca. The group I metals generally show the greater reactivity, for example with water.

We shall look at the reactions of group II metals with water, acids and oxygen.

Reactions with water

Magnesium only reacts well with water when heated in steam. Hydrogen and magnesium oxide are formed:

$$\mathbf{Mg(s) + H_2O(g) \rightarrow MgO(s) + H_2(g)}$$

Calcium reacts vigorously with cold water. Some of the calcium hydroxide that is formed dissolves to make the water alkaline. Hydrogen is also formed:

$$\mathbf{Ca(s) + 2H_2O(l) \rightarrow Ca(OH)_2(aq) + H_2(g)}$$

Barium reacts more vigorously than calcium and forms soluble barium hydroxide and hydrogen.

$$\mathbf{Ba(s) + 2H_2O(l) \rightarrow Ba(OH)_2(aq) + H_2(g)}$$

These reactions of the metals with water show how reactivity increases as group II is descended.

- *The more reactive group II metals are nearer the bottom of the group.*

(You will recall that a similar pattern was found in group I.)

Reactions with dilute acids

Magnesium reacts briskly with dilute acids. Hydrogen is usually formed, together with a salt:

$$\mathbf{Mg(s) + 2HCl(aq) \rightarrow MgCl_2(aq) + H_2(g)}$$

Calcium reacts too vigorously for you to try it practically, although your teacher might show you the reaction:

$$\mathbf{Ca(s) + 2HCl(aq) \rightarrow CaCl_2(aq) + H_2(g)}$$

Metals lower down the group cannot be reacted safely with acids in school laboratories. Once again, reactivity increases as the group is descended.

Reactions with oxygen

All the metals burn well in air and oxygen. Magnesium's reaction is well known. It forms white magnesium oxide:

$$\mathbf{2Mg(s) + O_2(g) \rightarrow 2MgO(s)}$$

Calcium reacts in a similar way:

$$\mathbf{2Ca(s) + O_2(g) \rightarrow 2CaO(s)}$$

You could probably predict the reaction of Ba with oxygen. All the group II metals show a close family resemblance in their reactions.

- *The chemical reactions of the group II metals show close similarities within the group.*

Compounds of group II metals

We found that compounds of group I elements generally have properties typical of ionic substances. The same applies to compounds of group II metals: most have high melting temperatures and are good electrolytes. Many are soluble in water (but not so many as in group I).

Oxides and hydroxides

The oxides can be formed by heating the carbonates. For example, CaO ('quicklime') is formed by roasting $CaCO_3$ (limestone or marble):

$$\mathbf{CaCO_3(s) \rightarrow CaO(s) + CO_2(g)}$$

(The carbonates of group I metals are harder to decompose. Group I oxides are *not* prepared by heating carbonates.)

All the group II oxides are white solids with high melting temperatures (like group I oxides). They also resemble group I oxides in their chemical behaviour. For example, they are *basic*: they react with acids to form salts:

$$\mathbf{MgO(s) + H_2SO_4(aq) \rightarrow MgSO_4(aq) + H_2O(l)}$$

$$\mathbf{CaO(s) + 2HNO_3(aq) \rightarrow Mg(NO_3)_2(aq) + H_2O(l)}$$

The oxides also react with water to form the hydroxides. For example, $Ca(OH)_2$ ('slaked lime') is formed from calcium oxide:

$$\mathbf{CaO(s) + H_2O(l) \rightarrow Ca(OH)_2(s)}$$

The hydroxides are more soluble at the bottom of group II. Calcium hydroxide is only

	Solubility (g per 100 g water at 20 °C)			
	Chlorides	*Carbonates*	*Sulphates*	*Hydroxides*
Mg	54	0.01	33	0.0009
Ca	76	0.001	0.2	0.156
Sr	54	0.001	0.01	0.80
Ba	36	0.002	0.0002	3.9

sparingly soluble. Its saturated solution is known as 'limewater'. Solutions of the hydroxides are *alkaline*.

- *Group II compounds resemble group I compounds in several ways, for example most are white ionic solids. Their oxides are basic and they form alkaline hydroxides.*

Salts of group II metals

These are mostly colourless, ionic solids. They often differ from salts of group I metals in their solubility in water. Most salts of the group I metals are soluble. In group II, nitrates and chlorides are soluble, but sulphates and carbonates are insoluble in some cases. If you look at the solubility data given in the table above you will see that solubilities sometimes show group trends.

What is the group trend for solubilities of sulphates? Which compounds show the reverse trend?

- *Group II compounds may differ from the corresponding group I compounds in several ways. Group II compounds may have lower thermal stabilities (e.g. carbonates) or lower solubilities (e.g. sulphates, hydroxides, carbonates).*

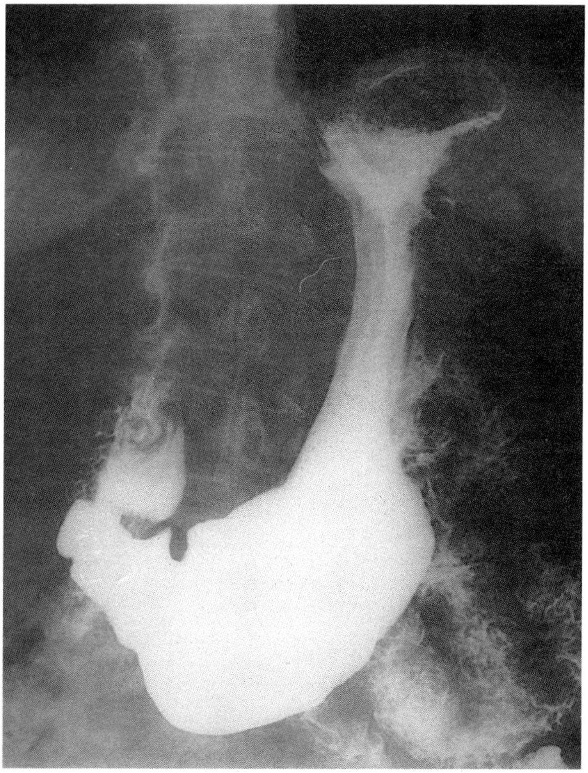

A 'barium meal' (of $BaSO_4$) is swallowed before an X-ray; it shows up as white in the stomach

Summary

1. The group II elements include Mg, Ca and Ba.
2. The group II elements are harder, more dense and with higher melting temperatures than are those in group I.
3. The group II elements have typical metallic structures with delocalized electrons.
4. The more reactive metals are found nearer the bottom of the group.
5. There are close similarities in chemical properties of the elements within the group, for example they all follow the same pattern in their reactions with water, dilute acids and oxygen.
6. Group II compounds resemble group I compounds in several ways, for example the hydroxides in both groups are alkaline.
7. Differences between compounds of group II and group I include lower thermal stabilities of group II carbonates, and lower solubilities of group II hydroxides.

Extension

1. Use your knowledge of group patterns in chemistry to write equations for the reactions of:
   - i Sr with water
   - ii Be with hydrochloric acid
   - iii Be with oxygen
   - iv $SrCO_3$ when heated
   - v SrO with nitric acid
   - vi BaO with water
2. This question is about the following group II metals:

   A Ba   *B* Be   *C* Ca
   D Mg   *E* Sr

   Which has the:
   - i largest atom
   - ii greatest reactivity with water
   - iii most insoluble sulphate
   - iv most soluble hydroxide
   - v highest melting temperature

   Do you think that the size of an element's atoms (within a group) is linked to the element's properties? Try to explain your answer.
3. i Precipitation of $BaSO_4$ is used in the usual chemical test for sulphates in solution. Acidified $BaCl_2(aq)$ or $Ba(NO_3)_2(aq)$ is used as the reagent.
   - *a* Complete the following equation: $Na_2SO_4(aq) + BaCl_2(aq) \rightarrow$
   - *b* Write another equation for the above reaction showing formulas for all the ions in the mixture.
   - *c* Rewrite the ionic equation in its simplest form, that is, exclude all spectator ions.

   ii Unless the solution is acidified, $BaCO_3$ could be precipitated from a solution containing dissolved carbonates. Both $BaCO_3$ and $BaSO_4$ are white, and could easily be confused.

   Explain how acidifying the mixture prevents precipitation of carbonate from the solution.

Revision

1. i What is the overall trend in melting temperatures for the elements in group II?

   ii How does this compare with the trend in melting temperatures in group I?

   iii Pick out any element which seems to have an unexpectedly high or low value.
2. If you wished to investigate the reaction of calcium with water, how would you:
   - i collect the gas formed
   - ii show that the gas is hydrogen
   - iii show that an alkali is formed
   - iv show that the alkali is limewater
3. Describe how you would attempt to prepare samples of the following salts by the method stated:
   - i $MgCl_2$ by synthesis
   - ii $Ba(NO_3)_2$ by neutralization
   - iii $BaSO_4$ from $Ba(NO_3)_2$ and Na_2SO_4
   - iv $BaCO_3$ from $Ba(OH)_2$ and CO_2
4. Write equations for the reactions in Revision 3 above.
5. Chlorides in group II have formulas of the type XCl_2, while those in group I have formulas of the type XCl.

   Explain how this difference arises using ideas about electronic structures of the metal atoms.
6. i What do you understand by the terms:
   - *a* close-packed structure
   - *b* delocalized electrons

   ii In potassium metal, each atom can provide only one electron for delocalization. Explain why.

   iii How many electrons per atom would you expect to be delocalized in calcium?

   iv How could ideas about the numbers of delocalized electrons be used to explain melting temperature differences between groups I and II?

Unit 21
Transition elements

What are transition elements?

The figure below shows where the transition elements are found in the periodic table. You will see that they form a 'bridge' between the left- and right-hand parts of the table.

All the transition elements have good conductivity. They can therefore be called *transition metals*.

● *All the transition elements are metals.*

Some familiar transition metals

Copper and iron are examples of transition metals that you will know about. You have probably heard the names of chromium, manganese, cobalt, nickel and platinum as well. They all have important uses. Some examples are given in the table on p. 94.

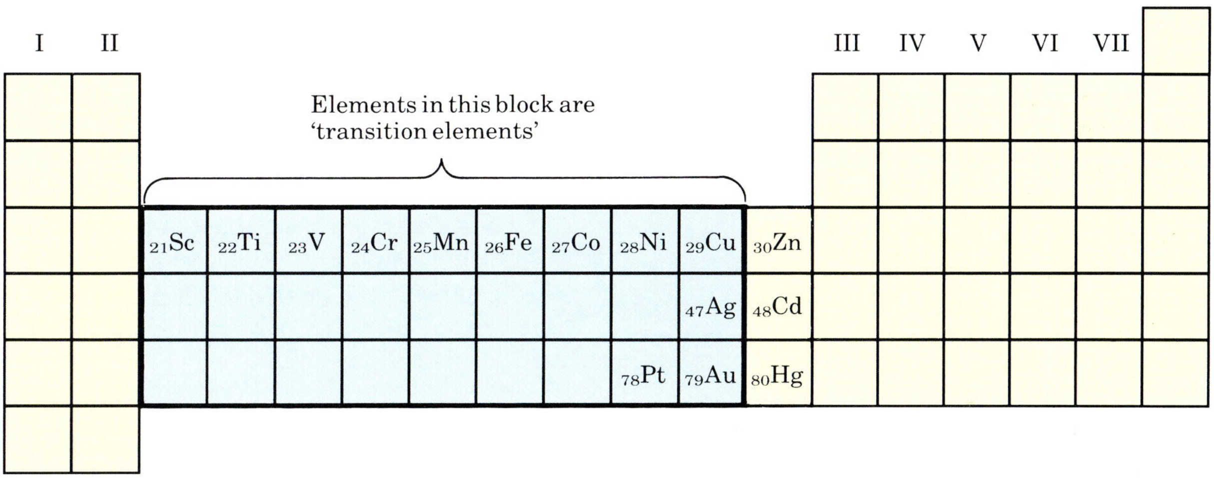

Transition elements in the periodic table

Transition metal oxides are used to colour glass, for example in stained glass windows (left); copper can be drawn out into fine wires for electrical use (centre); silver can be beaten to produce pots and bowls (right)

Transition metal	*Examples of use*
chromium	a constituent of stainless steel alloys; electroplating
cobalt	cobalt compounds used for blue glass
copper	electrical wiring; alloys (e.g. brass, bronze, coinage alloys); steam boilers and water tanks
iron	the main constituent in all steels
manganese	a constituent in many steel alloys
nickel	coinage alloys; a constituent of stainless steel; electroplating; industrial catalysts
platinum	jewellery; industrial catalysts

Uses of some transition metals

Properties of transition metals

How do transition metals compare with metals like sodium and calcium? There are important differences. For example, physical properties such as densities and melting temperatures of the transition metals are higher. The chemical reactivity of the transition metals is generally lower than in groups I and II.

Physical properties

Iron and copper are typical transition metals. Some physical properties of iron and copper are shown in the following table. Properties of sodium and calcium are also shown for comparison. The differences in density and melting temperature can be seen. The magnetism shown by iron is not shown by copper, but it is shown by other transition metals (nickel and cobalt).

● *Transition metals are generally dense metals with high melting temperatures.*

Chemical properties

Metals towards the left side of the transition block are more reactive than those on the right. (Thus, iron is more reactive than copper.) But none of the metals can match the metals of groups I and II for reactivity. The transition metals would appear near the bottom of a reactivity series.

How do the reactions of iron and copper, shown in the next table, compare with those of sodium and calcium?

	Reaction with water	*Reaction with dilute sulphuric acid*
Iron	reacts slowly when heated strongly in steam; hydrogen is formed	reacts slowly to form hydrogen
Copper	no reaction	no reaction

Reactions of iron and copper

Trends in the transition block

In earlier Units, we noticed how the properties of elements change as you cross the periodic table from left to right. In period 3, for example, properties change dramatically in the short space of a few elements. Thus, Na is very different from Si; and Si is very different from Cl.

However, this is not the case in the transition block. Change is very slow and gradual as you cross the transition block from left to right. Look at the graph showing *melting temperature variation* for the elements 19 to 36. You can see how the transition metals have values that are bunched together. In some cases, next-door neighbours in the transition block have almost the same melting temperatures: look at V and Cr, and Fe, Co and Ni.

Density variation shows the same kind of pattern: neighbouring elements in the

	Transition metals		*Group I and group II metals*	
	iron	*copper*	*sodium*	*calcium*
Density (*g cm*$^{-3}$)	7.86	8.92	0.97	1.55
Melting temperature (°*C*)	*1535*	*1083*	*98*	*850*
Magnetic properties	*magnetic*	*non-magnetic*	*non-magnetic*	*non-magnetic*

Physical properties of some metals compared

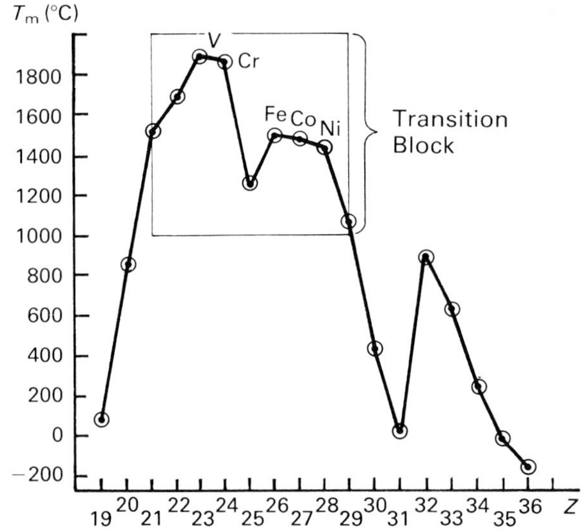

Graph showing melting temperature variation for elements 19 to 36

transition block often have very similar values, for example, Cr and Mn (7.19 and 7.20 g cm^{-3}), and Co, Ni and Cu (8.90, 8.90 and 8.92 g cm^{-3}).

● *Neighbouring elements in the transition block often have similar properties.*

Valency numbers of transition elements

Copper has two oxides, Cu_2O and CuO. It also has two chlorides, CuCl and $CuCl_2$. In fact, copper forms two sets of compounds that fit into two distinct families. In one family the copper has valency number +1 and in the other it has valency number + 2.

The same applies to iron. In its compounds Fe can have either valency number +2 or valency number +3. The situation is similar for other transition metals. See if you can work out valency numbers for the transition metals in the compounds given in the next table.

Compounds	*Formulas*
chlorides of iron	$FeCl_2$ $FeCl_3$
oxides of chromium	Cr_2O_3 CrO_3
chloride and oxides of manganese	$MnCl_2$ MnO_2 Mn_2O_7

What valency numbers have the transition metals got?

Transition metals are said to have variable valency. So far we have not met any non-transition metals with variable valency. Many non-transition metals have only one valency number (e.g. Na: +1; Ca: +2; Al: +3).

● *Variable valency is a feature of transition metal chemistry.*

Compounds of transition metals

It is useful to compare the properties of transition metal compounds with those of, say, sodium and calcium. There are several important differences. One of the differences is a special feature of transition metal compounds in general: transition metal compounds are usually coloured. Other differences are connected with the lower reactivity of transition metals compared with that of group I and group II metals.

A property typical of transition metal compounds: colours

Oxides, hydroxides and salts of sodium and calcium are nearly always colourless. Compounds of transition metals, however, usually have colours. The table below gives examples.

In the examples given below you can see that the same colour occurs for each aqueous solution that contains a particular transition

Compound (and state)	*Colour*
CuO(s) $CuCO_3$(s) $CuSO_4$(aq) $Cu(NO_3)_2$(aq)	black green blue blue
$FeSO_4$(aq) $Fe(OH)_2$(s) $FeCl_3$(aq) $Fe_2(SO_4)_3$(aq) $Fe(OH)_3$(s)	green green yellow yellow brown
$CoCl_2$(aq) $Co(NO_3)_2$(aq)	pink pink
$Ni(NO_3)_2$(aq)	green
$Cr_2(SO_4)_3$(aq) K_2CrO_4(aq)	green yellow
MnO_2(s) $KMnO_4$(aq)	black purple

Colours of some transition metal compounds

The colours of minerals may be due to traces of transition metals; corundum (Al_2O_3) is colourless when pure, but traces of chromium make *ruby*, and traces of titanium make *sapphire*

metal ion. For example, both $CoCl_2(aq)$ and $Co(NO_3)_2(aq)$ contain the ion $Co^{2+}(aq)$ and both solutions are pink. Also, in the case of solutions containing iron(II) and iron(III) compounds, the colours are different for the different valency states, that is, solutions containing $Fe^{3+}(aq)$ are yellow and those containing $Fe^{2+}(aq)$ are green.

● *Coloured compounds are a special feature of transition metal chemistry.*

Properties typical of less reactive metals

1. Basic properties of oxides are weaker than those of group I and group II metals. For example, CuO shows no reaction with water and reacts only slowly with dilute acid:

$$\mathbf{CuO(s) + H_2SO_4(aq) \xrightarrow{slow} CuSO_4(aq) + H_2O(l)}$$

Oxides of group I and group II metals (e.g. Na_2O and CaO) are strongly basic.

2. Reduction of oxides is easier than with those of group I and group II metals. For example, CuO can be reduced to copper by heating in a stream of laboratory gas (methane and hydrogen):

$$\mathbf{CuO(s) + H_2(g) \rightarrow Cu(s) + H_2O(g)}$$

Oxides of group I and group II metals cannot be reduced by heating in laboratory gas.

3. Thermal stability of salts is lower than those of group I and group II metals. For example, carbonates decompose at quite low temperatures:

$$\mathbf{CuCO_3(s) \rightarrow CuO(s) + CO_2(g)}$$

Carbonates of the group I and group II metals need much higher temperatures.

● *Oxides of transition metals are weak bases and quite good oxidizing agents compared with oxides of alkali metals. Salts of transition metals generally have lower thermal stability than do those of alkali metals.*

Summary

1. Transition elements are found in the central block of the periodic table.
2. All the transition elements are metals, and many have important uses.
3. Transition metals generally have high densities and high melting temperatures.
4. Transition metals are less reactive than metals in groups I and II.
5. Trends in crossing the transition block are slow and gradual (compared with crossing period 3, for example).
6. Variable valency is a feature of transition metal chemistry.
7. Coloured compounds are usual for transition metals.
8. Compared with the reactive metals in groups I and II, transition metals often have:
   a oxides that are weaker bases and stronger oxidizing agents;
   b salts with lower thermal stability.

Extension

1. i A green powder 'L' was heated in a test-tube. A colourless gas 'M' was released that turned limewater cloudy. A black powder 'N' remained in the test-tube. Half of 'N' was dissolved in warm dilute $HNO_3(aq)$ and produced a blue solution 'P'. The other half of 'N' was heated in a stream of laboratory gas and produced a red powder 'Q'.
   Identify L, M, N, P and Q.
   ii Write equations for the reactions described above.

2. i The colours of transition metal salt solutions are often due to hydrated cations in the solution. For example, solutions containing $Cu^{2+}(aq)$ are blue. What colours are associated with:

a $Fe^{2+}(aq)$
b $Fe^{3+}(aq)$
c $Co^{2+}(aq)$
d $Cr^{3+}(aq)$

ii Most hydroxides are insoluble in water (apart from those of group I metals, for example).

When alkali is added to a solution containing a dissolved salt, an insoluble hydroxide is frequently precipitated. For example a blue precipitate is formed when alkali is added to a solution of a copper salt:

$$\mathbf{Cu^{2+}(aq) + 2OH^{-}(aq) \rightarrow Cu(OH)_2(s)}$$

Write equations to show the precipitation of:

a a green hydroxide from $FeSO_4(aq)$
b a brown hydroxide from $FeCl_3(aq)$

Revision

1. This question is about the following elements:

A copper
B iron
C magnesium
D manganese
E phosphorus

Which element:

i is not a metal
ii has the symbol Mn
iii has a white basic oxide
iv forms salts that have blue aqueous solutions
v has only one valency number
vi is magnetic

2. This question is about the following transition metals:

A Co
B Cr
C Cu
D Fe
E Pt

Which is:

i the principle constituent of steel
ii the main metal used for electrical wiring
iii used in expensive jewellery
iv used for electroplating
v used (as its oxide) for colouring glass blue

3. This question is about the metals Mg and Ni. Which would you expect to have the:

i higher melting temperature
ii higher density
iii more stable carbonate
iv more basic oxide
v easier oxide to reduce
vi greater reactivity with dilute acid

4. This question is about the following valency numbers:

A +1
B +2
C +4
D +6
E +7

Which is the valency number of the transition metal in the following compounds:

i CrO_3
ii $CuCl$
iii $CuSO_4$
iv MnO_2
v Mn_2O_7

5. Non-transition elements may show variable valency, for example non-metals such as Cl and S, or metals such as Pb.

Write the formula for the oxide of each of the following elements (valency number given in brackets):

i Cl (+1)
ii Cl (+7)
iii S (+4)
iv S (+6)
v Pb (+2)
vi Pb (+4)

6. An unidentified element has the following properties:

A good conductivity
B high density
C melts below 400 °C
D low reactivity
E valency numbers + 2 and +4
F forms coloured oxides
G forms colourless salts

i Which of the above properties could be used to support the idea that the element is:

a a transition element
b not a transition element

ii Which of the following elements best fits the description of the unidentified element above?

C, Mn, Na, Pb, S

Unit 22
Reactivity of metals

All metals are not equally reactive

Earlier in your work in chemistry you will have tried comparing the reactivity of different metals. For example, you can compare iron, magnesium and copper by *burning* them and watching to see how vigorous the reactions are. Or you can try their reactions with *water* and *dilute acids*. It is quite easy to compare the speeds of the reactions in these cases.

In general, magnesium is more reactive than iron, and iron is more reactive than copper. In other words, magnesium seems to have high reactivity, which shows itself in most of its reactions. On the other hand, copper has low reactivity in most of its reactions.

If more metals are compared, the same sort of conclusion can be reached: *a metal that is more reactive in one way is usually more reactive in other ways*. This means that the overall reactivity of metals can be compared (instead of comparing them in one reaction at a time). Eventually, you could build up a list of the metals in 'reactivity order'. This kind of list can be called a *reactivity series*.

- *A reactivity series is a list of metals that puts them in order of reactivity compared with one another.*

The table below shows the results of some experiments and puts the metals in order of reactivity.

Other approaches to the reactivity series

If you were investigating the reactions of metals with, say, dilute hydrochloric acid, how would you compare 'reactivity'? One way would be to measure the *speed of hydrogen formation*. (You would have to make sure the metals were compared under the same conditions.)

However, there are other ways to compare 'reactivity'. For example, you could try measuring the *heat change* in each reaction. In other words, you could find out which metals give more heat when they react, and which give less. You could put the metals in order again. You would find that the metals are not in exactly the same order as they were when compared by the speed method. (But there are similarities.)

- *The reactivity of metals can be compared by looking at the speed of reaction (for instance with a dilute acid), and heat change in reaction.*

Metal	*Reaction when heated in oxygen*	*Reaction with water*	*Reaction with dilute hydrochloric acid*
Na	burn more vigorously near the top of the list	release hydrogen from cold water	explosive reaction at the top of the list; decreasing reactivity going down; hydrogen formed; very slow reaction for lead
Ca			
Mg		react to give hydrogen when heated in steam	
Zn			
Fe			
Pb		no reaction with pure water or steam	
Cu			no reaction
Ag	will not burn		

Comparing some metals

Platinum is very unreactive; it is one of the few elements found in a native (uncombined) state

Displacement reactions

If iron filings are put into copper(II) sulphate solution, the solution loses its blue colour and a brown sludge of copper metal is formed. The reaction that happens can be represented like this:

$$\mathbf{Fe(s) + CuSO_4(aq) \rightarrow FeSO_4(aq) + Cu(s)}$$

This type of change is called a *displacement reaction*. The copper is displaced (pushed out) of the compound by the iron.

Iron will displace other metals, for example silver and lead. But it will not displace zinc, magnesium or calcium.

You can investigate displacement reactions using other metals and salt solutions. The results of some investigations are shown in the figure below.

You will notice that Mg (the most reactive metal on the list) displaces all the others. But Ag (the least reactive metal in the list) displaces none of the others. The conclusion you can draw from experiments of this sort is that *metals only displace other metals that are lower down in the reactivity series*. As we have seen, Fe displaces Cu and Ag, but not Mg and Zn.

● *A metal will displace another metal below it in the reactivity series.*

You can see how investigating displacement reactions gives you another method for making a reactivity series.

Reactivity and simple cells

Simple electrical cells can be used to compare metals. The figure on p. 101 shows how a cell can be made. When the electrodes consist of a piece of copper foil and a piece of zinc foil, the e.m.f. (voltage) measured is about 1 volt. When other metals are used, different voltages are recorded. The best way to organize the experiment is to keep one electrode the same each time. For example, make one electrode copper each time, and try several metals as the other electrode in turn. When Mg/Cu is used a higher voltage is recorded than for Zn/Cu. When Fe/Cu is used,

Displacement reactions

	$MgSo_4(aq)$	$ZnSO_4(aq)$	$FeSO_4(aq)$	$CuSO_4(aq)$	$AgNO_3(aq)$
$Mg(s)$					
$Zn(s)$					
$Fe(s)$					
$Cu(s)$					
$Ag(s)$					

Key

signs of displacement

no change

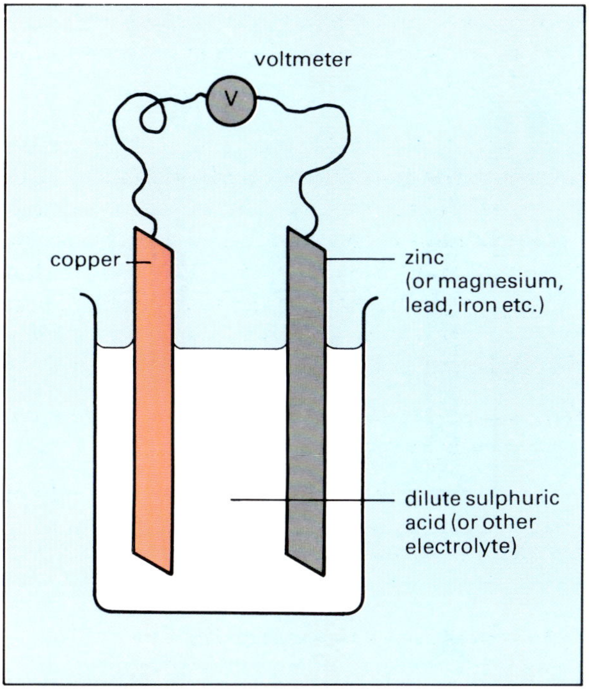

A simple cell

Reactive and less reactive metals are used together in electric cells

the voltage is lower. If Ag is used with Cu, current flows in the reverse direction.

The results of experiments with cells show that there is a connection between the e.m.f. value of the cell and the relative reactivities of the metals of the electrodes. High voltages are recorded when the metals are far apart in reactivity: low voltages are recorded when the metals are close together.

- *The e.m.f. value of a cell depends on the relative reactivities of the metals of the electrodes.*

Experimenting with simple cells is yet another way to work out a reactivity series of the metals.

Reduction of oxides

Oxides of metals can often be reduced in a variety of ways. For example, you can heat the oxide in hydrogen:

$$\mathbf{PbO(s) + H_2(g) \rightarrow Pb(s) + H_2O(l)}$$

Or in carbon monoxide:

$$\mathbf{Fe_2O_3(s) + 3CO(g) \rightarrow 2Fe(s) + 3CO_2(g)}$$

Or with carbon:

$$\mathbf{ZnO(s) + C(s) \rightarrow Zn(s) + CO(g)}$$

Hydrogen, carbon monoxide and carbon are good *reducing agents.*

However, not all oxides can be reduced with equal ease. You can compare oxides only by heating them with the same reducing agent under the same conditions. For example, the oxides CaO, CuO, MgO, PbO and ZnO could all be heated with hydrogen. At the temperature of a bunsen burner flame, only PbO and CuO are reduced. If the oxides Na_2O and Fe_2O_3 are heated with carbon, only the iron oxide is reduced at red heat.

You will have noticed that the hardest oxides to reduce are those of metals at the top of the reactivity series (Na, Ca, Mg, Zn). Oxides of metals near the bottom of the list are easier to reduce. We can draw the same conclusion in the following way:

- *Reactive metals are more stable in oxidized states. Unreactive metals are more stable in reduced states.*

Ease of reduction of oxides can be used to compare the reactivities of metals.

Summary

1. Metals differ in their reactivities.
2. A reactivity series is a list of metals that puts them in order of reactivity compared with one another.
3. Reactivities of metals can be compared by reacting them with a substance (e.g. oxygen, water, hydrochloric acid) under the same conditions and observing differences in reaction speeds.
4. Other ways to draw up reactivity series include:
   a comparing heat changes in reactions;
   b comparing e.m.f. values of simple cells;
   c investigating displacement reactions;
   d investigating reduction of oxides.
5. In general, a metal will displace another metal below it in a reactivity series.
6. In general, the greater the difference in reactivity of the metals of the electrodes, the greater is the e.m.f. of a cell.
7. Reactive metals are more stable in oxidized states; unreactive metals are more stable in reduced states.

Extension

1. **Simple cells and ionization of metals**

Why should e.m.f. values of simple cells depend on relative reactivities of the electrode metals?

An explanation starts with the idea that *different metals have different tendencies to form positive ions.* If two metals are connected together and dipped into a solution (as in a simple cell) they 'compete' with one another; only the metal with the stronger tendency is able to ionize. So, the stronger ionizer 'wins' the competition.

For example, if the metal atoms (M) pass into the solution as ions (e.g. M^{2+}) electrons that are left behind flow through the wires of the circuit to the other metal (see figure).

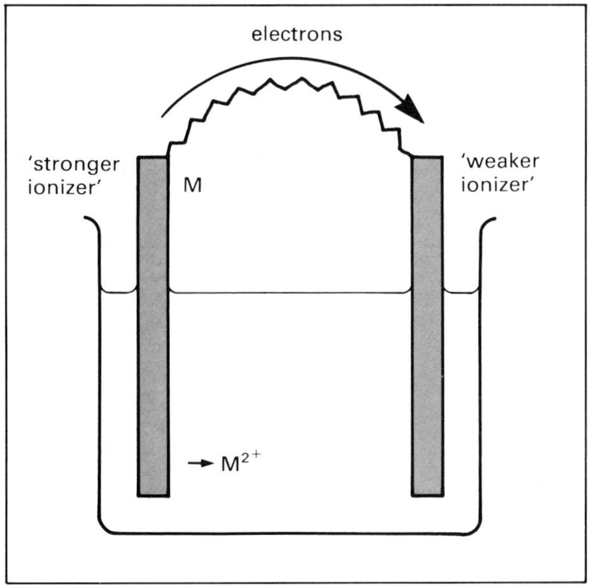

To get a more complete understanding, we must assume that *more reactive metals have a stronger tendency to form positive ions*. So, Mg is a 'stronger ionizer', and Cu is a 'weaker ionizer'.

Explain how these ideas about strong and weak ionizers can be used to account for the following observations:

i reactive metals displace less reactive metals from salt solutions, for example:

$$Zn(s) + Cu^{2+}(aq) \rightarrow Zn^{2+}(aq) + Cu(s)$$

ii reactive metals displace hydrogen from acid solutions, for example:

$$Zn(s) + 2H^{+}(aq) \rightarrow Zn^{2+}(aq) + H_2(g)$$

but less reactive metals do not, for example:

$$Cu(s) + 2H^{+}(aq) : \text{no change}$$

iii oxides of reactive metals are harder to reduce, for example:

$$CaO(s) + H_2(g) : \text{no change}$$

but oxides of less reactive metals are easier to reduce, for example:

$$CuO(s) + H_2(g) \rightarrow Cu(s) + H_2O(g)$$

2. **Simple cells and corrosion**

You can attempt this extension if you have completed the one above.

i In general, corrosion of a metal involves oxidation of it. The ease of corrosion of a metal depends on its reactivity: *more reactive metals corrode more rapidly.* This is in agreement with the observation that the more reactive metals are more stable in their oxidized states.

In each of the following cases, state which of the metals would tend to be more readily corroded under the same conditions:

a Fe, Mg
b Fe, Pb
c Fe, Zn

ii A useful method of preventing corrosion uses knowledge of the reactivity series and simple cells. For example, it may be necessary to protect an underground iron pipe from corrosion. If the pipe is connected (by an electrical conductor) to a piece of more reactive metal then, in the moist conditions underground, the situation is like that in a simple cell. The result is that the more reactive metal corrodes and the iron is protected. This is called *cathodic protection*.

a Name another object, apart from an underground pipe, that might benefit from cathodic protection.
b Suggest a metal other than zinc that would be useful for the cathodic protection of iron.
c Suggest an explanation for the fact that *galvanized* (zinc-coated) iron does not rust if the zinc coating cracks, while tin-plated iron rusts rapidly if the coating is damaged.

Hot-dipping steel in molten zinc

d In terms of corrosion, what would be the likely result of using copper rivets on the steel hull of a ship?
e Explain why cathodic protection only works if the two metals are connected by an electrical conductor.

3. **Aluminium**
Where will aluminium appear in a reactivity series?

i Al is often shown in a reactivity series between the metals Mg and Zn. However, look at these observations about aluminium:

- Al does not react with steam.
- Aluminium oxide is not reduced by carbon at red heat.

What do the observations suggest about aluminium's position in the reactivity series?

ii The odd behaviour of aluminium is explained by the idea that its surface is protected by a thin coating of oxide (Al_2O_3). How would the idea of a *protective coating* explain the following observation?

- A simple cell with Al and Cu electrodes gives a low e.m.f. unless the aluminium is first treated (e.g. with hydrochloric acid)

Revision

1. This question is about the following elements:

A Ag
B Cu
C Fe
D Na
E P

i Which is not a metal?
ii Which metal will react with water most vigorously?
iii Which metal will react with steam but not with cold water?
iv Which metal is most stable in oxidized states?
v Which metal is most stable in reduced states?

2. Here are some observations about five metals, A, B, C, D and E.
   i A will not react with steam but reacts slowly with hydrochloric acid to form hydrogen.
   ii B reacts with steam to form hydrogen.
   iii B is displaced from solutions of its salts by C.
   iv D is displaced by A, but not by E.

   Place the five metals in order of reactivity (most reactive first).

3. This question is about the following metals:

   A Ag
   B Ca
   C Cu
   D Fe
   E Pb

   Which metal will:
   i react with cold water to form hydrogen
   ii react with steam but not with cold water
   iii react slowly with dilute acid, but not with water or steam
   iv burn in oxygen, but will not react with dilute acid
   v not react with oxygen, water or dilute acid
   vi most often be found in a reduced state in nature
   vii have the oxide that is most difficult to reduce in the laboratory
   viii be displaced from aqueous solutions by all the other metals in the list

4. Look at the chart showing the results of displacement reactions (p. 100). Write equations for all the reactions that involve Mg.

5. Read the information that follows about the metals A–E.

   What can you deduce about their reactivities compared with the other metals?
   i Zn, Fe and A are all found to react with dilute hydrochloric acid, but only A reacts with cold water.
   ii Oxides of Mg, Cu and B are placed in a tube and hydrogen is passed through it. The tube is gradually heated up. The CuO is reduced first and then the oxide of B. MgO is not reduced.
   iii Metal C is displaced from aqueous solutions of its salts by Zn, but not by Cu.
   iv Equal amounts of Mg and D are each reacted with 100 cm^3 of dilute acid. A temperature rise of 20 °C is recorded in the case of the Mg, but only 5 °C in the case of D.
   v When Fe is connected to Cu in a simple cell, a voltmeter in the circuit deflects to the right. When E is used instead of the Fe, the deflection is to the left.

6. The importance of metals in history is connected with their positions in the reactivity series. Comment on the following observations:
   i Copper was widely used as long ago as 4000 BC.
   ii Iron smelting did not begin until about 1300 BC.
   iii Aluminium (the most abundant metal in the Earth's crust) was not put to use until after AD1800.

Unit 23
Electrolytes and electrolysis

What is an electrolyte?

● *An electrolyte is a substance that conducts electricity when melted or dissolved, but not when solid.*

Results of experiments to investigate electrolytes

Observations about electrolytes can be summarized like this:

1. Electrolytes include salts, bases and acids.
2. Decomposition of the electrolyte happens at the electrodes when electricity flows (this decomposition is called *electrolysis*).
3. Products at the positive electrode (*anode*) include non-metals (often oxygen from aqueous solutions) but not usually hydrogen.
4. Products at the negative electrode (*cathode*) include metals (and hydrogen, especially from aqueous solutions).

Explaining electrolysis observations

● *Electrolysis is best explained by the ionic theory.*

The main points of the ionic theory can be summarized like this:

1. Electrolytes are composed of positively and negatively charged particles called *ions*.
2. Ions are only free to move when electrolytes are melted or dissolved.
3. Positive ions are formed from metal atoms (or hydrogen atoms) and they migrate to the cathode during electrolysis. Positive ions are called *cations*.
4. Negative ions in general are formed from non-metal atoms (except hydrogen) and they migrate to the anode. Negative ions are called *anions*.
5. When they reach their destinations (i.e. the electrodes), the cations and anions may be *discharged*. This happens by the *transfer of electrons*. The anions may give up electrons to the anode. The cations may accept electrons from the cathode. Unless electrons are 'handed over', there will be no flow of electricity round the circuit.

● *Electrolytes conduct electricity because of transfer of electrons between ions and the electrodes during electrolysis.*

It is the discharge of ions that produces the new substances formed during electrolysis. We shall consider these changes in more detail later in this Unit. But first, let us look at the names and formulas of cations and anions found in some electrolytes. These are shown in the table below.

Electrolyte		*Cation*		*Anion*	
name	*formula*	*name*	*formula*	*name*	*formula*
aluminium oxide	Al_2O_3	aluminium	Al^{3+}	oxide	O^{2-}
ammonium sulphate	$(NH_4)_2SO_4$	ammonium	NH_4^+	sulphate	SO_4^{2-}
calcium hydroxide	$Ca(OH)_2$	calcium	Ca^{2+}	hydroxide	OH^-
copper (II) sulphate	$CuSO_4$	copper (II)	Cu^{2+}	sulphate	SO_4^{2-}
lead (II) bromide	$PbBr_2$	lead (II)	Pb^{2+}	bromide	Br^-
potassium iodide	KI	potassium	K^+	iodide	I^-
silver nitrate	$AgNO_3$	silver	Ag^+	nitrate	NO_3^-
sodium chloride	NaCl	sodium	Na^+	chloride	Cl^-
sodium hydroxide	NaOH	sodium	Na^+	hydroxide	OH^-
sodium carbonate	Na_2CO_3	sodium	Na^+	carbonate	CO_3^{2-}
zinc nitrate	$Zn(NO_3)_2$	zinc	Zn^{2+}	nitrate	NO_3^-

Cations and anions found in some electrolytes

Discharge of ions during electrolysis

Equations are written to represent these discharge processes. The symbol e^- is used to show each electron that is transferred. Here are some examples:

Discharge of cations at cathodes

1. cation provided by electrolyte → $Na^+ + e^- \rightarrow Na$ ← neutral atom of product; ↑ electron provided by cathode

2. $Pb^{2+} + 2e^- \rightarrow Pb$
3. $Mg^{2+} + 2e^- \rightarrow Mg$
4. $K^+ + e^- \rightarrow K$
5. $Al^{3+} + 3e^- \rightarrow Al$

Discharge of anions at anodes

2. anion provided by electrolyte → $Br^- \rightarrow e^- + Br$ ← neutral atom of product; ↑ electron accepted by anode

(**Note:** After formation at anodes, atoms of many non-metals combine to give diatomic molecules, for example $2Br \rightarrow Br_2$.)

2. $Cl^- \rightarrow e^- + Cl$
   $(2Cl \rightarrow Cl_2)$
3. $I^- \rightarrow e^- + I$
   $(2I \rightarrow I_2)$
4. $O^{2-} \rightarrow 2e^- + O$
   $(2O \rightarrow O_2)$
5. $OH^- \rightarrow e^- + OH$
   $(4OH \rightarrow O_2 + 2H_2O)$

(**Note:** Many complex anions, e.g. CO_3^{2-}, SO_4^{2-}, NO_3^-, are not discharged at anodes. Salts containing these anions cannot be melted without decomposing, and they are not discharged from aqueous solutions because of the part played by ions formed from H_2O; see below.)

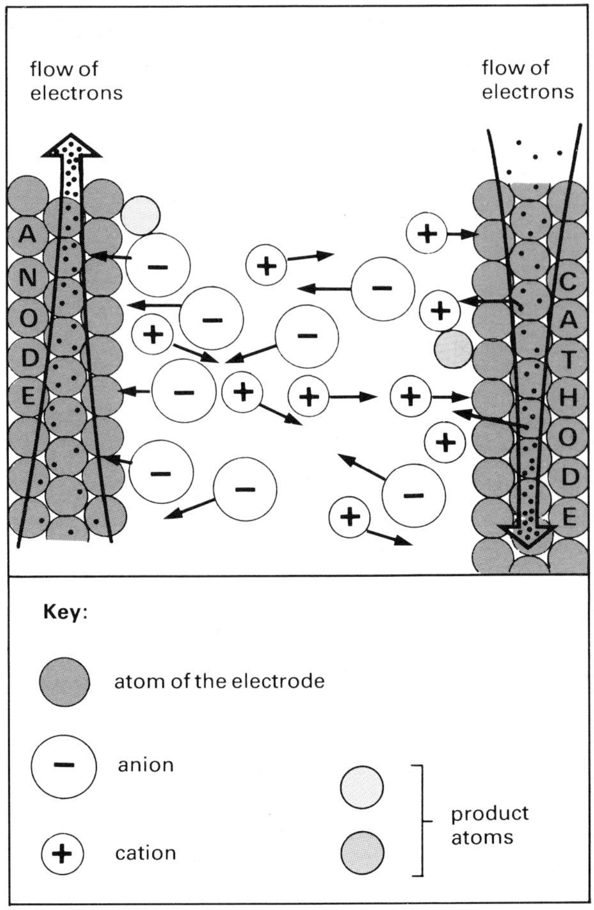

Migration and discharge of ions during electrolysis

Electrolysis of aqueous solutions

Both aqueous solutions of electrolytes and molten electrolytes conduct electricity. But the products at the electrodes are not always what you might expect. An aqueous electrolyte often gives different products at the electrodes to the products formed when the same electrolyte is molten. For example, when molten salt (sodium chloride) is electrolysed, the product at the cathode is sodium. But when aqueous salt solutions are electrolysed, the product at the cathode is *hydrogen*. The table on p.107 shows the results of some electrolysis experiments using aqueous electrolytes.

The results of experiments with aqueous solutions like these show that, in many cases, the salt cation is not discharged at the cathode. Instead, hydrogen is formed. And the salt anion is not always discharged at the anode. Instead, oxygen is formed at the anode.

● *Oxygen is formed at the anode, and hydrogen is formed at the cathode, during the electrolysis of many aqueous solutions.*

Electrolyte	*Anode product*	*Cathode product*
copper (II) sulphate (aq)	oxygen	copper
sodium chloride (aq)	chlorine and oxygen	hydrogen
potassium iodide (aq)	iodine	hydrogen
lead (II) nitrate (aq)	oxygen	lead

The part played by water in electrolysis of aqueous electrolytes

How can the behaviour of aqueous electrolytes be explained? The best approach is to consider the part played by the solvent (water) in the solution.

Pure water has been shown to be a very, very weak electrolyte, and this is thought to be due to the following ionization process:

$$H_2O(l) \rightarrow H^+(aq) + OH^-(aq)$$

We can calculate the proportion of water molecules that will be ionized at any particular time. Water is such a weak electrolyte that millions of water molecules would only contain one H^+ ion and one OH^- (on average). However, it is these ions from water that play a part in electrolysis processes of aqueous solutions.

If H^+ ions are discharged at the cathode, hydrogen will be formed.

$$H^+ + e^- \rightarrow H$$
$$(2H \rightarrow H_2)$$

If OH^- ions are discharged at the anode, oxygen is formed:

$$OH^- \rightarrow e^- + OH$$
$$(4OH \rightarrow O_2 + 2H_2O)$$

● *Water is a weak electrolyte and its ions may play a part in electrolysis processes.*

Summary

1. Electrolytes conduct electricity when melted or dissolved, but not when solid.
2. Decomposition of electrolytes by passing electricity through them is called electrolysis.
3. Electrolysis is best explained by the ionic theory.
4. The theory suggests that electrolytes conduct because of transfer of electrons between ions and the electrodes during electrolysis.
5. Positive ions (cations) are discharged at the cathode by accepting electrons.
6. Negative ions (anions) are discharged at the anode by giving up electrons.
7. Oxygen is formed at the anode and hydrogen is formed at the cathode when many aqueous solutions are electrolysed.
8. Water is a weak electrolyte and its ions may play a part in electrolysis processes.

Extension

Competition between ions during electrolysis

You have learned that aqueous solutions contain H^+ and OH^- ions, as well as any ions coming from the solute.

If NaF(aq) was electrolysed, we would expect *Na^+ and H^+* ions to arrive at the cathode. *F^- and OH^-* ions would arrive at the anode. The results of experiments suggest that the ions *compete for discharge* at the electrodes. In the case of NaF(aq), hydrogen is normally formed at the cathode (not sodium). And oxygen is formed at the anode. We can conclude that H^+ is discharged at the cathode (not Na^+) and OH^- is discharged at the anode (not F^-).

In general, under ordinary circumstances, H^+ will be discharged more easily than Na^+, and OH^- will be discharged more easily than F^-.

What happens with other cations and anions? A few results of electrolysis experiments are shown above. As a result of further investigation, we can draw up the following 'rules' (they are oversimplifications, but often apply):

Cations	*Anions*
H^+ is discharged rather than K^+, Na^+, Ca^{2+}.	OH^- is discharged rather than SO_4^{2-}, NO_3^{2-}, CO_3^{2-}.
Zn^{2+}, Pb^{2+}, Cu^{2+}, Ag^+ are discharged rather than H^+.	Br^- and I^- are discharged rather than OH^-.
(In general, more reactive metals are more difficult to discharge.)	(Cl^- may be discharged rather than OH^- depending on concentration.)

1. Copy and complete the following table to show probable anode and cathode products:

Electrolyte	*Anode product*	*Cathode product*
Na_2SO_4(aq)		
HI(aq)		
$CuBr_2$(aq)		
$AgNO_3$(aq)		
KOH(aq)		

2. Write equations for the electrode processes that occur at the anode and cathode during electrolysis of:

i $PbBr_2$(l)
ii Al_2O_3(l)
iii H_2SO_4(aq)
iv NaI(aq)
v K_2SO_4(aq)

Revision

1. This question is about the following substances:

A CCl_4(l)
B $CuSO_4$(aq)
C H_2SO_4(aq)
D KCl(l)
E NaOH(aq)

Choose one that:

i is not an electrolyte
ii is a laboratory acid
iii is a strong base
iv would produce chlorine at the anode during electrolysis

Choose two that, during electrolysis, would produce:

v hydrogen at the cathode
vi a metal at the cathode

2. The table below shows the names and formulas of some electrolytes and their ions, but gaps have been left in places. Copy the table and complete it.

3. Write equations to show the changes that happen at the anode and the cathode during electrolysis of the following substances:

i NaCl(l)
ii KI(l)
iii NaOH(l)

Electrolyte		*Cation*		*Anion*	
name	*formula*	*name*	*formula*	*name*	*formula*
aluminium oxide	Al_2O_3	aluminium	Al^{3+}	oxide	O^{2-}
calcium hydrogencarbonate	$Ca(HCO_3)_2$	calcium	Ca^{2+}	hydrogencarbonate	
copper (II) nitrate	$Cu(NO_3)_2$	copper (II)		nitrate	NO_3^-
magnesium nitrate		magnesium	Mg^{2+}	nitrate	NO_3^-
		potassium	K^+	hydroxide	OH^-
silver acetate (ethanoate)		silver	Ag^+	acetate (ethanoate)	CH_3COO^-
		zinc		bromide	

Unit 24
Redox changes

Gaining and losing oxygen

You have met the terms *oxidation* and *reduction* before. You should remember that a chemical reaction in which a substance combines with oxygen is called an oxidation. And a reaction in which oxygen is removed from a compound is called a reduction. Clearly, *reduction is the opposite of oxidation*.

● *In chemical change, gain of oxygen is called oxidation and loss of oxygen is called reduction.*

Burning, respiration and rusting are familiar examples of oxidation, for example:

burning methane:

$$\mathbf{CH_4(g) + \underset{\text{(from air)}}{2O_2(g)} \rightarrow CO_2(g) + 2H_2O(g)}$$

oxidizing glucose:

$$\mathbf{C_6H_{12}O_6(s) + \underset{\text{(from air)}}{6O_2(g)} \rightarrow 6CO_2(g) + 6H_2O(g)}$$

Many metals are extracted from ores by reduction processes, for example:

smelting of iron:

$$\mathbf{Fe_2O_3(s) + 3CO(g) \rightarrow 2Fe(l) + 3CO_2(g)}$$

production of aluminium:

$$\mathbf{2Al_2O_3(l) \xrightarrow{\text{electrolysis}} 4Al(l) + 3O_2(g)}$$

Redox

When carbon monoxide reduces iron(III) oxide (see equation above), the carbon monoxide gains oxygen while the iron(III) oxide loses it. In other words, both oxidation and reduction happen in one reaction. This is usually the case. Here is an example of a reaction that is easy to demonstrate in the laboratory:

oxidation

$$\mathbf{H_2(g) + PbO(s) \rightarrow H_2O(g) + Pb(l)}$$

reduction

When hydrogen and lead(II) oxide are heated together, the hydrogen is oxidized to form water vapour; the lead(II) oxide is reduced to form molten lead. Changes like this that involve reduction and oxidation are commonly called *redox reactions*.

Look at the following examples. What is oxidized and what is reduced in each case?

a $\mathbf{CuO(s) + H_2(g) \rightarrow Cu(s) + H_2O(g)}$

b $\mathbf{C(s) + H_2O(g) \rightarrow CO(g) + H_2(g)}$

c $\mathbf{SO_2(aq) + H_2O_2(aq) \rightarrow SO_3(aq) + H_2O(l)}$

● *Oxidation and reduction take place together in redox reactions.*

Oxidizing agents and reducing agents

Substances that cause oxidation are called *oxidizing agents*.

Some of the oxidizing agents we have met in the reactions above are: oxygen (burning methane), iron(III) oxide (smelting iron), steam (reaction *b*). Any substance that oxidizes another is an oxidizing agent. But some oxidizing agents are stronger than others. Iron(III) oxide and steam are not very strong oxidizing agents. Examples of strong oxidizing agents that you may use in the laboratory include the following:

$O_2(g)$, $KMnO_4(aq)$, $H_2O_2(aq)$, $HNO_3(aq)$, $K_2Cr_2O_7(aq)$

Substances that cause reduction are called *reducing agents*. In the reactions above, the reducing agents included carbon monoxide (smelting iron), hydrogen (reaction *a*) and carbon (reaction *b*). Reducing agents also vary in strength. Good reducing agents that you may use in the laboratory include the following:

$H_2(g)$, $Mg(s)$, $SO_2(g)$, $H_2S(g)$, $KI(aq)$, $CO(g)$

● *Substances that cause oxidation are called oxidizing agents. Substances that cause reduction are called reducing agents.*

Hydrogen and redox changes

Hydrogen plays a part in many redox changes; take the reaction of potassium manganate(VII) with hydrochloric acid, for example. This reaction is used for the usual laboratory preparation of chlorine. When concentrated hydrochloric acid is mixed with potassium manganate(VII) crystals, the manganate(VII) provides oxygen for the following change:

$$2HCl(aq) + [O] \rightarrow H_2O(l) + Cl_2(g)$$

Clearly, the chlorine is produced by oxidation of the HCl. You will notice that this oxidation has involved the removal of hydrogen from the HCl. This leads us to an additional definition of oxidation. *Oxidation may involve removal of hydrogen from a compound.* Similarly, *gain of hydrogen is reduction.*

Look at this reaction:

$$Cl_2(g) + H_2S(g) \rightarrow 2HCl(g) + S(s)$$

Here, the chlorine is reduced by gain of hydrogen from the H_2S. The H_2S is oxidized by loss of hydrogen. The chlorine is therefore acting as an oxidizing agent.

- *Removal of hydrogen from a compound is oxidation. Gain of hydrogen is reduction.*

Reactive metals are reducing agents

The list of good reducing agents given above includes Mg. All reactive metals are good reducing agents. Reactions that illustrate this include:

magnesium reducing steam:

$$Mg(s) + H_2O(g) \rightarrow MgO(s) + H_2(g)$$

aluminium reducing iron(III) oxide:

$$2Al(s) + Fe_2O_3(s) \rightarrow 2Fe(s) + Al_2O_3(s)$$

sodium reducing cold water:

$$2Na(s) + 2H_2O(l) \rightarrow 2NaOH(aq) + H_2(g)$$

Of course, all of these changes cause oxidation of the metal. (You will have realized by now that reducing agents always get oxidized in redox changes.) But all the changes also involve the formation of cations from the metal atoms.

$Mg \rightarrow Mg^{2+}$ (in MgO)
$Al \rightarrow Al^{3+}$ (in Al_2O_3)
$Na \rightarrow Na^+$ (in NaOH)

These changes happen by the *removal of electrons* from the metal atoms. The more closely we look at redox changes, the more it seems that *removal of electrons is oxidation.* As always, reduction may be defined as the opposite of oxidation: *gain of electrons is reduction.*

- *Oxidation of a particle happens if it loses one or more electrons: reduction is gain of electrons.*

Take the following displacement reaction, for example:

$$CuSO_4(aq) + Zn(s) \rightarrow ZnSO_4(aq) + Cu(s)$$

The zinc atoms change as follows:

$$Zn(s) - 2e^- \rightarrow Zn^{2+}(aq)$$

that is, they lose two electrons each and are oxidized.

The copper(II) ions are reduced by gaining electrons:

$$Cu^{2+} + 2e^- \rightarrow Cu(s)$$

As we know, a metal lower in the reactivity series is displaced by one higher in the series. Clearly, metals higher in the series are better reducing agents than those lower down.

Half reactions

As we saw in the last section, redox reactions can be represented by equations that show the oxidation and reduction separately. Take the following displacement reaction, for example:

$$Mg(s) + Fe^{2+}(aq) \rightarrow Fe(s) + Mg^{2+}(aq)$$

The equation can be split up like this:

$Mg(s) \rightarrow Mg^{2+}(aq) + 2e^-$ (oxidation)
$Fe^{2+}(aq) + 2e^- \rightarrow Fe(s)$ (reduction)

The parts of the whole reaction are called *half reactions*.

Laboratory investigation of oxidizing agents

Potassium iodide (KI) is a salt. It has colourless crystals and dissolves in water to form colourless solutions:

$$K^+I^-(s) + aq \rightarrow K^+(aq) + I^-(aq)$$

The iodide ion is a good reducing agent. It is easily oxidized to form iodine, especially if the solution is acidified:

$$2I^-(aq) \xrightarrow[\text{by oxidizing agent}]{\text{electrons removed}} I_2(aq)$$

The iodine formed is slightly soluble in water. Aqueous solutions of iodine vary from yellow to brown, depending on concentration. So, if a solution of KI goes brown, we can tell that an oxidizing agent is working.

Test each of the following chemicals in turn by mixing them with 1 or 2 cm^3 of KI(aq). Record your observations and rinse out the test-tube before trying the next test.

1. Dilute sulphuric acid.
2. Dilute nitric acid.
3. 50 per cent nitric acid (see safety note).
4. Potassium dichromate(VI) solution.
5. Potassium dichromate(VI) solution acidified with dilute sulphuric acid.
6. Hydrogen peroxide solution.
7. Hydrogen peroxide solution acidified with dilute sulphuric acid.
8. Chlorine water.

Safety note: Oxidizing agents can be corrosive. Wear safety goggles.

50 per cent nitric acid (equal amounts of concentrated HNO_3 and water) should be prepared by the teacher and used with care.

Conclusions

Which of the chemicals tested are good oxidizing agents?

Laboratory investigation of reducing agents

Potassium manganate(VII) is a salt with dark purple crystals. It dissolves in water to form purple solutions:

$$K^+MnO_4^-(s) + aq \rightarrow K^+(aq) + MnO_4^-(aq)$$

The manganate(VII) ion is a strong oxidizing agent, especially in acidic solutions. The reduction product is colourless, that is, the purple colour disappears during the reaction:

$$MnO_4^-(aq) \xrightarrow[\text{reducing agent}]{\text{electrons given by}} \textbf{colourless solution}$$

So, if the purple colour of manganate(VII) disappears during a reaction, it suggests that a reducing agent is working.

Test the following chemicals with a few drops of $KMnO_4(aq)$ acidified with dilute sulphuric acid:

1. Laboratory gas (methane, hydrogen).
2. Glucose solution.
3. Iron filings.
4. Magnesium ribbon.
5. Copper metal.
6. Sulphur dioxide gas.

   (**Safety note:** Use fume cupboard.)
7. Hydrogen sulphide gas.

   (**Safety note:** Use fume cupboard.)
8. Acidified KI(aq).

Conclusions

Which of the chemicals are good reducing agents?

Summary

1. Oxidation is gain of oxygen, or loss of hydrogen, or loss of electrons.
2. Reduction is loss of oxygen, or gain of hydrogen, or gain of electrons.
3. Oxidation and reduction take place together in reactions called redox reactions.
4. Substances that cause oxidation are called oxidizing agents, and substances that cause reduction are called reducing agents.
5. Good oxidizing agents include $O_2(g)$, $KMnO_4(aq)$, $H_2O_2(aq)$, $HNO_3(aq)$, $K_2Cr_2O_7(aq)$.
6. Good reducing agents include $H_2(g)$, $Mg(s)$, $SO_2(g)$, $H_2S(g)$, $KI(aq)$, $CO(g)$.

Extension

1. Iron is manufactured in a blast furnace. A mixture of iron ore (containing iron(III) oxide), coke and limestone is fed into the furnace. A powerful blast of hot air is blown into the furnace at the bottom and the following reactions happen:

   i $\mathbf{C(s) + O_2(g) \rightarrow CO_2(g)}$

   ii $\mathbf{CO_2(g) + C(g) \rightarrow 2CO(g)}$

   iii $\mathbf{3CO(g) + Fe_2O_3(s) \rightarrow 2Fe(l) + 3CO_2(g)}$

   The melted iron is collected at the base of the furnace. Most of it is transferred to 'converters' where it is converted into steels.

   i In reaction (i), which substance is being oxidized?
   ii In reaction (ii), which substance is being reduced?
   iii Name the reducing agent in reaction (iii).
   iv Steels are alloys. Find out more about alloy steels and write an account of their important properties and uses.

2. When copper is dissolved in concentrated nitric acid, copper(II) nitrate solution is formed:

   A $\mathbf{Cu(s) + 4HNO_3(aq) \rightarrow Cu(NO_3)_2(aq) + 2NO_2(g) + O_2(g)}$

   Solid copper(II) nitrate can be obtained from the solution. The action of heat on the solid causes decomposition:

   B $\mathbf{Cu(NO_3)_2(s) \rightarrow CuO(s) + NO_2(g) + O_2(g)}$

   i Which of the changes (A or B) involves oxidation of the copper? Explain your answer.
   ii Rewrite equation B and balance it.
   iii The overall effect of the reactions A and B is to convert copper into copper(II) oxide. Another way to bring about this change is summarized below:

   $$\mathbf{Cu(s) \xrightarrow{(C)} Cu(NO_3)_2(aq) \xrightarrow{(D)} Cu(OH)_2(s) \xrightarrow{(E)} CuO(s)}$$

   Describe how you would attempt to carry out the changes C, D and E.
   iv How could copper(II) oxide be converted back to copper?

3. **Redox in electrolysis**
   The changes that happen at the electrodes during electrolysis are oxidations or reductions. Ions are oxidized by the loss of electrons at the anode. (Anodes act as oxidizing agents.) Ions are reduced by gaining electrons at the cathode. (Cathodes act as reducing agents.)

   Write half reactions to show the redox changes that happen:

   i at the anode during electrolysis of:
      a molten lead(II) bromide
      b aqueous sodium hydroxide
   ii at the cathode during electrolysis of:
      a molten aluminium oxide
      b aqueous copper(II) sulphate
      c dilute sulphuric acid

4. **Redox in photography**
   Photographic emulsions. Photographic papers and photographic films have a thin coating of light-sensitive emulsion on one side. The emulsion is made from gelatin jelly mixed with millions of colourless, microscopic crystals of silver bromide. Each square centimetre contains thousands of millions of crystals.
   Exposure. When a light ray hits a crystal, the following change happens to a pair of Ag^+Br^- ions on the surface of the crystal:

   $$\mathbf{Ag^+ + Br^- \rightarrow Ag + Br}$$

Over a long period of exposure, the emulsion gradually goes dark as more and more grey/black Ag is formed. However, in photography the emulsion is exposed to light for only a short time, for example a fraction of a second for film in a camera, or several seconds for paper when printing in the darkroom. Under these conditions, so few Ag atoms are formed that the emulsion appears to be unchanged.

Development. If the emulsion is treated with a developer solution, any crystals that have been affected by light are rapidly darkened as the remaining Ag^+ ions within those crystals are converted to Ag. Any crystals in the film or paper that contain no Ag atoms stay clear or white.

i Scientists define *emulsion* as a mixture of one finely divided liquid in another (immiscible) liquid, so a photographic 'emulsion' is not strictly an emulsion. Explain.

ii During exposure of AgBr to light, which ion is *oxidized*? Explain in terms of electron exchange.

iii The chemical hydroquinone is used as a *developer*. Is hydroquinone an oxidizing agent or a reducing agent? Explain your answer.

iv Metallic silver could be said to *catalyse* the action of hydroquinone during development. Explain why this is important for the formation of the image.

v Find out more about photography and explain why:

a *fast emulsions* give grainy images

b *fixers* are an essential part of processing.

Revision

1. Give the name of the oxidizing agent in each of the following reactions:

i $ZnO(s) + C(s) \rightarrow Zn(s) + CO(g)$

ii $H_2(g) + PbO(s) \rightarrow H_2O(g) + Pb(s)$

iii $Fe_2O_3(s) + 3CO(g) \rightarrow 3CO_2(g) + 2Fe(s)$

iv $H_2S(g) + Cl_2(g) \rightarrow 2HCl(g) + S(s)$

v $Cl_2(g) + 2Fe^{2+}(aq) \rightarrow 2Cl^-(aq) + 2Fe^{3+}(aq)$

2. i Complete the following equations:

a $Mg(s) + 2H^+(aq) \rightarrow$

b $CuO(s) + 2H^+(aq) \rightarrow$

c $C(s) + H_2O(g) \rightarrow$

d $SO_2(g) + H_2O_2(aq) \rightarrow$

ii Which does *not* show a redox reaction?

3. This question is about the following equations:

A $2Al_2O_3(l) \rightarrow 4Al(l) + 3O_2(g)$

B $Cu^{2+}(aq) + Zn(s) \rightarrow Zn^{2+}(aq) + Cu(s)$

C $H_2(g) + CuO(s) \rightarrow H_2O(g) + Cu(s)$

D $H_2O(g) + C(s) \rightarrow CO(g) + H_2(g)$

E $Pb^{2+}(aq) + 2Cl^-(aq) \rightarrow PbCl_2(s)$

Which of them:

i does not involve oxidation or reduction

ii is a displacement reaction

iii shows a metal acting as a reducing agent

iv would be carried out by electrolysis

v is a precipitation reaction

vi shows a reducing agent written first

vii shows water acting as an oxidizing agent

4. This question is about the following chemicals:

A Cl_2

B HNO_3

C KI

D $KMnO_4$

E SO_2

At room temperature, which is:

i a solid oxidizing agent

ii a gaseous oxidizing agent

iii a liquid oxidizing agent

iv a gaseous reducing agent

v a solid reducing agent

5. A redox reaction is used for the usual laboratory preparation of chlorine.

i Name the oxidizing agent usually used.

ii Name the reducing agent usually used.

iii Draw a diagram to show the apparatus you would use.

iv A test for chlorine involves oxidation of pigments in indicator papers, for example litmus or universal indicator paper. What happens to the indicator papers when they are oxidized by chlorine?

6. This question is about the following colour changes that may be observed when certain solutions react:

A blue → red
B colourless → brown
C green → yellow
D orange → green
E purple → colourless

i Which colour change would you observe when:

a an alkaline solution containing litmus is acidified
b acidified $KMnO_4(aq)$ is treated with $SO_2(g)$
c acidified $K_2Cr_2O_7(aq)$ is treated with $SO_2(g)$
d a solution containing $Fe^{2+}(aq)$ is treated with $Cl_2(g)$
e acidified KI(aq) is treated with $Cl_2(g)$

ii Which change is not the result of a redox change?

7. Three reactions are described below:

A When iron(II) sulphate is mixed with sodium hydroxide solution a green precipitate is formed.
B After boiling iron(II) sulphate solution with nitric acid the colour of the solution is yellow.
C After cooling, the yellow solution from B gives a brown precipitate when mixed with sodium hydroxide solution.

i Name the precipitate formed in reaction A.
ii What kind of change has happened in reaction B?
iii Write an equation for reaction C.

8. Write half reactions for the following redox processes:

i $Fe(s) + Cu^{2+}(aq) \rightarrow Fe^{2+}(aq) + Cu(s)$
ii $Zn(s) + 2Ag^{+}(aq) \rightarrow 2Ag(s) + Zn^{2+}(aq)$
iii $2Fe^{2+}(aq) + Cl_2(g) \rightarrow 2Cl^{-}(aq) + 2Fe^{3+}(aq)$
iv $Mg(s) + 2H^{+}(aq) \rightarrow H_2(g) + Mg^{2+}(aq)$
v $Cl_2(g) + 2I^{-}(aq) \rightarrow 2Cl^{-}(aq) + I_2(aq)$

Unit 25
Reversible reactions

Is chemical change a one-way process?

Everyday chemical reactions like burning often seem to be permanent. After petrol has been burned in a car engine, we don't have any way of getting the hydrocarbons back again. Heptane in petrol burns to form carbon and water:

$$C_7H_{16}(l) + 11O_2(g) \rightarrow 7CO_2(g) + 8H_2O(g)$$

But carbon dioxide and water cannot be reacted to make heptane and oxygen.

- *Many chemical reactions seem to be one-way processes.*

Synthesis versus decomposition

Compounds may often be made by *synthesis reactions*:

$$Fe(s) + S(s) \rightarrow FeS(s)$$

$$2Na(s) + Cl_2(g) \rightarrow 2NaCl(s)$$

$$2Mg(s) + O_2(g) \rightarrow 2MgO(s)$$

$$2H_2(g) + O_2(g) \rightarrow 2H_2O(l)$$

Many of these synthesis reactions seem to be one-way processes. Once formed, the compounds appear to be *stable*, that is, they cannot be decomposed. For example, magnesium oxide is unaffected by heating to very high temperatures, and there seems to be no direct way to get the magnesium and oxygen to separate.

However, some compounds that appear to be stable at ordinary temperatures may be decomposed by heating them to a higher temperature. Mercury(II) oxide is formed by a synthesis reaction by heating mercury in oxygen at about 300 °C:

$$2Hg(l) + O_2(g) \rightarrow 2HgO(s)$$

But the oxide decomposes if heated to 500 °C:

$$2HgO(s) \rightarrow 2Hg(l) + O_2(g)$$

Safety note: Mercury vapour is a poison. Vapour would be released into the air if the above synthesis or decomposition reactions were attempted in the laboratory. These experiments should only be carried out by the teacher on a very small scale and using a fume cupboard.

- *Some compounds are stable in certain conditions, but unstable in other conditions.*

Reversible reactions

The mercury(II) oxide reaction is an example of a *reversible chemical change*. The change can happen in either direction, depending on the conditions. In theory, any reaction could be reversed if we could achieve the right conditions. In practice, many reactions (like the synthesis of MgO above) seem to be *irreversible*.

However, you are probably familiar with several reactions that may be easily reversed. Three examples are given below:

1. Hydrogen chloride and ammonia react to form ammonium chloride when the gases are mixed at room temperature:

   $$NH_3(g) + HCl(g) \rightarrow NH_4Cl(s)$$

   The ammonium chloride formed can be *decomposed* by warming it in a test tube:

   $$NH_4Cl(s) \rightarrow NH_3(g) + HCl(g)$$

   As the temperature falls again after heating, ammonium chloride will reform (see figure p.116).

2. Copper(II) sulphate-5-water is dehydrated by gentle warming, and anhydrous (white) copper(II) sulphate is formed:

   $$CuSO_4.5H_2O(s) \rightarrow CuSO_4(s) + 5H_2O(l)$$

   If cold water is added to the anhydrous product, the original blue compound is formed again:

   $$CuSO_4(s) + 5H_2O(l) \rightarrow CuSO_4.5H_2O(s)$$

Lavoisier's investigations into combustion depended on reversible reactions

3. When calcium carbonate reacts with water and carbon dioxide (as in the figure right), calcium hydrogencarbonate is formed:

$$\mathbf{CaCO_3(s) + CO_2(g) + H_2O(l) \rightarrow Ca(HCO_3)_2(aq)}$$

If the temperature rises, the calcium hydrogencarbonate decomposes:

$$\mathbf{Ca(HCO_3)_2(aq) \rightarrow CO_2(aq) + H_2O(l) + CaCO_3(s)}$$

Each of these pairs of equations could be combined into single equations, like this:

1. $\mathbf{NH_4Cl(s) \rightleftharpoons NH_3(g) + HCl(g)}$
2. $\mathbf{CuSO_4.5H_2O(s) \rightleftharpoons CuSO_4(s) + 5H_2O(l)}$
3. $\mathbf{CaCO_3(s) + CO_2(aq) + H_2O(l) \rightleftharpoons Ca(HCO_3)_2(aq)}$

● *A reversible reaction is one that can be reversed if the conditions are altered.*

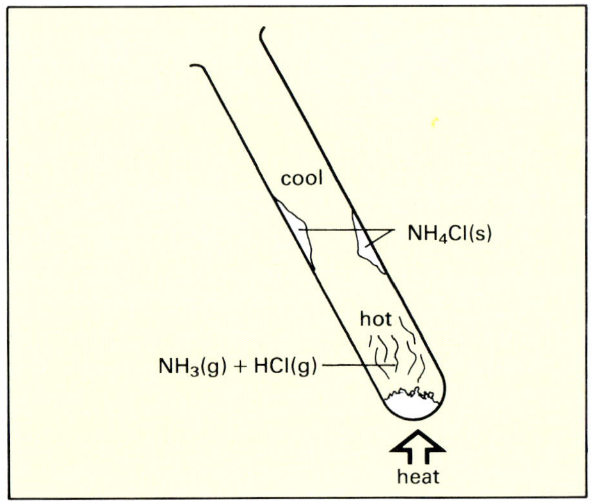

Decomposition of ammonium chloride on heating, and reformation on cooling

Stalactites form by the decomposition of calcium hydrogencarbonate found in hard water

Reversible reactions in the chemical industry

Reactions that are used for manufacturing important chemicals may be reversible. The *ammonia* and *sulphuric acid* processes will be dealt with more fully later (see Units 40 and 41), but it is probably worth mentioning here that both processes depend on reversible reactions:

ammonia synthesis (Haber process):

$$N_2(g) + 3H_2(g) \rightleftharpoons 2NH_3(g)$$

sulphur trioxide formation (contact process):

$$2SO_2(g) + O_2(g) \rightleftharpoons 2SO_3(g)$$

In each case, conditions must be adjusted so that the processes work at greatest efficiency. Two factors must be considered when deciding the best reaction conditions:

a restricting the reverse reaction;
b keeping the speed of the process reasonably high.

In the case of the Haber process, the reverse reaction (decomposition of NH_3) is favoured by increasing the temperature. At high temperatures the reverse reaction is faster than the forward reaction. Unfortunately, at low temperatures both forward and reverse reaction are so slow that there is hardly any change at all! So in practice, a temperature is chosen that balances the two factors:

a not too hot (decomposition very fast);
b not too cold (everything slows down).

Similar arguments apply to the contact process. In practice, both processes are carried out at temperatures of about 500 °C. If higher temperatures are used, decomposition (reversal) starts to take over. If lower temperatures are used, everything slows down.

- *The speed of the reverse reaction (as well as the speed of the forward reaction) must be considered if the best conditions for a reversible process are to be found.*

Summary

1. Many chemical reactions seem to be one-way processes.
2. Some compounds are stable in certain conditions, but unstable in others.
3. A reversible reaction is one that can be reversed in the laboratory if the conditions are altered.
4. The best conditions for a reversible process are found by taking the speeds of forward and reverse reactions into account.

Extension

Equilibrium in chemical change

If mercury and oxygen are heated at 300 °C, mercury(II) oxide is formed. If mercury(II) oxide is heated at 500 °C, mercury and oxygen are formed. What would happen if mercury, oxygen and mercury(II) oxide were all heated together at, say, 400 °C?

Experiments show that both synthesis and decomposition happen at the same time. At a low temperature, synthesis predominates: at a high temperature, decomposition becomes more important. Under certain circumstances the forward and reverse processes happen at the same speed: we say, *chemical equilibrium* is reached. The sign $\rightleftharpoons$ is used to show chemical equilibrium.

$$2Hg(l) + O_2(g) \rightleftharpoons 2HgO(s)$$

1. Write equations to show chemical equilibrium in the reactions of:
   i hydrogen and nitrogen
   ii oxygen and sulphur dioxide
   iii ammonia and hydrogen chloride
2. $BiCl_3$ reacts with water to form BiClO and HCl. BiClO reacts with HCl to form $BiCl_3$ and water. The two reactions reach equilibrium when the four substances are all present in certain concentrations.
   Write a balanced equation to show the equilibrium.

Revision

1. This question is about the following substances:
   A H_2O
   B NH_3
   C MgO
   D SO_3
   E HgO
   Choose one that is:
   i a solid oxide stable at high temperatures
   ii a liquid oxide stable at high temperatures
   iii a solid oxide that decomposes into its elements at high temperatures

iv an oxide that decomposes to a more stable oxide at high temperatures

v a substance that is not an oxide

2. In 1774, Lavoisier extracted samples of oxygen from air, using a reversible reaction involving mercury.

   Explain how you would attempt to repeat Lavoisier's experiments in a modern laboratory. Give detail of the necessary safety precautions. Draw diagrams of apparatus you would use and write equations to illustrate the changes.

3. Write a paragraph to explain how reversible reactions are important in:

   i a laboratory test for water

   ii the formation of stalactites in hard water areas

   iii the industrial manufacture of chemicals

   Include equations in your answers.

Unit 26
Chemical arithmetic

Calculating M_r values

The masses of molecules can be compared using the same scale as the one for atomic masses (on which H = 1: see p. 54). The mass of a molecule compared with a hydrogen atom is called the *relative molecular mass* (M_r). The M_r value of a compound can be worked out from A_r values if the formula of the compound is known. For example, the M_r value of CO_2 can be worked out as follows:

1. A_r values of the elements in CO_2:
   $A_r(C) = 12, A_r(O) = 16$.
2. Calculation of M_r for CO_2:
   $M_r(CO_2) = 12 + (16 \times 2) = 12 + 32 = 44$.

● *M_r values for substances can be worked out using knowledge of formulas and A_r values.*

Check the following calculations:

a $M_r(H_2O) = (1 \times 2) + 16 = 18$.
b $M_r(CaCO_3) = 40 + 12 + (16 \times 3) = 100$.
c $M_r(NH_3) = 14 + (1 \times 3) = 17$.
d $M_r(NaCl) = 23 + 35.5 = 58.5$.
e $M_r(S_8) = 32 \times 8 = 256$.

Calculating percentage compositions from formulas

The theoretical percentage of an element in a compound can be worked out using A_r values and the M_r value of the compound. For example, the percentage of carbon in CO_2 can be calculated as follows:

1. A_r and M_r values:
   $A_r(C) = 12; M_r(CO_2) = 44$.
2. Calculation of %:
   $\%(C) = \frac{12}{44} \times 100 = 27.3\%$.

● *The theoretical percentage of an element in a compound can be worked out from the formula of the compound.*

How can you work out the percentage of oxygen in CO_2? This can be done in two ways:

1. $\%(O) = 100 - \%(C) = 100 - 27.3 = 72.7\%$.

or, if the percentage of carbon has not been worked out:

2. $\%(O) = \frac{16 \times 2}{44} \times 100 = 72.7\%$.

Check the following calculations:

a $\%(Cu)$ in $CuO = \frac{64}{80} \times 100 = 80\%$.

b $\%(S)$ in $SO_2 = \frac{32}{64} \times 100 = 50\%$.

c $\%(O)$ in $CaCO_3 = \frac{48}{100} \times 100 = 48\%$.

d $\%(H)$ in $H_2O = \frac{2}{18} \times 100 = 11.1\%$.

e $\%(Cu)$ in $Cu_2O = \frac{64 \times 2}{144} \times 100 = 88.9\%$.

Calculating percentage compositions from experimental results

Two examples are given:

1. Analysis of black copper oxide

A weighed amount of copper oxide is reduced to copper by heating it in a stream of laboratory gas. The mass of copper obtained is recorded. The experiment is illustrated in the figure on p.120 (top), with specimen results.

The percentage of copper in the oxide can be worked out from these results as follows:

mass of oxide used $= 27.84 - 26.41 = 1.43$ g
mass of copper obtained $= 27.55 - 26.41 = 1.14$ g
$\%(Cu) = \frac{1.14}{1.43} \times 100 = 79.7\%$.

2. Synthesis of magnesium oxide

A weighed amount of magnesium ribbon is heated in a crucible until all of it is converted to magnesium oxide. The lid of the crucible must be kept on to stop the oxide escaping as smoke. The experiment is shown in the bottom figure on p.120. (How can you tell from the specimen results that the conversion of magnesium to oxide is complete?)

Analysis of black copper oxide

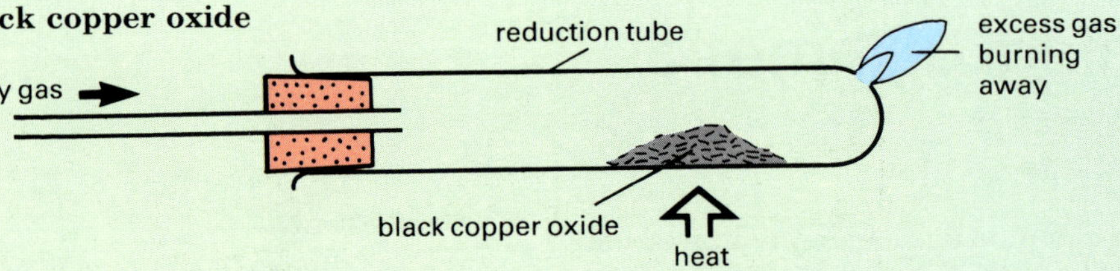

Safety note
The excess gas must not be lit until air is flushed from the tube. This should be done under supervision of the teacher.

Results

Mass of reduction tube	= 26.41 g
Mass of reduction tube + copper oxide	= 27.84 g
Mass of reduction tube + contents after heating	= 27.56 g
Mass of reduction tube + contents after reheating	= 27.55 g

Note
Reheating the tube (with laboratory gas flowing) shows that reduction is virtually complete because the mass is almost constant.

Synthesis of magnesium oxide

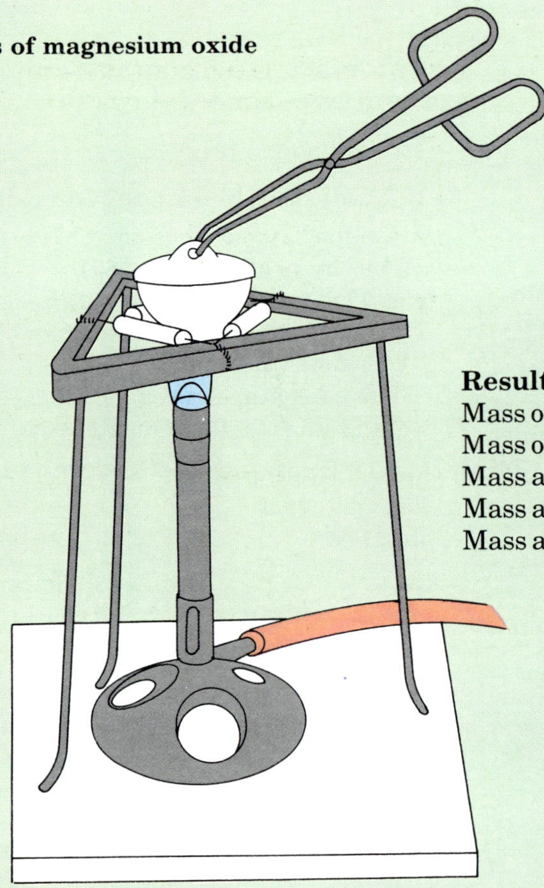

Results

Mass of crucible + lid	= 15.78 g
Mass of crucible, lid + magnesium	= 16.63 g
Mass after first heating	= 17.14 g
Mass after second heating	= 17.19 g
Mass after third heating	= 17.19 g

The percentage of magnesium in the oxide can be worked out from the results given:

mass of magnesium used = 16.63 − 15.78 = 0.85 g
mass of oxide formed = 17.19 − 15.78 = 1.41 g

$$\%(\mathrm{Mg}) = \frac{0.85}{1.41} \times 100 = 60.3\%.$$

● *The percentage composition of a compound can be worked out from the results of experiments in the laboratory.*

Which formula is correct?

Two oxides of copper are known: CuO and Cu_2O. Which of them is the black oxide used in the reduction experiment?

You can answer the question by comparing the theoretical percentages of copper (worked out from the formulas) with the percentage calculated from experimental results. The percentage of Cu in CuO is 80 per cent, and the percentage of Cu in Cu_2O is about 89 per cent. Analysis of the black oxide by reduction gave a percentage close to 80 per cent. We can conclude that black copper oxide is the oxide with formula CuO.

However, we can approach the problem of formulas from another angle. Take the case of magnesium oxide, for example. The specimen results given above lead to the following conclusion:

mass of magnesium used = 16.63 − 15.78 = 0.85 g
mass of oxide formed = 17.19 − 15.78 = 1.41 g
mass of oxygen combined with the magnesium = 1.41 − 0.85 = 0.56 g.

So, the ratio of magnesium to oxygen (by mass) in the oxide is 0.85 : 0.56.

This ratio can be converted to a ratio of numbers of atoms by using the A_r values ($A_r(\mathrm{Mg})$ = 24; $A_r(\mathrm{O})$ = 16). The calculation looks like this:

number of Mg atoms : number of O atoms

$$= \frac{0.85}{A_r(\mathrm{Mg})} : \frac{0.56}{A_r(\mathrm{O})}$$

$$= \frac{0.85}{24} : \frac{0.56}{16}$$

$$= 0.0354 : 0.0350$$

$$= 1 : 1 \text{ (approximately)}.$$

Our conclusion must be that there are equal numbers of Mg and O atoms in the oxide. The formula is Mg_1O_1, which is usually written as MgO.

● *The ratio of atoms in a compound can be calculated from the ratio of masses of the elements and their A_r values.*

Check the following calculations:

a Mass of aluminium in 1.02 g of aluminium oxide = 0.54 g.
∴ Ratio of Al : O (by mass) = 0.54 : 0.48

ratio of atoms of Al : atoms of O

$$= \frac{0.54}{A_r(\mathrm{Al})} : \frac{0.48}{A_r(\mathrm{O})} = \frac{0.54}{27} : \frac{0.48}{16} = 0.02 : 0.03 = 2 : 3.$$

∴ The simplest formula of the oxide = Al_2O_3.

b The masses of the elements C, H, K and O in a compound of the four elements were found to be 2.4 g, 0.2 g, 7.8 g and 9.6 g respectively.
∴ Ratio (by mass)
C : H : K : O = 2.4 : 0.2 : 7.8 : 9.6

ratio of atoms

$$= \frac{2.4}{A_r(\mathrm{C})} : \frac{0.2}{A_r(\mathrm{H})} : \frac{7.8}{A_r(\mathrm{K})} : \frac{9.6}{Ar(\mathrm{O})}$$

$$= \frac{2.4}{12} : \frac{0.2}{1} : \frac{7.8}{39} : \frac{9.6}{16}$$

$$= 0.2 : 0.2 : 0.2 : 0.6$$

$$= 1 : 1 : 1 : 3.$$

∴ Simplest formula of the compound = $CHKO_3$.

c The percentage by mass of sulphur in an oxide of sulphur is found to be 50%.
∴ Ratio (by mass) of S : O = 50 : 50

ratio of atoms of S : atoms of O

$$= \frac{50}{A_r(\mathrm{S})} : \frac{50}{A_r(\mathrm{O})} = \frac{50}{32} : \frac{50}{16} = 1 : 2.$$

∴ Simplest formula of the oxide = SO_2.

Summary

1. The relative molecular mass of a substance can be worked out from its formula by using the relative atomic masses of its elements.
2. The theoretical percentage composition of a compound can be calculated if its formula is known.
3. Laboratory investigations (e.g. analysis experiments) can be used to calculate percentage compositions.
4. The ratio of atoms in a compound can be calculated from the ratio by mass of the elements it contains.

Revision

The following approximate A_r values may be needed to calculate answers to the questions:

Element	H	C	N	O	Mg	S	Cl	K	Ca	Fe	Cu
A_r	1	12	14	16	24	32	35.5	39	40	56	64

1. Work out M_r values for the following substances:
   - i CO
   - ii Cl_2
   - iii H_2O_2
   - iv $CuSO_4$
   - v H_2SO_4
2. Calculate the percentage (by mass) of each element in the following compounds:
   - i SO_3
   - ii CuS
   - iii $CuSO_4$
   - iv CH_4
   - v $KHCO_3$
3. Calculate the percentage (by mass) of the element whose symbol is first in each compound:
   - i $CaCl_2$
   - ii N_2O
   - iii $Cu(NO_3)_2$
   - iv $MgSO_4.7H_2O$
   - v HNO_3
4. Oxides of iron were reduced in the laboratory.
   The masses recorded during the experiments are given in the next table.

Oxide	I	II	III
Mass of iron oxide (g)	1.16	0.72	1.00
Mass of iron (g)	0.84	0.56	0.70

   - i What mass of oxygen was combined with the iron in oxide I?
   - ii What is the percentage of iron in oxide II?
   - iii Oxide III is known to be either FeO, Fe_2O_3 or Fe_3O_4. Calculate the percentage of iron in the oxides with the given formulas. Compare the values with the percentage of iron in oxide III. Which formula is the formula of oxide III?

5. The next table shows the results of experiments carried out to investigate five compounds. Each is a compound of two elements only. Use the data to work out formulas for each compound.

Compound	*Elements*		*Mass of element 1 (g)*	*Mass of element 2 (g)*
	1	*2*		
I	copper	sulphur	1.28	0.64
II	iron	oxygen	0.28	0.08
III	copper	chlorine	0.32	0.36
IV	calcium	oxygen	1.20	0.48
V	oxygen	hydrogen	1.28	0.08

Unit 27
Moles

In chemistry we use A_r and M_r values to help us define the standard amount of a substance. The standard amount of a substance is called the *mole*.

● *In chemistry, the mole is a standard amount of a substance.*

How much is a mole of substance?

You can work out the mass of a mole of substance by using the M_r value of the substance. One mole of substance has a mass equal to the M_r value in grams.

Here are some examples:

1. **CO_2** $M_r = 12 + (16 \times 2) = 44$; one mole of CO_2 is 44 g.
2. **NaCl** $M_r = 23 + 35.5 = 58.5$; one mole of NaCl is 58.5 g.
3. **Fe** $A_r = 56$; one mole of iron is 56 g.
4. **H_2** $M_r = 1 \times 2 = 2$; one mole of H_2 is 2 g.
5. **He** $A_r = 4$; one mole of helium is 4 g.

● *A mole of a substance is given by the* M_r *(or* A_r*) value of the substance taken in grams.*

The abbreviation for mole is mol.

What is special about moles?

From the way the mole has been defined, it follows that one mole of any substance contains the same number of particles. Take CO_2 and Fe for example: the masses of one molecule of CO_2 and one atom of Fe are in the ratio 44:56. Thus, the number of molecules in 44 g of CO_2 is the same as the number of atoms in 56 g of Fe.

The number of particles in a mole of substance has been worked out from the results of experiments. The number is about 6×10^{23} per mole, which is an extremely large number! The value 6×10^{23} particles per mole is called the *Avogadro constant*. To calculate the number of particles in a given amount of a substance, you have to multiply the amount (number of moles) by the Avogadro constant. If the number of moles is given the symbol n, and the Avogadro constant has the symbol L, then:

$$\textit{number of particles} = L \times n$$

● *Different substances contain the same number of particles per mole: this number is called the Avogadro constant.*

What about substances like NaCl? Our knowledge of the properties of sodium chloride tells us that it does not contain 'NaCl' particles. It consists of Na^+ ions and Cl^- ions. So, care is needed when statements are made about the numbers of particles in ionic substances. Thus the number of Na^+ ions in one mole of NaCl is the same as the number of Cl^- ions, and the same as the number of molecules in one mole of H_2.

Check these examples:

a 28 g of N_2 and 2 g of H_2 have the same number of molecules (one mole of each).

b 4 g of He contains more atoms than 4 g of Ca (4 g of He is one mole, but 4 g of Ca is only 0.1 mol).

c 40 g of MgO and 30 g of Li_2O have the same number of anions (each amount is one mole).

d 40 g of MgO has half as many cations as 30 g of Li_2O.

Moles of gases

A balloon filled with H_2 gas floats in air, but a balloon filled with CO_2 gas sinks. The density of CO_2 is 22 times that of H_2 (under the same conditions). The gas SF_6 is even denser: it is about 72 times denser than H_2 at the same temperature and pressure.

If we compare the M_r values, these facts about gas densities begin to make sense:

$M_r(H_2) = 2$
$M_r(CO_2) = 44$
$M_r(SF_6) = 144$

We can see that the gas with the biggest molecules has the greatest density, and the gas with the smallest molecules has the lowest density. This relationship between molecular mass and density is a general one for all gases.

● *The density of a gas is related to its M_r value.*

However, the relationship only makes good sense if equal volumes of gases contain the same number of molecules (under the same conditions of temperature and pressure). In other words, when we compare the densities of different gases, we are comparing the masses of the same number of molecules each time.

This idea (about the number of molecules in volumes of different gases) was first suggested by an Italian scientist called Amedeo Avogadro in 1811. It did not become accepted for many years, but it is now recognized to be generally true for all gases. The idea is now commonly called Avogadro's law.

If a mole of any substance has a certain number of particles, it follows from Avogadro's law that a mole of any gas has a fixed volume (if the temperature and pressure are fixed). So, 2 g of H_2, 44 g of CO_2 and 144 g of SF_6 (one mole of each) all take up the same amount of space at room temperature and pressure. Experiments show that at *normal* room temperature and pressure, the volume of a mole of any gas is *about* 24 dm^3.

● *Under the same conditions of temperature and pressure, a mole of any gas has the same volume.*

If the volume of a mole of any gas (at room temperature and pressure, or r.t.p.) is 24 dm^3:

1. 0.1 mol of CO_2 at r.t.p. has a volume of 2.4 dm^3
2. 10 mol of H_2 at r.t.p. has a volume of 240 dm^3
3. 2 mol of SF_6 at r.t.p. has a volume of 48 dm^3

Similarly, at room temperature and pressure,

4. 12 dm^3 of N_2 contains 0.5 mol of gas
5. 2400 dm^3 of HCl contains 100 mol of gas
6. 2400 cm^3 of SO_2 contains 0.1 mol of gas

Concentrations of solutions

It is convenient to express concentrations of solutions in units of moles of solute per litre of solution. (A litre is the same as a cubic decimetre and is written dm^3.) Some examples are given:

1. Bench (dilute) sulphuric acid has an approximate concentration of 1 mol dm^{-3}.
2. Oxygen in tap water has an approximate concentration of 0.001 mol dm^{-3}.
3. Saturated salt solution (at room temperature) has an approximate concentration of 5 mol dm^{-3}.

The units of concentration *mol dm^{-3}* are usually abbreviated to M, that is, 1M means 1 mol dm^{-3}, 0.001M means 0.001 mol dm^{-3}, and so on.

● *A solution with concentration 1M contains 1 mole of solute in every litre (dm^3) of solution.*

You can work out the mass of solute in a certain volume of solution if you know the solution's concentration. For example, a solution of NaCl with concentration 0.5M contains 0.5 mol dm^{-3}, so 100 cm^3 of solution will contain 0.05 mol. The M_r value for NaCl is 58.5, so the mass of salt in 100 cm^3 of the solution at a certain temperature is $0.05 \times 58.5 = 2.925$ g.

The table below gives more examples. Can you fill in the gaps?

Solution	*Volume*	*Amount of solute (mol)*	*M_r(solute)*	*Mass of solute (g)*
1M NaCl	2 dm^3	2	58.5	117
10M HCl	1 dm^3	10	36.5	365
0.1M NaOH	100 cm^3	0.01	40	0.4
0.5M KOH	2 dm^3			
2M H_2SO_4	500 cm^3			
0.1M $CuSO_4.5H_2O$	50 cm^3			

Summary

1. In chemistry, the mole is a standard amount of substance.
2. A mole of a substance is given by the M_r (or A_r) value of the substance in grams.
3. A mole of any substance contains the same number of particles.
4. The density of a gas is proportional to its M_r value.
5. A mole of any gas has the same volume (at the same temperature and pressure).
6. A solution containing one mole of solute per litre is a 1M solution.

Revision

1. This question is about the following masses:

   A 17 g
   B 18 g
   C 38 g
   D 40 g
   E 44 g

   Which is the mass of one mole of:

   i Ar
   ii F_2
   iii H_2O
   iv C_3H_8
   v NH_3

2. This question is about the following numbers:

   A 0.01
   B 0.10
   C 0.50
   D 1.00
   E 10.00

   Which is the number of moles in:

   i 0.2 g of H_2
   ii 1.0 g of $CaCO_3$
   iii 4.0 g of Ar
   iv 4.4 g of CO_2
   v 6.0 g of C
   vi 12.0 g of Mg
   vii 40.0 g of He
   viii 40.0 g of NaOH
   ix 180.0 g of $C_6H_{12}O_6$
   x 180.0 g of H_2O

3. In each of the following cases, select the *greater* number of moles:

   i 10 g of $CaCO_3$ or 10 g of $KHCO_3$
   ii 20 g of Ar or 10 g of NaOH
   iii 44 g of CO_2 or 22 g of C_3H_8
   iv 10 g of He or 10 g of H_2
   v 4 g of MgO or 8 g of NaOH
   vi 64 g of CuO or 64 g of Cu_2O
   vii 64 g of S_2 or 64 g of S_8
   viii 32 g of O_2 or 64 g of S_8
   ix 18 g of Be or 18 g of H_2O
   x 25 g of $CuSO_4.5H_2O$ or 20 g of $CuSO_4$

4. In each of the following cases, choose the gas with the higher density (under the same conditions of temperature and pressure):

   i CH_4 or C_2H_6
   ii C_2H_6 or C_2H_4
   iii O_2 or H_2S
   iv CO_2 or CO
   v Cl_2 or HBr

5. As you know, air is a mixture of N_2 and O_2, with small amounts of other gases.

   i If five similar balloons were filled with the following gases at the same pressure, which would sink fastest in air?

      A CH_4
      B C_2H_4
      C C_2H_6
      D C_3H_6
      E C_3H_8

   ii Which of the above gases is likely to have a density closest to that of air?

6. This question is about the numbers of molecules in each of the following:

   A 1.0 g of H_2
   B 4.0 g of He
   C 6.4 g of SO_2
   D 7.3 g of HCl
   E 11 g of CO_2

   Which mass of gas contains:

   i most molecules
   ii least molecules
   iii the same number of molecules as 1.6 g of CH_4

7. Copy the following table and finish it.

Solution	*Volume of solution*	*Amount of solute(mol)*	M_r*(solute)*	*Mass of solute(g)*
1M NaCl(aq)	1 dm^3		58.5	
0.1M NaOH(aq)	2 dm^3	0.2		
2M Na_2CO_3(aq)	100 cm^3			
0.5M $KMnO_4$(aq)	500 cm^3			
0.2M $AgNO_3$(aq)		0.2		

8. The following electrolytes can be considered to be fully ionic. Which contains more cations?

   i 1 mol of CaO or 1 mol of K_2O

   ii 5.6 g of CaO or 9.4 g of K_2O

   iii 8 g of NaOH or 4 g of MgO

   iv 1 dm^3 of 1.0M Na_2SO_4(aq) or 1 dm^3 of 1.0M $MgSO_4$(aq)

   v 100 cm^3 of 1.0M $(NH_4)_2SO_4$(aq) or 200 cm^3 of 0.5M $CuSO_4$(aq)

9. Copy the following table and finish it.

Substance	*Mass(g)*	M_r	*n(mol)*	*Number of molecules*
CO_2	4.4	44	0.1	$0.1 \times 6 \times 10^{23} = 6 \times 10^{22}$
$C_6H_{12}O_6$	180			
O_2	3.2×10^{-3}			
H_2O	1000			

10. i The number of seconds in one year is about 30 million, i.e. 3×10^7 seconds. If you could count at the rate of 1 atom per second without stopping, how many years would it take to count the atoms in 12 g of carbon?

   ii How does your answer to (i) compare with the age of the Earth (thought to be about 5×10^9 years)?

Unit 28
Calculations from equations

Equations and quantities

Equations tell us about the relative numbers of particles (reacting and formed) in a reaction. In other words, equations tell us about the ratio of moles of reactants and products in chemical change. Some examples should make this clear:

1. $CaCO_3(s) \rightarrow CaO(s) + CO_2(g)$

1 mol of $CaCO_3$ would form 1 mol each of CaO and CO_2 if it were decomposed completely.

2. $N_2(g) + 3H_2(g) \rightarrow 2NH_3(g)$

If nitrogen and hydrogen were completely converted to ammonia, 1 mol of N_2 would require 3 mol of H_2 and 2 mol of NH_3 would be formed.

3. $2NaOH(aq) + H_2SO_4(aq) \rightarrow 2H_2O(l) + Na_2SO_4(aq)$

2 mol of NaOH would be needed to neutralize 1 mol of H_2SO_4, and 2 mol of water would be formed together with 1 mol of salt.

● *Equations show the ratio of moles of reactants and products involved in a chemical change.*

Working out masses

We can work out the masses of reactants and products using information given in an equation. For example, we can work out the mass of calcium oxide formed in the decomposition of a certain mass of calcium carbonate. The equation (given above) indicates that 1 mol of $CaCO_3$ when completely decomposed gives 1 mol of CaO. The M_r values are: $M_r(CaCO_3) = 100$, and $M_r(CaO) = 56$. So, we can calculate that 100 g of calcium carbonate will produce 56 g of CaO; 10 g of carbonate will produce 5.6 g of oxide; 1 kg of carbonate will produce 560 g of oxide, and so on.

● *Equations can be used to calculate masses of reactants and products involved in a reaction.*

Working out volumes of gases involved in reactions

Under the same conditions of temperature and pressure, the volumes of gases are proportional to their numbers of moles. Therefore, we can use equations to work out the volumes of gaseous products if we know the amounts of reactants involved. For example, in the Haber synthesis (equation above), 1 mol of N_2 requires 3 mol of H_2 and will produce 2 mol of ammonia if the reaction is complete; 100 cm^3 of N_2 will produce 200 cm^3 of ammonia if the reaction is complete. Similarly, 1 dm^3 of N_2 will produce 2 dm^3 of ammonia, and so on.

● *Equations can be used to calculate volumes of gaseous reactants and products.*

Working out volumes of solutions involved in reactions

If we look at the equation for the neutralization reaction given earlier, we can see how volumes of the reactants can be calculated:

$$\underset{2\text{ mol}}{2NaOH(aq)} + \underset{1\text{ mol}}{H_2SO_4(aq)} \rightarrow Na_2SO_4(aq) + 2H_2O(l)$$

If the reactants are both of 1M concentration, then we can see from the equation that the volume of NaOH(aq) needed will be twice the volume of $H_2SO_4(aq)$. In other words, 100 cm^3 of 1M $H_2SO_4(aq)$ would need 200 cm^3 of 1M NaOH(aq), 1 dm^3 of 1M H_2SO_4 would need 2 dm^3 of 1M NaOH(aq), and so on.

If the reactants do not have equal concentration, we can still work out the reacting volumes, providing we remember that each mole of H_2SO_4 needs two moles of NaOH. If 2M NaOH(aq) is reacted with 1M $H_2SO_4(aq)$, equal volumes would be needed for neutralization. If 1M NaOH(aq) is reacted with 2M H_2SO_4(aq), each litre of H_2SO_4(aq) needs four litres of NaOH(aq), and so on.

● *Equations can be used to calculate the volumes of reactant solutions needed for complete reaction.*

Summary

1. The proportions of moles of reactants and products involved in a reaction are shown by the equation for the reaction.
2. Masses of reactants and products involved in a reaction can be calculated from the equation for the reaction if M_r values are known.
3. Equations can be used to calculate volumes of gaseous reactants and products.
4. The volumes needed for complete reaction when solutions of reactants are mixed can be calculated using information given in equations.

Extension

When a solution of lead(II) salt is mixed with a solution of an iodide, a yellow precipitate is formed. This question is about an experiment to investigate the *formula* of the yellow precipitate.

Two solutions, A and B, were prepared. Solution A contained iodide anions of concentration 1.0M and solution B contained lead(II) cations of the same concentration. 5 cm^3 volumes of solution A were placed in each of 10 numbered test tubes. Then different volumes of solution B were added to the tubes, as shown in the table. After stirring the mixtures and then centrifuging, the depth of precipitate formed in each tube was measured. The depths are also shown in the table.

Tube	1	2	3	4	5	6	7	8	9	10
Volume of solution B added (cm^3)	0.5	1.0	1.5	2.0	2.5	3.0	3.5	4.0	4.5	5.0
Depth of precipitate formed (mm)	2	4	6	8	10	10	9	11	10	10

1. Name the yellow precipitate.
2. Name a soluble lead(II) salt that could be used to prepare solution B.
3. If the iodide chosen for solution A is KI, what mass of it should be dissolved in water to make 500 cm^3 of 1.0M solution?
4. Plot a graph to show *depth of precipitate* (vertical axis) against *volume of solution B added*.
5. Account for the shape of the graph, including any irregularities.
6. Which tubes contain *excess* of iodide ions? How could you prove this?
7. In which tubes have all iodide ions been precipitated?
8. In which tube have all the iodide ions and all the lead(II) ions been precipitated?
9. Calculate the amounts of lead(II) ions and iodide ions in the tube you have chosen in (8).
10. Give the formula of the yellow precipitate and show how it derives from your answer to (9).

Revision

1. In each of the following reactions, a solid reacts to form a gas. How many moles of solid are needed to form one mole of gas in each case?

   i $Ca(s) + 2H_2O(l) \rightarrow H_2(g) + Ca(OH)_2(aq)$
   ii $2Na(s) + 2H_2O(l) \rightarrow 2NaOH(aq) + H_2(g)$
   iii $Mg(s) + H_2SO_4(aq) \rightarrow MgSO_4(aq) + H_2(g)$
   iv $2HNO_3(aq) + CaCO_3(s) \rightarrow CO_2(g) + H_2O(l) + Ca(NO_3)_2(aq)$
   v $3Fe(s) + 4H_2O(g) \rightarrow Fe_3O_4(s) + 4H_2(g)$

2. The reaction of magnesium with steam is described by the following equation:

   $$Mg(s) + H_2O(g) \rightarrow MgO(s) + H_2(g)$$

   i What mass of magnesium is needed to react completely with:

   a 0.18 g of steam
   b 0.36 g of steam
   c 0.72 g of steam

   ii What mass of magnesium oxide would be formed by complete reaction of:

   a 0.24 g of magnesium
   b 0.48 g of magnesium

3. The following reactions were carried out at room temperature and pressure. In each case, 1 mole of the first reactant in the equation was completely used up. What volume of gas would be formed in each reaction? (1 mole of gas at room temperature and pressure has a volume of about 24 dm^3.)

   i $H_2(g) + Cl_2(g) \rightarrow 2HCl(g)$
   ii $S(s) + O_2(g) \rightarrow SO_2(g)$
   iii $2H_2O_2(aq) \rightarrow 2H_2O(l) + O_2(g)$
   iv $Mg(s) + 2HCl(aq) \rightarrow MgCl_2(aq) + H_2(g)$
   v $N_2(g) + 3H_2(g) \rightarrow 2NH_3(g)$

4. The following equation shows the reaction of marble chips (calcium carbonate) with dilute nitric acid.

   $$CaCO_3(s) + 2HNO_3(aq) \rightarrow Ca(NO_3)_2(aq) + CO_2(g) + H_2O(l)$$

   i What volume of carbon dioxide would be collected at room temperature and pressure from

   a 100 g of marble
   b 10 g of marble

   ii Draw a diagram to show how you would collect the carbon dioxide over water.

   iii In practice, less than the theoretical amount of gas is collected when the experiment is done. Suggest a reason for this.

5. Methane burns in oxygen to form CO_2 and H_2O:

   $$CH_4(g) + 2O_2(g) \rightarrow CO_2(g) + 2H_2O(l)$$

   If all volumes were measured. at room temperature and pressure:

   i What volume of oxygen would be used in completely burning 100 cm^3 of methane?

   ii What volume of gas would remain if 100 cm^3 of methane was reacted with 300 cm^3 of oxygen?

   iii What mass of water would be formed if 240 cm^3 of methane was completely burned? (1 mole of gas has a volume of about 24 dm^3 at room temperature and pressure.)

6. i How much solute is there in:

   a 500 cm^3 of 1.0M solution
   b 10 cm^3 of 1.0M solution
   c 1000 cm^3 of 0.5M solution
   d 500 cm^3 of 2.0M solution

   ii What mass of NaOH is there in:

   a 1000 cm^3 of 1.0M NaOH(aq)
   b 50 cm^3 of 1.0M NaOH(aq)
   c 500 cm^3 of 2.0M NaOH(aq)
   d 25 cm^3 of 0.1M NaOH(aq)

7. This question is about the following neutralization reaction:

   $$2NaOH(aq) + H_2SO_4(aq) \rightarrow Na_2SO_4(aq) + 2H_2O(l)$$

   i How many moles of sodium hydroxide are needed to neutralize:

   a one mole of sulphuric acid
   b 1000 cm^3 of 0.5M sulphuric acid

   ii What volume of 1.0M sodium hydroxide solution is needed to neutralize:

   a one mole of sulphuric acid
   b 200 cm^3 of 2.0M sulphuric acid solution

Unit 29
Energy from chemicals

Heat from chemicals

Whenever a chemical reaction happens, energy changes also happen. Often the chemicals that are reacting give *heat* energy to the surroundings. Reactions that give heat (lose energy) to the surroundings are called *exothermic reactions*.

● *Reactions that give out energy are called exothermic reactions.*

If a test tube gets hot in your hand while a reaction is going on, you know that the reaction is exothermic. The chemicals are losing heat; your hand (the surroundings) is gaining heat. Most reactions are exothermic and many can be investigated on a test-tube scale, for example:

a dissolving magnesium in dilute acid:

$$\mathbf{Mg(s) + 2H^+(aq) \rightarrow Mg^{2+}(aq) + H_2(g)}$$

b adding water to anhydrous copper(II) sulphate:

$$\mathbf{CuSO_4(s) + 5H_2O(l) \rightarrow CuSO_4.5H_2O(s)}$$

c reacting calcium with water:

$$\mathbf{Ca(s) + 2H_2O(l) \rightarrow Ca(OH)_2(aq) + H_2(g)}$$

d neutralizing dilute acid with alkali:

$$\mathbf{H^+(aq) + OH^-(aq) \rightarrow H_2O(l)}$$

Combustions

The most familiar exothermic reactions are combustions. Whenever a substance burns in air or oxygen, heat is released. Oxygen is not the only gas that supports combustion. Metals may burn in chlorine, for example, to release heat energy in the process.

$$\mathbf{2Fe(s) + 3Cl_2(g) \rightarrow 2FeCl_3(s)}$$

A red-hot reaction!

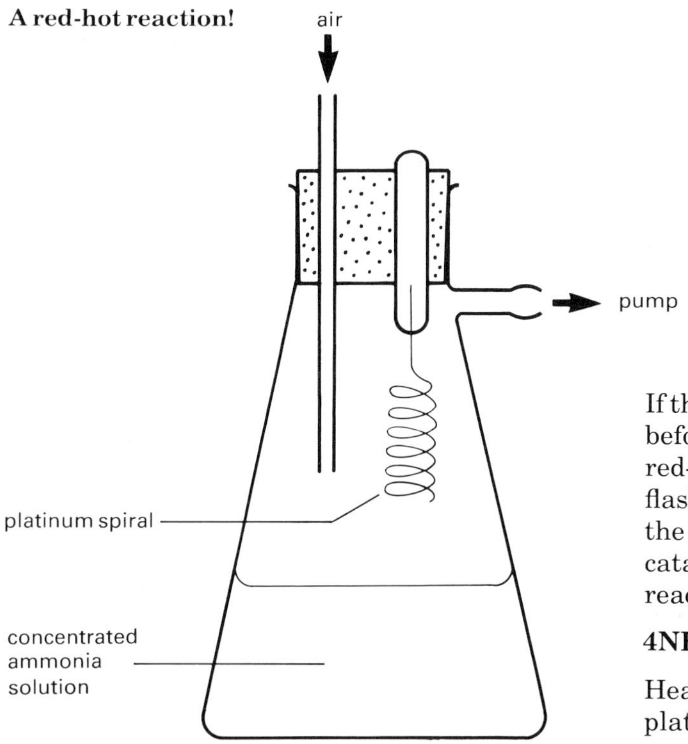

If the platinum wire is heated in a flame before placing it in the flask, it can be kept red-hot simply by sucking air through the flask. Oxygen and ammonia gas react on the surface of the platinum. The platinum catalyses the following exothermic reaction:

$$\mathbf{4NH_3(g) + 5O_2(g) \rightarrow 4NO(g) + 6H_2O}$$

Heat released in the reaction keeps the platinum hot.

Most of our energy comes from chemical change: a coal fire; gunpowder is discovered; blasting with dynamite; an athlete exercising

In addition to heat, other forms of energy may be released, for example light. Fuels are used for lighting as well as heating. Candles are not used often nowadays, but hydrocarbons still provide light energy sometimes, for example burning propane in camping gas cylinders:

$$C_3H_8(g) + 5O_2(g) \rightarrow 3CO_2(g) + 4H_2O(g)$$

Photographers' flash bulbs contain magnesium, which produces a great deal of light energy when it burns.

● *Combustions are exothermic reactions.*

Endothermic changes

Not all reactions are exothermic. Some involve the *absorption* of energy. Reactions in which energy is taken in (absorbed) are called *endothermic* reactions.

The most important endothermic reaction is probably photosynthesis.

$$6CO_2 + 6H_2O \xrightarrow[\text{(chlorophyll)}]{\text{sunlight absorbed}} C_6H_{12}O_6 + 6O_2$$

● *Changes (like photosynthesis) that absorb energy are said to be endothermic.*

Chlorophyll is a catalyst for the process. The glucose, which is the final product, has a high chemical energy content.

However, endothermic changes that are easy to demonstrate in the laboratory are not so common. You could try mixing solutions of ammonium carbonate and propanoic acid and measuring the temperature change. Alternatively, you could investigate some dissolving processes.

Compare temperature changes when solid electrolytes are dissolved in water. The list in the figure (right) gives some suggestions. Try a few spatula measures of each in test-tubes half full with water.

Electrical energy

Most of our electricity is obtained from chemical change, either directly or indirectly.

In a power station, the first step is to get heat from a fuel by burning it. Some of the heat energy then gets converted into electrical

Oil lamps were used for lighting in the last century

Dissolving and energy changes

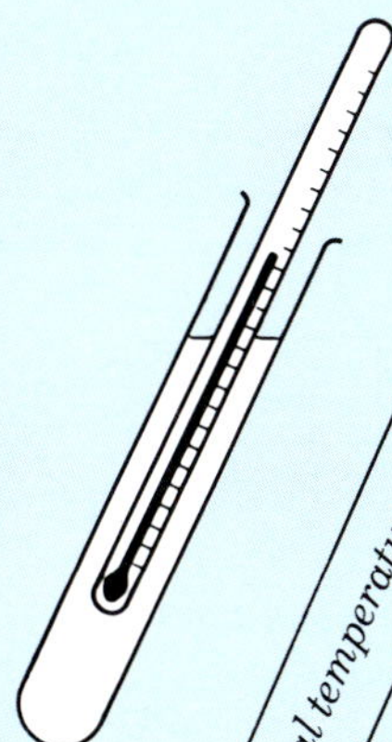

Solute	Initial temperature (°C)	Final temperature (°C)	Temperature change (°C)	Exothermic or endothermic dissolving?
NH_4NO_3				
$CaCl_2$				
Na_2CO_3				
NaOH				
$NaNO_3$				
K_2CO_3				
KCl				
KNO_3				

energy. But more than half the energy is wasted.

Chemical energy may be changed directly into electrical energy. This is done in *electrical cells* (see Unit 22). For example, in a *Daniell cell* the following overall change happens:

$$\mathbf{Zn(s) + Cu^{2+}(aq) \rightarrow Cu(s) + Zn^{2+}(aq)}$$

The reaction between Zn(s) and $CuSO_4$(aq) produces heat if the metal is simply placed in the solution. But the chemical change may be divided into two 'half reactions', which can be carried out in different places:

$$\mathbf{Zn(s) \rightarrow Zn^{2+}(aq) + 2e^-}$$

$$\mathbf{Cu^{2+}(aq) + 2e^- \rightarrow Cu(s)}$$

This is exactly how a Daniell cell works. The electrons are carried from the zinc rod to the copper through the connecting wire, that is, some of the energy of the reaction is released as electrical energy.

● *Chemical energy may be changed into electrical energy in an electrical cell.*

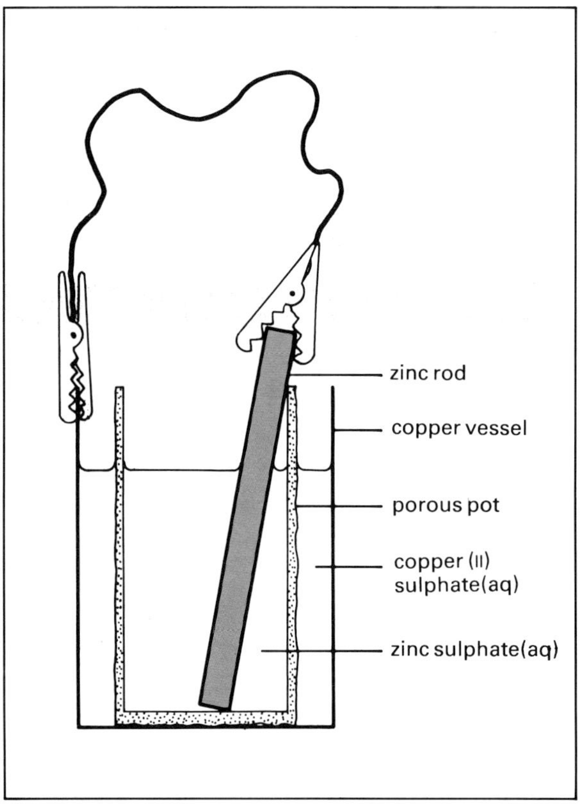

A Daniell cell

Fuel cells

In the Daniell cell, the fuel (reducing agent) is zinc. The Cu^{2+} ions do the oxidizing. Both the oxidizing agent and the reducing agent get used up while the cell is providing electric current, so eventually the cell is exhausted. It must then be thrown away.

However, some cells can use a continuous supply of oxidizing agent and fuel. Electricity may be generated directly from reactions like these:

$$\mathbf{2H_2(g) + O_2(g) \rightarrow 2H_2O(l)}$$

$$\mathbf{CH_4(g) + 2O_2(g) \rightarrow CO_2(g) + 2H_2O(l)}$$

(Metal electrodes are still required, but they act as catalysts, and are not used up.)

● *Cells that provide electricity using reducing agents like hydrocarbons are called 'fuel cells'.*

Summary

1. Reactions (e.g. combustions) that give out energy are called exothermic reactions.
2. Changes (e.g. photosynthesis) that absorb energy are said to be endothermic.
3. Chemical energy can be converted directly into electrical energy in a cell.
4. Fuel cells provide electricity by the oxidation of reducing agents such as hydrocarbons or hydrogen.

Extension

1. **Forms of energy**
   Energy for industry is most usefully supplied in the form of *heat* or *electricity*. Most heat energy is generated by *combustion*, but *nuclear reactions* also release energy. (The energy content of uranium is millions of times greater than that of coal.)
   i What is a 'nuclear reaction'? What happens to the uranium atoms in the core of a nuclear reactor?
   ii What are the advantages and disadvantages of nuclear power stations compared with ordinary power stations?

2. **Cells and displacement reactions**

Heat is released when displacement reactions happen, for example:

$$Zn(s) + FeSO_4(aq) \rightarrow Fe(s) + ZnSO_4(aq)$$

The above reaction may be represented by two half equations as follows:

$$Zn(s) \rightarrow Zn^{2+}(aq) + 2e^-$$

$$Fe^{2+}(aq) + 2e^- \rightarrow Fe(s)$$

If a cell is constructed using the same metals and solutions, some of the energy from these two changes is released as electrical energy. Thus, if Zn and Fe are placed in dilute $FeSO_4(aq)$, the potential between them is about 0.3 volts. If similar simple cells are made using other pairs of metals, the following potentials may be recorded:

Cell	*Electrodes*	*Potential (volts)*
A	Zn and Cu	1.0
B	Zn and Pb	1.5
C	Fe and Pb	0.2
D	Fe and Cu	0.7
E	Cu and Ag	0.3

i In cell A, which metal would you expect to be the negative electrode? Explain.

ii Place the five metals Ag, Cu, Fe, Pb and Zn in order of reactivity (see Unit 22).

iii Is there any connection between the relative positions of pairs of metals in the reactivity list, and the potentials of the cells containing them? Explain.

iv If the same pairs of metals were involved in direct displacement reactions, which pair would you expect to give the most heat per mole?

Revision

1. i What are the advantages of electrical energy compared with other forms of energy?

ii How could you use electrical energy to give:
a heat; *b* light; *c* chemical energy; *d* kinetic energy

2. This question is about the following equations:

A $Zn(s) + 2AgNO_3(aq) \rightarrow Zn(NO_3)_2(aq) + 2Ag(s)$

B $2NH_4OH(aq) + H_2SO_4(aq) \rightarrow (NH_4)_2SO_4(aq) + 2H_2O(l)$

C $CH_4(g) + 2O_2(g) \rightarrow CO_2(g) + 2H_2O(g)$

D $C_6H_{12}O_6 + 6O_2 \rightarrow 6CO_2 + 6H_2O$

E $6H_2O + 6CO_2 \rightarrow C_6H_{12}O_6 + 6O_2$

Which equation shows:

i a combustion

ii an endothermic change

iii respiration of glucose

iv a neutralization

v a displacement

Unit 30
Measuring energy changes

Suppose you wanted to measure the amount of heat given out by a flame, how would you set about it?

One way would be to try to 'catch' all the heat coming out of the flame. For example, you could use the heat to warm up some water. The simplest approach is to stand a beaker of water over the flame. The temperature change in the water can then be recorded.

However, that is not the end of the matter. *Temperature change* and *amount of heat* are not the same. If the water starts at, say, 20 °C and the temperature goes up to 40 °C, this does not tell you how much heat has gone into the water. The *amount of water* being heated must be taken into account.

You can work out the amount of heat absorbed by the water, providing you know the mass of water being heated. Each gram of water requires 4.2 joules for a temperature rise of 1 °C. (We say, the *specific heat capacity* of water is 4.2 J per g per °C.) So, if the temperature rise of a gram of water were 20 °C, the quantity of heat absorbed would be 20×4.2 joules. And if 100 grams of water were being heated, the quantity of heat would be $100 \times 20 \times 4.2$ joules.

In general, the quantity of heat needed to heat m g of water by t °C is $m \times t \times 4.2$ joules.

● *If **m** grams of water has a temperature change of **t** °C, the amount of heat involved is **m** × **t** × **4.2 joules**.*

When reactions are carried out in solution, most of the heat of reaction is absorbed by the solvent in the case of exothermic reactions (or from the solvent in the case of endothermic reactions). So, the temperature change of the solution can be used to work out the heat change directly.

Practical problems

In laboratory investigations of heat changes, not all the heat is accounted for. For example, when a beaker of water is placed over a flame, only part of the flame's heat goes into the water. Some is absorbed by the beaker, and a lot of it escapes into the air. These heat losses affect the accuracy of measurements a great deal. In practice, perhaps only half the heat of the flame is trapped in the water.

You can improve the accuracy of measurements by improving the design of the apparatus used. For example, you can cut down heat losses by using draught shields round the flame. Some alternative pieces of apparatus are shown in the next diagram.

● *Heat losses in experiments lead to inaccurate values for heats of reactions.*

Comparing fuels

Which fuels give most heat? How can you compare them?

The sensible way would be to burn equal amounts of different fuels and compare the quantity of heat released in each case. As usual in comparisons of this sort, we compare a mole of each fuel (i.e. equal numbers of molecules).

The practical approach is simple. A certain mass of fuel is burned using an apparatus like those shown on p.137. For example, a liquid fuel could be weighed in a lamp before and after burning. The heat released is absorbed in a known mass of water. The quantity of heat can be worked out if the temperature rise of the water is recorded. If the relative molecular mass of the fuel is known, the heat released by one mole of fuel can be calculated.

The following specimen results show the method of calculation. (Ethanol is the fuel chosen as an example.)

Specimen results

Mass of lamp containing fuel:

a before burning = 47.28 g
b after burning = 46.88 g

mass of water heated = 50 g
temperature of water before heating = 19 °C
temperature of water after heating = 39 °C.

Measuring the heat given out by a flame

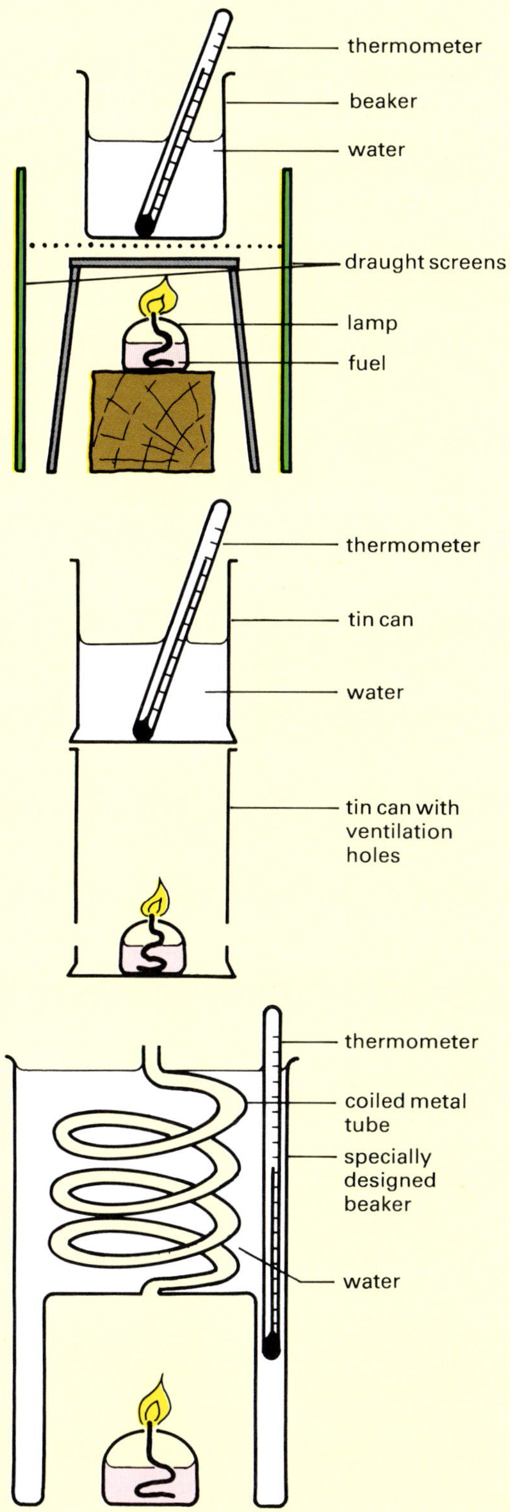

Deductions from results

Mass of fuel burned = 47.28 − 46.88 = 0.40 g
temperature rise of water = 39 − 19 = 20 °C
heat absorbed by water = 50 × 20 × 4.2 = 4200 joules.
∴ Therefore, the heat released by burning 0.40 g of fuel is 4200 joules (assuming all the heat was absorbed). If 1 g of fuel was burned, the heat released would be $4200 \times \frac{1}{0.4}$ joules.

The mass of one mole of ethanol is 46 g. If one mole of ethanol was burned, the heat released would be:

$$4200 \times \frac{46}{0.4} \text{ joules}$$
$$= 483\,000 \text{ joules}$$
$$= 483 \text{ kJ}.$$

Conclusion

The heat released when a mole of ethanol burns is 483 kJ.

Positive and negative heat changes

The conclusion written above is often written as follows:

$$\Delta H_m(C_2H_5OH + 3O_2 \rightarrow 2CO_2 + 3H_2O) = -483 \text{ kJ mol}^{-1}$$

ΔH_m is the symbol used for molar heat change. The Δ is called 'delta'. The units are 'kilojoules per mole'. Why is there a negative sign before the number?
The negative sign tells you that the reaction is exothermic. A positive sign would indicate an endothermic reaction.

- *Exothermic changes are given negative heat values and endothermic changes are given positive values.*

Hydrocarbon	*ΔH_m(combustion) (kJ mol^{-1})*
methane, $CH_4(g)$	−890
ethane, $C_2H_6(g)$	−1560
propane, $C_3H_8(g)$	−2220
butane, $C_4H_{10}(g)$	−2880
pentane, $C_5H_{12}(l)$	−3510
hexane, $C_6H_{14}(l)$	−4190
heptane, $C_7H_{16}(l)$	(see Extension 4)
octane, $C_8H_{18}(l)$	−5510

Some ΔH_m (combustion) values for hydrocarbons

Energy diagrams

When an exothermic reaction is finished, there must be less heat energy in the new substances formed (products) than there was in the original substances (reactants). The opposite must be true of an endothermic change: products will contain more energy than reactants.

We can show this information in the form of the following energy diagrams:

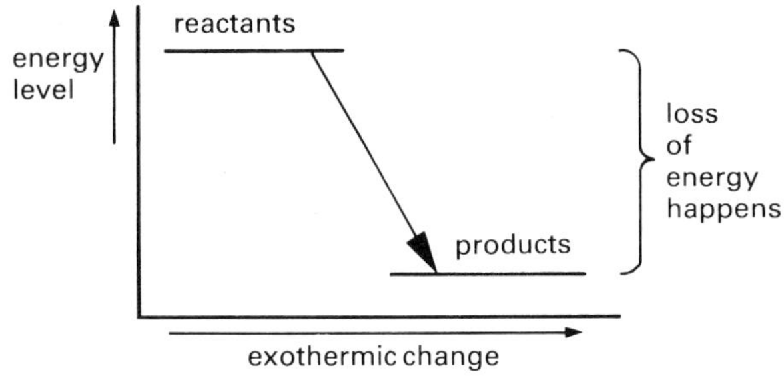

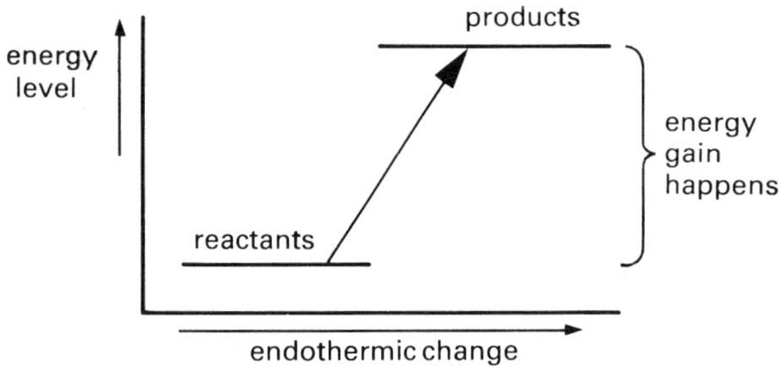

Energy diagrams for exothermic and endothermic changes

● *Energy diagrams can be used to show energy changes in chemical reactions.*

Summary

1. If *m* g of water has a temperature change of *t* °C, the amount of heat involved is $m \times t \times 4.2$ joules.
2. The specific heat capacity of a substance is the amount of heat required to raise 1 g of the substance by one degree celsius. The specific heat of water is 4.2 J g^{-1} $°C^{-1}$.
3. Heat losses in experiments lead to inaccurate values for heats of reactions.
4. Exothermic changes are given negative heat values, and endothermic changes are given positive values.
5. Energy diagrams are useful for showing energy changes in chemical reactions.

Extension

1. Look at the diagram on p.137 of pieces of apparatus used for the determination of ΔH values of combustion reactions.
   i Which would you expect to reduce heat losses most efficiently? Explain your answer.
   ii Suggest how the design of the apparatus might be improved.
2. Approximate values for the molar heats of combustion of some alcohols are given in the table:

Alcohol	*Formula*	ΔH_m *(combustion) (kJ mol 1)*
methanol	CH_3OH	−700
ethanol	C_2H_5OH	−1400
propan-l-ol	C_3H_7OH	−2000
pentan-l-ol	$C_5H_{11}OH$	−3300

   i Work out the *Mr* values of the alcohols.
   ii Draw a graph to show how ΔH_m values change as M_r increases. What do you conclude from your graph?
   iii Use your graph to estimate the ΔH_m value for combustion of butan-l-ol (C_4H_9OH).
   iv The ΔH_m (combustion) value for ethanol given in the table is greater than the value found in the experiment described in this Unit. Suggest a reason for the difference.
3. An experiment was carried out to find the temperature rise when 50 cm^3 of 1M alkali was mixed with 50 cm^3 of 1M acid. The experiment was repeated with several acids and alkalis. The temperature rise in each case was about 12 °C.
   i Write an equation for the reaction of:
   a HCl(aq) and NaOH(aq)
   b HNO_3(aq) and KOH(aq)
   ii Rewrite each of the equations in its simplest ionic form, that is, leave out all spectator ions.
   iii Explain why the neutralization reactions gave the same temperature rise.
4. i Use the ΔH_m (combustion) values for hydrocarbons given in this Unit to estimate the ΔH_m (combustion) value for

heptane. Explain how you arrive at your estimate.

ii On complete combustion, which fuel gives more heat *per gram*, butane or octane? Show your working.

iii The density of liquid butane is 580 kg m^{-3} and that of octane is 700 kg m^{-3}. Which fuel gives the most heat *per* dm^3*?* *Show your working.*

iv Which of the two fuels would you choose to power the following:

a a satellite launch vehicle

b a long-range submarine

Explain the reasons for your choice.

Revision

1. i **How is respiration like combustion?** Write a word equation for the combustion of a fuel (e.g. methane). How is this similar to the word equation for respiration? What other similarity is there between the two processes?

ii Some foods burn well, especially those with oil in them. Peanut is a good example. So, peanuts could give energy in either combustion or respiration.

You could try comparing the energy content of a food (e.g. peanut) with a fuel (e.g. meths) by burning both. Describe the experimental arrangements you could make so that you could:

a measure the heat given out

b compare equal amounts of peanut and meths.

2. Four experiments were done to measure the heat released when a fuel is burned. The heat was absorbed by a known mass of water each time. The results are shown in the next table.

Experiment	*Mass of water (g)*	*Temperature (°C) at start*	*Temperature (°C) at finish*
I	100	20	30
II	50	21	47
III	75	19	38
IV	117	18	26

i Calculate the amount of heat absorbed by the water in each experiment. (Note: Specific heat capacity of water = 4.2 J g^{-1} °C^{-1}.)

ii The same mass of the same fuel was burned in each experiment. In which experiment were the heat losses:

a least

b greatest

3. In the experiment described above (Q2), the M_r value (relative molecular mass) of the fuel was 46. The mass of fuel burned in each experiment was 0.5 g.

i Work out an *average* value for the heat released per g of fuel (ignoring heat losses).

ii Calculate a value for ΔH_m for the reaction.

4. Draw energy diagrams to represent the following changes:

i $CH_4(g) + 2O_2(g) \rightarrow CO_2(g) + 2H_2O(g)$; exothermic change

ii $C_2H_5OH(l) + 3O_2(g) \rightarrow 2CO_2(g) + 3H_2O(g)$; heat is released

iii $NH_4NO_3(s) + aq \rightarrow NH_4^+(aq) + NO_3^-(aq)$; $\Delta H_m = +25$ kJ mol^{-1}

iv $Zn(s) + 2H^+(aq) \rightarrow Zn^{2+}(aq) + H_2(g)$; ΔH_m is negative

v $HCl(aq) + NaOH(aq) \rightarrow NaCl(aq) + H_2O(l)$; $\Delta H_m = -57$ kJ mol^{-1}

5. A neutralization reaction was investigated as follows: 50 cm^3 of 1M $HNO_3(aq)$ was mixed with 50 cm^3 of 1M NaOH(aq). A temperature rise of 12 °C was recorded.

i Assume that the heat capacities of the solutions are 4.2 J g^{-1} °C^{-1} and work out the heat change in this reaction.

ii What would be the heat released per mole of acid and alkali?

iii If 500 cm^3 of the same acid were reacted with 500 cm^3 of the same alkali, which of the following would you expect the temperature rise to be:

A 0.12 °C *B* 1.2 °C

C 12 °C *D* 120 °C

E 1200 °C

Some plants and animals contain acids: rhubarb; red ants; a bee; nettles

Unit 31
Laboratory acids

Mineral acids and organic acids

The common laboratory acids are *mineral acids*. They are called mineral acids because they may be derived from substances found in the Earth's crust. The acids and their corresponding minerals are shown in the next table.

Mineral acid	*Corresponding minerals*
hydrochloric acid, $HCl(aq)$	rock salt (sodium chloride, $NaCl$)
nitric acid, $HNO_3(aq)$	saltpetre (potassium nitrate, KNO_3); Chile saltpetre (sodium nitrate, $NaNO_3$)
sulphuric acid, $H_2SO_4(aq)$	sulphur

Acids and their minerals

Hydrochloric acid and sulphuric acid are manufactured from their corresponding minerals, that is, the minerals are the *raw materials*. But nowadays nitric acid is not manufactured from mineral nitrates. Instead it is manufactured mainly from *ammonia*. This means that indirectly it is manufactured from nitrogen of the air.

There are many acids that are not mineral acids. These are the *organic acids*. They are derived from hydrocarbons. Some are shown in the next table.

Organic acid	*Corresponding hydrocarbon*
methanoic acid, $HCOOH(aq)$ (commonly called 'formic acid')	methane, CH_4
ethanoic acid, $CH_3COOH(aq)$ (commonly called 'acetic acid')	ethane, C_2H_6

Organic acids and their hydrocarbons

Acid strength

By definition, all acid solutions contain hydrogen ions, $H^+(aq)$. The hydrogen ions are produced by reaction of the acid molecules with water molecules. For some acids, the reaction with water is complete. In effect, 100 per cent of the dissolved acid reacts to produce ions and there are no molecules of acid left, for example:

$$\mathbf{HCl(g) + aq \rightarrow H^+(aq) + Cl^-(aq)} \quad (1)$$

$$\mathbf{H_2SO_4(l) + aq \rightarrow 2H^+(aq) + SO_4^{2-}(aq)} \quad (2)$$

In these cases where *ionization is complete* the acids are said to be *strong acids*. The three principal mineral acids mentioned above are all strong acids.

In other cases there is only partial reaction with the water. Only a fraction of the dissolved molecules react. Only a small proportion of hydrogen ions and anions are formed. These acids are called *weak acids*. Organic acids are generally weak acids, for example.

$$\mathbf{CH_3COOH(l) + aq \rightleftharpoons H^+(aq) + CH_3COO^-(aq)} \quad (3)$$

- *Strong acids react completely with water, but weak acids react only partially.*
  Mineral acids are strong acids, but organic acids are generally weak.

Basicity of acids

The molecules of an acidic substance may contain one, two or more hydrogen atoms that can be lost to form hydrogen ions. In the examples we have met so far, hydrochloric acid has one hydrogen atom that can be ionized per molecule, and sulphuric acid has two (equations 1 and 2 above).

Acids that lose only one hydrogen atom per molecule are called *monobasic* acids. Acids that can lose two hydrogen atoms per molecule are called *dibasic* acids. Phosphoric acid can lose three hydrogen atoms per molecule; it is *tribasic*. The table (p. 142) illustrates the idea. (Notice that ethanoic and methanoic acids have more than one hydrogen atom per molecule, but since only one atom can be ionized in each case they are both monobasic.)

Basicity	*Formula*	*Name*	*Anion formed by ionization*
1 monobasic	HCl CH_3COOH HNO_3 $HCOOH$	hydrochloric acid ethanoic acid nitric acid methanoic acid	Cl^-, chloride CH_3COO^-, ethanoate NO_3^-, nitrate $HCOO^-$, methanoate
2 dibasic	H_2SO_4 H_2CO_3	sulphuric acid carbonic acid	SO_4^{2-}, sulphate CO_3^{2-}, carbonate
3 tribasic	H_3PO_4	phosphoric acid	PO_4^{3-}, phosphate

Basicity of acids

Normal and acid salts

In the neutralization of *monobasic acids*, all the hydrogen ions are replaced by metal cations (or ammonium cations) as follows:

$$\mathbf{NaOH(aq) + HCl(aq) \rightarrow NaCl(aq) + H_2O(l)}$$

$$\mathbf{Mg(OH)_2(s) + 2HNO_3(aq) \rightarrow Mg(NO_3)_2(aq) + 2H_2O(l)}$$

In reactions like the examples above, *one* mole of hydroxide ions is supplied for each mole of acid in solution. (Remember, they are monobasic acids, so there is only one mole of $H^+(aq)$ per mole of acid dissolved.)

Dibasic acids can release *two* moles of hydrogen ions per mole of acid dissolved. If all the $H^+(aq)$ is to be neutralized, two moles of $OH^-(aq)$ must be supplied for each mole of acid:

$$\mathbf{2NaOH(aq) + H_2SO_4(aq) \rightarrow Na_2SO_4 + 2H_2O(l)}$$

$$\mathbf{Mg(OH)_2(aq) + H_2SO_4(aq) \rightarrow MgSO_4(aq) + 2H_2O(l)}$$

If only one mole of hydroxide ions is available per mole of acid, then only half the hydrogen ions of the dibasic acid are used up:

$$\mathbf{NaOH(aq) + H_2SO_4(aq) \rightarrow NaHSO_4(aq) + H_2O(l)}$$

$$\mathbf{NaOH(aq) + H_2CO_3(aq) \rightarrow NaHCO_3(aq) + H_2O(l)}$$

Salts that are formed by replacement of all the available hydrogen of an acid are called *normal salts.* If only a part of the hydrogen is replaced, the salts are called *acid salts.* It follows from this that monobasic acids can form only normal salts; dibasic (and tribasic) acids may form normal or acid salts.

The table below shows some examples of normal salts and acid salts.

The pH of acid solutions

Can we work out the concentration of the *ions* in a solution of an acid?

Suppose, for example, we have a 1.0M solution of hydrochloric acid. According to equation 1 above, every mole of HCl(g) that reacts with water produces a mole of $H^+(aq)$. Hydrochloric acid is a strong acid, so reaction is complete, that is, all of the HCl molecules are used up. So the concentration of $H^+(aq)$ produced is 1.0M. (The chloride ion concentration is also 1.0M of course.)

Acid	*Normal salts*	*Acid salts*
$HCl(aq)$	sodium chloride, $NaCl$ calcium chloride, $CaCl_2$	—
$HNO_3(aq)$	magnesium nitrate, $Mg(NO_3)_2$ potassium nitrate, KNO_3	—
$H_2SO_4(aq)$	sodium sulphate, Na_2SO_4 potassium sulphate, K_2SO_4	sodium hydrogensulphate, $NaHSO_4$ potassium hydrogensulphate, $KHSO_4$
$H_2CO_3(aq)$	potassium cabonate, K_2CO_3 sodium carbonate, Na_2CO_3	potassium hydrogencarbonate, $KHCO_3$ sodium hydrogencarbonate, $NaHCO_3$

Normal and acid salts

What happens with dibasic acids? Suppose we have 1.0M sulphuric acid. If you look at equation 2 above you will be able to work out the concentrations of the $H^+(aq)$ and the $SO_4^{2-}(aq)$. They are 2.0M and 1.0M respectively.

Weak acids

The concentrations of ions in solutions of weak acids cannot be worked out from equations in the same way. For example, the ethanoic acid in reaction 3 on p. 141 may have concentration 1.0M. But how much of the ethanoic acid has reacted with the water to form ions? We don't know. All we can say with certainty about the concentration of $H^+(aq)$ in 1.0M ethanoic acid solution is that it is *less than* 1.0M. (Remember, only a fraction of the acid molecules have reacted with the water at any time.)

pH values show the *relative acidity* of solutions. The pH values are related to the concentration of the hydrogen ions. Higher concentrations of $H^+(aq)$ correspond to lower pH values, as the figure below shows.

Each of the following pairs of acids is arranged so that the acid solution with the *lower* pH value is on the left. Check through the list and see if you agree.

2.0M HCl(aq) and 1.0M HCl(aq)
1.0M HCl(aq) and 1.0M $CH_3COOH(aq)$
1.0M $H_2SO_4(aq)$ and 1.0M HCl(aq)

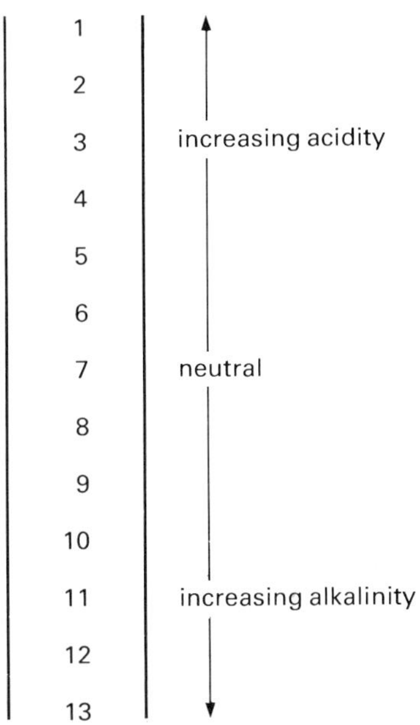

pH values and relative acidity

Properties of the mineral acids in solution

Reaction with carbonates

Mineral acids react as typical acids. Salts, carbon dioxide and water are formed, for example:

$$\mathbf{H_2SO_4(aq) + CuCO_3(s) \rightarrow CuSO_4(aq) + CO_2(g) + H_2O(l)}$$

$$\mathbf{H_2SO_4(aq) + ZnCO_3(s) \rightarrow ZnSO_4(aq) + CO_2(g) + H_2O(l)}$$

$$\mathbf{2HCl(aq) + Na_2CO_3(aq) \rightarrow 2NaCl(aq) + CO_2(g) + H_2O(l)}$$

$$\mathbf{2HNO_3(aq) + K_2CO_3(aq) \rightarrow 2KNO_3(aq) + CO_2(g) + H_2O(l)}$$

Each of these equations (and all other similar equations) may be written as an *ionic equation*. Taking the last one from the list above as an example, we obtain:

$$\mathbf{2H^+(aq) + 2NO_3^-(aq) + 2K^+(aq) + CO_3^{2-}(aq) \rightarrow 2K^+(aq) + 2NO_3^-(aq) + CO_2(g) + H_2O(l)}$$

The spectator ions may be ignored (since they are not involved in a chemical change). We arrive at the simplest form of the equation:

$$\mathbf{2H^+(aq) + CO_3^{2-}(aq) \rightarrow CO_2(g) + H_2O\ (l)}$$

This simplest equation shows the change that is common to all reactions of carbonates and acids.

Since carbon dioxide is formed when any carbonate reacts with an acid, we can use the reaction with acid as *the chemical test for a carbonate*, as follows:

1. Add dilute nitric acid to the unknown solution or solid.
2. Test any gas formed with limewater. (See next figure.)

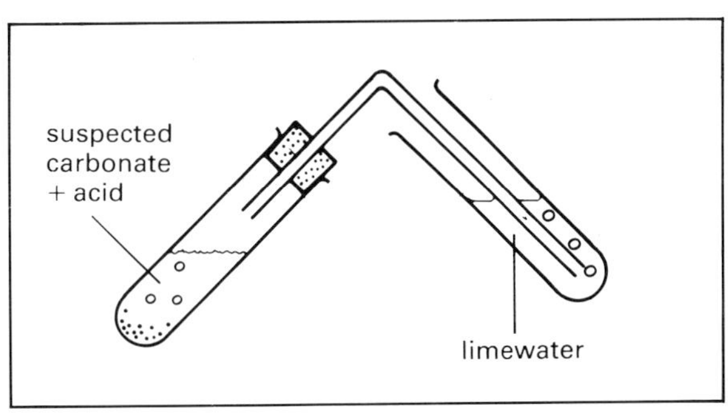

Chemical test for carbonates

Reaction with bases

The mineral acids react as typical acids with bases. Salts and water only are formed, for example:

$$\mathbf{H_2SO_4(aq) + CuO(s) \rightarrow CuSO_4(aq) + H_2O(l)}$$

$$\mathbf{HNO_3(aq) + NaOH(aq) \rightarrow NaNO_3(aq) + H_2O(l)}$$

$$\mathbf{HCl(aq) + NH_4OH(aq) \rightarrow NH_4Cl(aq) + H_2O(l)}$$

$$\mathbf{2HNO_3(aq) + Cu(OH)_2(s) \rightarrow Cu(NO_3)_2(aq) + 2H_2O(l)}$$

● *The three mineral acids follow a common pattern in their reactions with carbonates and bases.*

Reaction with metals

Hydrochloric acid and sulphuric acid follow one pattern: hydrogen gas is produced in reaction with the more reactive metals (together with a salt), for example:

$$\mathbf{H_2SO_4(aq) + Zn(s) \rightarrow ZnSO_4(aq) + H_2(g)}$$

$$\mathbf{2HCl(aq) + Mg(s) \rightarrow MgCl_2(aq) + H_2(g)}$$

Nitric acid behaves differently from the typical acids above. Little hydrogen is produced, even with the most reactive metals. Instead, brown nitrogen oxide gas may be formed, depending on how concentrated the acid is. This behaviour of nitric acid is a result of its oxidizing nature (see next Unit).

● *Dilute nitric acid does not behave like a typical acid in its reactions with metals.*

Summary

1. The common mineral acids are hydrochloric acid, nitric acid and sulphuric acid.
2. Strong acids react completely with water: weak acids react only partially.
3. Mineral acids are strong acids: organic acids are generally weak acids.
4. Dibasic acids can release two moles of hydrogen ions per mole of acid dissolved, and may form either normal or acid salts.
5. Dilute solutions of hydrochloric acid and sulphuric acid behave as typical acids in their reactions with carbonates, bases and reactive metals.
6. Nitric acid behaves as a typical acid in its reactions with carbonates and bases, but not with metals.

Extension

The pH value of a solution is related to its hydrogen ion concentration, $[H^+]$, by the following mathematical equation:

$$\mathbf{pH = -\log[H^+]}$$

where $[H^+]$ has units of mol dm^{-3}.

Consider the hydrogen ion concentrations of the following solutions, *A* to *E*:

Solution	*$[H^+]$*(mol dm^{-3})
A	10^{-2}
B	10^{-4}
C	10^{-5}
D	10^{-7}
E	10^{-9}

1. Which solution has the highest hydrogen ion concentration?
2. Which solution has the highest pH?
3. Which solution is neutral?
4. Which solution has a hydrogen ion concentration 1000 times greater than that of a neutral solution?
5. Which two solutions have pH values that differ by one unit?

Revision

1. This question is about the following acids:

   A HNO_3
   B H_2CO_3
   C H_2SO_4
   D H_3PO_4
   E CH_3COOH

   Choose one that is:

   i an organic acid
   ii a tribasic acid
   iii a monobasic mineral acid
   iv a weak dibasic acid
   v a strong dibasic acid

2. Give the name and formula of:

   i the normal salt that may be formed by reaction of phosphoric acid and potassium hydroxide
   ii the acid salt that may be formed by reaction of sulphuric acid and sodium hydroxide

3. In each of the following cases state true or false:

   A 1.0M solution of hydrochloric acid would have a *higher* pH than:

   i 1.0M $CH_3COOH(aq)$
   ii 1.0M $H_2SO_4(aq)$
   iii 0.5M $HCl(aq)$
   iv 2.0M $HNO_3(aq)$
   v 10.0M $HCl(aq)$

4. Write balanced equations to show the reactions of dilute sulphuric acid with:

   i $Mg(s)$
   ii $MgO(s)$
   iii $Mg(OH)_2(s)$
   iv $NaOH(aq)$
   v $Na_2CO_3(aq)$

5. Write balanced equations to show the reactions between:

   i $H_2SO_4(aq)$ and $NH_3(aq)$
   ii $HNO_3(aq)$ and $ZnCO_3(s)$
   iii $HNO_3(aq)$ and $CuO(s)$
   iv $HCl(aq)$ and $Zn(s)$
   v $HCl(aq)$ and $Mg(s)$

6. Write each of the following equations in the form of:

   i a full ionic equation, that is, including spectator ions
   ii the simplest ionic equation, that is, without spectator ions

   a $Mg(s) + H_2SO_4(aq) \rightarrow MgSO_4(aq) + H_2(g)$
   b $NaOH(aq) + HNO_3(aq) \rightarrow NaNO_3(aq) + H_2O(l)$
   c $2HCl(aq) + Na_2CO_3(aq) \rightarrow 2NaCl(aq) + H_2O(l) + CO_2(g)$
   d $CuO(s) + 2HNO_3(aq) \rightarrow Cu(NO_3)_2(aq) + H_2O(l)$
   e $NH_4OH(aq) + HCl(aq) \rightarrow H_2O(l) + NH_4Cl(aq)$

Unit 32
Concentrated acids

> **Safety note:** Concentrated acids are dangerous chemicals. This applies to concentrated sulphuric acid and nitric acid especially. They should be used by the teacher only. The risks are increased many times if the acids are *hot* and concentrated. Hydrogen chloride gas, which escapes by evaporation from concentrated hydrochloric acid, is extremely toxic.

How concentrated is 'concentrated'?

Hydrogen chloride is a *gas* so even the most concentrated hydrochloric acid must contain some water. But nitric acid and sulphuric acid are *liquids*. So concentrated forms of these acids could be prepared that contained no water. However, the concentrated laboratory acids normally contain some water. Ordinary concentrated sulphuric acid is 98 per cent H_2SO_4.

Are concentrated acids acidic?

This is not such a silly question as it might at first seem. As we know, water plays a vital part in acidity. Dilute laboratory acids contain a large amount of water and their main properties are those of *typical acids*. But in the absence of sufficient water, other properties of the substances become more obvious. Typical acid behaviour may take second place. This applies to sulphuric acid and nitric acid especially.

● *The acidity of concentrated acids may be masked by other properties.*

Redox behaviour

Nitric acid

If a drop of concentrated nitric acid is added (with great care) to potassium iodide crystals there is a very vigorous reaction. Purple fumes of iodine vapour are formed. The following change happens to the iodide ions:

$$2I^-(s) \rightarrow I_2(g) + 2e^-$$

The electrons are removed from the iodide ions by the nitric acid. This means it has *oxidized* the iodide ions.

Nitric acid is a *powerful oxidizing agent.*

The fate of an oxidizing agent is to get reduced. (You can't *remove* electrons without *accepting* them.) When nitric acid is reduced the products include the brown gas nitrogen dioxide.

$$HNO_3 \xrightarrow{\text{reducing agent}} NO_2$$

Formation of nitrogen dioxide is a sign that the nitric acid is behaving as an oxidizing agent rather than (or as well as) a typical acid. (In more dilute solutions, the oxidizing ability of HNO_3 diminishes and typical acidic properties become more obvious, for example its effect on indicators.)

● *Nitric acid is a powerful oxidizing agent in concentrated solution.*

Metals are reducing agents. Their atoms easily lose electrons. This explains why hydrogen is rarely formed in reactions of nitric acid with metals. The nitric acid is reduced and $NO_2(g)$ is formed instead of $H_2(g)$. Even the less reactive metals will reduce nitric acid. Copper, for example, is below hydrogen in the activity series and would not be expected to form hydrogen in reaction with nitric acid. But copper will dissolve in nitric acid, forming a blue solution of copper nitrate and releasing nitrogen dioxide gas.

Because of its oxidizing nature, nitric acid is very damaging to skin and clothing and must be used with great care in the laboratory.

Sulphuric acid

Sulphuric acid is not such a strong oxidizing agent as nitric acid (and again its oxidizing power diminishes rapidly on dilution). But hot concentrated sulphuric acid has got oxidizing ability. Copper is slowly attacked by the hot acid. It is oxidized to copper oxide and copper sulphate. The reduction products of sulphuric acid include the colourless, sharp-smelling gas sulphur dioxide. Whenever sulphur dioxide is formed in the reactions of sulphuric acid it shows that the acid is acting as an oxidizing agent.

$$H_2SO_4 \xrightarrow{\text{reducing agent}} SO_2$$

Hydrochloric acid

Concentrated hydrochloric acid has no oxidizing ability. It behaves as a *reducing agent*. Strong oxidizing agents generate chlorine from concentrated solutions of hydrochloric acid.

$$HCl \xrightarrow{\text{oxidizing agent}} Cl_2$$

This appears to be oxidation by removal of hydrogen from the HCl. It could equally well be considered to be oxidation by removal of electrons from the chloride ion, Cl^-.

$$Cl^- \xrightarrow{\text{oxidizing agent}} Cl_2$$

Suitable oxidizing agents are manganese(IV) oxide, potassium manganate(VII) and potassium dichromate(VI) (see Unit 24).

- *Concentrated hydrochloric acid has reducing properties.*

Concentrated sulphuric acid as a dehydrating agent

Concentrated sulphuric acid has a strong *affinity* for water, that is, it has a strong tendency to combine with water. This is a most important feature of the behaviour of the concentrated acid. Affinity for water is at the root of many of its properties and uses, as we shall see.

Hygroscopy

Hygroscopy means 'the absorption of water from the atmosphere'. Many chemicals are *hygroscopic*, but concentrated sulphuric acid shows the property very well. As water is absorbed the acidic solution becomes more dilute and increases in mass, as shown in the figure below.

The ability of sulphuric acid to absorb water makes it a useful *drying agent* in the laboratory preparation of gases. Water vapour mixed with a gas is removed by bubbling the gas through the concentrated acid (figure p. 148).

Dilution

Mixing concentrated sulphuric acid with water releases large amounts of heat. Great care must be taken in doing this. The acid must always be added slowly (with stirring) *to the water*. Pouring water into the acid can be very dangerous since steam and acid spray are likely to be formed.

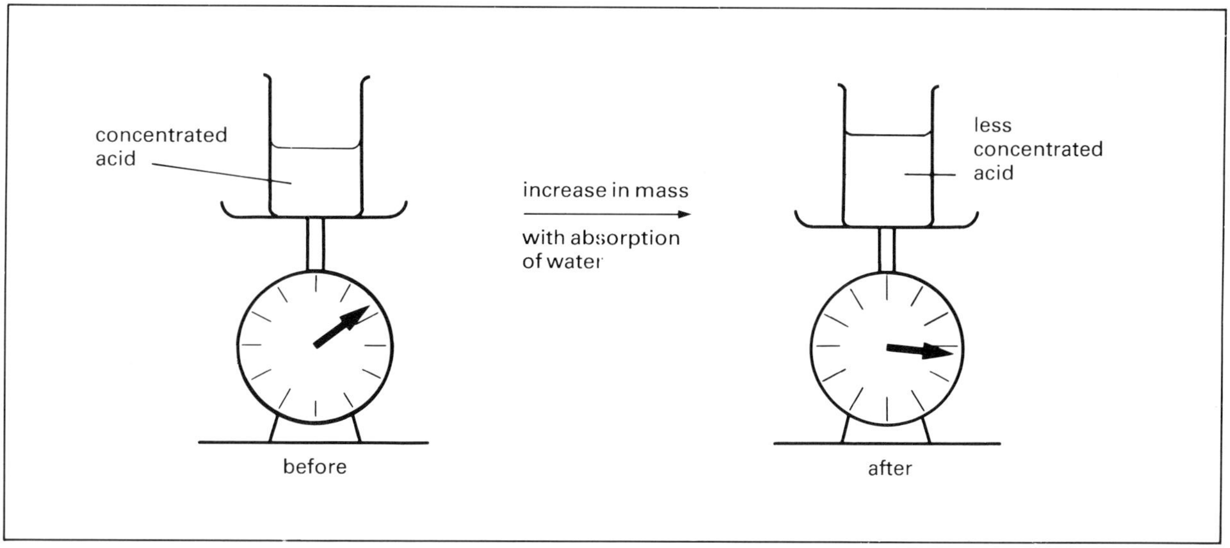

Water absorption from the atmosphere by concentrated sulphuric acid

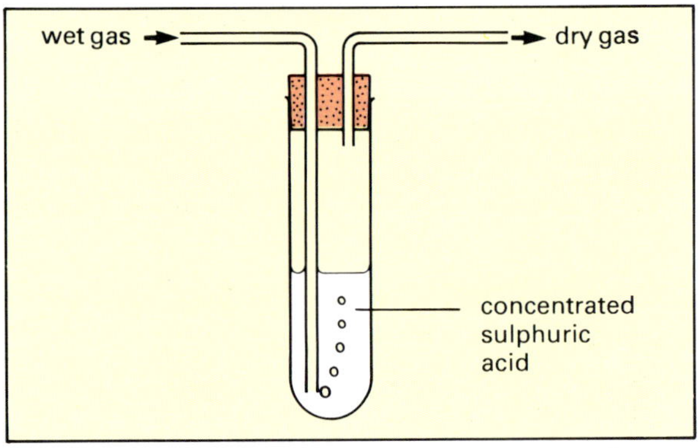

Concentrated sulphuric acid as a drying agent for gases

Dehydration

This is the removal of water, that is, water molecules or the elements of water, from compounds. Dehydration of the tissues of the skin causes serious acid 'burns' when concentrated sulphuric acid is spilled on the skin.

The following reactions illustrate the behaviour of the acid as a *dehydrating agent*:

1. **Dehydration of blue copper sulphate crystals**

   Molecules of water of crystallization are removed from the hydrated salt.

   $$\underset{\text{blue}}{\mathbf{CuSO_4.5H_2O(s)}} \xrightarrow[\text{sulphuric acid}]{\text{concentrated}} \underset{\text{grey}}{\mathbf{CuSO_4(s)}}$$

2. **Dehydration of sugar**

   $$\underset{\text{sucrose}}{\mathbf{C_{12}H_{22}O_{11}(s)}} \xrightarrow[\text{sulphuric acid}]{\text{concentrated}} \mathbf{C(s) + H_2O(g) + CO(g)}$$

   This is a complex reaction involving more than simple dehydration. There is no molecular water in sucrose. However, the elements of water (hydrogen and oxygen) are present in sucrose in the molar ratio 2:1. (This is true for all carbohydrates: see Unit 33.) So, in simple terms, the change may be regarded as the removal of water from the carbohydrate leaving a residue of carbon. Escaping steam and carbon monoxide turn the hot mixture into a spongy mass of black carbon.

● *Concentrated sulphuric acid is a powerful dehydrating agent.*

Summary

1. Concentrated acids show properties not shown by the same acids in dilute solution.
2. Nitric acid is a strong oxidizing agent in concentrated solution. Nitrogen dioxide gas is formed during its oxidizing reactions.
3. Concentrated sulphuric acid is a weaker oxidizing agent than nitric acid but a powerful dehydrating agent.
4. Concentrated hydrochloric acid has reducing properties.
5. Concentrated acids are corrosive and cause acid burns because of their oxidizing and dehydrating action on the tissues of the skin.

First aid: As with most spillages of chemicals, swilling the skin with plenty of water *as quickly as possible* is the best action to take if concentrated acid is spilled on the skin. Clothing that is soaked by a spillage of the acid should be removed without delay.

Extension

1. i Concentrated sulphuric acid is 98 per cent H_2SO_4, that is, 100 g contains only 2 g of water. What mass of H_2SO_4 is contained in 1 kg of concentrated sulphuric acid?

   ii What amount (in moles) of H_2SO_4 is contained in 1 kg of concentrated acid?

   iii The density of concentrated sulphuric acid is 1.84×10^3 kg m^{-3}. What volume of concentrated acid should be mixed with water to make 1 dm^3 of 1.0M solution?

2. i What gaseous product is generally formed when H_2SO_4 acts as an oxidizing agent?

   ii The non-metals C and S may be oxidized to CO_2 and SO_2 respectively by warming with concentrated sulphuric acid. Construct balanced equations for the two reactions. (Hint: H_2O is a product in both cases.)

3. i Which of the following gases could *not* be dried by bubbling through concentrated H_2SO_4?

   Cl_2, CO_2, H_2, NH_3, O_2

   ii Explain why concentrated H_2SO_4 could not be used to dry the gas you have chosen, and name an alternative drying agent that could be used.

Revision

1. Describe a reaction you could do to demonstrate each of the following properties and state what you would expect to observe in each case:

   i the acidity of dilute sulphuric acid
   ii the dehydrating action of concentrated sulphuric acid
   iii the oxidizing action of concentrated nitric acid
   iv the reducing nature of concentrated hydrochloric acid

2. State what you understand by:

   i typical acid behaviour
   ii dehydrating agent
   iii hygroscopic substance
   iv acid burn
   v oxidizing agent

3. Write an account of the possible dangers associated with the use of concentrated acids. What emergency action should be taken if concentrated acids are spilled?

Unit 33
Organic chemistry

Carbon in living things

Many chemical compounds can be obtained from living things. For example, sugars like glucose and sucrose can be obtained from the juices of fruits and plants. Ethanol is produced in the fermentation of fruit juices. Methane ('marsh gas') is formed when vegetation decomposes. Methanoic acid (formic acid) is found in ant and nettle stings. Urea can be crystallized from animal urine. If you look at the formulas of these compounds in the next table, you will see that they all have something in common.

glucose	$C_6H_{12}O_6$
sucrose	$C_{12}H_{22}O_{11}$
ethanol	C_2H_5OH
methane	CH_4
methanoic acid	HCOOH
urea	N_2H_4CO

Formulas of some natural substances

What all these compounds have in common are the elements carbon and hydrogen. In particular, carbon is found in nearly all compounds obtained from living things.

- *Nearly all compounds obtained from living things are carbon compounds.*

Organic chemicals: sugar from plant juices (top); ethanol from fermentation of fruit juices, such as grapes (left); methane (marsh gas) from decaying vegetation (right)

Organic chemicals

In the early days of chemistry, it was thought that the compounds obtained from living things could not be made in the laboratory. The idea was that there were special processes going on inside the organism (living thing). The special

processes were thought to be essential for the formation of the compounds. So, chemists believed that the compounds from organisms were somehow special and different from 'ordinary' chemicals that could be made in the laboratory. They called chemicals from living things *organic chemicals* and the others *inorganic chemicals*.

However, in 1828 a chemist called Wohler showed that organic chemicals were just ordinary chemical substances. He did this by converting an inorganic chemical into an organic chemical, simply by heating it in the laboratory. Gradually, more and more organic chemicals were shown to be just like ordinary chemicals. But we still use the terms 'organic' and 'inorganic' to divide chemicals into two classes. Nowadays, however, we use the term organic compounds to mean *carbon compounds*. (There are some carbon compounds that are classed as inorganic compounds, for example carbon oxides and carbonates. But these are exceptions to the rule.)

● *Organic chemistry is the study of compounds of carbon.*

Most of the organic chemicals we have nowadays are man-made and are not obtained directly from organisms. However, the main raw material for manufacturing organic chemicals is *petroleum*. (This was formed in the past from marine organisms.)

● *Most man-made organic chemicals are derived from petroleum.*

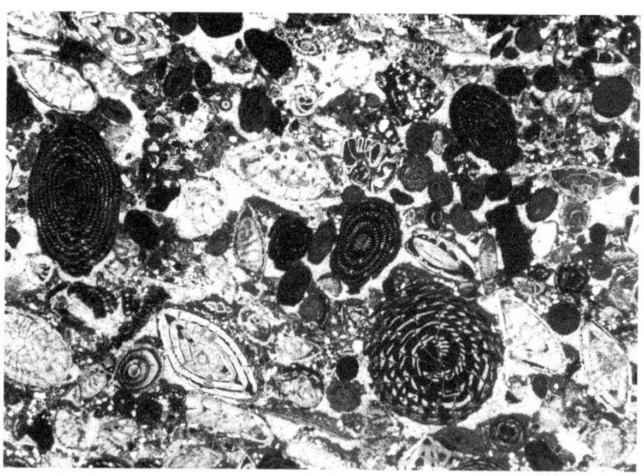

Oil-bearing rock, showing the dead remains of organisms

There are millions of carbon compounds

Why do we have a separate branch of chemistry just for carbon compounds? Couldn't its compounds be included with those of other elements?

There's a simple reason for keeping carbon compounds separate: there are just too many of them. *There are more compounds of carbon than compounds of all the other elements put together.* Organic chemistry is a very large branch of chemistry. It includes millions of compounds. Most of these are compounds of carbon involving just a few other non-metallic elements, for example hydrogen, nitrogen, oxygen and the halogens.

Why does carbon have so many more compounds than other elements? What is special about carbon? The answer to these questions is, carbon atoms have the special property of being able to join together to form chains of atoms. The chains may be short, or they may be hundreds or thousands of atoms long. The atoms of a few other elements can form very short chains, but no other element can form chains so well as carbon.

● *Carbon atoms have a special property: they can join together to form stable chains.*

How does forming chains increase the number of compounds? You can see the answer to this question if you look at the molecular structures of some carbon hydrides. These carbon hydrides are usually called *hydrocarbons*. Some examples are shown in the figure on p.152 (top).

(Could you draw structures for hydrocarbons with three, four and six carbon atoms per molecule?)

Because the carbon chain can be practically any length, and because there can be branched as well as straight chains, the number of possible hydrocarbons is enormous. For example, it has been calculated that hundreds of thousands of different 'carbon hydride' molecules could be constructed by different arrangements of just 20 carbon atoms and 42 hydrogen atoms. By comparison, nitrogen has got only *two* hydrides, NH_3 and N_2H_4.

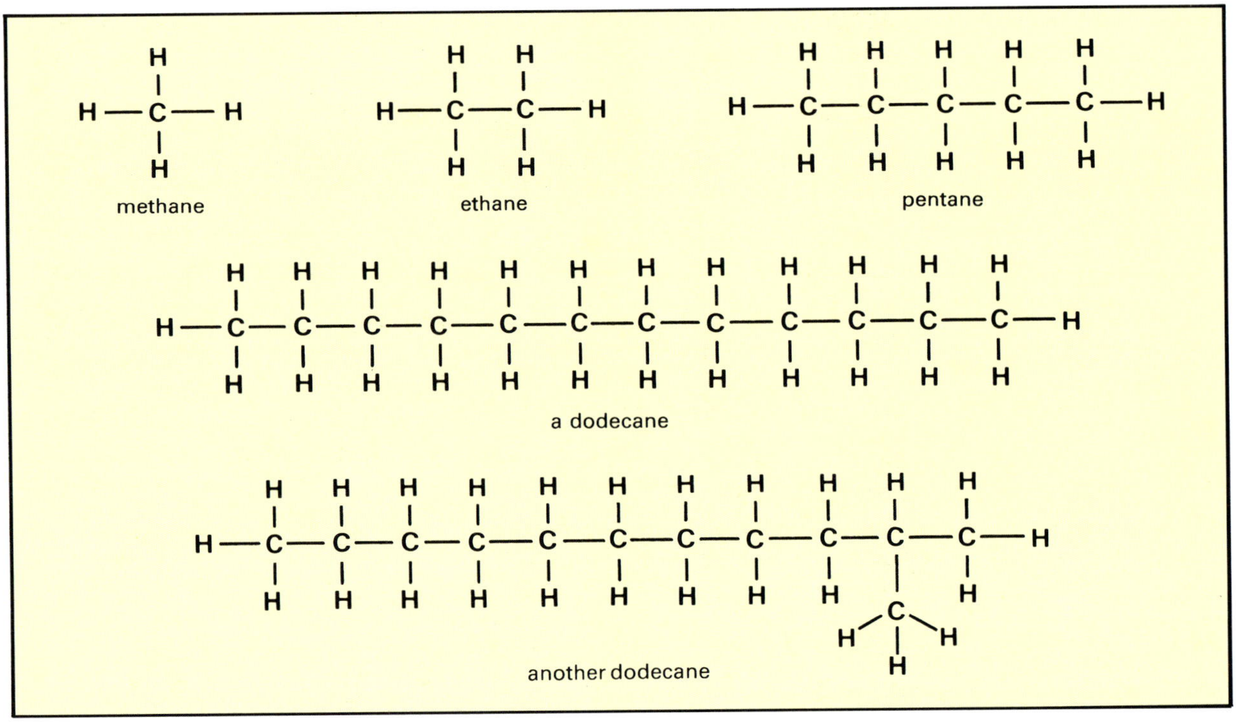

Some hydrocarbons

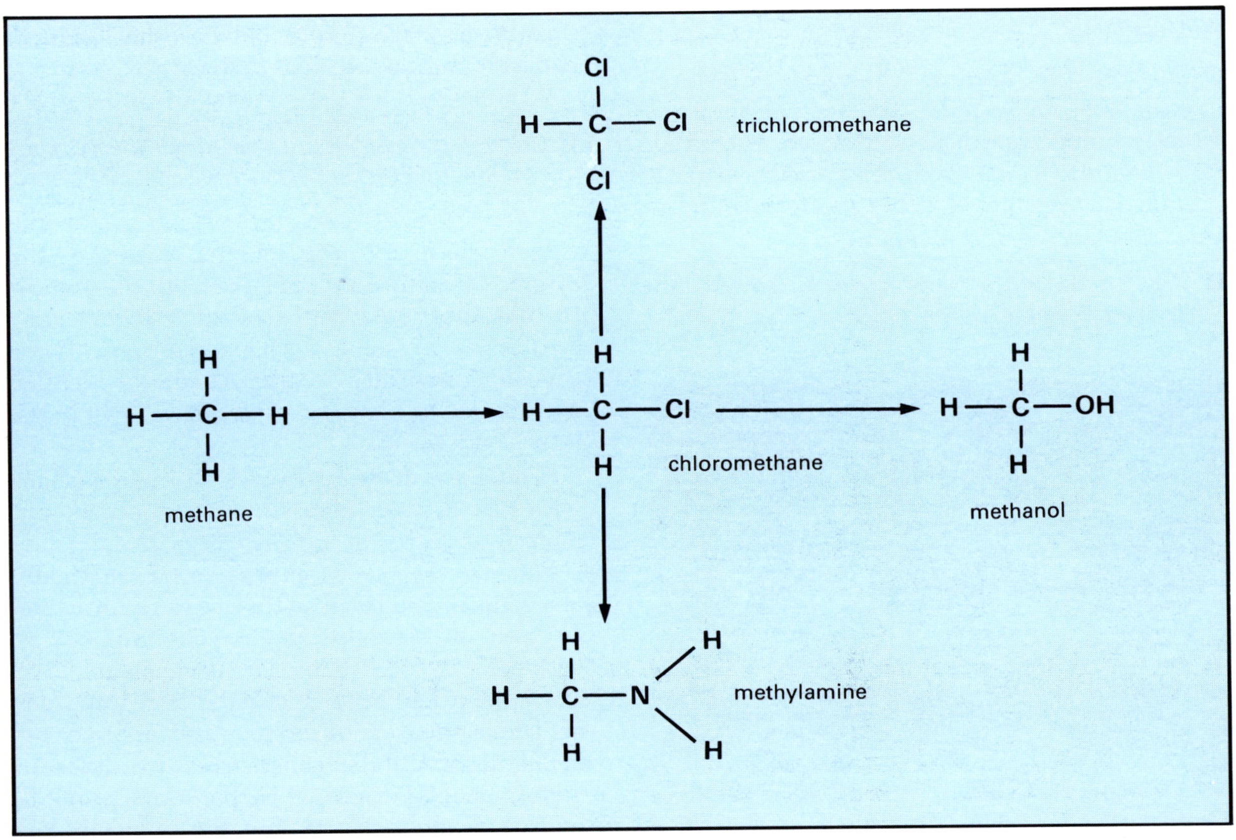

Compounds from methane

Class	*Characteristics*	*Examples*
Hydrocarbons	all compounds of carbon and hydrogen only	
(i) alkanes	only single bonding between carbon atoms in the chains	ethane, C_2H_6 dodecane, $C_{12}H_{26}$
(ii) alkenes	double bonding between some carbon atoms	ethene, C_2H_4 propene, C_3H_6
(iii) alkynes	triple bonding between some carbon atoms	ethyne, C_2H_2
Carbohydrates	compounds of carbon, hydrogen and oxygen, with twice as many H atoms as O atoms	glucose, $C_6H_{12}O_6$ sucrose, $C_{12}H_{22}O_{11}$ starch, $(C_6H_{10}O_5)n$
Alcohols	compounds of carbon, hydrogen and oxygen, containing OH groups of atoms in their molecules	methanol, CH_3OH ethanol, C_2H_5OH

Classes of organic compounds

More carbon compounds

There are still more possibilities. The chains we have looked at so far have all had carbon atoms joined by *single* covalent bonds. But *double* and *triple* bonds between carbon atoms are possible. So, there are molecules with structures like the next figure.

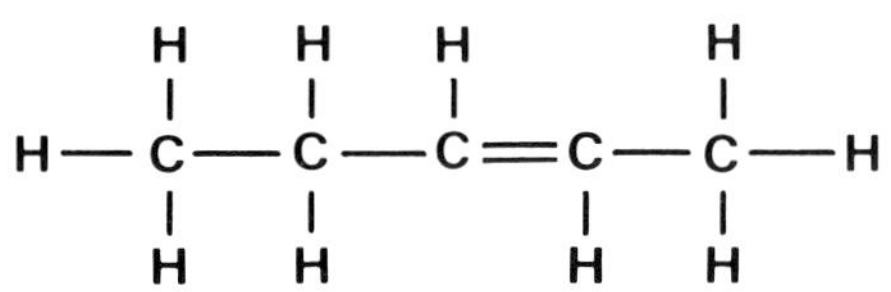

A hydrocarbon with a double bond

This increases the number of possible hydrocarbons even further.

We should also consider compounds with oxygen, or nitrogen, or halogens. A single hydrocarbon can lead to a lot of new compounds if hydrogen atoms are 'replaced' by atoms of other elements. We can take methane as a simple example, as shown in the figure on the left.

Now you can see why there are so many compounds of carbon to think about.

Classifying organic chemicals

There are so many organic compounds to consider. The only way to cope with them all is to sort them out into families (or classes).

Some examples of classes of organic compounds are shown in the table above.

Summary

1. Nearly all compounds obtained from living things are carbon compounds.
2. The study of carbon compounds is called organic chemistry.
3. Most synthetic organic compounds are derived from petroleum.
4. There are more compounds of carbon than compounds of all the other elements put together.
5. Carbon atoms can join together to form chains of atoms. This explains why there are so many organic compounds.
6. Organic compounds are sorted into classes such as alkane hydrocarbons, alkene hydrocarbons and carbohydrates.

Extension

1. In 1828, for the first time, an organic compound was made in the laboratory by heating an inorganic compound. Can you explain why this was considered remarkable at the time?
2. The inorganic compound used was ammonium cyanate. When it is heated, urea is formed. The two compounds have the same molecular formula although the atoms are arranged differently. This is an example of

isomerism. The molecular formula of both isomers is N_2H_4CO.

Which two of the following formulas are formulas of isomers of N_2H_4CO?

A $(NH_2)_2CO$
B $(NH)_4CO$
C NH_4CNO
D NH_4CO
E $(NH_4)_2CO_3$

3. One of the isomers includes the ammonium group of atoms and is ammonium cyanate. The urea molecule does not contain the ammonium group: its atoms are grouped differently.

Give the formula of urea selected from *A* to *E* above, that is, to show the grouping of the atoms.

4. Use normal valency rules to draw a structure of the urea molecule, that is, with the grouping of atoms suggested in 3 above but showing bonds between the atoms.
(Hint: six single bonds and one double bond are needed.)

Revision

1. This question is about the following formulas:

A CH_4
B $CHCl_3$
C C_2H_5OH
D $C_6H_{12}O_6$
E NH_3

Which is the formula of:

i glucose
ii methane
iii trichloromethane
iv ethanol
v ammonia
vi a hydrocarbon
vii a carbohydrate
viii an inorganic compound

2. This question is about the following compounds:

A ethane
B ethanol
C ethene
D ethyne
E starch

Which of the compounds belongs to the class called:

i carbohydrates
ii alkane hydrocarbons
iii alkene hydrocarbons
iv alkyne hydrocarbons
v alcohols

3. This question is about the following molecular structures:

A 

B 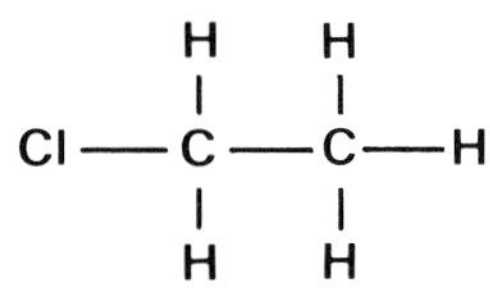

C 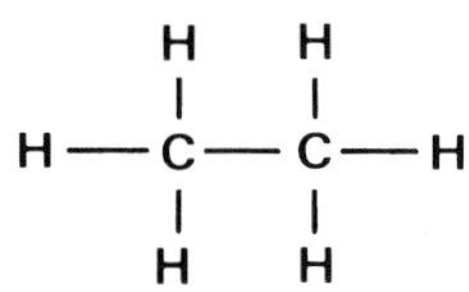

D 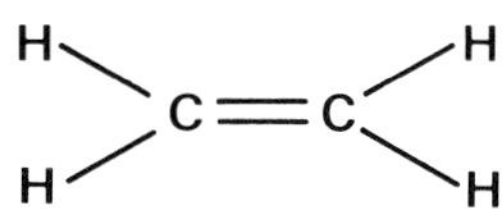

E 

Which is the structure of an:

i alkane
ii alkene
iii alkyne
iv organic compound that is not a hydrocarbon
v inorganic compound

Unit 34
Alkanes

Saturated hydrocarbons

Alkanes are organic compounds of carbon and hydrogen only. In other words, they are *hydrocarbons*. All the carbon atoms in alkane molecules are joined by single covalent bonds. Compounds of this type with no double or triple bonds are said to be *saturated*.

● *Alkanes are saturated hydrocarbons.*

The general formula of the alkanes

Examples of the alkanes include the following substances:

methane	CH_4
ethane	C_2H_6
propane	C_3H_8
butanes	C_4H_{10}
pentanes	C_5H_{12}
hexanes	C_6H_{14}

All of these substances have molecules that can be represented by the formula C_nH_{2n+2}.
The value of n in this formula can be any whole number. Thus, when $n = 1$ the formula of the alkane is CH_4 because $2n+2 = 4$. When $n = 2$ the formula of the alkane is C_2H_6 because $2n + 2 = 6$, and so on.

The formula C_nH_{2n+2} is known as the *general formula* of the alkanes.

● *The general formula of the alkanes is* C_nH_{2n+2}.

Physical properties of alkanes

Only a few of the alkanes are gases. The rest are liquids or solids with low melting temperatures.

The gaseous alkanes are methane, ethane, propane and butane. Their formulas are shown above. You will notice that these *gaseous hydrocarbons* are the ones with the *smallest molecules*. Is this just a coincidence? Or is there a pattern in the melting and boiling temperatures of the alkanes? This idea can be checked by looking at the boiling temperatures of some individual alkanes. The information is given in the next table.

Alkane	*Boiling temperature* (°C)
methane, CH_4	−162
ethane, C_2H_6	−87
propane, C_3H_8	−42
butane, C_4H_{10}	0
pentane, C_5H_{12}	36
hexane, C_6H_{14}	69
decane, $C_{10}H_{22}$	174

Boiling temperatures of some alkanes

The figures show a clear link between the boiling temperature and the size of the molecules. You could illustrate the relationship by drawing a graph of boiling temperature (vertical axis) against number of carbon atoms per molecule (horizontal axis) (see Revision Q 2). There is a similar pattern with melting temperatures.

These observations have led to the idea that the weak force of attraction *between* molecules varies according to the size of the molecule. Larger molecules attract one another more strongly than do small molecules.

● *The larger the hydrocarbon molecules the more strongly they attract one another and the less volatile is the alkane.*

Homologous series

Compounds with similar chemical properties and which can be represented by a general formula are said to belong to a *homologous series*. The alkanes belong to a homologous series of saturated hydrocarbons. In Unit 35 we will meet another homologous series, the alkenes. If the members of the alkanes are placed in order of increasing molecular size, there is a steady increase in boiling temperature. In general, if the members of a homologous series are put in order of increasing M_r values, there is a steady change in their physical properties.

A North Sea oil and gas rig

Chemical properties of alkanes

Alkanes are very largely *inert*. In other words, they are unreactive with most other chemicals.

One of their few reactions is *combustion*. However, this reaction is of great importance. After all, the combustion of alkanes (from natural gas and petroleum) provides a great deal of our energy for heating and transport.

If there is enough oxygen, the combustion of alkanes always produces the same products: carbon dioxide and water. As an example, the equation for the combustion of methane is given as:

$$\mathbf{CH_4(g) + 2O_2(g) \rightarrow CO_2(g) + 2H_2O(l)}$$

If there isn't enough oxygen, carbon monoxide or carbon (soot) is formed instead of carbon dioxide. Carbon monoxide is a poison. Exhaust gases from car engines may contain carbon monoxide, which pollutes the atmosphere.

- *Alkanes burn well and are important fuels. Carbon dioxide and water are formed if there is excess of oxygen.*

Isomerism of alkane hydrocarbons

You can draw the structure of one of the smaller alkane molecules quite easily. Just use the normal rules of valency to work it out. The valency number of hydrogen is 1 and that of carbon is 4. So, for example, you could work out the structure of a propane (C_3H_8) molecule to be:

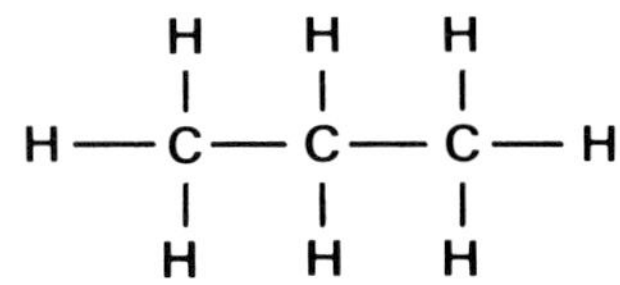

This is the only possible way to join up the three carbon atoms and eight hydrogen atoms if they have their normal valencies.

But in most cases, there is more than one way to join up the atoms in a given molecular formula. For example, there are two butanes, C_4H_{10}:

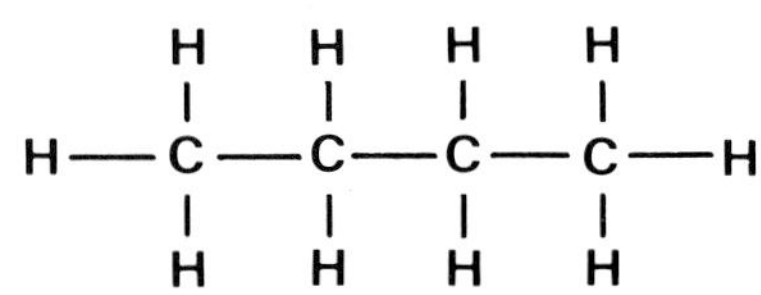

and

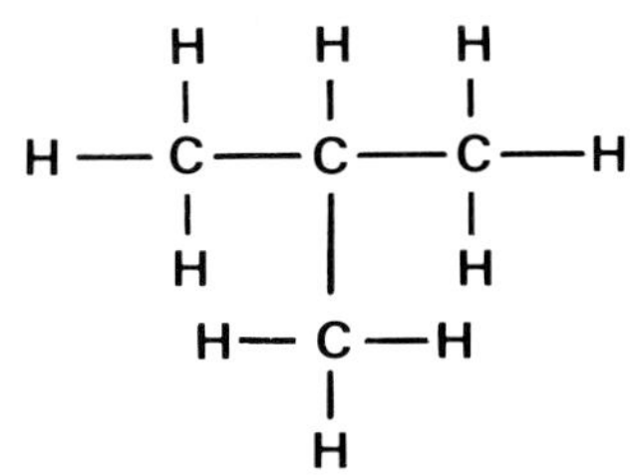

These are molecules of *different compounds*, not different forms of the same compound.

Substances like the butanes, which have molecules with the same formula but different structures, are called *isomers*.

- *Isomers are compounds with the same molecular formula but different molecular structures.*

There are three isomeric pentanes (C_5H_{12}). See if you can work out their molecular structures. There are nearly 2000 isomers with formula $C_{14}H_{30}$.

Summary

1. Alkanes are saturated hydrocarbons.
2. The general formula of alkanes is C_nH_{2n+2}
3. The less volatile the alkane, the larger are its molecules.
4. Alkanes burn well and are important fuels.
5. Carbon dioxide and water are produced when alkanes burn if there is excess oxygen.
6. Isomers are compounds with the same molecular formula but different molecular structures.

Extension

In the last Unit we discovered that there are many hydrides of carbon, but only two hydrides of nitrogen. The nitrogen hydrides have the formulas NH_3 and N_2H_4. Their structures are:

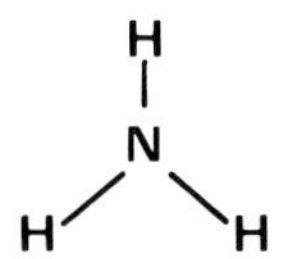

and

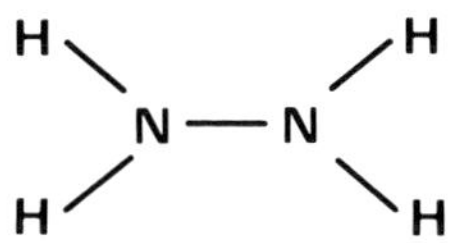

The reason for this important difference between carbon and nitrogen is that carbon atoms can form long chains, but nitrogen atoms cannot.

1. What name is usually given to 'hydrides of carbon'?
2. What is the name of the nitrogen hydride, NH_3?
3. What is the valency of nitrogen atoms in the two hydrides?
4. If nitrogen could form long chains of atoms, the following hydrides might exist:

   N_3H_5 and N_4H_6

   Draw structures of these hypothetical (imaginary) hydrides of nitrogen.
5. What would be the formula of the hypothetical hydride with five nitrogen atoms?
6. What is the general formula of this family of hypothetical nitrogen hydrides?
7. Suggest a reason for the fact that nitrogen cannot form long chains of atoms.

Revision

1. Which of the following formulas is *not* the formula of an alkane?

   A $C_{10}H_{20}$
   B $C_{17}H_{36}$
   C $C_{19}H_{40}$
   D $C_{27}H_{56}$
   E $C_{30}H_{62}$

2. Look at the boiling temperature data given on p.155. Draw a graph using the data to show how the boiling temperatures of the alkanes vary with the number of carbon atoms per molecule. (Use the vertical axis for the boiling temperatures, and the horizontal axis for the number of carbon atoms.)

   Use your graph to estimate the boiling temperatures of the alkanes with seven, eight and nine carbon atoms per molecule.

3. This question is about the equation for the combustion of the alkane propane. Which of the following equations shows the correct number of molecules of water and carbon dioxide?

   A $C_3H_8(g) + 5O_2(g) \rightarrow CO_2(g) + H_2O(l)$
   B $C_3H_8(g) + 5O_2(g) \rightarrow 2CO_2(g) + 2H_2O(l)$
   C $C_3H_8(g) + 5O_2(g) \rightarrow 2CO_2(g) + 3H_2O(l)$
   D $C_3H_8(g) + 5O_2(g) \rightarrow 3CO_2(g) + 3H_2O(l)$
   E $C_3H_8(g) + 5O_2(g) \rightarrow 3CO_2(g) + 4H_2O(l)$

4. The following are structures of pentane molecules:

(a)

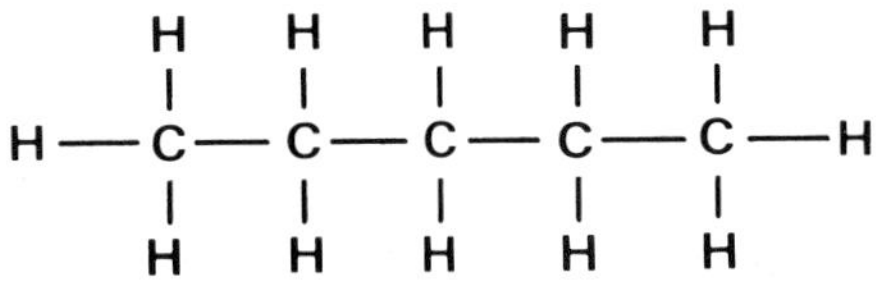

(b)

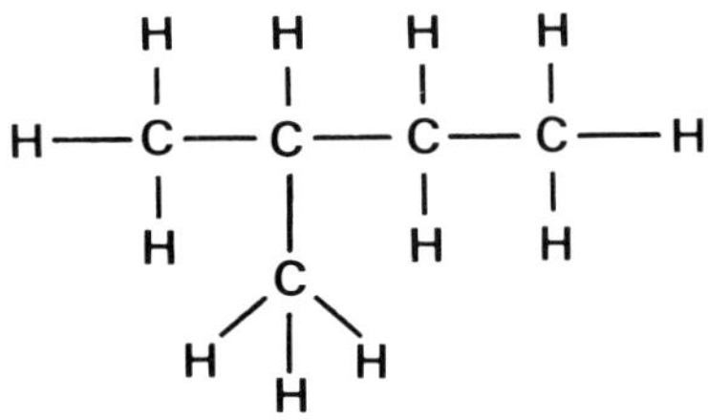

(c)

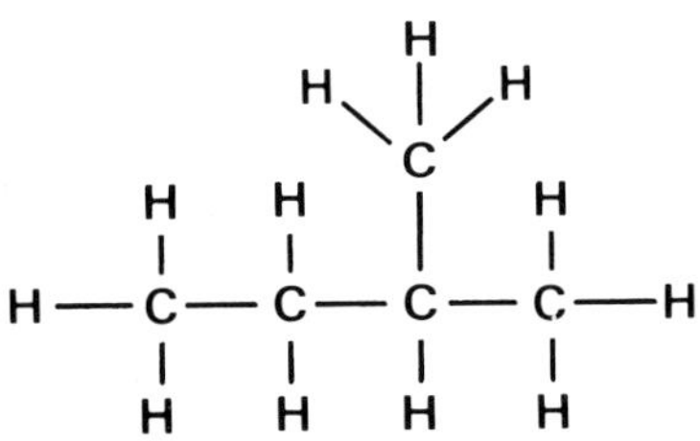

(d)

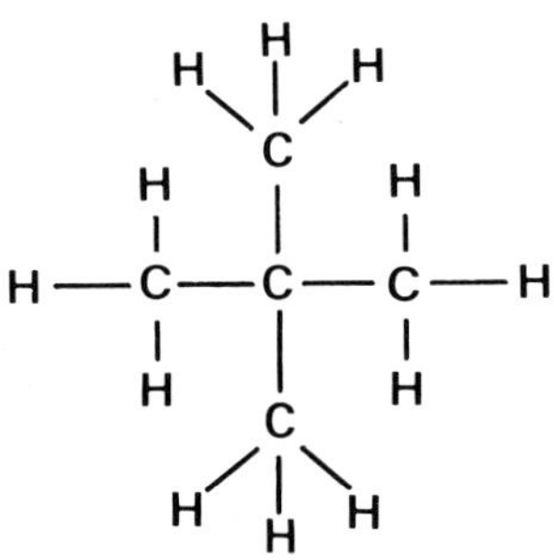

(e)

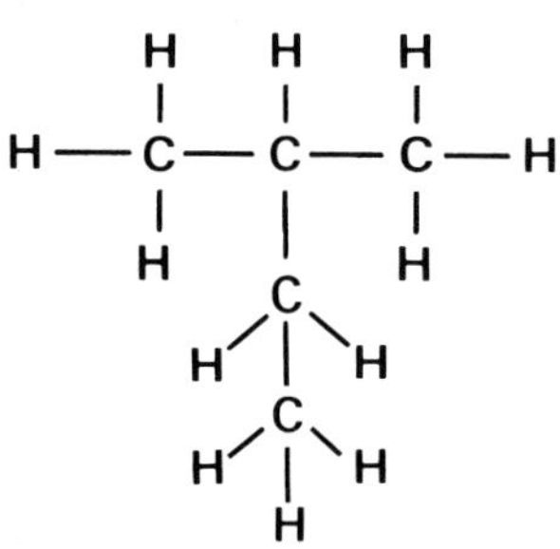

If you examine the structures carefully, you will find that in three cases the carbon atoms are joined up in the same order. In other words, three of the structures are just different ways of showing the *same molecule*. In other cases, the structures really are different: they belong to *isomeric pentanes*.

The structures are grouped together in threes below:

A (a) (b) (c)
B (a) (b) (d)
C (a) (c) (e)
D (b) (c) (e)
E (c) (d) (e)

i Which is a group of three identical molecules?

ii Which is a group of three isomeric molecules?

5. i Name the hydrocarbons with the following molecular formulas:

(a) C_2H_6 (b) C_5H_{12}

ii Draw structures for molecules with formulas (a) and (b) above.

iii Other hydrocarbons in the same class include propane (C_3H_8) and butanes (C_4H_{10}). Draw structures for these hydrocarbons.

Unit 35
From alkenes to polymers

Alkane hydrocarbons can be decomposed by heating them to a high temperature in the absence of air. Decomposition of hydrocarbons like this is usually called *'cracking'*, and it often results in the formation of a gas. The gas that is formed can be called 'cracked gas'. An experiment to show cracking in the laboratory is illustrated in the figure below.

It is interesting to compare the 'cracked gas' with natural gas, that is, to compare it with the laboratory gas supply.

Comparing 'cracked gas' with natural gas

There are several similarities between the gases: both cracked gas and laboratory gas are colourless gases. Both are insoluble in water. Both are flammable and produce carbon dioxide and water when burned.

However, there are important differences between cracked gas and natural gas. These differences are best illustrated by two chemical tests, which can be done in the laboratory. The first test is the effect of the gas on *bromine water*. The second is a similar test using *acidified potassium manganate(VII)*. The results of these tests together with other observations about the gases are given in the figure on p. 160.

Quite clearly there is an important difference between the hydrocarbons in natural gas and the hydrocarbons in cracked gas. The difference is the chemical reactivity of hydrocarbons in cracked gas.

- *Hydrocarbons in the gas formed by cracking alkanes will react with bromine water and acidified potassium manganate(VII), and decolourize them.*

Unsaturated hydrocarbons

Laboratory gas (natural gas) contains alkane hydrocarbons such as methane. As we know, the alkane hydrocarbons are unreactive compounds. Apart from combustion, they have few other chemical properties (see Unit 34). The tests with bromine water and potassium manganate(VII) confirm this.

On the other hand, the hydrocarbons in cracked gas have special reactivity. They are said to be *unsaturated*. The reactions with

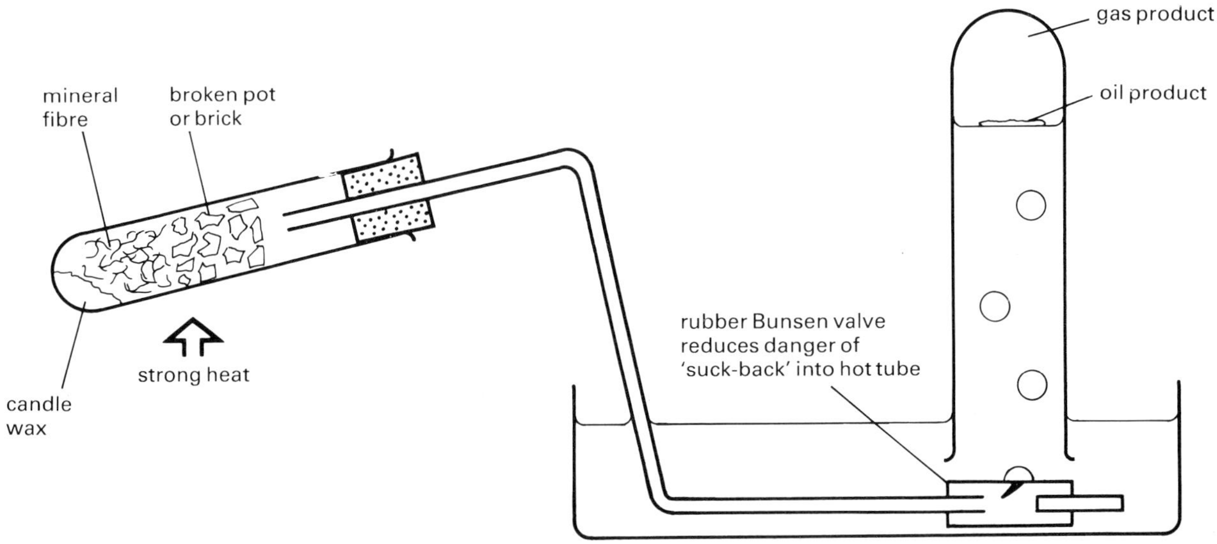

Cracking in the laboratory

Properties of gaseous hydrocarbons

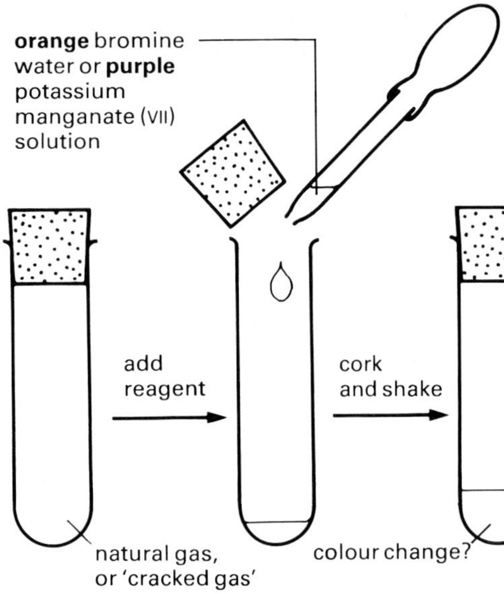

Summary of observations

Observation	*Natural gas (laboratory gas)*	*Cracked gas*
colour of gas	colourless	colourless
reaction with aqueous bromine	no reaction	solution decolourized
reaction with acidified potassium manganate (VII)	no reaction	solution decolourized

bromine water and acidified potassium manganate(VII) are *tests for unsaturation* in hydrocarbons.

- *Unsaturated hydrocarbons decolourize bromine water or potassium manganate(VII).*

It can be shown that the unsaturated hydrocarbons in cracked gas include the compounds ethene, propene and butene. These are members of the *alkene* family. Their molecules have double bonds between some carbon atoms. Two examples of alkene molecules are shown in the next figure.

ethene, C_2H_4

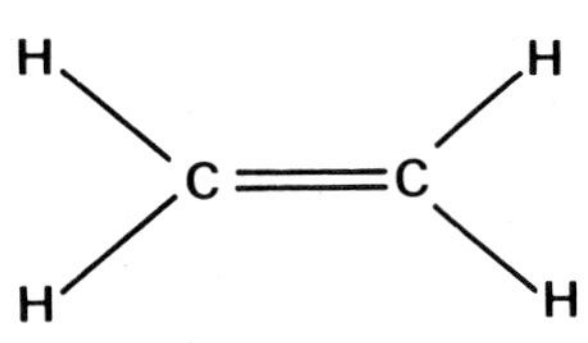

propene, C_3H_6

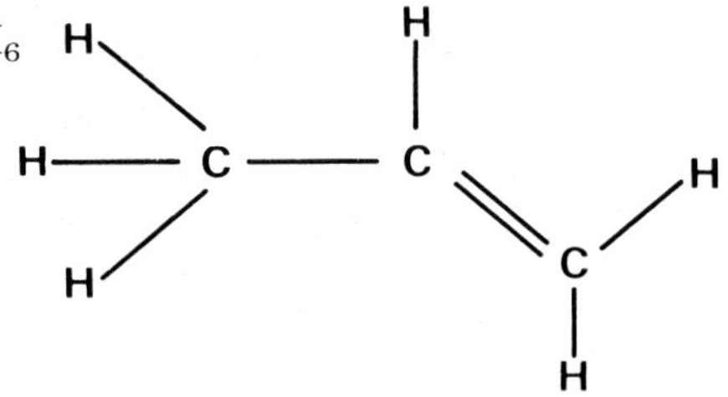

Molecular structures of alkene molecules

The general formula of alkenes

The formulas of alkenes fall into a pattern. Their molecules have twice as many hydrogen atoms as carbon atoms. So alkenes can be represented by the general formula C_nH_{2n} (n can be any whole number except 1; the compound CH_2 does not exist).

- *Alkenes are unsaturated hydrocarbons with general formula C_nH_{2n}.*

Addition reactions

The special reactivity of alkenes is caused by the double bonds in their molecules. These double bonds are *4-electron bonds* (see Unit 10).

Double bonds between carbon atoms can be broken open so that two of the electrons are used to join the carbon atoms to other atoms. This type of reaction is called an *addition reaction*.

- *Most of the special reactions of alkenes are addition reactions.*

Reaction of ethene with bromine, Br_2

Remember, the reaction with bromine is used as a test for unsaturation. It works at room temperature. The colour of the bromine disappears.

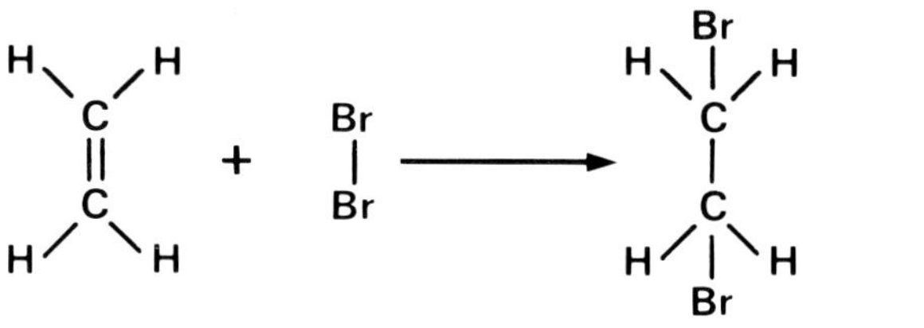

ethene 1, 2 – dibromoethane

$C_2H_4 + Br_2 \rightarrow C_2H_4Br_2$

Reaction of propene with hydrogen, H_2

This addition reaction needs a catalyst and high pressure.

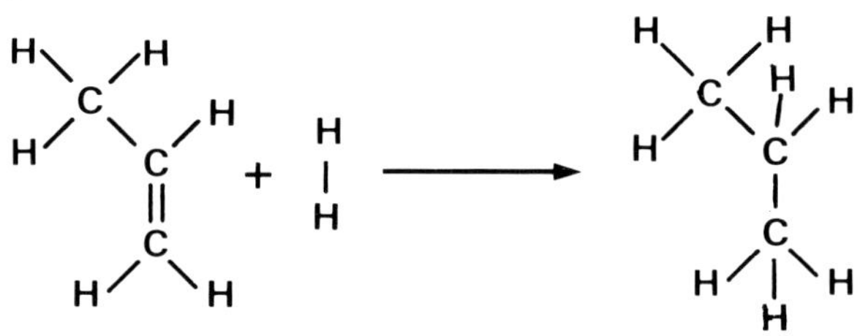

propene propane

$C_3H_6 + H_2 \rightarrow C_3H_8$

Reaction of ethene with water, H_2O

This addition reaction needs a catalyst and a high temperature.

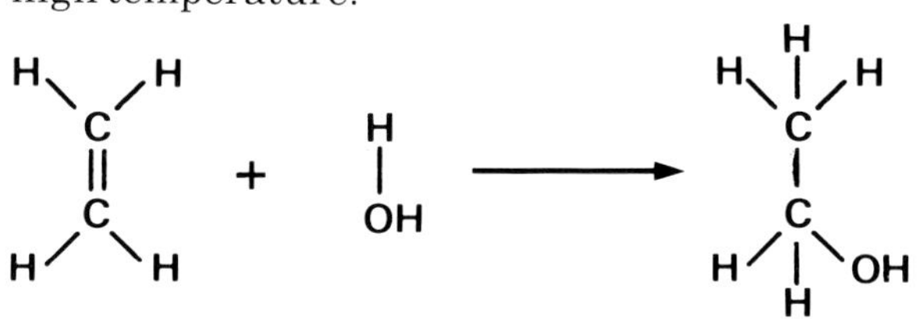

ethene ethanol

$C_2H_4 + H_2O \rightarrow C_2H_5OH$

Polymerization of ethene

This is a special kind of addition reaction called *addition polymerization*. In this type of reaction, many molecules of the same type join together to form long-chain molecules. The long-chain molecules are called *polymers*. The reactant molecules are like links in a chain. They are called *monomers*. When the monomer is ethene, the polymer is called poly(ethene) or polythene. Many polymer materials are familiar to us as *plastics* (see Extension 2).

● *Addition polymerization is the reaction of many unsaturated monomer molecules of the same kind to make a long-chain molecule.*

The number of monomer units in a polymer chain is usually very large, but it varies from one chain to the next. In the equation below, the symbol n is used to represent the number.

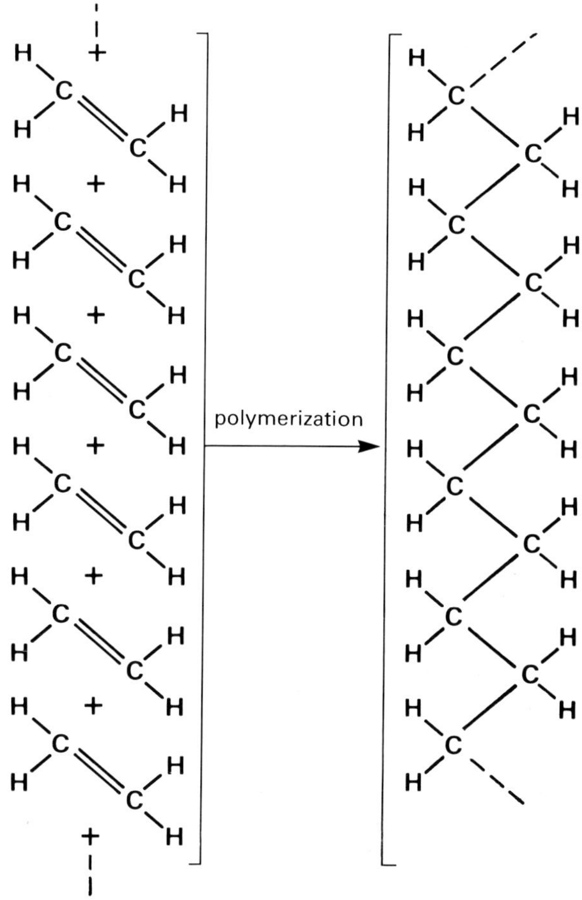

$nC_2H_4 \longrightarrow (C_2H_4)n$

Summary

1. Hydrocarbons that decolourize bromine water and acidified potassium manganate(VII) are unsaturated hydrocarbons.
2. The gas formed by cracking alkanes contains unsaturated hydrocarbons.
3. Unsaturated hydrocarbons with the general formula C_nH_{2n} are called alkenes.
4. Most of the special reactions of alkenes are addition reactions.
5. Polymerization of ethene to form polythene is an example of an addition polymerization reaction.

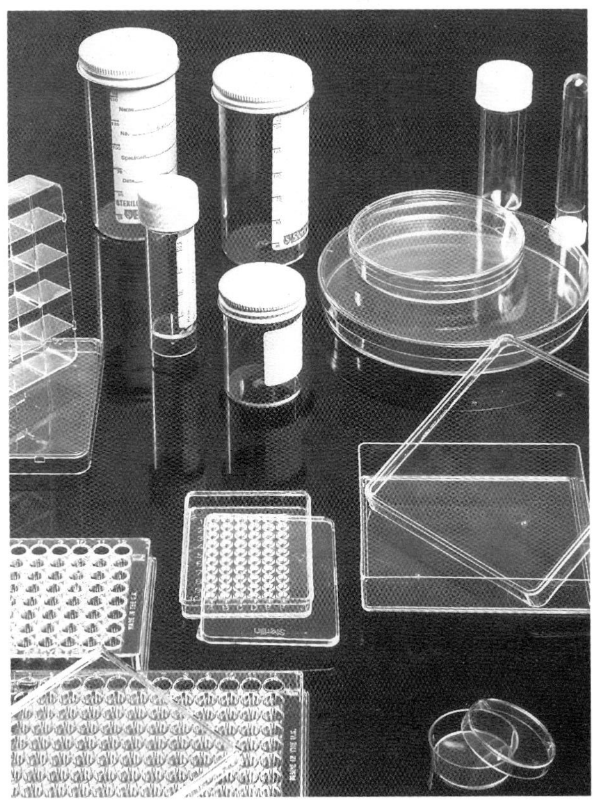

Uses of plastics: polybutene tubing for laying underground; polypropene fruit boxes; polymers used for greenhouses; expanded polystyrene packaging to keep breakable goods safe; crystal polystyrene medical ware

Extension

1. i We have learned in this Unit that ethene molecules can join together in addition polymerization reactions. The product is the polymer called poly(ethene). Poly(ethene) is useful as a *plastic*.

   You can make other plastics in similar polymerization reactions using different starting materials (monomers). Some information about common plastics made by addition polymerization is given in the first table below. Copy the table and fill in the blank spaces.

   ii The properties of different plastics vary slightly, but they usually have many properties in common. For example, most plastics are:

   a water-proof;
   b lightweight (low density);
   c easily softened or melted by heat;
   d flammable;
   e electrical resistors;
   f easily moulded;
   g flexible;
   h rot and corrosion resistant;

   Sometimes these properties give plastics advantages over other materials. Sometimes they result in disadvantages.

   The second table is about the uses of some plastics in everyday life. Copy the table and fill in the spaces.

2. **Thermosets and thermoplastics**
   One of the properties of plastics such as those mentioned in Extension 1 is that they soften when warmed. This is a useful property from the manufacturer's point of view because it means that products from these plastics can be made in two separate stages:

   Stage 1: synthesis of the plastic material, for example as powder or chips;
   Stage 2: manufacture of the plastic product by warming the powder in a mould.

   Plastics of this type are called thermosoftening plastics or (usually) *thermoplastics*.

   Some plastics behave differently from thermoplastics. Once formed, heating does not soften them. In fact, warming is often the method chosen to speed up the setting of these materials, and they are therefore

Plastics made from polymerization

Plastic (common name)	*Polymer (chemical name)*	*Monomer*
polythene	poly(ethene)	ethene
PVC	poly(chloroethene)	chloroethene
polystyrene	poly(phenylethene)	
PTFE		tetrafluoroethene
perspex		methyl–1, 2–methylpropenoate

Uses of plastics

Use	*Traditional or old-fashioned material*	*Plastic substitute*	*Advantages of plastic*	*Disadvantages of plastic*
drainpipes and gutters	cast iron	PVC	lightweight rust-free	none
spectacle lenses		perspex		easily scratched
bottles		polythene or PVC		
food wrappers and bags		polythene		
flower pots		polystyrene		

called thermosetting plastics or simply *thermosets*.

The monomer molecules for thermosetting plastics differ from those we have met so far in an important way: as well as forming chains, they can form *cross-links* between the chains. Thus, if a thermoplastic is represented as:

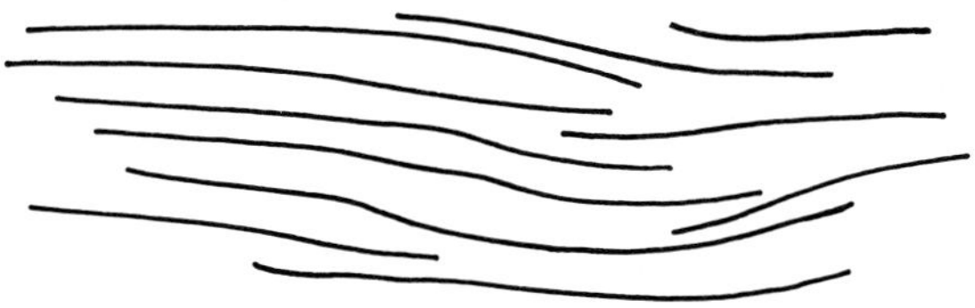

then a thermoset would be:

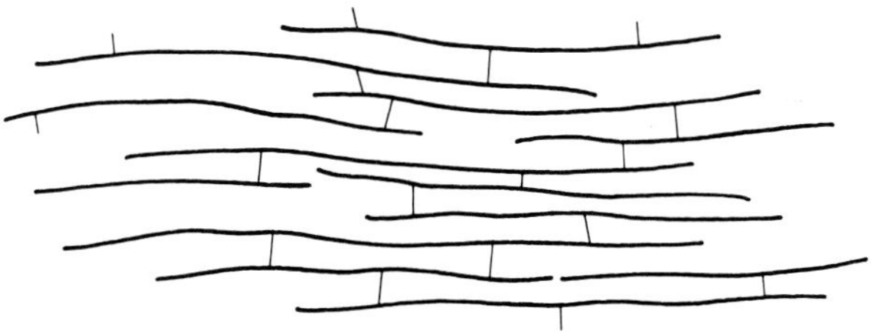

i Thermosets are used for making items such as pan handles and coffee cups. Explain why thermoplastics would not be useful for these purposes.

ii List some other uses of plastics that you think would be appropriate for thermosets rather than thermoplastics. Explain your reasons in each case.

iii Explain (in terms of their structures) why thermoplastics can be softened by warming while thermosets cannot.

3. The formula of chloroethene is C_2H_3Cl. The chloroethene molecule contains a double bond between the C atoms, similar to that in the ethene molecule.

   i Draw a structure for the chloroethene molecule.

   ii Write an equation to show the polymerization of chloroethene.

   iii Draw the structure of part of the poly(chloroethene) chain molecule.

4. Use the information included in Extensions 1 and 2 above to help you write an essay about plastics.

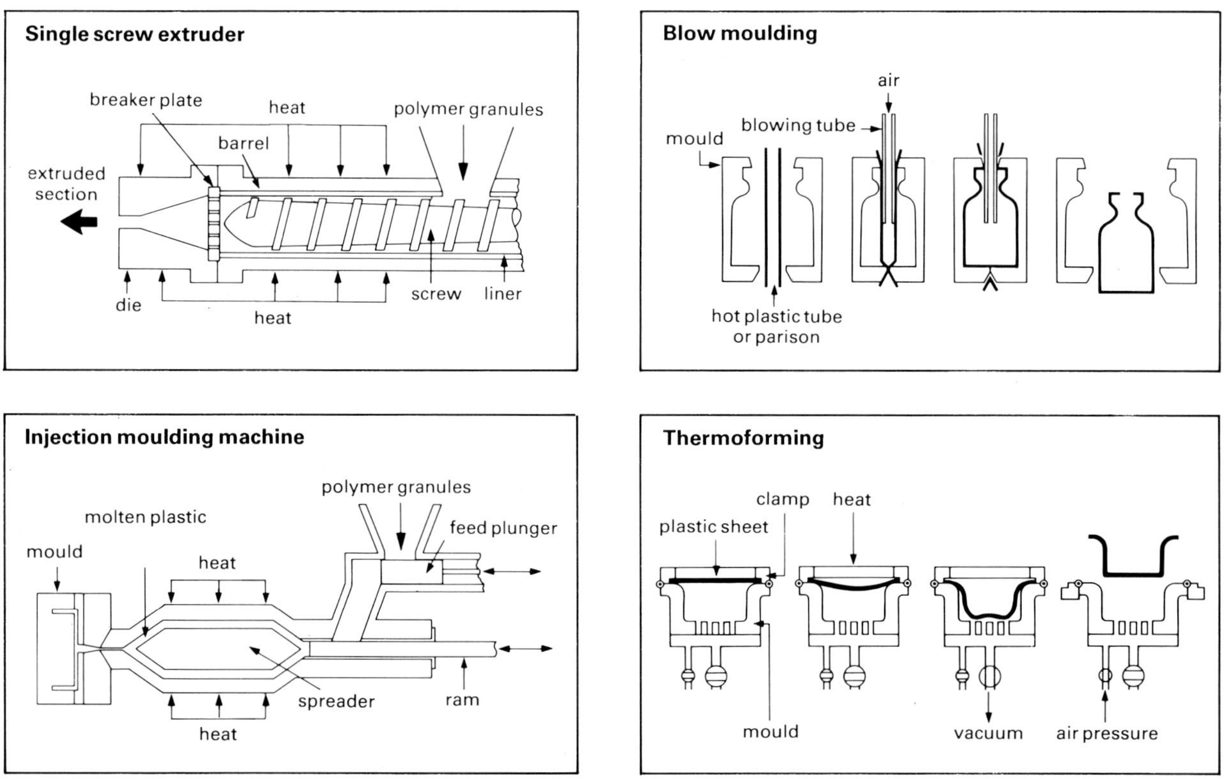

Techniques for shaping thermoplastics: extrusion; injection moulding; blow moulding; thermoforming

Revision

1. Some addition reactions are mentioned on p.161 in this Unit. They are only examples. Any unsaturated molecule can do addition reactions. Write equations to show the reaction of:
   - i bromine with propene
   - ii ethene with hydrogen
2. Carbon dioxide and water are formed when hydrocarbons burn. You can do experiments to prove it. The following diagram shows an apparatus you could use to investigate the combustion of laboratory gas.
   - i Copy the diagram and label it to show any parts that you think are missing.
   - ii How would you use the apparatus to identify carbon dioxide and water, which are produced in the flame?
   - iii What control experiment would you need to do before you could draw conclusions from the results?
3. This question is about the five gases whose properties are listed in the table below.

   Which of the gases could be:
   - i carbon dioxide
   - ii carbon monoxide
   - iii ethene
   - iv hydrogen
   - v methane

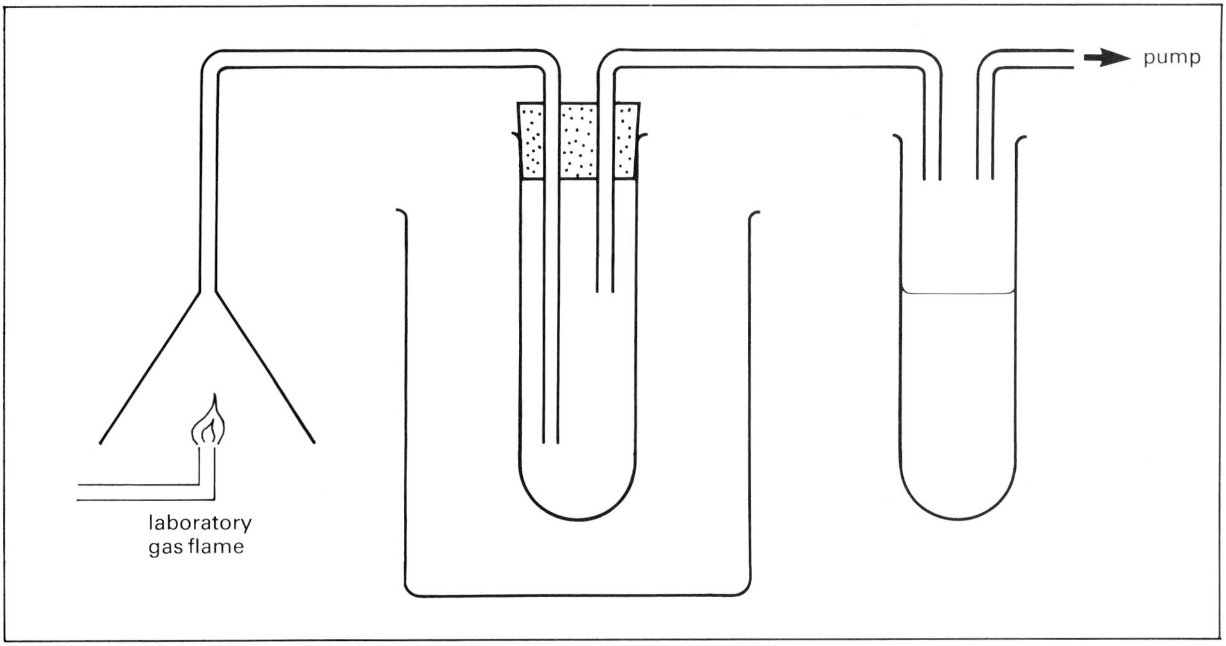

Gas	*Reaction with bromine water*	*Flammability*	*Products of combustion*
A	no reaction	flammable	water
B	no reaction	flammable	carbon dioxide
C	decolourizes bromine water	flammable	carbon dioxide and water
D	no reaction	flammable	carbon dioxide and water
E	no reaction	non-flammable	—

4. Look at the illustration on p.215. It shows the changes that happen to a hydrocarbon molecule during the reaction called *cracking*. The molecule chosen as an example to be cracked is $C_{14}H_{30}$. This is a *saturated* molecule. The products of the reaction include two *unsaturated* hydrocarbons.
   - i Explain what the term 'cracking' means.
   - ii Explain what the term 'unsaturated' means.
   - iii What family does the saturated hydrocarbon belong to?
   - iv Name the other product formed in this reaction that is not a hydrocarbon.
   - v Draw structures of the two unsaturated molecules to show their bonding, that is, use lines for covalent bonds.

5. The hydrocarbon CH_2 does not exist. If it did, it would break the *normal rules of valency*.
   - i What are the normal rules of valency for carbon and hydrogen?
   - ii How would CH_2 break these rules?

Unit 36
Ethanol

Ethanol, commonly called *alcohol*, is one of the oldest chemical products used by man. It has been manufactured by fermentation since ancient times. We still make some ethanol by fermentation today.

- *Ethanol has been made by fermentation for thousands of years.*

Fermentation

A fermentation is a chemical process that uses micro-organisms to change a raw material. The micro-organisms may be bacteria or yeasts. When ethanol is made by fermentation, the micro-organisms used are yeasts. The yeasts provide enzymes, which are catalysts for the chemical changes that happen in the fermentation process.

A variety of substances may be used as raw materials for making ethanol by fermentation, but they are usually sugars like glucose, $C_6H_{12}O_6$, or sucrose, $C_{12}H_{22}O_{11}$. (Sucrose is familiar to us as table sugar.)

When sugars are changed by the action of enzymes in yeasts, the final products are ethanol and carbon dioxide. The fermentation of glucose can be represented by an equation for the overall change, as follows:

$$C_6H_{12}O_6(aq) \rightarrow 2C_2H_5OH(aq) + 2CO_2(g)$$

- *Glucose can be converted to ethanol and carbon dioxide by the action of enzymes in yeast.*

An experiment to investigate fermentation is described on p.168.

Structure of ethanol molecules

Ethanol's formula is written C_2H_5OH (rather than C_2H_6O) because experiments have shown that its molecules contain the $-OH$ group of atoms. (Other molecules with $-OH$ groups may also belong to the alcohol family.)

The name *ethanol* suggests that ethanol is related to *ethane* and *ethene*. Investigations have shown that the three compounds have molecules with structures as shown in the next figure.

Ethene can be prepared from ethanol in the laboratory. The process is similar to the cracking of a hydrocarbon: its vapour is heated in the absence of air and the molecules decompose. The decomposition of the ethanol molecules can be called a *dehydration*, as the equation shows:

$$C_2H_5OH(g) \rightarrow C_2H_4(g) + H_2O(g)$$

(As we shall see, it is more useful to be able to do the reverse of this dehydration process.)

- *Ethanol molecules are related to molecules of ethane and ethene.*

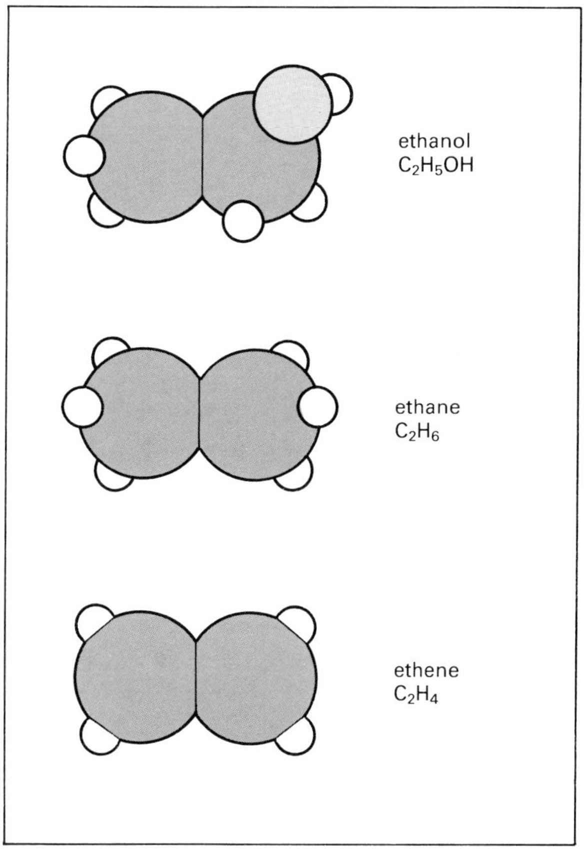

Molecules of ethanol, ethane and ethene compared

Investigating fermentation

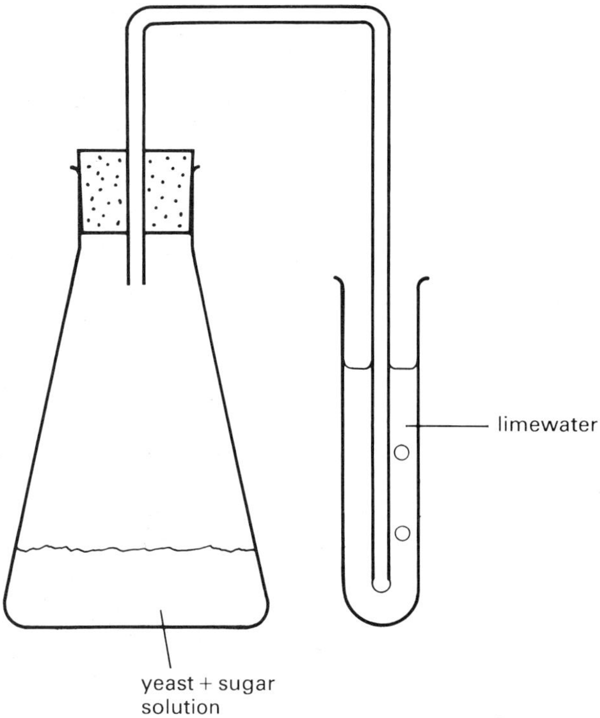

The mixture in the flask should be kept in a warm (but not hot) place for several days. Gas is formed and the limewater goes cloudy. The contents of the flask smell 'alcoholic' afterwards.

Almost pure ethanol can be obtained by distilling the contents of the flask. As the first drops are collected, the thermometer records a temperature close to the boiling temperature of ethanol (78 °C). The distillate is flammable, although the fermented mixture will not burn *before* distillation.

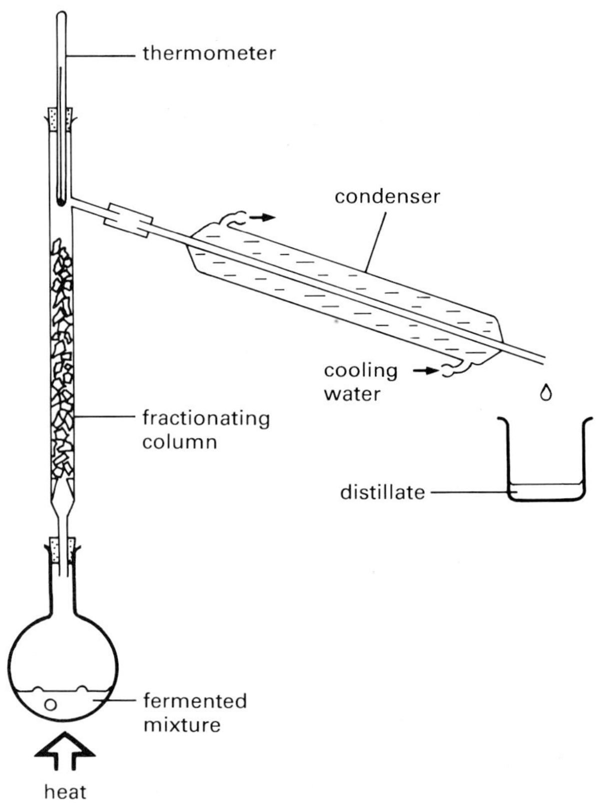

Distillation of spirit manufacture increases alcohol strength

Uses of ethanol

1. Ethanol is an important ingredient in many drinks. Alcoholic drinks vary in strength from about 10 per cent ethanol (beer, wine, cider) to 40 per cent ethanol (spirits such as whisky, brandy, gin).
2. Ethanol is a useful solvent, for example in perfume, after-shave, ink and varnish.
3. Ethanol is a raw material for making other chemicals, for example ethyl ethanoate (acetate), ethoxyethane (ether) and trichloromethane (chloroform).
4. Ethanol is used as a fuel in methylated spirits.

● *Ethanol is used in drinks, as a solvent, as a fuel and as a raw material for chemicals.*

Industrial ethanol

Alcoholic drinks are made by fermentation, and some industrial ethanol is made by fermentation, for example from molasses. However, we cannot make all the ethanol we need nowadays from carbohydrates. Most ethanol for industry uses *petroleum* as a raw material. The petrochemical ethene (obtained by cracking petroleum fractions) is converted to ethanol by reaction with steam. A catalyst (phosphoric acid) and high temperature and pressure (300 °C and 70 atmospheres) are needed.

$$C_2H_4(g) + H_2O(g) \rightarrow C_2H_5OH(g)$$

This is a *hydration* reaction and is the reverse of the dehydration reaction mentioned earlier in this Unit.

● *Industrial ethanol is manufactured by the hydration of ethene.*

Properties of ethanol

Ethanol is a colourless liquid that boils at 78 °C. It is completely miscible with water, that is, the liquids dissolve one another in all proportions. It is flammable and forms carbon dioxide and water when burned in excess oxygen:

$$C_2H_5OH(l) + 3O_2(g) \rightarrow 2CO_2(g) + 3H_2O(l)$$

Formation of ethyl ethanoate by esterification

Safety note: Concentrated sulphuric acid and glacial ethanoic acid must be used only by the teacher and with great care.

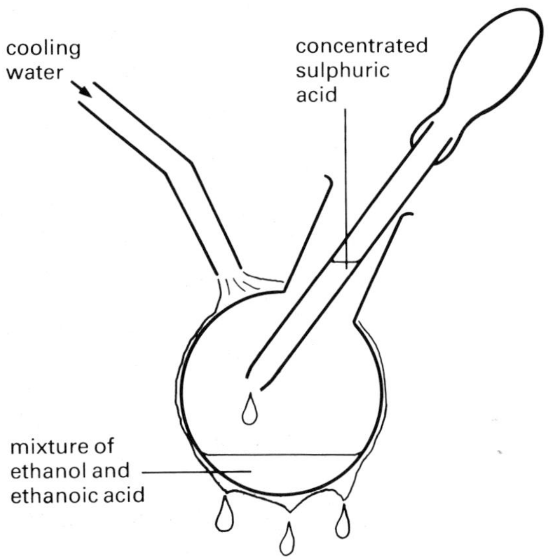

Ethanol (5 cm^3) and concentrated ('glacial') ethanoic acid (5 cm^3) are mixed in a flask. Note the smell of the mixture at this stage. Concentrated sulphuric acid (1 cm^3) is added, one drop at a time. The flask is cooled under cold water as the sulphuric acid is added.

After mixing, the mixture is warmed with a reflux condenser fitted. (A long glass tube will do.) This prevents loss of vapour and reduces the risk of fire. After warming for a few minutes, cool the mixture and remove the condenser tube. Note the smell of ethyl ethanoate.

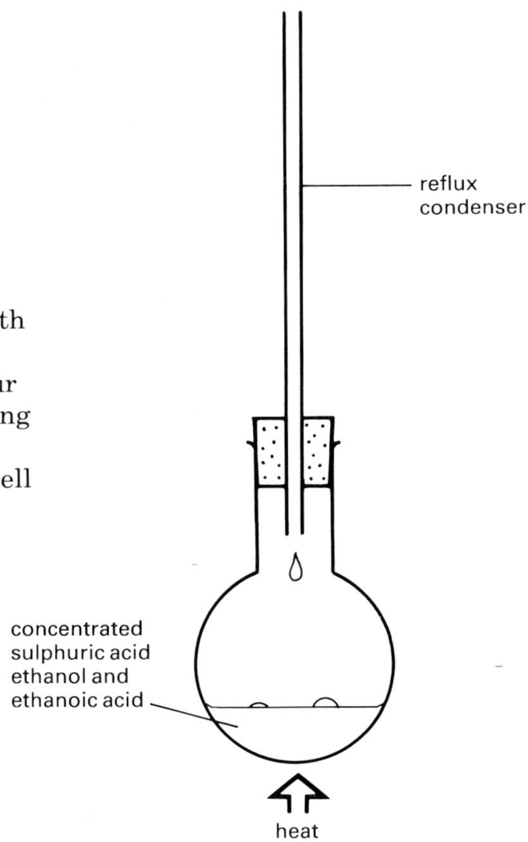

Equation $\mathbf{C_2H_5\,CO\boxed{OH + H}OC_2H_5 \rightarrow C_2H_5\,COOC_2H_5 + H_2O}$

(Concentrated sulphuric acid is a catalyst in this reaction.)

Ethanol may be oxidized by oxidizing agents such as potassium dichromate (see extension 5). It forms ethanoic acid (acetic acid, CH_3COOH). Ethanol in wine or beer may be oxidized by reaction with oxygen of the air if certain enzymes are present to catalyse the reaction; the wine or beer goes sour due to the formation of ethanoic acid.

$$\mathbf{C_2H_5OH \xrightarrow{\text{oxidation}} CH_3COOH}$$

As we have seen, ethanol can be dehydrated to form ethene, C_2H_4. Ethanol also reacts with organic acids like ethanoic acid (acetic acid) to form compounds called *esters*. The reaction of an alcohol with an acid to form an ester is called *esterification*. An esterification reaction is described in the figure on p.170.

● *Ethanol can be oxidized, and dehydrated, and will form esters.*

The ester formed when ethanol reacts with ethanoic acid is called *ethyl ethanoate*. Ethyl ethanoate is an important solvent. (Other esters have uses as food flavourings, and as raw materials for plastics.)

The sails and mast of this sailboard are made from polyester

Summary

1. Ethanol has been made by fermentation for thousands of years.
2. Ethanol molecules are related to molecules of ethane and ethene.
3. Ethanol is used in drinks, as a solvent, as a fuel and as a chemical raw material.
4. Most ethanol for industry is manufactured from ethene, a petrochemical.
5. The chemistry of ethanol can be summarized in a chart like the next figure.

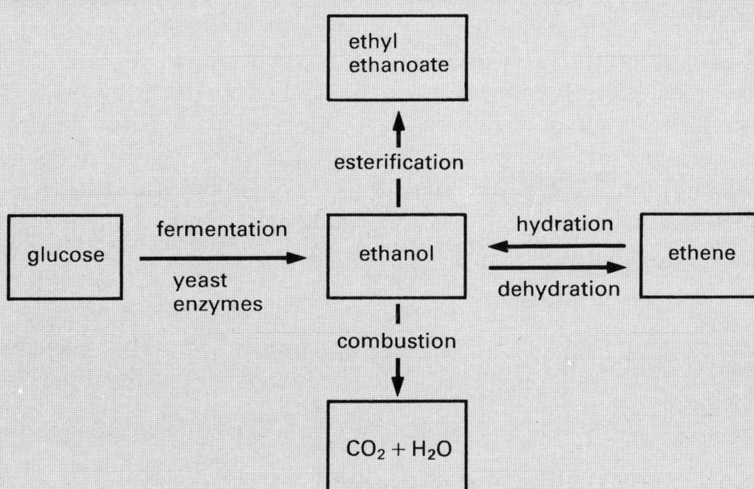

Extension

1. **Smaller and smaller molecules**
Starch can be changed, step by step, to ethene:

starch → glucose → ethanol → ethene

The molecules change from very large (polymeric starch), to large (glucose), and finally to small (ethanol and ethene). The physical properties of the substances change at the same time: starch and glucose are solids, ethanol is a liquid and ethene is a gas. This is what we have come to expect: *substances with smaller molecules are generally more volatile than substances with larger molecules.*

Illustrate this general principle by reference to:

i alkane hydrocarbons (methane, ethane, propane, butane, etc.)
ii halogen elements (fluorine, chlorine, bromine, iodine)

2. The products of fermentation (carbon dioxide and ethanol) are simply waste products as far as the yeast is concerned. The carbon dioxide can escape from the solution as bubbles of gas, but the ethanol accumulates (builds up) in the solution. The concentration of ethanol may get so high that further growth of the yeast is prevented, that is, the yeast is poisoned by its own waste products. In practice, this means that the alcohol content of wines and beers has a natural limit.

Nowadays, the alcohol content of wine, beer, etc. is usually printed on the label of the can or bottle. It is usually given as a percentage by volume. Carry out a *survey* (perhaps with other members of your class) to find out about the alcohol content of different kinds of alcoholic drink.

3. Simple alcohols have the *general formula* $C_nH_{2n+1}OH$. (For ethanol, $n = 2$.) Write the molecular formula for:

i methanol ($n = 1$)
ii propanols ($n = 3$)
iii butanols ($n = 4$)

4. **Starch, enzymes and hydrolysis**
The raw material for many fermentation processes is starch, for example from grain or potatoes. The first step in the process is to break down the molecules in starch to form glucose.

We believe that starch is a *natural polymer* with molecules consisting of chains of glucose units. The breakdown of the chains is achieved by hydrolysis, that is, reaction with water. This change is catalysed by enzymes in two stages. For example, to make beer, barley is first allowed to germinate. Starch molecules in the grain are changed to maltose (a sugar) by the action of the group of enzymes called diastase, which is found in the germinating barley. In the second stage, maltose can be converted to glucose by the yeast enzyme called maltase.

The glucose can next be converted to ethanol and carbon dioxide by another group of yeast enzymes (called zymase).

i Explain the meanings of:

a polymer
b hydrolysis
c enzyme

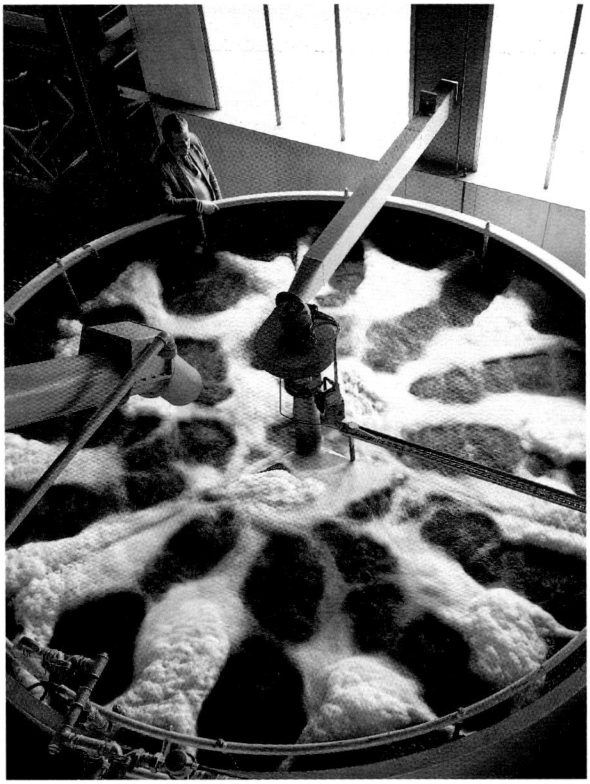

Barley germinating in a vat

ii The series of changes in the hydrolysis and fermentation processes can be summarized as follows:

$$\text{starch, }(C_6H_{10}O_5)_n \xrightarrow[\text{enzymes}]{\text{malt}} \text{maltose, } C_{12}H_{22}O_{11}$$

$$\text{maltose, } C_{12}H_{22}O_{11} \xrightarrow[\text{enzyme I}]{\text{yeast}} \text{glucose, } C_6H_{12}O_6$$

$$\text{glucose, } C_6H_{12}O_6 \xrightarrow[\text{enzyme II}]{\text{yeast}} C_2H_5OH \text{ and } CO_2$$

Name the malt enzymes and yeast enzymes I and II mentioned in the summary above.

5. **Breathalysers**

Ethanol can be oxidized by strong *oxidizing agents* (see Unit 24). One such oxidizing agent is potassium dichromate(VI), an *orange* crystalline solid. In the presence of acids such as sulphuric acid it can be reduced by ethanol vapour to form *green* chromium(III) compounds. (The ethanol is converted to colourless ethanoic acid.)

i How could the chemical changes described above be used as a way of testing the alcohol content of breath? (Briefly outline the principle of the method.)

ii Sketch a design for a 'breathalyser' instrument, based on the idea in (i) above.

Revision

1. This question is about the following equations:

A $C_2H_4 + 3O_2 \rightarrow 2CO_2 + 2H_2O$
B $C_2H_4 + H_2O \rightarrow C_2H_5OH$
C $C_2H_5OH + 3O_2 \rightarrow 2CO_2 + 3H_2O$
D $C_2H_5OH \rightarrow C_2H_4 + H_2O$
E $C_6H_{12}O_6 \rightarrow 2C_2H_5OH + 2CO_2$

Which is the equation for:

i combustion of ethanol
ii combustion of ethene
iii dehydration of ethanol
iv fermentation of glucose
v hydration of ethene

2. i What sort of chemical change is:

a a dehydration
b an esterification
c a fermentation
d a hydration
e a polymerization

ii Give an example of each of the above types of chemical change, with an equation.

3. i Draw the molecular structures of ethane and ethanol. What are the similarities and differences in their structures?

ii In what ways are the physical and chemical properties of ethane and ethanol similar? How are they different?

4. i List the physical properties of ethanol.

ii Which of ethanol's physical properties support the idea that it has a *molecular* structure?

iii Draw a 'dot and cross' picture to show the electronic structure of ethanol given the following atomic numbers: $Z(C) = 6, Z(O) = 8, Z(H) = 1$.

5. Energy is released when yeast ferments glucose solutions. The yeast cells use the energy for growth and reproduction. More advanced organisms get most of their energy from glucose by respiration. Respiration involves a more complete breakdown of the glucose and greater release of energy.

i What name is used for reactions that release energy?

ii Write an equation for the fermentation of glucose.

iii Write an equation for the respiration of glucose.

iv In what ways are fermentation and respiration different?

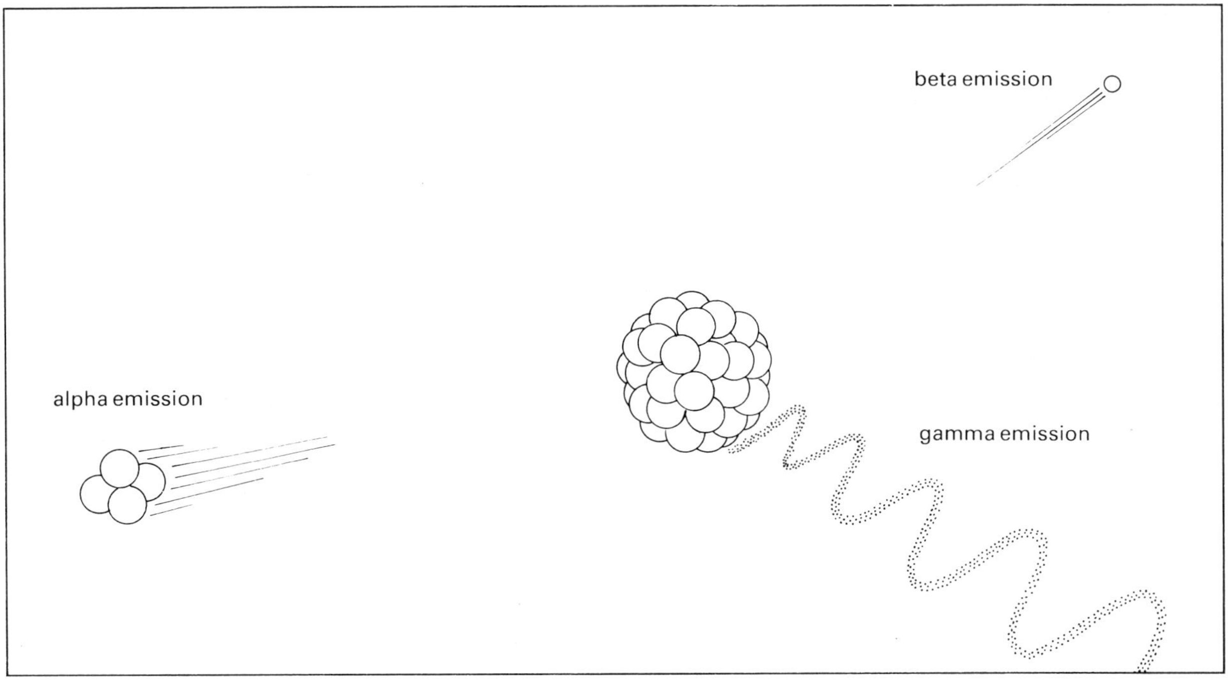

Types of emission

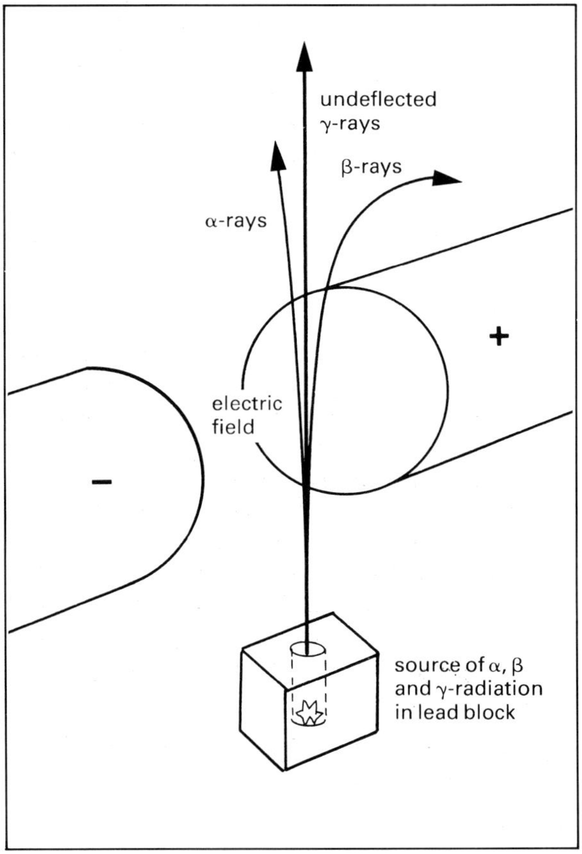

Deflection of radiation by an electric field

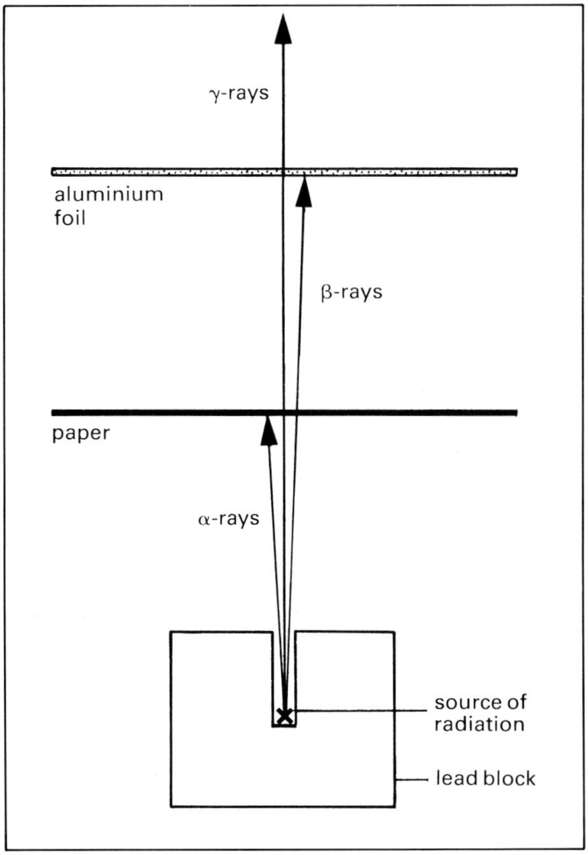

Penetrating power of radiations

Unit 37
Radioactivity

Protons, neutrons and isotopes

We have already met ideas about the atomic nucleus, protons, neutrons and isotopes. Let us refresh our memories:

Nucleus: Most of the mass of an atom is concentrated in a positively charged centre called a nucleus (see Unit 2).

Protons: The positive charge of the nucleus is carried by positively charged particles called protons. Atoms of different elements have different numbers of protons in their nuclei. The proton number of the atoms of a particular element is given by Z, its atomic number (see Units 2 and 12).

Neutrons: Neutrons are neutral particles with the same mass as protons. They are found in the nuclei of all atoms except ${}^{1}_{1}H$ (see Units 2 and 12).

Isotopes: Varieties of an element with different numbers of neutrons in the nucleus are called isotopes. Isotopes of an element have different mass numbers (A), but the same atomic number. The ${}^{A}_{Z}X$ notation is used as a shorthand for describing nuclei (see Unit 12).

Unstable nuclei

Most natural nuclei never change, that is, they are stable. However, some nuclei are unstable. They decompose, one nucleus at a time, by emitting (giving out) a ray of energy or fast-moving particle of matter. Isotopes that 'decay' like this are said to be *radioactive*.

- *A radioactive substance has atoms with unstable nuclei.*

Natural nuclei that show radioactivity include potassium-40 (${}^{40}_{19}K$), uranium-235 (${}^{235}_{92}U$) and uranium-238 (${}^{238}_{92}U$). Substances containing these natural radioactive nuclei are found in the earth and contribute to 'background radiation'. The level of background radioactivity varies from place to place.

More than one thousand kinds of artificial nuclei have also been manufactured in nuclear reactors. These include nuclei of several *new elements* that are not found in the earth, for example plutonium ($Z = 94$). All artificial nuclei are radioactive.

Types of radiation

Early experiments showed that there are three important kinds of emission from radioactive nuclei. They are called α, β and γ rays (alpha, beta and gamma rays). The properties of these radiations are summarized below and illustrated in the diagrams on the left.

α-rays

These are deflected by electrical forces (towards negative charges and away from positive charges), and they are cut off by even thin sheets of paper. Evidence like this suggests that α-rays are high-velocity particles with positive charge. We now believe that α-particles have a mass that is four times greater than the proton's mass, and have twice as much *positive* charge as protons. This leads to the conclusion that:

- *α-rays have the characteristics of high-velocity helium nuclei,* ${}^{4}_{2}He$.

β-rays

These are deflected by magnetic and electrical forces, but in the opposite direction to α-rays. They penetrate sheets of paper (and several metres of air), but are cut off by thin sheets of metal foil. We believe that β-rays are high-velocity particles with *negative* charge. The mass of the particles turns out to be very much less than the mass of α-particles. In fact, the mass of a β-particle is the same as the mass of an electron. The amount of negative charge they carry is also the same as the charge of an electron.

- *β-rays have the characteristics of high-velocity electrons.*

γ-rays

This radiation is not deflected by electrical or

magnetic fields, and it is very penetrating, for example it will penetrate lead sheet, or several kilometres of air. Evidence like this, together with other evidence, leads us to the conclusion that γ-rays are very-high-frequency forms of electromagnetic radiation (similar to X-rays) with zero mass.

● *γ-rays are high-energy forms of electromagnetic radiation.*

Biological effects of radiation

Most people have experienced sunburn at one time or another. It is a painful effect caused by exposure to strong sunlight. Clearly, the amount of damage caused by sunlight depends on the intensity of the light, and how long the exposure lasts. Unfortunately, the damage is not visible until hours afterwards. Similar factors apply to the damage caused by nuclear radiations.

Background radiation

There has always been radiation. Human beings have evolved in a radioactive environment. The rocks of the Earth themselves are radioactive. Our bodies are not damaged by the low level of background radiation. Similarly, the damaging effects of low levels of man-made radioactivity would be slight.

High levels of radiation

The effects of prolonged exposure to radiation, or exposure to intense radiation, may be dangerous.

Alpha rays are stopped by the top layer of dead skin on our bodies and are harmless if absorbed in that way. However, if an α-radiation source is swallowed or inhaled, the effects are very damaging because the radiation is very concentrated (localized). Beta rays are more penetrating, and external sources can cause internal damage to the body. Gamma rays are so penetrating that their effects are very spread out through the whole body.

In general, the effects of radiation can be divided into three types, depending on how long they take to show themselves:

1. **Immediate effects**
   Severe damage by intense radiation shows itself within hours. Cells will die, and there are effects similar to acute sunburn.
2. **Delayed effects**
   Radiation damage may result in faulty reproduction of the body's cells. This may lead to cancers. Bone marrow (blood-forming) cells are especially sensitive, and leukaemias (blood cancers) are common results of exposure to radiation.
3. **Effects on future generations**
   If our reproductive cells are affected, future generations may be damaged because of genetic changes.

● *Exposure to high levels of radiation may have damaging effects on us or on our unborn children.*

Nuclear fission

Massive nuclei (e.g. $^{235}_{92}U$) may split into two roughly equal fragments if bombarded with neutrons. This splitting is called *nuclear fission*. It is accompanied by a release of huge amounts of energy. In addition, neutrons are also released, which can cause more nuclei to split, so a *chain reaction* may result. Nuclear power stations generate energy by controlled fission of uranium or plutonium nuclei.

Chain reactions are described in Unit 45, together with the applications of nuclear energy and radioactivity (Unit 46).

● *Nuclear fission is the splitting of massive nuclei by neutron bombardment.*

Summary

1. A radioactive substance has atoms with unstable nuclei.
2. The three types of radiation that can be given out by unstable nuclei are:
   i α-rays (high-velocity helium nuclei);
   ii β-rays (high-velocity electrons);
   iii γ-rays (high-energy forms of electromagnetic radiation).
3. Exposure to radiation can cause cancers or genetic changes.
4. Nuclear fission is used to generate energy in nuclear power stations.

The discovery of radioactivity

Henri Becquerel (1852–1908): Henri, a Frenchman, discovered in 1896 that a photographic plate wrapped in black paper could be affected if left near a uranium salt. After development, the plates were 'fogged' as though they had been exposed to light. Further investigation by Becquerel led him to conclude that the uranium was giving out invisible but very penetrating radiation in a constant stream.

Pierre and Marie Curie: Marie (1867–1934) was Polish but worked in France. She and Pierre took up the investigation of radioactivity, which had been started by Becquerel. In 1899 they were able to announce the discovery of two radioactive elements, which they had extracted from the uranium ore called *pitchblende*. They named the elements *polonium* and *radium*.

Becquerel and the Curies shared the Nobel Prize for physics in 1903 for their work in this field.

Marie continued her researches alone after Pierre's death in a road accident in 1906. She was awarded a second Nobel Prize (for chemistry) in 1911. Marie Curie died of leukaemia.

Marie Curie (1867–1934) was awarded two Nobel Prizes for her researches into radioactivity

Lord Rutherford (1871–1937): Lord Rutherford was a New Zealander who worked in Montreal, Manchester and Cambridge. He showed that radiations could be divided into at least two types (α and β) according to their penetrating power and charge.

His experiments led him to develop the idea of the nuclear atom.

Lord Rutherford (1871–1937) (on the right) first suggested the idea of the atomic nucleus

Sir James Chadwick discovered the neutron

1. Read the passage about the history of the discovery of radiation and then answer the questions that follow.
   i What was remarkable about the radiation that Becquerel discovered in 1896?
   ii The Curies named one of the elements they discovered in pitchblende 'polonium'. Can you suggest why this name was chosen? What was the other element called?
   iii Marie Curie suffered from leukaemia before her death in 1934. How might this have been connected with her work?
   iv What new ideas were put forward by Lord Rutherford following his researches into radioactivity?
2. **Half-life**
   The rate of decay of a radioactive substance can be measured, for example by using a Geiger–Müller tube to 'count' the β-particles emitted. The radioactivity of a sample of radioactive substance is generally found to get less and less as time goes on (although it never disappears altogether). This is because, as time goes on, there are fewer and fewer radioactive nuclei left in the sample. A graph of the number of emissions against the time can be used to show the drop in radioactivity. Graphs for different radioactive substances are found to have the same general form, although the time-scale can vary enormously.

   To compare the rates of radioactive decay of different nuclear species, we use the idea of *half-life*. The half-life is the time taken for the count rate to drop to exactly half its initial level. For a particular nuclear species, the half-life is constant, that is, it does not matter what the initial count rate is, the time taken for the rate to reduce to one-half is the same. Some examples of half-life are given in the next table.

$^{A}_{Z}X$	$^{14}_{6}C$	$^{40}_{19}K$	$^{234}_{91}Pa$
Half-life	5570 years	1.3×10^9 years	1.18 minutes

   In an experiment, some protoactinium ($^{234}_{91}Pa$) was extracted from uranyl ethanoate solution using an organic solvent. The protoactinium solution was placed in a Geiger–Müller liquid counter. Counts for 20-second intervals were recorded as follows:

Interval (seconds)	*Mean time (seconds)*	*Count*
0–20	10	6600
30–50	40	5000
60–80	70	3900
90–110	100	3000
120–140	130	2400
150–170	160	1800
180–200	190	1400
210–230	220	1100
240–260	250	800
270–290	280	600
300–320	310	500
330–350	340	350
360–380	370	300

   Plot a graph of count (vertical axis) against mean time.

   From the graph, measure the time taken for the count to drop from:

   a 6600 to 3300
   b 4000 to 2000
   c 2000 to 1000

   and hence work out a mean value for the half-life of $^{234}_{91}Pa$.

Revision

1. This question is about the following particles and radiations:

   A α-particle *B* neutron
   C γ-ray *D* proton
   E electron

   Which of them:

   i has mass but no charge
   ii has negligible mass and no charge
   iii has mass and charge like that of a normal He nucleus
   iv has negative charge
   v has the same mass and charge as a β-particle at rest
   vi is the nucleus of ^1_1H

2. Copy the following table and fill in the gaps to show the characteristics of nuclear radiations.

	Radiation		
	α	β	γ
Approximate mass (on the scale $^1_1H = 1$*)*		0.0005	0
Charge (on the scale proton's charge = +1)	+2		
Approximate penetration in air	5 cm		

3. This question is about the three main types of nuclear radiation (α, β and γ). Which type:

   i carries negative charge
   ii has greatest mass
   iii is most penetrating
   iv is least penetrating
   v is undeflected by magnetic fields

SECTION III
CHEMISTRY IN INDUSTRY

In some countries salt is obtained by evaporation of sea water

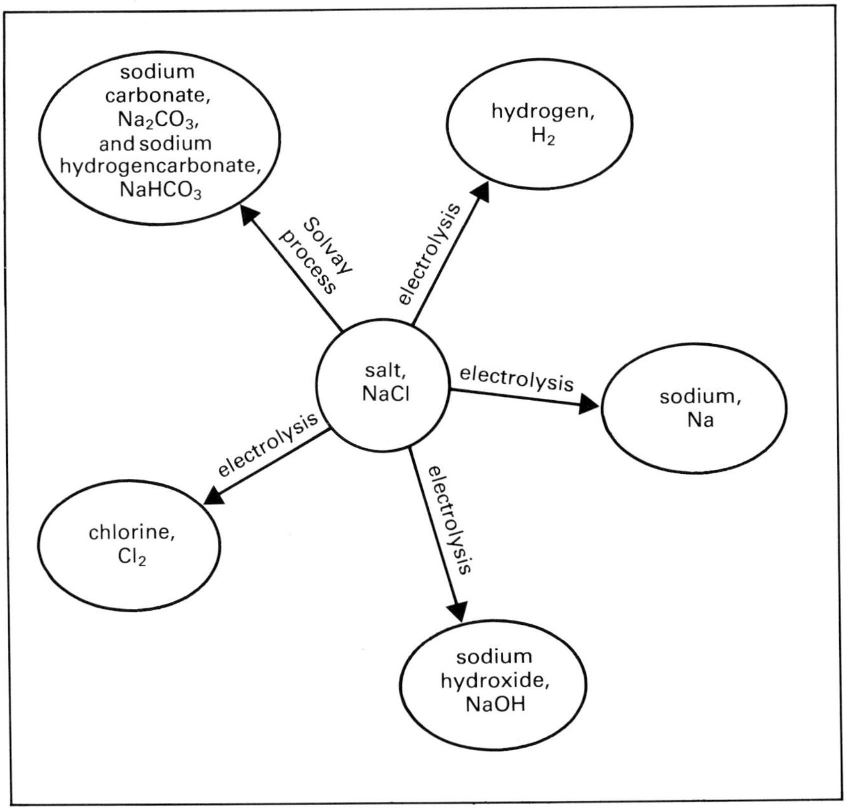

Chemicals from salt

Unit 38
Salt as a raw material

Common salt (sodium chloride) is familiar to all of us because of its use for cooking and on the dinner table. However, salt has a much greater value as a raw material for chemical products. In this Unit we shall be looking at the main processes and products associated with salt.

Where do we get salt?

Sea water contains immense amounts of various salts. The main product formed when sea water is evaporated is sodium chloride, common salt. In sunny parts of the world, salt supplies are obtained by evaporation of sea water.

In ancient Britain, salt was obtained by evaporation of water from salt springs. Iron Age people in Lincolnshire, and the Romans in Cheshire, got salt like this by heating salty water over fire.

However, we have large reserves of underground *rock salt* in Britain. This was deposited about 200 million years ago by evaporation of inland seas, long before the British Isles were formed. In places the deposits of salt are hundreds of metres thick.

Mining of rock salt started in the 17th century. Later, mine workings filled with water and underground reservoirs of *brine* (salt-water) were formed. This led to the method of pumping brine to the surface instead of going underground to dig out the rock salt. The brine was then evaporated by heating the water. During this century, evaporation under reduced pressure has been used.

In places like Cheshire, where salt works were common, subsidence and land collapse used to be a serious problem. Nowadays, replacement water is pumped underground to prevent this happening.

● *In Britain, salt for industry is obtained by evaporation of brine from underground salt deposits.*

In recent times, rock-salt mining has been taken up again on a large scale. The crude rock salt is used for treatment of ice on roads in winter.

Properties of salt

Salt is soluble in water and crystallizes to form cubic crystals. The freezing temperature of aqueous solutions of salt is lower than that of water. (So, salt added to ice or snow causes it to melt even on very cold days.) Aqueous solutions of salt and molten salt conduct electricity, that is, salt is an electrolyte. This property of salt in general is explained by the ionic theory. The structure of sodium chloride, Na^+Cl^-, is illustrated on p. 28.

When molten sodium chloride or concentrated NaCl(aq) is electrolysed, chlorine is formed at the anode. The product at the cathode depends on the conditions: molten sodium chloride produces sodium at the cathode, but aqueous solutions under ordinary conditions produce hydrogen at the cathode. However, sodium may be formed in the electrolysis of NaCl(aq) if a *mercury cathode* is used (see Extensions).

● *Salt is an electrolyte and is composed of Na^+ and Cl^- ions.*

Industrial uses of salt

Most of the salt needed by the chemical industry is used in electrolysis processes. Products from these processes include *sodium hydroxide*, *hydrogen*, *chlorine* and *sodium*. Two important industrial electrolysis processes are described below.

A lot of salt is also required for the manufacture of sodium carbonate (and sodium hydrogencarbonate) in the *ammonia-soda process*. The ammonia-soda process is also called the *Solvay process*.

The products obtained from salt in the electrolysis processes and the Solvay process are summarized in the chart on p. 182.

Electrolysis processes

1. Molten sodium chloride is electrolysed industrially in a specially designed cell called a Downs cell. Molten sodium is produced at a steel cathode:

$$Na^+(l) + e^- \rightarrow Na(l)$$

Chlorine is formed at a carbon anode:

$$2Cl^-(l) \rightarrow Cl_2(g) + 2e^-$$

● *Sodium and chlorine are formed by the electrolysis of molten sodium chloride.*

2. Aqueous sodium chloride normally produces chlorine at the anode and hydrogen at the cathode when it is electrolysed in concentrated solution, for example with carbon electrodes. The anode reaction is the same as that for molten NaCl (above). At the cathode, H^+ ions (from H_2O) are discharged in preference to Na^+ ions (see p. 107).

$$2H^+(aq) + 2e^- \rightarrow H_2(g)$$

The solution in the cathode region becomes concentrated with two kinds of ion:

i $Na^+(aq)$ (these positive ions migrate to the cathode);

ii $OH^-(aq)$ ions (these result from H_2O when H^+ is discharged).

Thus, the NaCl(aq) solution gradually becomes NaOH(aq).

● *Hydrogen, chlorine and aqueous sodium hydroxide are produced by the electrolysis of concentrated aqueous sodium chloride.*

There are two serious problems to be overcome before this apparently simple process can be operated on an industrial scale. Firstly, chlorine reacts with sodium hydroxide solutions to produce chlorates, NaClO and $NaClO_3$. Secondly, hydrogen and chlorine gas form an explosive mixture when they meet. Industrial electrolysis cells have been specially designed to avoid these difficulties. These include *diaphragm cells*, *membrane cells* and *mercury cells* (see Extensions).

The ammonia-soda process

This process was first operated successfully by Ernest Solvay in Belgium in 1864. The firm ICI are manufacturing sodium carbonate by essentially the same process in Cheshire to this day.

The main raw materials are *limestone*, *salt* and *ammonia*. There are several chemical steps in the process, which is complicated. A flow diagram for the process is given below. The overall change is:

$$2NaCl + CaCO_3 \rightarrow CaCl_2 + Na_2CO_3$$

(It is worth pointing out that there is no reaction if sodium chloride and calcium carbonate are simply mixed together in the laboratory. See also Unit 39.)

● *In the ammonia-soda process, sodium carbonate ('soda') is manufactured using sodium chloride as a raw material.*

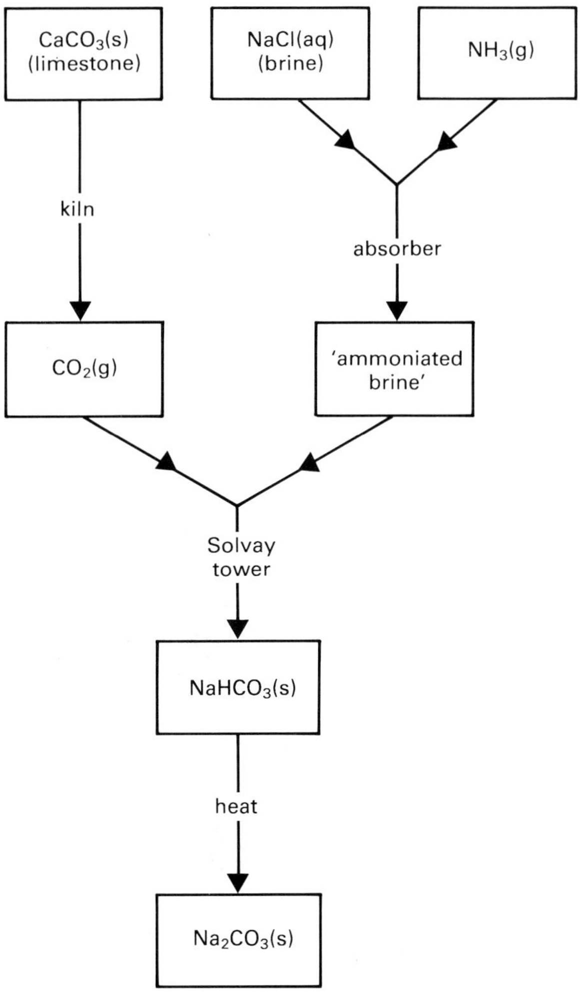

A simplified flow diagram for the ammonia-soda process

Uses of salt products

We have seen how salt is the basis for manufacturing sodium hydroxide, chlorine, sodium carbonate, sodium and hydrogen. How are these chemicals useful to us?

Uses of sodium hydroxide

The largest single use of sodium hydroxide is for the manufacture of rayon, a fibre made from cellulose. It is also required for the manufacture of paper and soap. Pure alumina (aluminium oxide), which is used for aluminium manufacture, is obtained from bauxite by a precipitation process involving the use of sodium hydroxide. In general, whenever a manufacturing process needs an alkali for neutralization or synthesis, sodium hydroxide is used.

Uses of chlorine

Chlorine is used in the manufacture of organic chlorine compounds. The most important of these is chloroethene ('vinyl chloride'), which is the monomer for PVC plastics. Other organic chlorine compounds have uses as refrigerants, pesticides, aerosol propellants and solvents. Chloromethane and chloroethane are used in the manufacture of petrol additives.

Chlorine is used in the sterilization of water at water treatment plants, and in swimming pools. Chlorine is also used as a bleach, for example in paper manufacture.

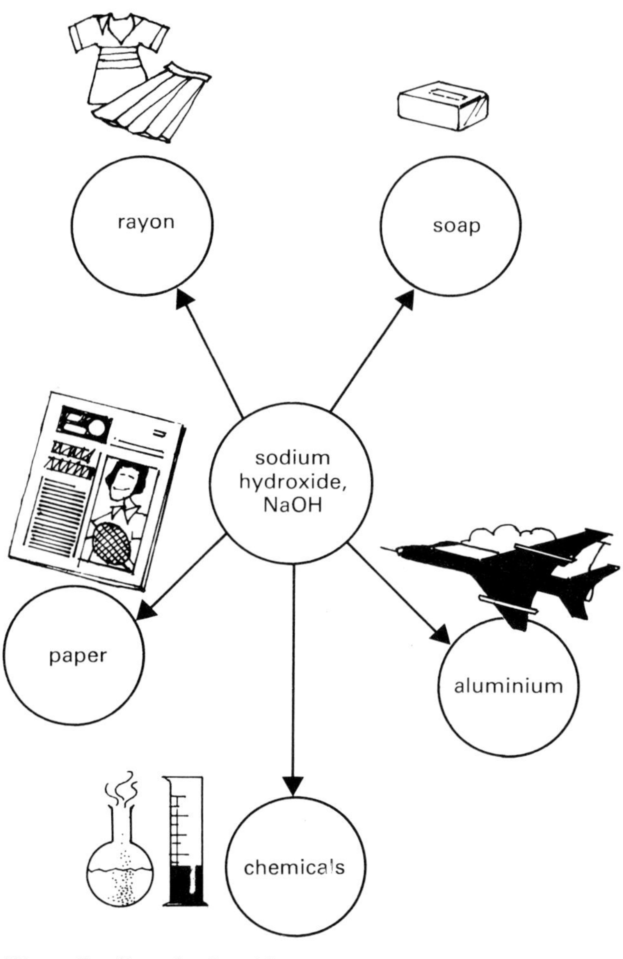

Uses of sodium hydroxide

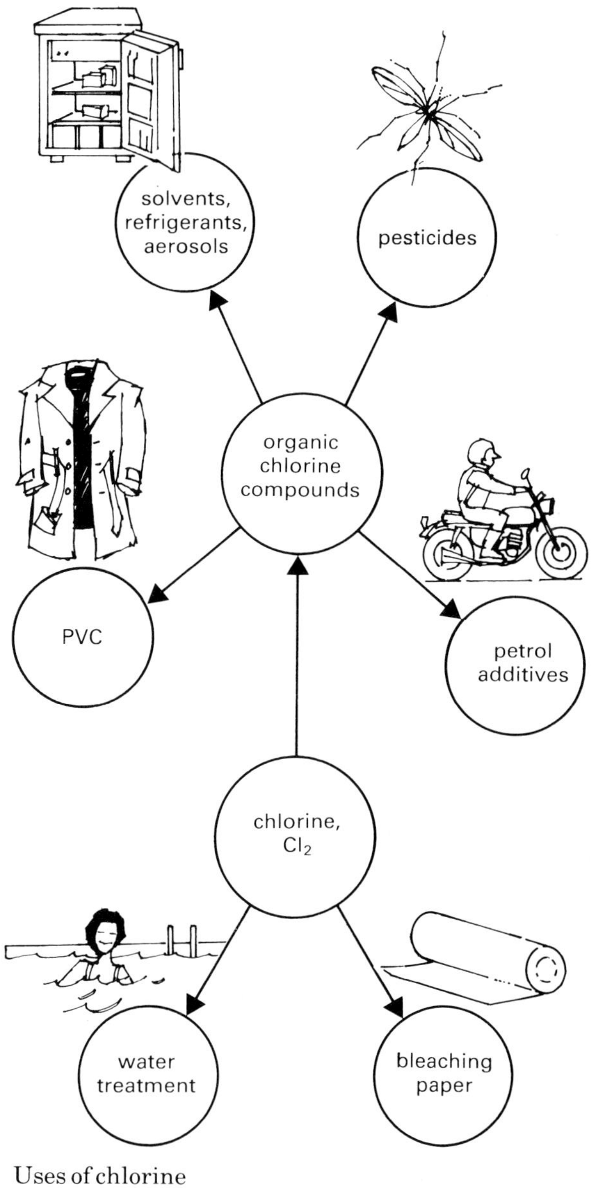

Uses of chlorine

Uses of hydrogen

Hydrogen is burned in chlorine to produce pure hydrogen chloride for hydrochloric acid. It is also used as a reducing agent, for example in the manufacture of a nylon monomer from benzene. Hydrogen gas (in cylinders) is also used for welding.

Uses of sodium

Liquid sodium is used as a coolant (i.e. for heat transfer) in some nuclear reactors (see Fast reactors, Unit 45, p. 231). Sodium is also used as a reducing agent, for example in the manufacture of titanium metal.

$$TiCl_4 + 4Na \rightarrow 4NaCl + Ti$$

(Titanium is used in the manufacture of certain alloy steels.)

Uses of sodium carbonate

More than half of all the sodium carbonate manufactured in the Solvay process is used in the glass industry. The rest is used in a very wide range of chemical processes, for example in the textile, dye and food industries.

Uses of sodium hydrogencarbonate

The main uses of sodium hydrogencarbonate ('bicarb') are in the food trade, for example baking powder, antacids and self-raising flour. Each of these uses depends on the release of CO_2 from $NaHCO_3$ by the effect of acid or heat.

Uses of hydrogen, sodium, sodium carbonate and sodium hydrogencarbonate are summarized in the next table.

hydrogen	hydrochloric acid manufacture; manufacture of nylon monomer; welding
sodium	coolant in fast reactors; titanium manufacture
sodium carbonate	glass manufacture; textile, dye and food industries
sodium hydrogencarbonate	baking powder, antacids; self-raising flour.

Uses of hydrogen, sodium, sodium carbonate and sodium hydrogencarbonate

Summary

1. The salt industry in Britain uses brine from underground salt deposits as a raw material.
2. Salt is an electrolyte and is composed of Na^+ and Cl^- ions.
3. Chemical products from salt are manufactured by electrolysis and by the ammonia–soda (Solvay) process.
4. Electrolysis of molten sodium chloride produces sodium and chlorine.
5. Electrolysis of aqueous sodium chloride produces hydrogen, chlorine and sodium hydroxide.
6. Salt is a raw material for sodium carbonate ('soda') in the ammonia–soda process.
7. Chemicals from salt are used in the manufacture of many important products, for example rayon, PVC, paper and glass.

Extension

1. Electrolysis of salt solution (brine) may be carried out on an industrial scale in *diaphragm cells*. A diagrammatic diaphragm cell is shown on p. 187.

   i What gas would be collected at A?
   ii Write an equation to show the formation of gas A at the cathode.
   iii Write an equation to show the formation of gas B at the anode.
   iv Why is it important to keep gases A and B apart?
   v The diaphragm separates gas B (anode region) from NaOH(aq) (cathode region). Why is this necessary?
   vi The 'caustic liquor' that is removed from the cathode region contains unused sodium chloride as well as sodium hydroxide. How would you attempt to separate the two solutes?

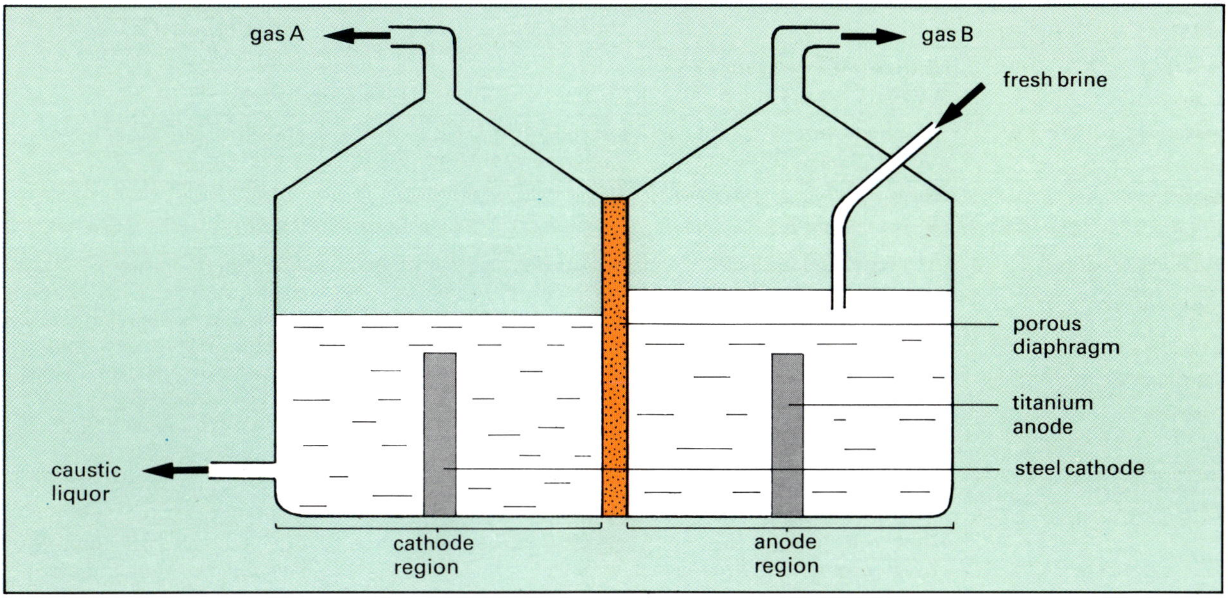

A diaphragm cell

2. The *mercury cell* has a mercury cathode. The mercury constantly flows through the cell.

   Mercury is used because sodium ions are discharged instead of hydrogen ions at a mercury cathode. (Normally, sodium would not be the expected product at the cathode in the electrolysis of aqueous sodium salts.)

   The sodium formed dissolves in the cathode to form an *amalgam* (mercury alloy). The amalgam that leaves the cell is treated with water, and hydrogen is formed in the reaction. The mercury that remains is used again in the electrolysis cell.

   i Name the gas A formed at the anode in the mercury cell.

   ii Write an equation to show the discharge of sodium ions at the cathode.

   iii When the sodium amalgam is reacted with water, what products are formed?

   iv Write an equation to show the reaction of sodium with water.

   v How does the use of a mercury cathode get round the difficulties involved in producing hydrogen and chlorine in a single process?

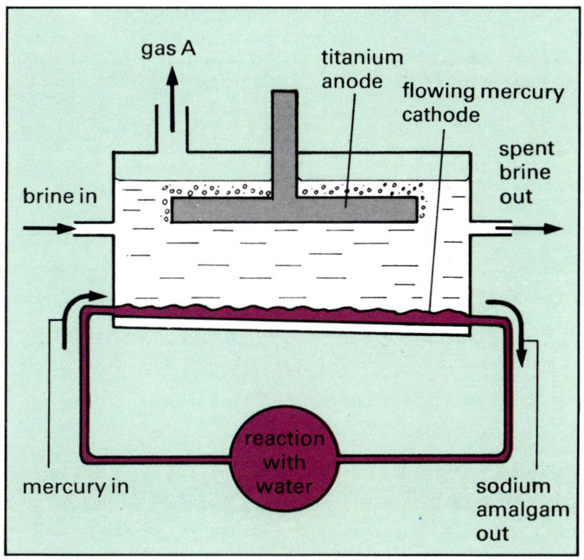

A mercury cell

3. Modern *membrane cells* are similar to diaphragm cells except that the porous diaphragm is replaced by an *ion exchange* membrane. The membrane allows cations to pass through, but not anions, that is, it is permeable to cations. (The material of the membrane is a polymeric fluorinated hydrocarbon with anionic groups substituted into the chain molecule. These groups repel OH^- and Cl^-, but allow Na^+ to enter the membrane.)

   If present trends continue, membrane cells will eventually replace other types of cell used in the chloro-alkali industry.

   Examine the table on p. 188 comparing the three types of cell.

	Mercury cells	*Diaphragm cells*	*Membrane cells*
Capital costs	High, mainly because of expensive mercury.	Less expensive.	
Maintenance costs	No membranes or diaphragms to replace.	Diaphragms need frequent replacement.	Membranes last for 2 or 3 years.
Energy costs (1) electricity	Higher voltage, therefore more expensive.	Less expensive.	
Energy costs (2) heat	Concentrated caustic liquor is produced, which does not need evaporation, so no heating needed.	Steam heating required to concentrate the caustic liquor (to crystallize the unwanted NaCl); high heating cost.	The NaOH is not contaminated with NaCl, so no crystallization is needed. However some concentration of the liquor is needed before sale to reduce transport costs; low heating cost.
Operating difficulties	Mercury is a health hazard and must not be allowed to pollute the environment. All wastes must be purified as much as possible. (However, mercury is 'lost' at the rate of a few grams per tonne of product formed.)	Constant current needed (other cells work at varying currents).	High purity brine is needed (e.g. low Ca^{2+} or Mg^{2+} concentrations) because of the nature of the ion exchange membrane.
Product purity	High purity NaOH is produced. (The NaOH formed from the amalgam does not come into contact with NaCl.)	Low purity NaOH is produced: NaOH is contaminated by NaCl that seeps through the porous membrane.	High purity NaOH is produced. (The ion exchange membrane prevents passage of chloride ions into the cathode region.)

i Write an account comparing the mercury and diaphragm cell processes from the point of view of *economics*, pointing out the advantages and disadvantages of the two processes.

ii Use the information given in the table to help you explain why the membrane cells are likely to replace other types of cells in the future.

Revision

1. This question is about the following uses of chemical products obtained from salt:

   A glass making
   B PVC manufacture
   C rayon manufacture
   D titanium manufacture
   E welding

   Which use requires:

   i chlorine
   ii hydrogen
   iii sodium
   iv sodium carbonate
   v sodium hydroxide

2. Chemicals obtained from salt are involved in the manufacture of the following products:

   a aluminium;
   b pesticides;
   c glass.

   For each of the above manufactured products:

   i name the chemical involved that is obtained from salt
   ii state how the chemical is made from salt
   iii mention the part it plays in the manufacturing process

3. Write a short essay under the heading 'Salt, a useful chemical'.
4. Aqueous sodium chloride was electrolysed in a laboratory experiment. Platinum electrodes were used and a gas was collected at each of them.
   i Draw and label a suitable electrolysis cell and show how the gases could be collected.
   ii Name the gas that was collected at the cathode and state how it could be tested to confirm its identity.
   iii The gas collected at the anode had bleaching properties. Name the gas and state one other property you would expect it to have.
   iv The solution was found to be alkaline at the end of the experiment. Explain.
   v The experiment was repeated using a much more dilute salt solution and a different gas was collected at the anode. What would you expect this gas to be?

Silicon is the major element in igneous rocks . . .

. . . and in sedimentary rocks such as clay

Quartz

Granite

Unit 39
Silicon, sand and limestone

Silicon in the Earth's crust

It is calculated that about a quarter (28 per cent) of the mass of the Earth's crust is silicon. The crust is mainly made of *igneous rocks* such as granite and basalt, and silicon is the major element in most of them. Silicon is also the main component in many *sedimentary rocks* such as sandstone and clay. Of all the elements, only oxygen is more abundant in minerals.

- *Next to oxygen, silicon is the major constituent of minerals in the Earth's crust.*

Silicon and oxygen

It is not surprising, in view of the fact that together they make up three-quarters of the mass of the crust, that silicon and oxygen are by far the most frequent partners in minerals. Si is directly combined with O in all its minerals. Three examples are given in the next table.

Some minerals containing Si and O

Name of mineral	*Sources of the mineral (rocks)*	*Formula of mineral*
quartz	granites, sandstones	SiO_2
orthoclase	granites	$KAlSi_3O_8$
kaolinite	clays	$Al_2Si_2O_5(OH)_4$

Note: Orthoclase belongs to the felspar group of minerals.

It is estimated that 60 per cent of the Earth's crust is composed of these minerals.

Extraction of silicon

Very pure silicon is needed for microchips, which are used in computer hardware. How is it obtained?

Silicon is extracted from silicon(IV) oxide (silica) by reduction with carbon at a high temperature in an electric furnace.

$$\mathbf{SiO_2(s) + 2C(s) \rightarrow 2CO(g) + Si(s)}$$

This reaction is feasible at temperatures above 1500 °C.

Purification processes involve:

a formation of a volatile halide, for example $SiCl_4$, by reaction of Si with chlorine;
b distillation of the halide to separate it from impurities;
c thermal decomposition (or reduction) of the halide to reform pure silicon;
d finally, super-pure silicon can be made by the process known as zone refining.

- *Silicon is extracted from silica by high-temperature reduction with carbon.*

Physical properties of silicon

Silicon is in period 3 and group IV of the periodic table.

We have compared it with other members of period 3 before (see Unit 15.) From the point of view of its physical properties, Si was seen to occupy a position part-way between the metals and non-metals in the period. How does it compare with carbon in group IV?

The comparison between Si and C is complicated by the fact that carbon shows allotropy. If you look at the table of physical properties given, you will see that Si bears some resemblance to both the carbon allotropes; for

	III	IV	V	VI	VII	0
						He
period 2	B	C	N	O	F	Ne
period 3	Al	Si	P	S	Cl	Ar
period 4	Ga	Ge	As	Se	Br	Kr
period 5	In	Sn	Sb	Te	I	Xe
period 6	Tl	Pb	Bi	Po	At	Rn

Silicon in the periodic table

example, all three solids are involatile, which indicates that they have giant structures. However, in some respects silicon shows a greater resemblance to the graphite allotrope than it does to the diamond allotrope. For example, silicon and graphite have similar density and colour, and both are electrical conductors, although silicon is a very weak conductor (see Semiconductors, below). However, silicon is hard, whereas graphite is soft. Although not as hard as diamond, silicon has a similar structure to diamond (see Diamond structure, Unit 5).

The next table compares the physical properties of silicon, graphite and diamond.

<table>
<tr><th></th><th>Si</th><th>C(graphite)</th><th>C(diamond)</th></tr>
<tr><td>Density
kg m⁻³</td><td>2330</td><td>2300</td><td>3500</td></tr>
<tr><td>T_m (°C)</td><td>1410</td><td colspan="2" rowspan="2">Sublimes above 3500</td></tr>
<tr><td>T_b (°C)</td><td>2700</td></tr>
<tr><td>Colour</td><td>grey-black</td><td>black</td><td>colourless</td></tr>
<tr><td>Electrical conductivity</td><td>weak</td><td>moderate</td><td>nil</td></tr>
<tr><td>Hardness</td><td>hard</td><td>soft</td><td>very hard</td></tr>
</table>

Physical properties of silicon, graphite and diamond

● *From the point of view of physical properties, silicon has properties part-way between those of metals and non-metals. It has some characteristics of both graphite and diamond.*

Semiconductors

The majority of elements are metals and show metallic conduction, that is, they have good electrical conductivity, which *decreases* as the temperature rises. Most non-metals are insulators, that is, they have electrical conductivities that are practically zero at all temperatures. Some of the elements fall into neither of these categories: they are weak conductors whose conductivity *increases* as they get hotter. These elements are called *semiconductors*; they include silicon (Si), germanium (Ge) and selenium (Se). (In the periodic table these elements are located near the diagonal division between metals and non-metals.) The computer revolution that is taking place in our society is based on the semiconducting properties of silicon.

● *Silicon's most important property is semiconductivity.*

Silicon microchips

Microchips are very thin rectangles of silicon measuring a few millimetres. They are manufactured from large, cylindrical *single crystals* of pure silicon. The crystals are sliced very thinly, and each slice produces a disc 10–20 cm in diameter, called a 'wafer'. Each wafer is then given a surface coating of light-sensitive material that hardens on exposure to ultraviolet (UV) light. Hundreds of copies of tiny microcircuits are printed onto the surface of the disc by using UV light and a 'negative'. Then chemical etching (dissolving) is used to remove a layer of the silicon that has not been affected (i.e. printed on). When the printing process is complete, the disc is broken up into separate chips, and each chip is joined to electrical connectors and sealed in plastic.

● *Microchips are manufactured by etching microscopic circuits onto crystalline silicon wafers.*

Silicon in silicones

Silicones are a useful group of silicon compounds. They are greasy, oily or rubbery materials with good electrical resistance and thermal stability. They are used as water-proofing agents, as non-stick linings for pans, as greases, and in oil–paint mixtures.

Silicones are *polymeric* materials with chain structures that should remind you of poly(ethene) (see Unit 35). Unlike poly(ethene), however, the 'back-bone' of a silicone molecule consists of alternate O and Si atoms, not C atoms. In a sense, silicones are artificial (synthetic) equivalents of materials such as asbestos (see p. 195). Part of the structure is shown in the next figure.

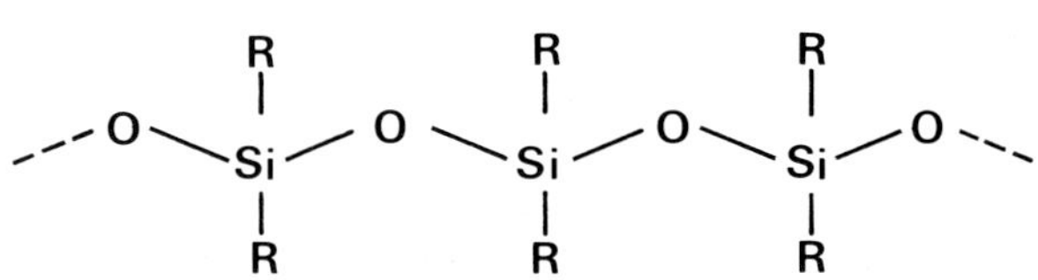

Part of the structure of a silicone molecule

A silicon chip: the microcircuits are etched onto the surface

To a certain extent, the silicone molecules also have the properties of hydrocarbons: the R-groups shown in the silicone structure are groups of atoms derived from alkane hydrocarbon molecules. For example, the R-group CH_3 is derived from methane, CH_4, and the R-group C_2H_5 is derived from ethane, C_2H_6. (Note: groups such as these derived from alkane molecules are called *alkyl groups*.) In some ways, silicone molecules resemble those of hydrocarbon oils.

- *Silicones are synthetic materials that have been engineered to combine heat-resistant properties with lubricating and water repellent properties.*

Silica, SiO_2

As we have seen, *silica* (silicon(IV) oxide) is one of the most abundant substances on Earth, being a major constituent of sand, sandstone and many igneous rocks. It is a practically insoluble material with a high melting temperature (1710 °C), and the properties of a non-electrolyte. Thus it has a giant structure with covalent bonding. Studies have shown that its structure resembles that of diamond (see Unit 5). Imagine the infinite pattern of tetrahedrally arranged C atoms replaced by a similar pattern of Si atoms with one O atom

Silicones are used in tyre manufacture to coat the inside of the tyre mould; they act as a non-stick surface to allow the tyre to be removed from the mould once it has been formed

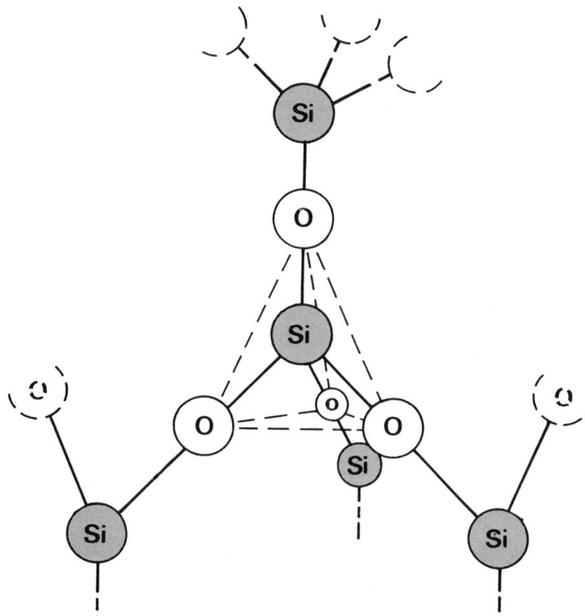

The silica structure

between every pair of Si atoms, as shown in the figure on p. 193.

Chemically, silica is inert and stable, that is, it resists chemical change under most conditions. It is attacked slowly by alkaline solutions, however, and dissolves in bases when molten, to form salts called *silicates*. Thus it has the properties of an *acidic oxide*.

- *Silica is an involatile, generally unreactive substance. One of its few properties is to dissolve in strong bases.*

The acidic nature of silica is important in the manufacture of glass, and helps to explain the abundance of natural silicates, for example those in igneous rocks, clays and asbestos materials. We shall also meet it later in slag formation in the blast furnace extraction of iron (Unit 43).

Glass manufacture

If silica is melted (T_m = 1710 °C) and cooled rapidly, solidification may be so rapid that the atoms are unable to achieve a regular pattern. The solid formed under these conditions has no regular structure, that is, it is not crystalline. This type of disordered solid is referred to as a *glass*. Silica (from sand) is the main ingredient in ordinary glass. However, glass is normally manufactured (at temperatures lower than 1710 °C) from molten mixtures of SiO_2 with various metal oxides. The metal oxides, being basic, form silicates by reaction with the silica.

Ordinary glass (soda glass) is made from mixtures of SiO_2, Na_2CO_3 (see Unit 38) and $CaCO_3$(limestone). The Na_2CO_3 and $CaCO_3$, when hot, provide the oxides Na_2O and CaO. Ordinary glass therefore contains sodium and calcium silicates. Ornamental 'crystal' glass contains silicates of sodium, potassium and lead. 'Pyrex' glass contains silicates of boron and aluminium and is sometimes called 'borosilicate glass'. Colours may be introduced into glass by adding small amounts of oxides of transition metals. Some examples of colours from particular oxides are listed on p. 195.

Glass manufacture: pouring molten glass into a 'cast'

Glass products (top); borosilicate glass is used in heat-proof laboratory glassware (bottom)

Oxide	*Colour*
CoO	blue
CuO	deep blue
Fe_2O_3	yellow
MnO_2	pink
NiO	brown

(How would you attempt to obtain green glass using the above oxides?)

● *Glasses are non-crystalline solids with no regular structure. Silica sand is the basis of ordinary glass manufacture.*

Asbestos is a fibrous material

Some silicate minerals

Asbestos

The term 'asbestos' is used for several kinds of fibre-like silicate minerals. Common (chrysotile) asbestos has a complex structure in which silicate sheets are twisted into cylinders. Some asbestos minerals have simpler structures that are easier to describe. These structures may be visualized as chains of silicate groups, carrying negative charge, and having Mg^{2+} and Ca^{2+} ions associated with them, as shown in the figure below.

This thread-like structure explains the fibrous nature of asbestos minerals, and the stability of the silicate groups explains the heat-resistant properties of asbestos. Asbestos is used for manufacturing protective clothing and for making brake linings. It is a recognized health hazard, however, and its use is now restricted. (Breathing microscopic asbestos fibres can cause lung disease.)

Clays

Clays contain minerals derived from igneous rocks. For example, changes in the composition of sodium aluminosilicates and potassium aluminosilicates (see 'orthoclase in granites', above) can form minerals like kaolinite, $Al_2Si_2O_5(OH)_4$. These changes are thought to have been caused by the action of warm

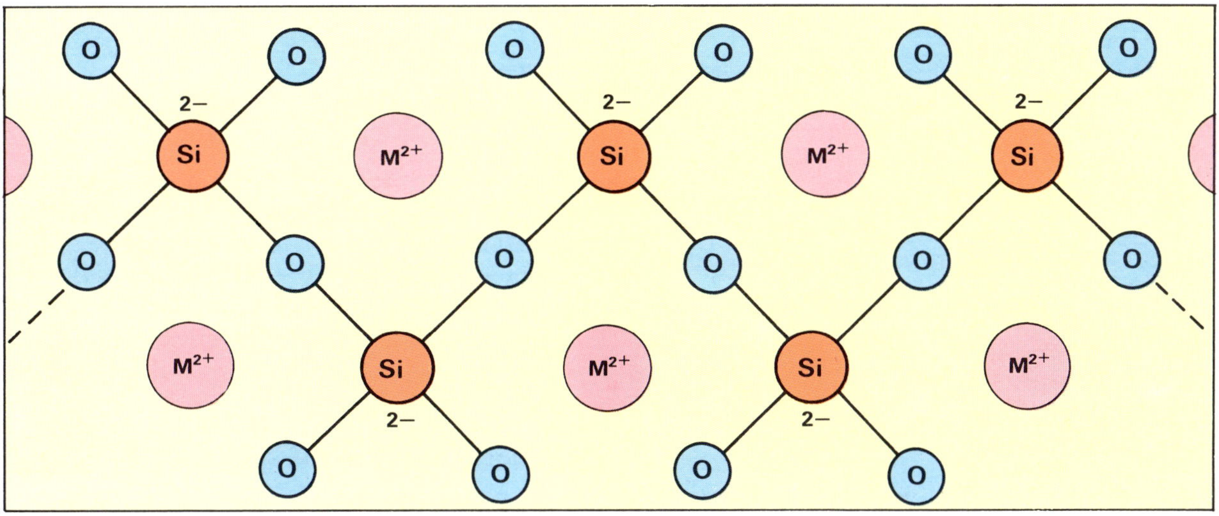

A simplified silicate chain in an asbestos mineral (M = Ca or Mg)

Clays are used for roof tile and brick making

A china clay pit in Cornwall; china clay is used for porcelain

underground water dissolving K^+ and SiO_2 from granite rocks (see Extension 1).

Clays are used for tile and brick making, and for cement manufacture (see p. 198). A special white clay called china clay (mainly kaolinite) is used for making porcelain, as a filler in rubbers and plastics and in coatings for high-grade paper. China clay is an important export from Britain. The main economic deposits are found in Devon and Cornwall. A problem of land dereliction is caused by large-scale exploitation of surface minerals such as china clay.

- *Silicate minerals that are important natural resources include clays and asbestos.*

Limestones

Limestones are *calcium carbonate* rocks. The various types include *organic limestones* (e.g. chalk and carboniferous limestones) derived from the shells of marine organisms, and limestones formed by *precipitation* of calcium carbonate deposits (e.g. oolitic limestone). This latter type may contain $MgCO_3$ and is then called Permian or magnesian limestone, or dolomite. The various forms of natural $CaCO_3$ occur widely in Britain.

Chemical reactions of $CaCO_3$

1. Although largely insoluble in pure water, $CaCO_3$ dissolves slowly in slightly acidic

Chalk cliffs are made of calcium carbonate

Limestone rocks also consist mainly of the calcium carbonate mineral, calcite

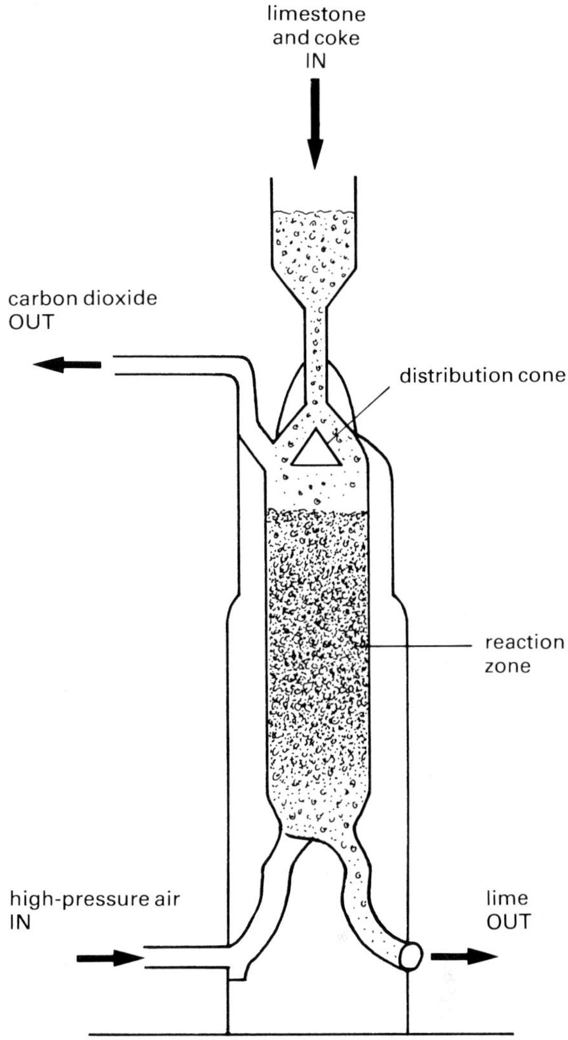

A lime kiln

natural water (i.e. water containing CO_2), forming calcium hydrogencarbonate, $Ca(HCO_3)_2(aq)$. The presence of calcium hydrogencarbonate in water accounts for the occurrence of *temporary hardness* of water in some areas, and for the formation of stalactites and stalagmites (see Book 1). In common with other carbonates, $CaCO_3$ dissolves in stronger acids releasing $CO_2(g)$.

2. $CaCO_3$ decomposes at high temperatures to form calcium oxide (lime) and carbon dioxide. This is the basis of 'lime burning' (see illustration on right of p.197).

$$\mathbf{CaCO_3(s) \rightarrow CaO(s) + CO_2(g)}$$

The 'lime' can react exothermically with water to form 'slaked lime', calcium hydroxide ($Ca(OH)_2$).

$$\mathbf{CaO(s) + H_2O(l) \rightarrow Ca(OH)_2(s)}$$

Both CaO and $Ca(OH)_2$ are basic. $Ca(OH)_2$ is only slightly soluble in water; its saturated solution is an alkali and is familiar as lime-water in the laboratory. Other more important uses of limestone and products obtained from it are given below.

Uses of limestone, lime and slaked lime

1. *Mortar and plaster:* $Ca(OH)_2$ when mixed with water forms a paste which sets on

drying. If left in contact with air, reaction with CO_2(g) produces calcium carbonate(s).

$$Ca(OH)_2(s) + CO_2(g) \rightarrow CaCO_3(s) + H_2O(g)$$

This reaction accounts for the usefulness of $Ca(OH)_2$ in plaster and early forms of cement (mortar).

(Note: In the long term, exposure of the mortar to CO_2 and H_2O produces $Ca(HCO_3)_2$ in solution, that is, the $CaCO_3$ is eroded away, so mortar of this kind needs frequent replacement.)

2. *The ammonia–soda process:* limestone is a raw material for the manufacture of Na_2CO_3 and $NaHCO_3$ by this process (see Unit 38).
3. *Agriculture:* lime and limestone may be spread on the land as soil conditioners. They have the effect of counteracting excess acidity (often associated with the long-term use of artificial fertilizers) and also help to break up heavy clay soils.
4. *Slag formation:* limestone is used in the blast furnace extraction of iron (see Unit 43). It reacts with silica in the ore to form slag and thus purifies the iron.
5. *Glass manufacture:* limestone is a minor ingredient in the mixture used to manufacture soda-glass.
6. *Portland cement:* this is made by roasting crushed limestone with clay. The product may be thought of as calcium aluminosilicate. When mixed with water it sets to a hard mass because of the formation of interlocking crystals. With sand, gravel and water the product is called concrete.

Concrete is the most widely used modern building material. Its use has revolutionized architecture and engineering. Concrete is extremely strong under pressure (that is, when squashed) and its strength under tension (that is, when stretched) may be increased by reinforcing it with steel rods.

Because of its use in making concrete, the manufacture of Portland cement is of very great economic importance.

● *Limestone and lime products have important uses in the chemical and glass industries, agriculture, iron production and cement manufacture.*

Laying mortar in a wall

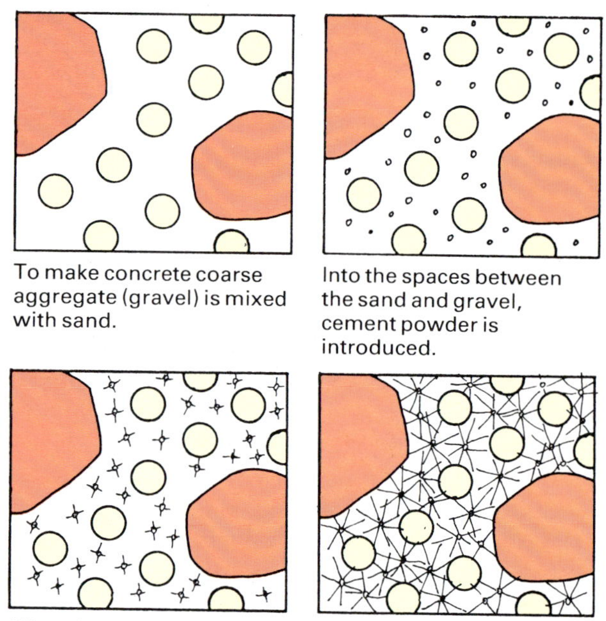

To make concrete coarse aggregate (gravel) is mixed with sand.

Into the spaces between the sand and gravel, cement powder is introduced.

Water is then added to the mix and the cement starts to grow crystals.

The crystals grow and interlock with the sand and gravel surfaces, binding the mass together.

How cement sets

Summary

1. About a quarter of the mass of the Earth's crust is silicon.
2. Silicon is extracted from SiO_2 by reduction with carbon.
3. Silicon has some characteristics of both graphite and diamond.
4. Silicon's most important property is semiconductivity.
5. Silicon is the basis of the microchip industry.
6. Silicones are synthetic polymers with heat-resistant and lubricating properties.
7. Silica is an involatile, generally unreactive substance with some acidic properties.
8. Silica sand is the main raw material for the glass industry.
9. Clays and asbestos are examples of economically important silicate minerals.
10. Limestones contain $CaCO_3$ and are useful in the chemical, glass, iron and cement industries.

Extension

1. **Leaching of granite to form kaolinite**
Orthoclase may react with hot water containing acid (H_2X) according to the following (unbalanced) equation:

$$\mathbf{KAlSi_3O_8(s) + H_2X(aq) + H_2O(l) \rightarrow Al_2Si_2O_5(OH)_4(s) + K_2X(aq) + SiO_2(aq)}$$

i SiO_2 is practically insoluble, but appears in the equation as $SiO_2(aq)$. What does this suggest about the speed of the above reaction?
ii Suggest the possible identity of the acid H_2X. What might be the source of the acid you have suggested?
iii Balance the above equation.

2. **Lime burning** is mentioned in this Unit. The principal reactions involved are:

Reaction 1: $\mathbf{C(s) + O_2(g) \rightarrow CO_2(g);\ \Delta H = -394\ kJ\ mol^{-1}.}$

Reaction 2: $\mathbf{CaCO_3(s) \rightarrow CaO(s) + CO_2(g);\ \Delta H = +178\ kJ\ mol^{-1}.}$

i What do the ΔH values tell you about each of the above reactions?
ii If most of the heat given out by one reaction is absorbed by the other, how many moles of $CaCO_3$ can be decomposed by the combustion of one mole of carbon (to the nearest mole)?
iii If the theoretical ratio of C to $CaCO_3$ calculated in (ii) is used in the lime-burning kiln, approximately what mass of coke will be needed to decompose 1 tonne (1000 kg) of limestone?
iv If the same ratio of C to $CaCO_3$ is used, what volume of CO_2 will be formed during the 'burning' of 1 tonne of $CaCO_3$?

3. **The float glass process**
This process, introduced by Pilkington of St Helens in 1959, has revolutionized the production of *plate glass*. The principle of the process is to float molten glass on the surface of molten tin, as illustrated in the figure on p.200.

i Before 1959, plate glass was manufactured by passing hot glass through rollers and then grinding and polishing the surfaces. What do you suppose is the advantage of the molten tin method?
ii Why do you think tin was chosen rather than any other metal?
iii 'Cullet' is recycled glass. What are the other raw materials that go into the furnace?
iv The molten glass in the furnace is stirred by platinum paddles. Why is platinum chosen for this job?

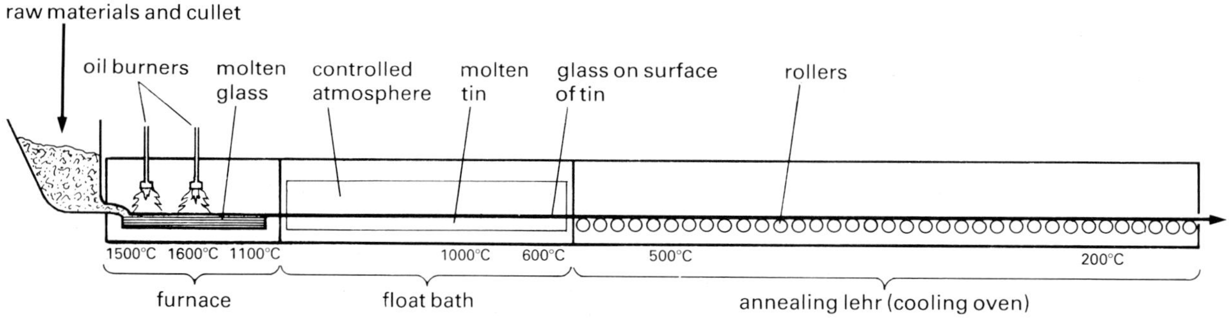

The float glass process

v The 'controlled atmosphere' is a *reducing gas*.

a Suggest a reducing gas for use in the float bath chamber.

b Why do you think a reducing gas is necessary?

vi The 'annealing lehr' is a cooling oven through which the ribbon of glass progresses slowly. Can you suggest why this stage of the process is necessary?

Revision

1. i Draw up a table to compare the physical and chemical properties of the two group IV oxides CO_2 and SiO_2.

   ii Explain why the two oxides have different physical properties by using your knowledge of their structures.

2. The figure (right) can be used to show the main uses of limestone.

   i Give the name and formula of the product A.

   ii Briefly describe the processes B and C.

   iii Name the products formed at D and E.

   iv Write equations for the reactions F and G.

   v Which of the reactions F and G is exothermic and which is endothermic?

   vi Copy the chart, inserting names as replacements for letters A–G, and finish it by indicating some uses of slaked lime.

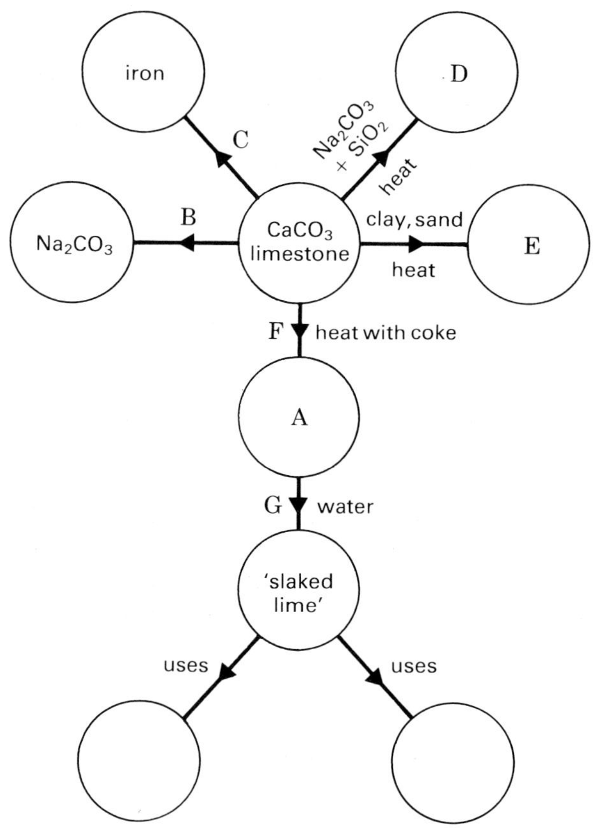

Uses of limestone

Unit 40
Ammonia and fertilizers

Ammonia is produced on a very large scale in Britain. It is mainly used for the manufacture of agricultural fertilizers. The production of food for a growing world population therefore depends on the manufacture of ammonia, and its synthesis affects the lives of all of us.

- *Ammonia is a raw material needed for increasing the world's food production.*

The Haber synthesis

The synthesis reaction in which ammonia is formed looks simple on paper:

$$N_2(g) + 3H_2(g) \rightleftharpoons 2NH_3(g)$$

However, it is a difficult reaction in practice. It is generally called the Haber synthesis, after Fritz Haber who, at the beginning of this century, made a study of the conditions needed to get the best results in the reaction.

The problem with the ammonia synthesis is that the reaction is reversible (see Unit 25). Under ordinary conditions, the forward reaction:

$$N_2(g) + 3H_2(g) \rightarrow 2NH_3(g)$$

is much slower than the reverse reaction:

$$2NH_3(g) \rightarrow N_2(g) + 3H_2(g)$$

Consequently, when nitrogen and hydrogen react, high concentrations of ammonia are difficult to achieve. However, the percentage yield of ammonia can be improved by careful control of reaction conditions. For the best results, the right *catalyst* must be used, and the *pressure* and *temperature* have to be carefully controlled.

- *The success of the Haber synthesis for the production of ammonia depends on choosing the best reaction conditions.*

Use of catalysts in the Haber synthesis

A catalyst is used to speed up the process. The catalyst chosen for the job is *iron*.

Catalysts affect forward and reverse reactions equally, so they do not change the proportion of ammonia that could be obtained in a reaction mixture. However, by the use of an iron catalyst, the small percentage of ammonia that is produced is formed quickly. If the ammonia is removed from the reaction mixture, the unused reactants can be recycled through the reaction vessel. Repeated contact with the catalyst leads to a higher conversion rate in a given time.

Pressure control of the Haber synthesis

The speed of a reaction involving gaseous reactants is always increased by increasing the pressure of the reaction mixture. However, there is another effect: pressure can change the proportion of product that is formed. This is the case for all reversible reactions involving gases in which the number of moles of gas changes as reaction proceeds.

In the Haber synthesis, the forward reaction involves a *decrease in the number of moles of gas*. (The equation shows that 4 moles of gaseous reactant are changed into only 2 moles of gaseous product.) Experiment shows that this type of change is *favoured by high pressure*. Reactions that involve an increase in the number of moles are favoured by low pressure. Low pressure would therefore favour the reverse reaction in the Haber process, that is, decomposition of the ammonia.

In practice, the synthesis is usually carried out at pressures of about 200 atmospheres in a special high-pressure reaction vessel. (Even higher pressures would give better yields, but would also require more expensive reinforced reaction vessels.) Recent developments in plant design and catalyst composition have allowed ICI to develop commercial ammonia production at lower pressures (70–80 atmospheres) while maintaining conversion efficiency at about 15 per cent. This process (the ICI 'AMV process') will result in improved efficiency, and therefore lower costs.

An ammonia synthesis tower

● *The Haber synthesis is carried out at 200 atmospheres pressure and using an iron catalyst.*

Temperature and the Haber synthesis

Changing the temperature at which a reaction is carried out has two important effects:

a all reactions are speeded up by increasing the temperature (and slowed down by decreasing the temperature);
b the percentage yield in reversible reactions may be increased or decreased by increasing the temperature.

Experiments have shown that, in general, *reversible exothermic processes are favoured by low temperature* and *reversible endothermic processes are favoured by high temperature*. In the case of the ammonia synthesis, the forward reaction is exothermic and the reverse reaction is endothermic. This suggests that low temperature would lead to a high yield. Unfortunately, the higher percentage yield would be achieved at a slower rate if the temperature were lower. Clearly, the two temperature effects, (i) and (ii) above, are in conflict in the case of ammonia synthesis. In practice it is found to be more economic to carry out the reaction at high temperatures. This allows reasonable yields of about 15 per cent to be achieved rapidly (which is better than higher yields being achieved very slowly). The best temperature is found to be 400–450 °C (see Extension 1).

● *In the Haber synthesis, a temperature of about 450 °C is chosen to give the most economic production of ammonia.*

Raw materials for ammonia production

We have seen that the Haber synthesis involves the combination of nitrogen and hydrogen. Where are these raw materials obtained? The answer is, nitrogen is obtained from the *air*, and hydrogen is obtained from *water and hydrocarbons*. Good sources of hydrocarbons are natural gas (i.e. North Sea gas) and naphtha (from petroleum). Natural gas is largely methane. Naphtha is a mixture of hydrocarbons and is similar to petrol.

Methane and steam can be reacted together as follows:

$$\mathbf{CH_4(g) + H_2O(g) \rightarrow CO(g) + 3H_2(g)}$$

$$\mathbf{CH_4(g) + 2H_2O(g) \rightarrow CO_2(g) + 4H_2(g)}$$

These changes are brought about by using a nickel catalyst and a high temperature and pressure. (Note: Sources of hydrocarbons for these reactions must be free of sulphur, which is a poison for nickel catalysts.) In both the reactions above, hydrogen is produced by reduction of steam and oxidation of methane. The next stage in the process is to add air to the gas mixture. The oxygen of the air is removed by reaction with some of the hydrogen, and this produces a mixture that is largely nitrogen, hydrogen, steam and oxides of carbon. The carbon monoxide can be converted to carbon dioxide (by reaction with the steam), and then the carbon dioxide can be removed by absorption in potassium carbonate solution. If the correct proportions of steam, methane, and air have been used, the final mixture of gases will contain three parts of nitrogen and one part of hydrogen, that is, the ratio needed for the Haber synthesis.

The important stages in the production of ammonia are summarized in the next figure.

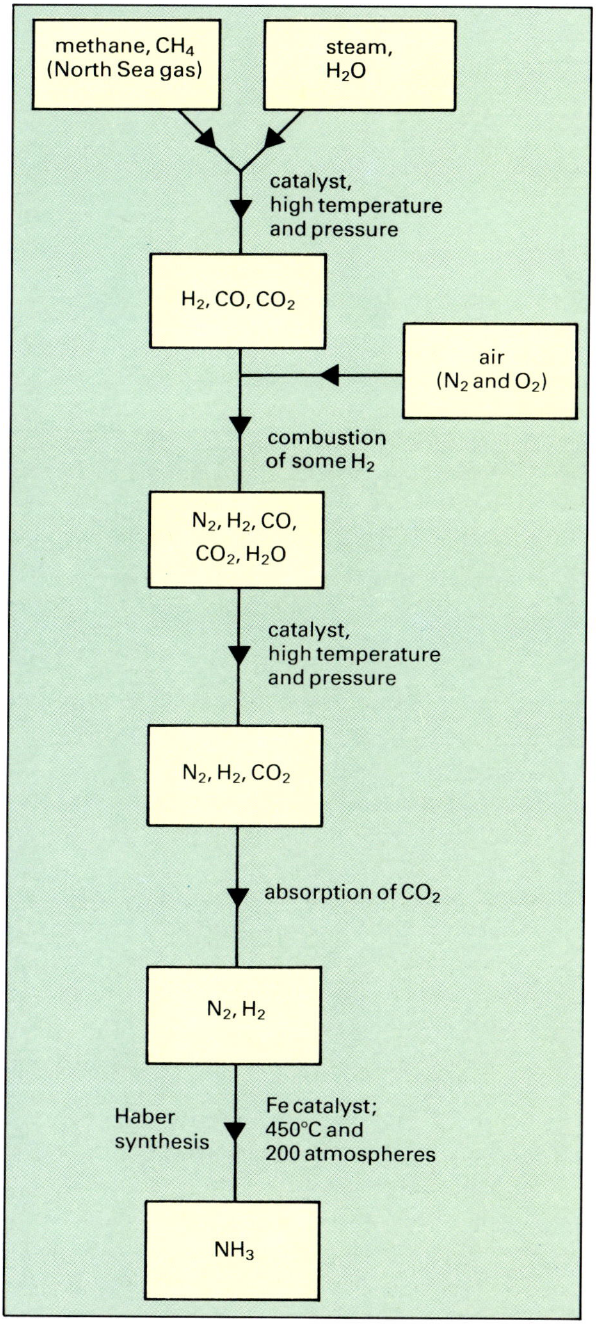

Flow chart for ammonia production

Uses of ammonia

As much as 80 per cent of ammonia is converted into *fertilizers*. Salts may be formed directly from the ammonia by neutralization. Alternatively, the ammonia may be oxidized to form nitric acid. Much of this nitric acid is used in the production of nitrates for fertilizers. Ammonium nitrate is the most widely used nitrogen compound in synthetic fertilizers.

The oxidation of ammonia is achieved using a platinum catalyst in the following reaction:

$$\mathbf{4NH_3(g) + 5O_2(g) \rightleftharpoons 4NO(g) + 6H_2O(g)}$$

The nitrogen monoxide is oxidized to nitrogen dioxide, which is then reacted with water to form nitric acid:

$$\mathbf{NO(g)} \xrightarrow[H_2O(l)]{O_2(g)} \mathbf{HNO_3(aq)}$$

Apart from fertilizer production, ammonia and nitric acid are needed for the manufacture of *polymers* (e.g. polyurethanes), *dyestuffs* (e.g. aniline dyes), *explosives* (e.g. TNT), and *synthetic fibres* (e.g. nylons). These uses of ammonia are summarized in the figure on p. 204.

Compound fertilizers

The term 'compound fertilizer' is used for any synthetic fertilizer that consists of more than one component. Most synthetic fertilizers used by farmers nowadays are compound fertilizers. They are usually manufactured into granules to make spreading on the land easier.

The components in the mixture are compounds of nitrogen, phosphorus and potassium. Each of these elements is important for strong growth of crops. Compounds of nitrogen that are incorporated into granules include *ammonium sulphate*, *ammonium nitrate* and *ammonium phosphate*. The raw material for these nitrogen compounds is, of course, ammonia. The raw material for the phosphorus component is calcium phosphate rock. This is reacted with sulphuric acid to produce phosphoric acid, which in turn is used to form ammonium phosphate. The raw material for the potassium component is potassium chloride. This needs no treatment before granulation.

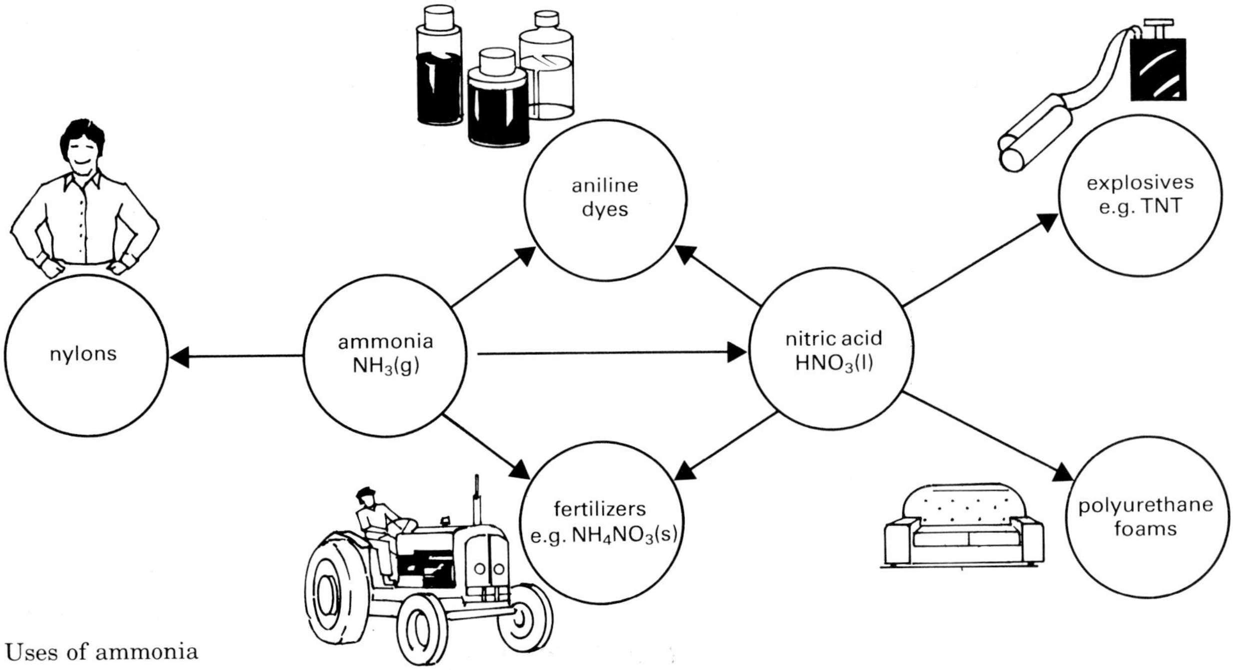

Uses of ammonia

The percentages of N, P and K vary from one compound fertilizer to the next. The farmer can choose a fertilizer to suit the condition of the soil, and the crop to be grown.

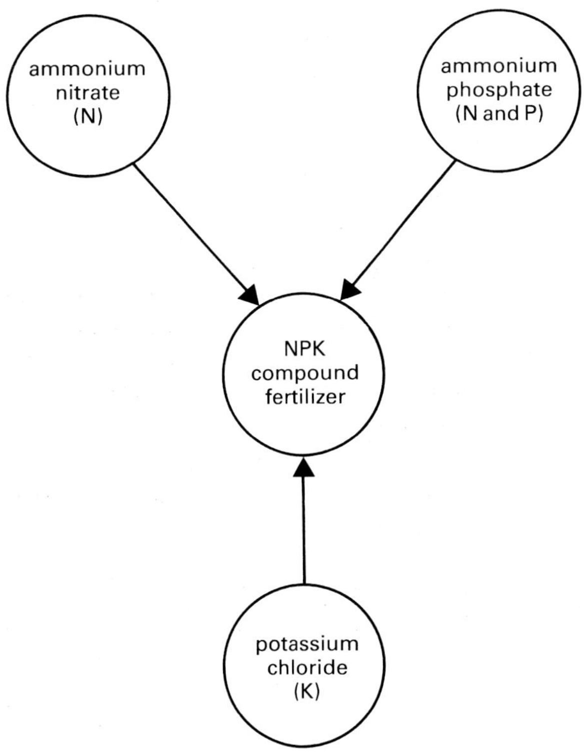

NPK compound fertilizers

Summary

1. Increasing the world's food production depends on the use of synthetic fertilizers manufactured from ammonia.
2. Ammonia is manufactured in the Haber synthesis:

$$N_2(g) + 3H_2(g) \rightleftharpoons 2NH_3(g)$$

3. For the best results in the Haber synthesis, a good catalyst must be chosen, and the pressure and temperature in the reaction vessel must be carefully controlled.
4. Reasonable yields are obtained in the Haber synthesis using an iron catalyst at 200 atmospheres pressure and 450 °C.
5. The raw materials for ammonia production are air, steam and hydrocarbons such as methane and naphtha.
6. Ammonia is used for the manufacture of nitric acid, plastics, dyes and explosives, as well as fertilizers.
7. Compound fertilizers are mixtures of N, P and K components such as ammonium nitrate, ammonium phosphate and potassium chloride.

Extension

1. **Percentage yield in the Haber synthesis**
The forward and reverse reactions in the Haber synthesis may be allowed to compete until no further change is apparent. The reaction is said to have reached equilibrium when this happens. The percentage of ammonia in the mixture at equilibrium varies with the pressure and temperature conditions, as shown in the table below.

		Pressure (atmospheres)			
		10	*100*	*200*	*600*
Temperature (°C)	*200*	50	80	90	95
	300	15	50	70	85
	400	4	25	40	65
	500	1	10	20	40

Approximate percentages (by volume) of ammonia in various equilibrium mixtures

i Which conditions given in the table would result in the best yield of ammonia at equilibrium?
ii Why are 'best theoretical conditions' similar to these *not* used in practice?
iii Which conditions in the table are closest to those most usually used in the ammonia industry?
iv What is the approximate theoretical yield for the conditions you have selected in (iii) above?
v Why is the lower yield considered acceptable in practice?

2. **Activation energy and active sites**
Chemical reactions, whether exothermic or endothermic, frequently need an energy input to get them going. This initial energy input can be called the '*activation energy*' of the reaction. Once started, exothermic reactions may produce enough energy to keep going. In a few cases, apparently stable mixtures may react explosively once started, for example some gaseous mixtures after sparking.

i Use ideas of the kinetic theory (moving particles) to explain why higher temperatures are better than lower temperatures for starting reactions off.
ii Use the activation energy idea, and your understanding of 'exothermic', to explain how apparently stable mixtures of gases can react rapidly once reaction starts.
iii *a* Molecules such as N_2 and H_2 (even those with more than enough energy) won't react unless they meet.
b Solids such as iron have active sites on their surfaces, onto which gaseous molecules congregate.

How could the points (*a*) and (*b*) above explain the catalytic effect of iron in the Haber synthesis?

Revision

1. This question is about the following equations:

A $CH_4(g) + H_2O(g) \rightleftharpoons CO(g) + 3H_2(g)$
B $CO(g) + H_2O(g) \rightleftharpoons CO_2(g) + H_2(g)$
C $N_2(g) + 3H_2(g) \rightleftharpoons 2NH_3(g)$
D $CH_4(g) + 2H_2O(g) \rightleftharpoons CO_2(g) + 4H_2(g)$
E $2H_2(g) + O_2(g) \rightleftharpoons 2H_2O(g)$

Choose one of the equations that shows:

i two moles of reactant converted to four moles of product
ii two moles of reactant converted to two moles of product
iii four moles of reactant converted to two moles of product
iv a reaction in which the yield would not be affected by pressure change
v two reactions in which the yield would be increased by decreasing the pressure
vi two reactions in which the yield would be increased by increasing the pressure

2. Mixtures of hydrogen and nitrogen (in the same proportions) were allowed to react in sealed vessels. The conditions in each vessel were as shown below:

Vessel	*Catalyst*	*Pressure (atmospheres)*	*Temp (°C)*
A	iron	10	1000
B	iron	100	100
C	none	100	100
D	iron	200	400
E	iron	2000	20

i In which two vessels would the eventual yield of ammonia be the same?

ii In which vessel do the conditions most closely resemble those usually used in the ammonia industry?

iii In which vessel would the eventual yield be *a* highest; *b* lowest?

3. Four of the following are manufactured using ammonia or nitric acid. Which is the exception?

A aniline dye
B DDT
C nylon
D synthetic fertilizer
E TNT

4. NH_4NO_3, $Ca(NO_3)_2$ and $(NH_4)_2SO_4$ are three substances that can be used as fertilizers. Which of the three substances has the lowest percentage of nitrogen?

5. Write an essay about the world food problem. Mention:

i the nitrogen cycle,
ii population growth and food shortage,
iii the problem of distributing food surpluses,
iv health problems resulting from unbalanced diets,
v the benefits and problems of using artificial fertilizers.

Unit 41
The contact process

Sulphuric acid and economic development

All advanced industrial countries make use of sulphuric acid. It plays an important part in many chemical manufacturing processes. In general, countries with higher levels of industrial development use more sulphuric acid. Almost one quarter of the total world production is manufactured in the USA. Most of the rest originates in the USSR, China, Japan or Western Europe. Perhaps a country's sulphuric acid manufacturing capacity is a good indication of its prosperity?

- *The wealth of a nation may be linked to its sulphuric acid production.*

Production has started to become more important in underdeveloped countries. Thus, Morocco, which once exported phosphate rock (for phosphoric acid manufacture) now manufactures its own sulphuric acid and uses it to produce phosphoric acid for export instead.

The contact process

Nearly all sulphuric acid is manufactured by one method nowadays. The method is called the *contact process*.

The most important reaction in the process is the oxidation of sulphur dioxide to form sulphur trioxide:

$$2SO_2(g) + O_2(g) \rightleftharpoons 2SO_3(g)$$

This reaction is *reversible*. It also needs a *catalyst*.

Catalysis in the contact process

Sulphur trioxide can be prepared from sulphur dioxide in the laboratory using a platinum catalyst. An apparatus is shown in the figure below.

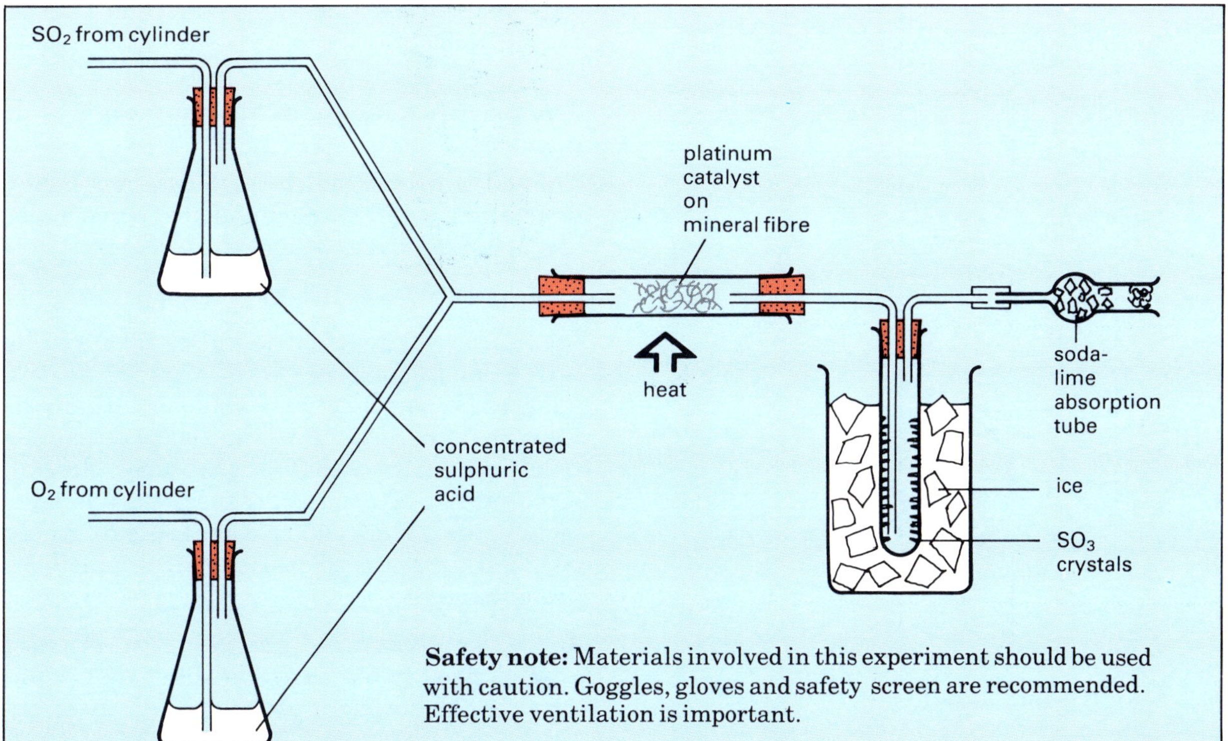

Safety note: Materials involved in this experiment should be used with caution. Goggles, gloves and safety screen are recommended. Effective ventilation is important.

A laboratory version of the contact process

A cheaper catalyst is available for the large-scale industrial method. Vanadium(V) oxide is used (in the form of silica pellets coated with the oxide). It is worth noting that the V_2O_5 catalyst only works at temperatures above 400 °C.

- *SO_3 is produced on a large scale in the contact process using V_2O_5 as a catalyst.*

In the industrial process, the gas mixture passes through four catalyst beds, one after another, to increase the percentage conversion of sulphur dioxide (figure below).

Temperature control in the contact process

The conversion of SO_2 to SO_3 is exothermic. In general, reversible exothermic processes are favoured at low temperatures. It follows from this that, in a given mixture of SO_2 and O_2, a larger percentage of SO_3 would *eventually* be formed at a lower temperature.

However, another factor must be taken into account: the reaction rate is greatly reduced by lowering the temperature. In the contact process, it is not worthwhile doing the reaction at a low temperature: a higher proportion of SO_3 might eventually be produced, but it could take days for the mixture to reach equilibrium. The most economic conversion is achieved by keeping the temperature of each catalyst bed as close as possible to 420 °C. This is done by cooling the gas after it passes through each bed.

After passing through four catalyst beds, about 2 per cent of the sulphur dioxide remains unconverted. This passes into the atmosphere. However, improved pollution control standards for new plant now require that less than 0.5 per cent of unconverted SO_2 should be emitted to the atmosphere. To achieve this standard, the 'double absorption' technique has been introduced. In this process, the gas mixture is treated to remove SO_3 after passing through bed 3; this results in an improved percentage conversion in the final catalyst bed and a better overall yield.

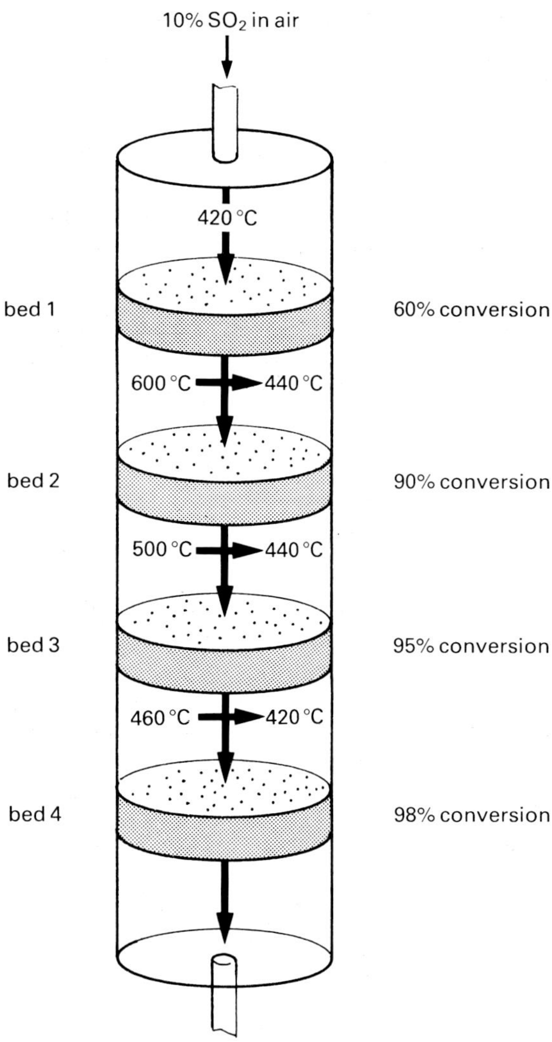

A four-stage SO_2 converter

The pressure factor in the contact process

The forward reaction in the formation of SO_3 results in a smaller amount of gas (three moles of reactant produce two moles of product):

$$2SO_2(g) + O_2(g) \rightarrow 2SO_3(g)$$

In theory, this reaction would be favoured by increasing the pressure of the mixture, that is, a larger proportion of SO_2 would eventually be converted to SO_3. However, in practice the reaction is carried out at pressures close to atmospheric pressure because of economic factors: the cost of using higher pressure would be high and would not improve efficiency dramatically.

- *The conversion of SO_2 to SO_3 is most economically carried out at 420 °C and normal atmospheric pressure.*

Note: Pollution control legislation may require the introduction of higher pressure processes in the future. In France, a sulphuric acid manufacturer (PCUK) achieves a conversion efficiency of 99.85 per cent by operating a process at 4 atmospheres pressure.

Absorption of sulphur trioxide

The final stage in manufacturing sulphuric acid is to produce H_2SO_4 from SO_3. If the SO_3 were simply cooled and mixed directly with water, much of the reaction would take place in the gas phase:

$$SO_3(g) + H_2O(g) \rightarrow H_2SO_4(l)$$

The product would be a fine mist of concentrated sulphuric acid, which could escape to the atmosphere.

A roundabout way of reacting SO_3 with H_2O is therefore used. The SO_3 is absorbed in concentrated (98 per cent) sulphuric acid, and water is gradually added to the mixture to keep the concentration at 98 per cent. A lot of heat is released in the process. The acid may be further diluted for sale.

● *SO_3 is reacted with water indirectly by absorbing it in H_2SO_4 and diluting the mixture.*

Raw materials for H_2SO_4 manufacture

Most of the sulphur dioxide needed for the contact process in Britain is manufactured from sulphur. (Elswhere, sulphide minerals are important raw materials.)

The sulphur used in Britain comes from two main sources: (i) imported sulphur from the USA, Mexico, Poland (extracted from underground deposits by the Frasch process); (ii) imported sulphur from France and Canada (extracted from crude oil and natural gas).
Note: Sulphur extracted from oil and gas is produced by oxidation of H_2S. This impurity may make up 25 per cent of natural gas from some sources. North Sea oil and gas are largely free from sulphur, however, so little sulphur is obtained from our own oil and gas sources.

Whatever the source of sulphur, it must be converted to SO_2 as a first step in the contact process. This is done by spraying liquid sulphur into a furnace:

$$S(l) + O_2(g) \rightarrow SO_2(g)$$

● *Sulphur is the main raw material for sulphuric acid manufacture.*

Uses of sulphuric acid

The use of dilute sulphuric acid in car batteries is well known. In fact this use is a relatively minor one. Large-scale uses of sulphuric acid for a wide variety of industrial processes are listed below and summarized in the chart.

1. *Fertilizers:* About one-third of all sulphuric acid is used in the manufacture of fertilizers. Phosphate rock (calcium phosphate) is treated with sulphuric acid to make the more soluble calcium dihydrogen phosphate ('super phosphate'). Sulphuric acid is used in the manufacture of phosphoric acid (for ammonium phosphate) and ammonium sulphate.
2. *Rayon:* Viscose 'syrup' (manufactured from wood pulp) is squirted into an acid bath to form long filaments.
3. *Detergents:* Detergents are manufactured from organic raw materials (derived from hydrocarbons) by reaction with H_2SO_4.

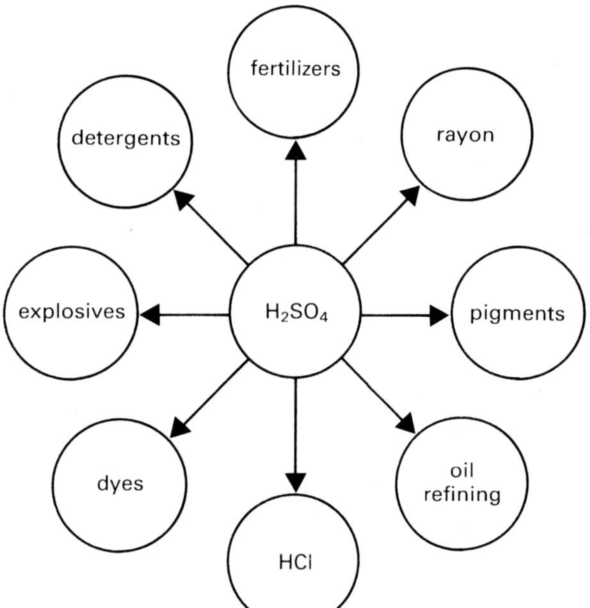

Uses of sulphuric acid

4. *Explosives and dyes:* Many of these are manufactured by the 'nitration' of hydrocarbons. The 'nitration' is carried out using a mixture of concentrated H_2SO_4 and concentrated HNO_3.
5. *Pigments:* The white pigment TiO_2 (widely used in paints) requires sulphuric acid in its manufacture.
6. *Oil refining:* Removal of sulphur from crude oil is achieved using sulphuric acid.
7. *Treatment of rock salt* to produce Na_2SO_4 (for glass) and HCl requires sulphuric acid.

Summary

1. The sulphuric acid capacity of a country is a good indicator of its economic strength.
2. The contact process for sulphuric acid manufacture involves oxidation of SO_2 using a V_2O_5 catalyst.
3. The conversion of SO_2 to SO_3 is carried out at about 420 °C and one atmosphere pressure.
4. Sulphur trioxide is reacted with water indirectly in the final stage of the contact process.
5. The main raw material for sulphuric acid manufacture in Britain is imported sulphur.
6. Sulphuric acid is used in a wide variety of industrial processes including the manufacture of fertilizers, detergents, rayon, explosives, dyes and pigments.

Revision

1. This question is about catalysts that you have met in chemistry.

   A a yeast enzyme
   B iron
   C manganese(IV) oxide
   D platinum
   E vanadium(V) oxide

   Which catalyst would be most useful for the:

   i laboratory preparation of SO_3 from SO_2
   ii economic manufacture of SO_3 from SO_2
   iii fermentation of glucose solution
   iv Haber synthesis of ammonia
   v oxidation of ammonia in the manufacture of HNO_3
   vi decomposition of ammonia to form nitrogen and hydrogen

2. This question is about the reversible reaction:

   $$2SO_2(g) + O_2(g) \rightleftharpoons 2SO_3(g)$$

   Copy the following sentences about the reaction choosing the words that correctly complete each of them:

   i Formation of SO_3 is favoured by *increasing/decreasing* the temperature because the forward reaction is *exothermic/endothermic*.
   ii Formation of SO_3 is favoured by *increasing/decreasing* the pressure because the forward reaction is accompanied by an *increase/decrease* in the total number of moles of gas.

3. This question refers to the following statements about the reaction of SO_2 and O_2. Read each and state whether it is *true* or *false*.

   i The source of oxygen for the industrial process is air.
   ii The catalyst used for the industrial process is platinum.
   iii The change happens faster the higher the temperature.
   iv The reaction is exothermic.
   v More product will eventually be formed at higher temperatures.
   vi Two moles of product are formed from two moles of reactants.
   vii Increasing the pressure favours product formation.

4. What conditions of temperature and pressure are considered to be 'best' for the contact process?

   How are decisions about the choice of these conditions based on:

   i scientific principles
   ii economic considerations
   iii concern for the environment?

Unit 42
The petroleum industry

A source of alkanes

We need alkanes to make many of the organic products that we use in every day life. Natural alkanes are used to make other types of hydrocarbon. All of these hydrocarbons are important starting points for the manufacture of materials such as plastics, detergents and fibres. So, alkanes are important. Where do we get alkanes from? The answer to the question is, *petroleum*.

● *Petroleum is the main source of alkanes.*

Separating petroleum

Crude petroleum oil is a complex mixture of hydrocarbons, mainly alkanes. We may think of it as a solution with thousands of component solutes. It would not be easy to get a single hydrocarbon from such a mixture, but it is relatively easy to divide it into a number of simpler mixtures. The method used is *fractional distillation*, which is often called *fractionation*.

Fractionation works when the components in solution have different boiling temperature (T_b) values. The T_b values of the components in crude oil range from very high to very low (see next table). If such a mixture is warmed, the vapour that escapes first from the liquid is richest in the components with lowest T_b values. In other words, the most volatile components will have the highest concentration in the vapour. If the part of the liquid that evaporates (say, between 40 °C and 100 °C) is collected and condensed, it forms a liquid that is a mixture of hydrocarbons with T_b values within that fairly narrow range. This simpler mixture obtained from petroleum is called a *petroleum fraction*. Other fractions with higher boiling ranges may be collected as the temperature is raised (table p.213).

● *The complex mixture of hydrocarbons in petroleum is simplified by fractional distillation.*

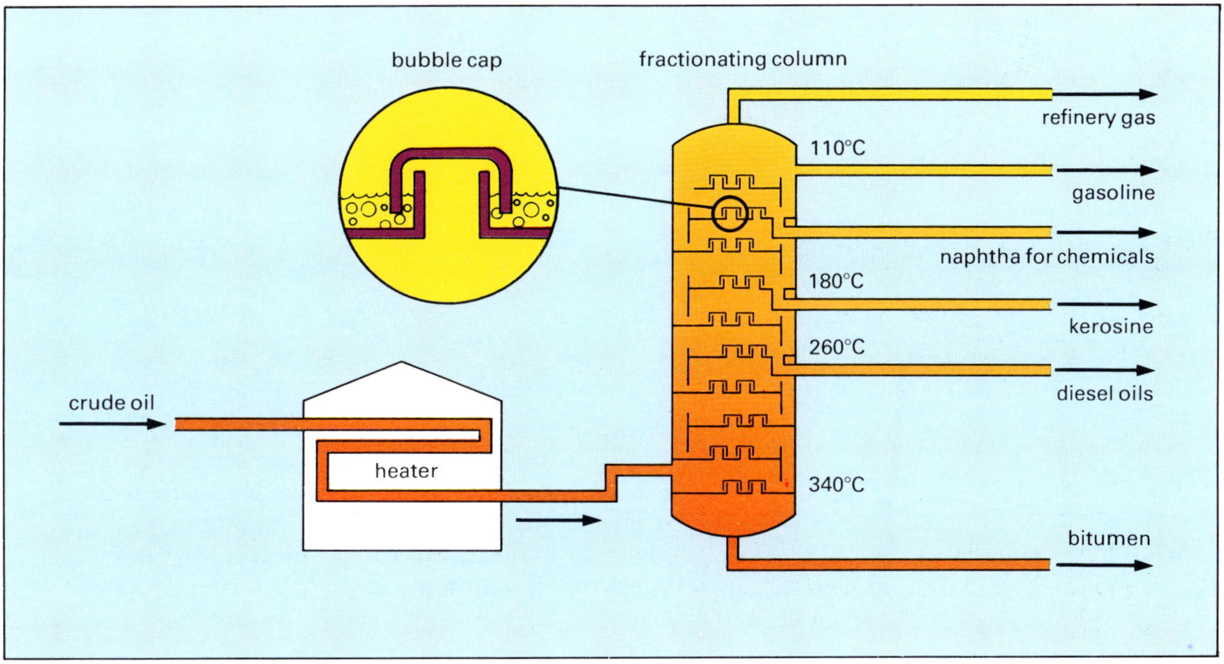

A refinery fractionating column

Experiment to do fractionation of crude oil

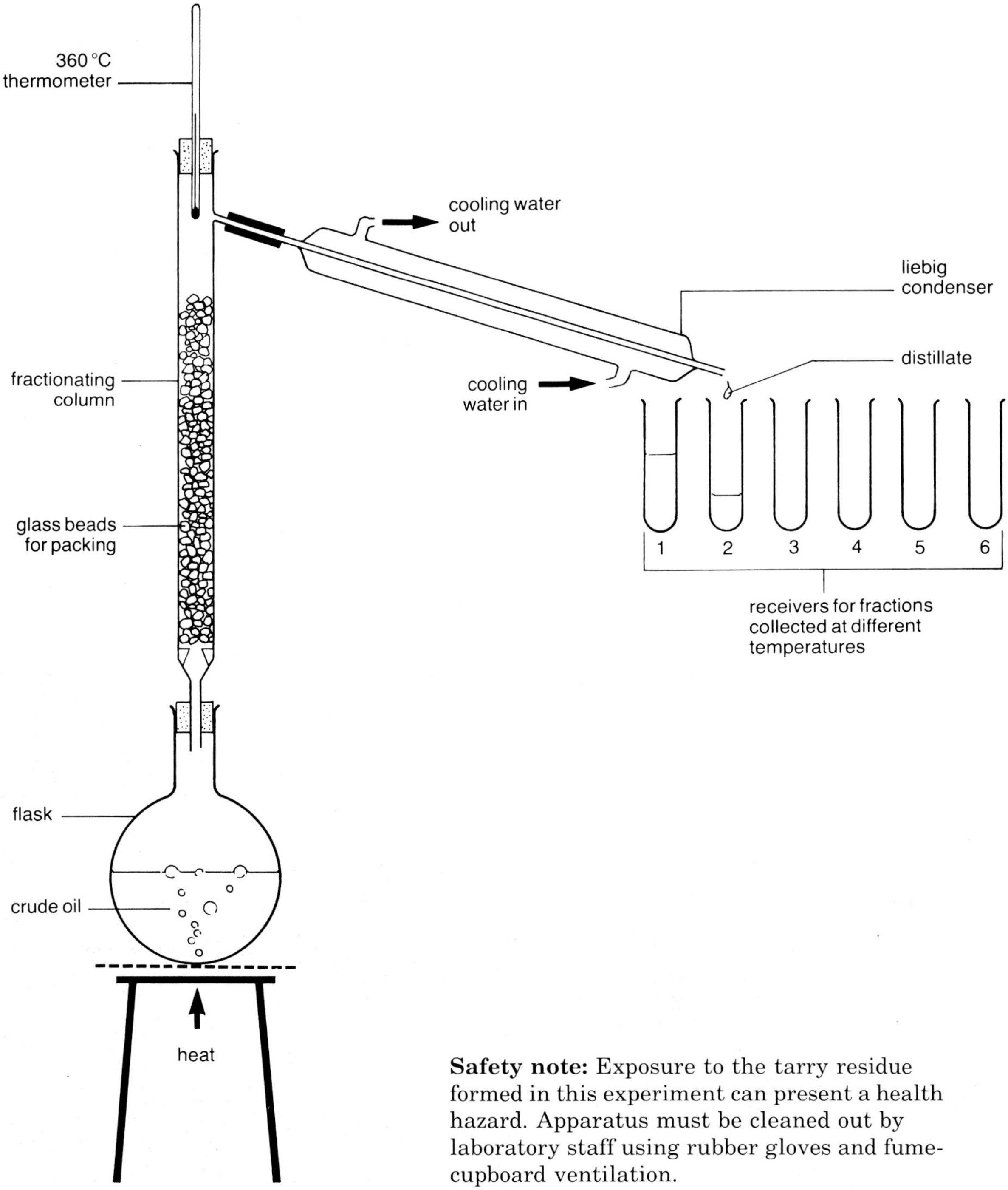

Safety note: Exposure to the tarry residue formed in this experiment can present a health hazard. Apparatus must be cleaned out by laboratory staff using rubber gloves and fume-cupboard ventilation.

Molecules sorted by size

You should recall that there is a link between the boiling temperature of an alkane and the size of its molecules (Unit 26). Thus, the hydrocarbons in each fraction separated from petroleum all have similar numbers of carbon atoms per molecule. In effect, fractionation is a method of sorting molecules of hydrocarbons by size.

Petroleum fraction	*Approximate percentage in crude petroleum*	*Boiling range (°C)*	*Carbon atoms per alkane molecule*
petroleum gas	3%	below 40	1–4
gasoline	7%	40–100	4–10
naphtha	7%	100–160	4–10
kerosine	13%	160–250	10–16
light gas oil	9%	250–300	16–20
heavy gas oil	9%	300–350	20–25
residue	52%	above 350	more than 25

Characteristics of petroleum fractions

Fractionation in practice

In the laboratory, fractionation is carried out by means of a fractionating column, as illustrated in the figure on p.212.

The column ensures that the less volatile components are condensed and returned to the flask. Only the most volatile components reach the top and enter the Liebig condenser. The temperature in the flask is raised gradually and one fraction after another is collected in the receivers.

An industrial fractionating column is not only much bigger (up to 50 metres), but also has design features that distinguish it from the laboratory version. First of all, instead of separating one fraction at a time (by gradually raising the temperature of the mixture), fractions constantly flow out at various levels of the column. This allows the refinery column to operate continuously; as fractions are taken off, more hot crude oil enters the column near the bottom. Secondly, trays with bubble caps or similar devices are built into the column. These force the rising vapours to pass through the liquid that condenses at each level. Bubble caps improve the efficiency of the separation (see p.211).

An oil refinery

Fuel	*Fraction used*	*Everyday uses*
liquid petroleum gas (LPG)	petroleum gases	portable heaters and cookers, camping lanterns, blow-lamps
petrol	gasoline (and other fractions after 'cracking', e.g. naphtha and heavy gas oil)	cars
paraffin oil	kerosine	jet engines, portable heaters, tractor engines, central heating boilers
diesel oil	light gas oil	buses, lorries, taxis, locomotives
fuel oil	heavy gas oil	ships' engines, factory generators, furnaces

Fuels obtained from petroleum fractions

A catalytic cracking tower

Alkanes as fuels

Many important fuels are produced from petroleum fractions. These include petrol, diesel oil and heating oil, in other words, *fuels for transport* and *fuels for heating and lighting*. Modern life could not carry on without these fuels.

● *Petroleum fractions give us fuels for transport, heating and lighting.*

Information about petroleum fuels is given in the table above.

Cracking alkane hydrocarbons

One of the problems in the oil refining business is that the gasoline fraction does not meet the demand for petrol. Only about 7 per cent of crude petroleum ends up in the gasoline fraction. On the other hand, more of some fractions is produced than we really need. For example, there is not much demand for naphtha and heavy gas oil as fuels. So, the refinery manager has a problem. If more crude oil is distilled (to get more petrol), a lot of the oil fractions will be wasted. How can the less useful fractions be disposed of?

Perhaps you could use some of the less useful fractions to make more petrol? This idea makes good economic sense, and it can be done. The process is called *cracking*.

● *Cracking converts less useful fractions into more useful ones.*

The change is carried out by heating the petroleum fraction to a high temperature using a solid catalyst. Heavy oils and waxes are converted to lighter oils and gases. Cracking helps the refinery to produce more petrol and uses up the surplus of less valuable fractions.

You can do experiments to illustrate cracking in the laboratory (see Unit 35, p. 159).

How does cracking work?

When a substance gets hot, the particles in it move more quickly. The movement can take different forms, for example shaking about (vibration) or moving from place to place. When the alkane molecules in the petroleum fractions

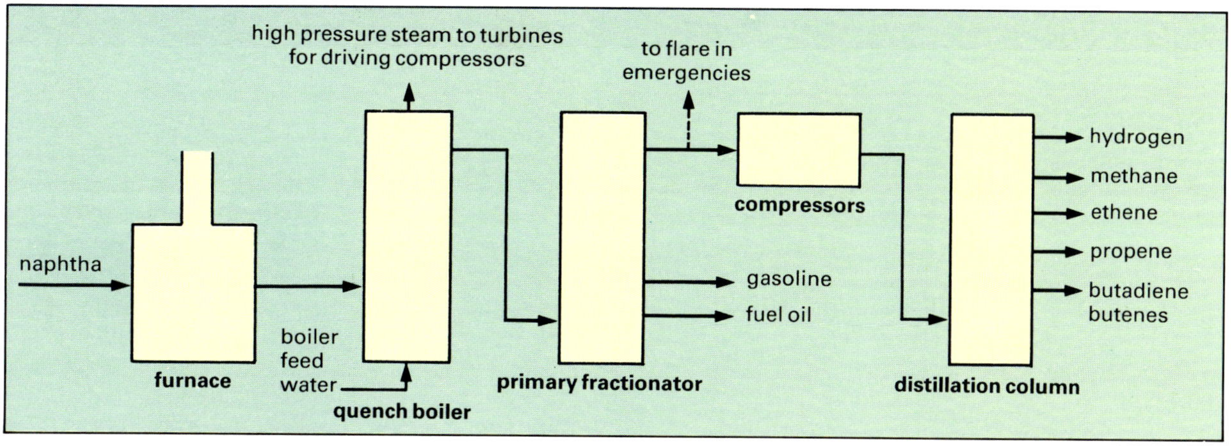

Cracking of naphtha molecules

are heated to high temperature, the more energetic movement can cause the molecules to split. The covalent bonds between some of the carbon atoms in the molecules are broken. The break in the molecule can happen anywhere in the chain of atoms. Since there are chains of many different sizes to begin with, splitting (or cracking) of the chains can result in very complicated mixtures.

One way of cracking just one hydrocarbon molecule is shown in the figure on the right.

Cracking is a kind of *thermal decomposition*. The molecules in the cracked products are smaller than those in the original fraction. This explains why the products of cracking are more volatile ('lighter') than the original fraction.

● *Cracking converts long molecules into shorter ones and produces light oils from heavy oils.*

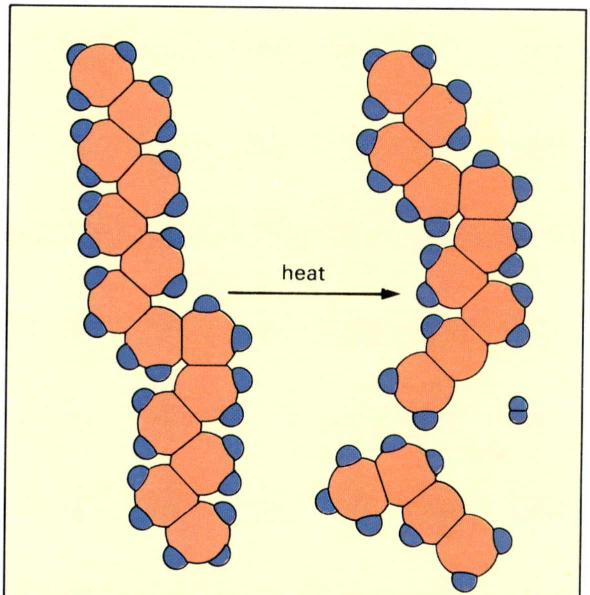

$$C_{14}H_{30} \longrightarrow C_4H_8 + H_2 + C_{10}H_{20}$$

Cracking of a hydrocarbon molecule

Summary

1. Petroleum (crude oil) is the main source of alkanes.
2. Petroleum is separated into parts called fractions by fractional distillation.
3. Petroleum fractions give us fuels for transport and heating.
4. Cracking converts less useful fractions into more useful ones.
5. Cracking works by decomposing long hydrocarbon molecules into shorter ones at high temperatures.
6. Light oils and gases are produced by cracking heavy oils and waxes.

Extension

Product	*Fractions used*	*Process*	*Uses*
petrochemicals e.g. ethene, butene, propene	petroleum gases, naphtha, heavy gas oil, residue	cracking	manufacture of plastics, detergents, synthetic fibres, solvents, glycol, synthetic rubbers, agricultural chemicals
lubricating oils and waxes	heavy gas oil and residue	low-pressure distillation	engine lubricants, candles, floor polish, petroleum jelly
bitumen	residue	low-pressure distillation	road surfacing, roofing felt, waterproofing

The information given in the table above tells you about products that are obtained from petroleum, apart from fuels.

Study the table and use the information in it to help you write an account of the production and uses of non-fuel petroleum products. Give details of examples of uses:

a in the home;
b in industry and engineering;
c in agriculture.

Revision

1. This question is about the following materials:

A gasoline
B kerosine
C meths
D naphtha
E petroleum gas

Which material:

i is not a petroleum fraction
ii is the petroleum fraction with the lowest boiling temperature
iii is the petroleum fraction with the highest boiling temperature
iv consists of the smallest molecules
v consists of the most volatile alkanes

2. Look at the table on p.214, which gives information about fuels obtained from petroleum.

Use the information given in the table to write a short account of petroleum fuels used for heating, lighting and transport. You can illustrate your essay with pictures from newspapers or magazines, or with your own drawings.

3. Which of the following is not part of the change called *cracking*?

A molecules of different sizes are separated from one another
B covalent bonds in molecules are broken
C large molecules are broken into smaller ones
D decomposition of molecules happens
E energetic vibrations cause the destruction of molecules

4. The following equations are incomplete. They should show the cracking of hydrocarbon molecules. *One* formula is missing in each case. Copy them and finish them properly.

i $\_\_\_\_ \rightarrow C_4H_{10} + C_6H_{12}$
ii $C_{15}H_{32} \rightarrow C_5H_{10} + H_2 + \_\_\_\_$
iii $C_{12}H_{26} \rightarrow C_6H_{14} + \_\_\_\_$
iv $C_{11}H_{24} \rightarrow H_2 + C_2H_4 + \_\_\_\_$
v $C_{14}H_{30} \rightarrow C_4H_8 + \_\_\_\_$

Unit 43
Iron and steel

The most widely used metal

Iron is more widely used than any other metal, although it is *not* the most abundant metal in the Earth's crust. This fact requires an explanation, and we shall begin this Unit by considering the reasons behind it.

Occurrence of metals

The Earth's crust is made up largely of the *non-metals* silicon and oxygen (about 75 per cent by mass). Mineral silicates are very common constituents of igneous rocks, sand and clays (see Unit 39). The most abundant metal in the rocks of the Earth is *aluminium* (about 10 per cent), and then comes iron (about 6 per cent). Both of these metals are widely used. However, in spite of its greater abundance, aluminium is used in smaller quantities, and has a much shorter history than iron. Why is this? The main reason is the relative ease of extraction of the two metals. In general, metals that are easy to extract from their ores have been in use longer than those that are difficult to extract.

- *The widespread use of a metal depends on the ease of its extraction as well as the natural abundance of its ores.*

What do we mean by 'ease of extraction'?

Many metals are found as oxides, and chemical reduction is often used to get the metal out (extract it). The reduction on a large scale requires a cheap source of reducing agent, and coke is a good choice. However, reduction of different oxides is achieved at different temperatures. Some metal oxides can only be reduced at very high temperatures. One way of thinking about 'ease of extraction' is to consider the temperature needed for reduction of the oxide. Those oxides that need only relatively low temperatures for reduction can be said to be 'easy' to extract.

Stability of oxides

One meaning of the word *stability* is 'resistance to change'. For example, a compound that resists change when heated (i.e. is not decomposed) is said to be thermally stable. A kind of stability that applies to some oxides is *resistance to reduction*. As we have seen, oxides of some metals resist reduction except at very high temperatures. This kind of stability of oxides is linked to the position of the metal in the reactivity series. Those metals that are high in the reactivity series generally have oxides that are 'stable', that is, they resist reduction when heated with reducing agents.

- *The ease of reduction of a metal oxide is connected with the position of the metal in the reactivity series.*

Mining iron ore

Chemical reduction or electrolysis?

Some metal oxides are too difficult to reduce using available reducing agents, and electrolysis is found to be a more feasible method for their extraction. Aluminium is the best example of a metal in this category. Similarly, other metals that are near the top of the reactivity series would also be extracted by electrolysis.

On the other hand, metals like iron, which are lower down in the series, can be extracted by chemical reduction methods, that is, by 'smelting'. The smelting of iron ore is carried out in blast furnaces.

- *Metals that are high in the reactivity series are extracted by electrolysis. Less reactive metals may be extracted by smelting.*

In the remaining part of this Unit we shall concentrate on the extraction of iron and on its usefulness in iron alloys (steels). (The extraction of aluminium is considered in the next Unit.)

Extraction of iron

Iron ores

Typical ores for the blast furnace are rocks containing Fe_2O_3 (haematite) or Fe_3O_4 (magnetite). The main job of the blast furnace is to bring about the *reduction* of these oxides, that is, remove the oxygen. A second important task is the *purification* of the iron by removal of minerals such as silicates, which are present in the ores and tend to make the iron brittle.

Reduction

Coke and air are the raw materials that bring about the reduction of the iron oxide. First of all, the coke is oxidized in the blast of hot air that enters the furnace at the base.

$$C(s) + O_2(g) \rightarrow CO_2(g); \quad \Delta H = -390\ kJ\ mol^{-1}$$

This reaction is strongly exothermic and keeps the temperature near the base of the furnace at about 1700 °C. At this high temperature, carbon dioxide and more coke can react to form carbon monoxide. (Like other reversible *endothermic* reactions, this one is favoured by high temperatures.)

$$CO_2(g) + C(s) \rightleftharpoons 2CO(g); \quad \Delta H = +170\ kJ\ mol^{-1}$$

Because the formation of carbon monoxide is endothermic, the higher regions of the furnace are cooler than the lower regions. At these lower temperatures (about 800 °C) the carbon monoxide can reduce the iron oxide:

$$Fe_2O_3(s) + 3CO(g) \rightleftharpoons 2Fe(s) + 3CO_2(g)$$

This reaction is slightly exothermic, so is favoured by the cooler conditions. Temperature conditions in the blast furnace are shown in the next illustration.

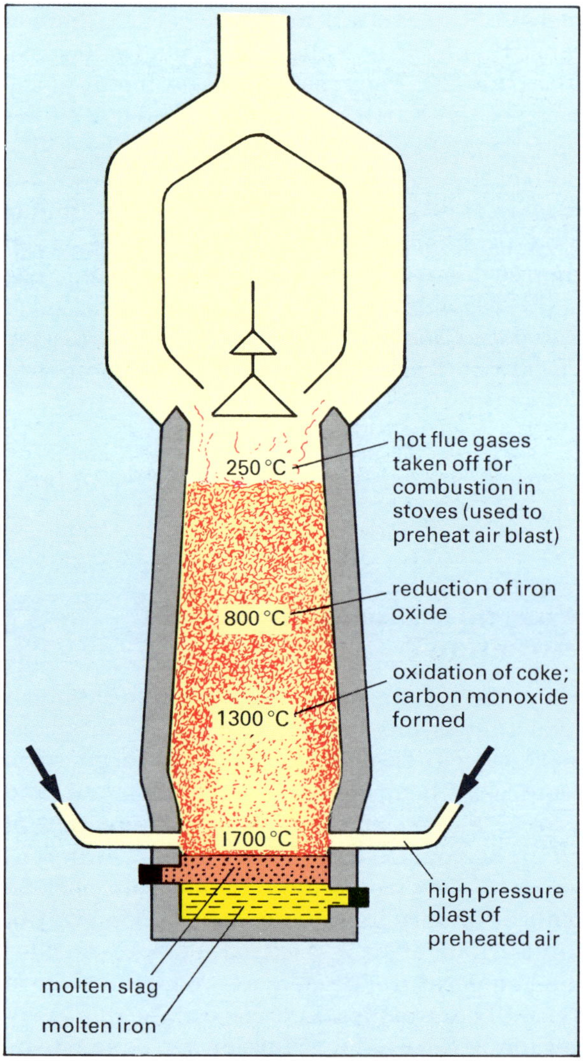

Temperatures inside a blast furnace

Purification

Limestone is added to the raw materials to do this job in the blast furnace. At high temperatures it decomposes to form calcium oxide as follows:

$$CaCO_3(s) \rightarrow CaO(s) + CO_2(g)$$

The calcium oxide is basic and reacts with acidic impurities in the iron. The main impurity is silica, which reacts to form calcium silicate:

$$CaO(s) + SiO_2(s) \rightarrow CaSiO_3(s)$$

The temperature is sufficiently hot at the base of the furnace to melt both the iron and the silicate, and both can be tapped off at intervals. The iron produced is referred to as *pig iron* and the calcium silicate as *slag*.

● *Raw materials for the extraction of iron in the blast furnace are iron ore, coke, air and limestone.*

Summary

1. Metals that are widely used are those that have abundant ores and are easy to extract.
2. Metals that are higher in the reactivity series are more difficult to extract from their ores than those that are lower down.
3. Less reactive metals may be extracted by smelting, but electrolysis is used for extracting more reactive metals.
4. Iron is extracted by smelting iron ore in a blast furnace, using coke as a reducing agent.

Extension

1. In the light of your knowledge of the reactivity series, comment on the information given for a few of the metals in the following table. It shows the time in history when they first became available, or their dates of discovery.

Metal	*History*
Al	First extracted by Oersted (Denmark) in 1825, but on a small scale. It only became widely available after 1886 following the availability of a large-scale method of extraction, developed independently by C.M. Hall (USA) and P.L.T. Heroult (France).
Cu	Early copper-smelting techniques developed around 4000 BC.
Fe	Secret iron-smelting techniques of the Hittites became more widely known after the decline of their empire (invaded by Assyrians after 1260 BC).
Sn	The discovery of tin around 2500 BC marked the start of the Bronze Age.

2. **Iron into steel**

a *The steel industry:* In spite of the closure of some steel works, and reduction of capacity at others, Britain is still one of the world's major steel-producing nations. The British Steel Corporation (BSC), a public corporation, accounts for 85 per cent of Britain's crude steel production.

b *Why make steel?* Crude iron straight from the blast furnace (sometimes called pig iron) is hard and brittle, even when hot. These properties make it unsuitable for engineering purposes. They are the result of impurity elements contained in the iron, as shown below:

C	3–4
Si	1
P	1
Mn	1
S	0.1

Approximate percentage of impurity elements in crude iron

The aim in steel-making is to reduce the proportion of the non-metals C, Si and P in the iron.

c *Steel production:* The principle of the steel-making process is to treat molten iron with a blast of pure oxygen to oxidize impurity elements in the hot metal. This *basic oxygen steel-making* (BOS) process is described in the diagrams on p. 220.

1

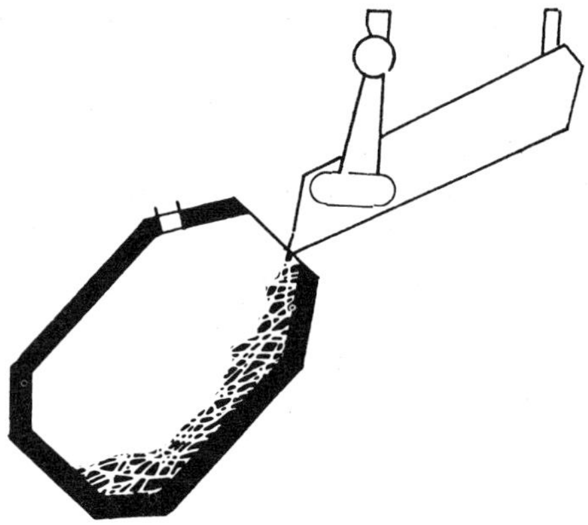

Scrap steel (which makes up about 30 per cent of the total 'charge') is put into the special tilting furnace.

2

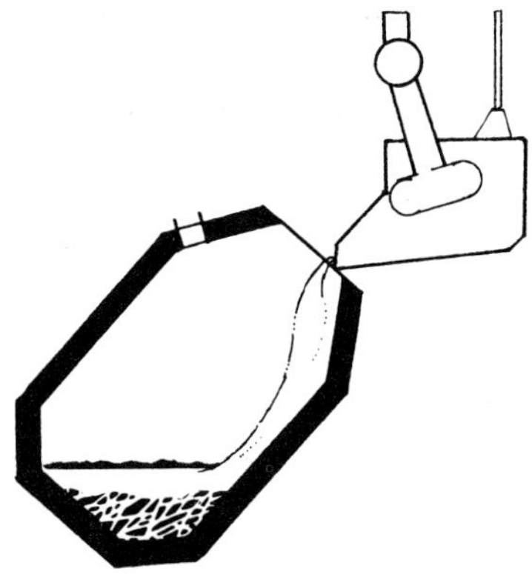

Molten iron makes up the rest of the charge, which can be 350 tonnes in total.

3

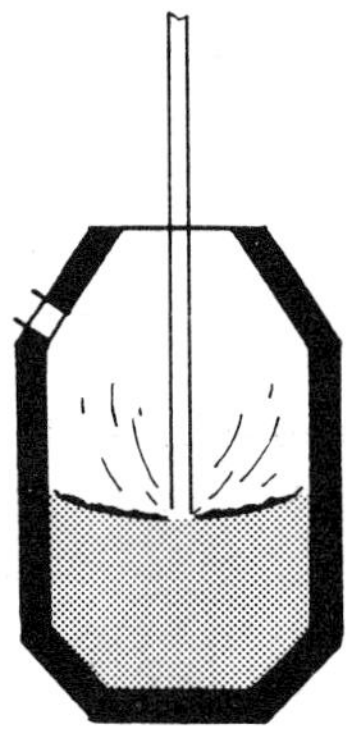

The 'blow' involves directing a high-speed blast of pure oxygen through a water-cooled lance onto the surface of the hot metal. At this stage, lime may also be added.

4

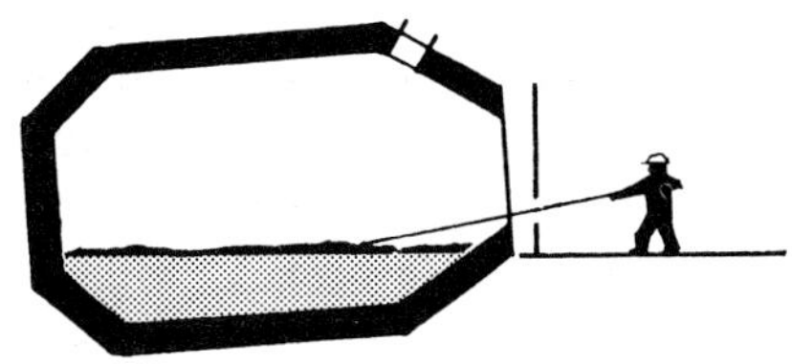

A sample of the product is analysed to check that the steel has reached the desired composition.

5

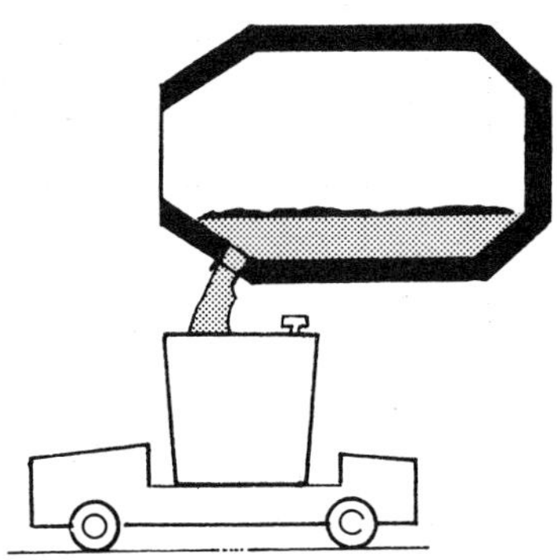

The molten steel is poured off ('tapped').

6

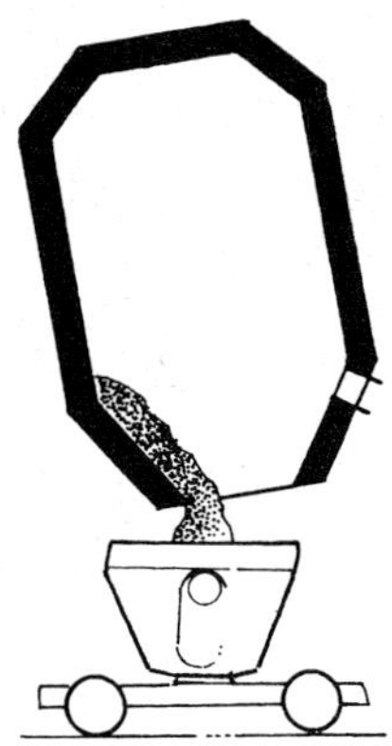

Finally, slag is removed. The whole process takes less than an hour.

Basic oxygen steel-making process

Notes: 1. The BOS process is sometimes called the LD process (from Linz–Donawitz who developed it).
2. The 'open-hearth' process is now obsolete.
3. The electric arc process is based on the recovery of scrap steel, not the treatment of crude iron, and will not be described.

i The BOS process has evolved over a long period. The original Bessemer process (1856) used a furnace lined with *silica* bricks. Why do you think silica was considered to be a suitable material for lining a furnace?

ii In 1878 the Thomas–Gilchrist modification was introduced. In this process, the silica lining of the furnace was replaced by a *basic* lining containing, for example, CaO or MgO. Explain the likely advantage of this innovation.

iii Until relatively recently, the molten iron was treated with a blast of *air* rather than oxygen. The steel produced then was more brittle than steel produced by the oxygen method nowadays. Suggest an explanation.

Casting molten steel into ingot moulds

iv Write *equations* for any reactions that you think might take place during the 'blow'.

v Which of the products in (iv) above are likely to be volatile?

vi What special measures would be needed to deal with these volatile products in a steel works? Explain why.

vii Which of the products in (iv) above are likely to be involatile?

viii Explain how the involatile products are removed from the steel.

3. **Carbon steels and alloy steels**

Steels consisting of iron and carbon only are called simply carbon steels. Any steel containing more than 0.5 per cent in total of elements other than carbon is referred to as an *alloy steel*. Alloy steels are more expensive than carbon steels and they generally have specialized uses, that is, they are not used for general large-scale engineering and building purposes.

The next table gives the compositions of some steels and their properties.

Steel	*Typical composition (%)*	*Notable properties*
A mild steel	Fe 99.8 C 0.2	relatively soft and easily worked, i.e. malleable and ductile, especially when hot
B high-carbon steel	Fe 99 C 1	relatively hard and tough
C	Fe 76 W 18 Cr 5 C 1	remains hard at high temperatures
D	Fe 69 Cr 20 Ni 10 C 1	good corrosion resistance
E	Fe 86 Mn 13 C 1	hard-wearing over long periods

Which steel would be useful for:

i high-speed metal-working tools
ii kitchen drainers and cutlery
iii rock-breaking machinery
iv wire, nails or sheet steel
v wood-working tools such as chisels

4. This question is about the following reactants that are involved in industrial processes for extracting metals. In each case: *a* name the reducing agent, and *b* suggest a balanced equation.

i iron (III) oxide and carbon monoxide
ii carbon and tin (IV) oxide
iii titanium tetrachloride and sodium
iv zinc oxide and carbon
v uranium (IV) oxide and magnesium

Revision

1. Read each of the following statements and say whether it is *true* or *false*:

i Aluminium is higher in the reactivity series than copper.
ii Zinc oxide is more stable than sodium oxide towards reducing agents.
iii Iron is more widely used than aluminium because of its greater natural abundance.
iv Aluminium only became readily available after the development of electrolytic methods of extraction.
v Carbon would be expected to reduce lead(II) oxide at a lower temperature than it could reduce magnesium oxide.

2. This question is about the following equations:

A $2Al_2O_3 \rightarrow 4Al + 3O_2$
B $CaCO_3 \rightarrow CaO + CO_2$
C $CaO + SiO_2 \rightarrow CaSiO_3$
D $C + O_2 \rightarrow CO_2$
E $CO_2 + C \rightarrow 2CO$

Which of them represents:

i slag formation in the blast furnace extraction of iron
ii the reaction that produces a reducing agent in the blast furnace
iii a thermal decomposition that happens in the blast furnace
iv the reaction that generates most heat in the blast furnace
v a change that can be brought about by electrolysis, but not by heat alone

3. State the meaning of the following chemical terms and give an example to illustrate each of them.

i decomposition
ii electrolysis
iii reduction
iv smelting
v stable

Unit 44
Getting metals by electrolysis

Industrial electrolysis

Electrolysis processes play an important part in the economy of developed countries. We have seen (Unit 38) that the *chlor-alkali industry* relies on electrolysis for the production of sodium hydroxide and chlorine. In the last Unit, you were reminded that for metals near the top of the reactivity series the only feasible method of extraction is electrolysis. This applies to aluminium, magnesium, calcium and the alkali metals such as sodium (see Unit 38, Downs cell). Electrolysis also plays a part in the *purification* of some metals after extraction, for example copper, and in the *electroplating* of metal objects.

In this Unit we shall concentrate on industrial electrolysis as it applies to metal extraction, purification and plating.

- *The extraction, purification and plating of metals are important applications of electrolysis.*

Extraction of aluminium

The principle of this process has remained unchanged since it was developed independently by Charles Hall (USA) and Paul Heroult (France) in the same year, 1886. (By coincidence, both men were born in 1843, and both died in 1914!)

An aluminium electrolysis plant, showing the electrolysis cells

Raw material

The ores of aluminium are called *bauxites* and they contain mineral forms of hydrated alumina ($Al_2O_3.3H_2O$ or $Al_2O_3.H_2O$). Ores that are economically useful at present generally contain 45 per cent Al_2O_3. Impurities include SiO_2, Fe_2O_3 and TiO_2.

The first stage in the extraction process is to obtain the pure aluminium oxide (alumina) from the ore. This is achieved by treating the crushed ore with hot sodium hydroxide solution. The aluminium oxide dissolves, forming sodium aluminate.

$$\mathbf{Al_2O_3(s) + 2NaOH(aq) + 3H_2O(l) \rightarrow 2NaAl(OH)_4(aq)}$$

Insoluble impurities, together with some undissolved Al_2O_3, are separated from the solution by sedimentation. Then the sodium aluminate is decomposed to form aluminium hydroxide, $Al(OH)_3$. This is achieved by dilution (which lowers the pH) and by cooling the solution.

$$\mathbf{NaAl(OH)_4(aq) \rightarrow NaOH(aq) + Al(OH)_3(s)}$$

A copper refinery

Crystallization of the $Al(OH)_3$ is encouraged by seeding the mixture with previously prepared crystalline $Al(OH)_3$. Finally, the aluminium hydroxide is decomposed (dehydrated) by heating it at 1200–1500 °C to form pure anhydrous alumina (Al_2O_3).

$$2Al(OH)_3(s) \rightarrow Al_2O_3(s) + 3H_2O(g)$$

Electrolysis

The main difficulty at this stage is the high melting temperature and insolubility of alumina. In practice, a suitable electrolyte is formed by dissolving the Al_2O_3 in molten cryolite, Na_3AlF_6. (Cryolite is found as a mineral or may be manufactured.) At 1000 °C, cryolite is a good solvent for Al_2O_3 and will dissolve about 15 per cent by mass of the oxide.

The electrodes are made of carbon that is manufactured from bitumen. The cathode is the carbon lining of the electrolysis tank, with a steel bar embedded in it (see figure below). This conducts the electricity into the molten mixture. The aluminium oxide is decomposed by the electricity passing through it. The anodes are carbon blocks in the centre of the tank. They conduct the electricity away again.

The electrode reactions are as follows:

i *At the anode:*

$$O^{2-} \rightarrow O + 2e^-$$
$$2O + C \rightarrow CO_2$$

As the second equation suggests, the carbon of the anode is slowly eaten away by oxidation to form carbon dioxide.

ii *At the cathode:*

$$Al^{3+} + 3e^- \rightarrow Al$$

Molten aluminium is formed as a pool at the base of the electrolysis tank, as illustrated in the next figure. Each cell is capable of producing about 1 tonne of aluminium per day in a continuous process.

● *Aluminium is manufactured by electrolysis of alumina dissolved in molten cryolite using carbon electrodes.*

Copper purification

Copper occupies a position near the bottom of the activity series. It can therefore be easily extracted from its ores by smelting, that is,

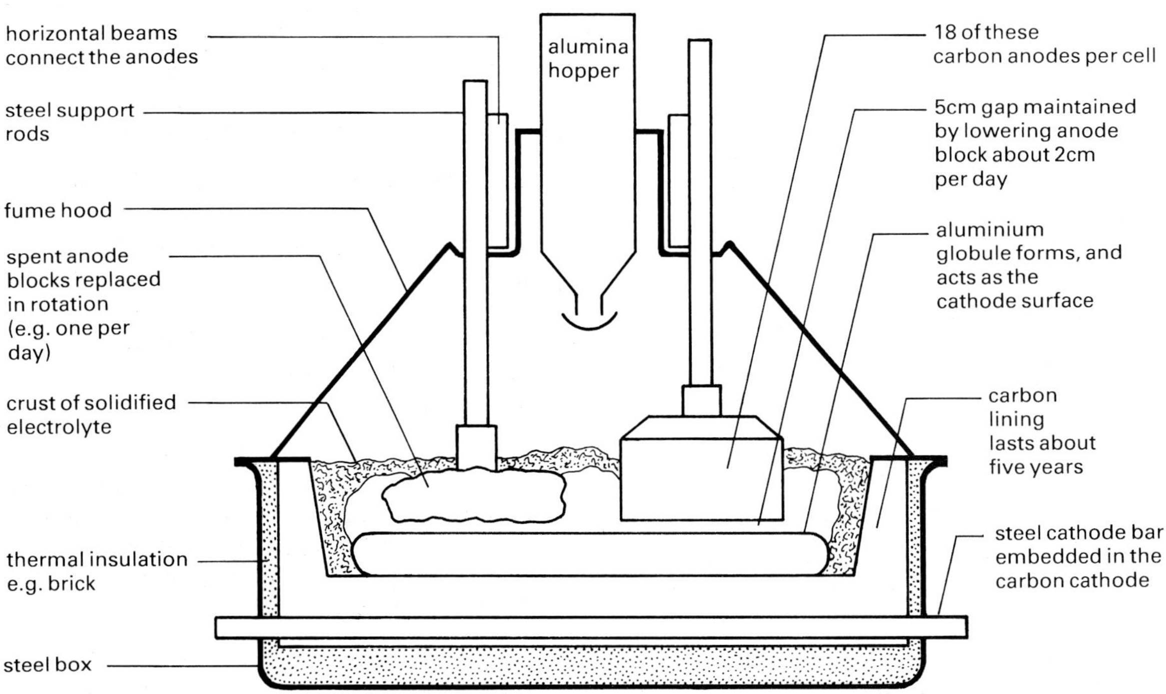

Cross-section of an electrolysis cell for the Hall-Héroult Process

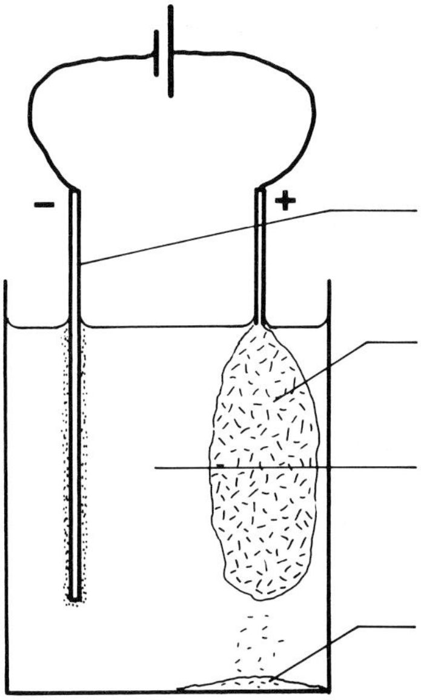

Electrolytic refining of copper

chemical reduction. However, the copper produced is impure and needs refining. (Copper is mainly used for electrical apparatus, and high purity results in high electrical conductivity.) The purest copper (99.95 per cent) is produced by *electrolytic refining*. The principle of this process is simple and is illustrated in the figure above.

The cell contains a mixed electrolyte of $CuSO_4(aq)$ and $H_2SO_4(aq)$ and operates at room temperature. The anodes are made of the impure copper to be refined, and the cathodes consist of very pure copper. At the start of the electrolysis the cathodes are thin sheets, but over a period of several days they get thicker and thicker as copper is deposited on them.

Cathode process:

$$\mathbf{Cu^{2+}(aq) + 2e^- \rightarrow Cu(s)}$$

At the same time, the copper of the anodes gradually dissolves into the solution.

Anode process:

$$\mathbf{Cu(s) \rightarrow Cu^{2+}(aq) + 2e^-}$$

Precious metals such as gold, silver and platinum may be present in the impure anode blocks. These metals do not dissolve into the electrolyte; instead they collect on the floor of the cell as sludge. The sludge is removed at intervals and processed to extract the precious metals. Metals such as iron that may be in the anode material dissolve into the electrolyte, but are not deposited at the cathode. Thus only copper collects at the cathode and the purity of the product is very high.

● *Highly purified copper is produced by electrolytic refining.*

Electroplating

Electroplating means coating a metal object with a layer of another metal by using electrolysis. This can have a number of purposes, for example:

a forming a protective coating to stop corrosion;
b forming a shiny, attractive surface;
c making a cheap metal look like an expensive one.

In theory, electroplating shou d be easy. Passing a current through a solutio. . many salts (those of less reactive metals) should cause the metal to be deposited at the cathode. In practice, unless conditions are just right, the coating that forms on the cathode is often an uneven, dull and powdery layer that soon flakes off. By contrast, what is needed is a thin but uniform coating, firmly bonded to the material of the cathode, and with a hard, shiny surface. Conditions must be carefully controlled to get this desired result; these conditions include:

a the surface of the cathode object (it must be degreased and cleaned thoroughly, for example by acid 'pickling', before starting);
b the composition and concentration of the electrolyte;
c the current flowing through the cell;
d the temperature of the electrolyte;
e the pH of the electrolyte.

Metals that may be used to electroplate objects include chromium, nickel, zinc, cadmium, tin, copper and silver. The chosen metal is used as the anode in the electrolysis cell. An appropriate compound of the metal is used as the electrolyte in solution.

● *The durability and appearance of metal objects can be improved by electroplating with other metals.*

Some examples of electroplating

More nickel is used for electroplating than any other metal, often as an 'undercoat' for another metal, for example, underneath electroplated chromium or silver. Electrolyte solutions of nickel(II) sulphate and nickel(II) chloride are commonly used. The pH of the electrolyte is kept between 2 and 5.

For chromium plating, the electrolytes that work best are found to be acidic solutions of chromate(VI) compounds. Hydrogen is liberated at the cathode, as well as chromium. In practice, the finished article may have a first coat of copper, then nickel and finally chromium. The spray produced during chromium plating is known to be a health hazard. Tools, door-handles, taps and bicycle parts are examples of items that may be chromium plated.

Tin-plated steel is used in the drinks and food-canning industry. A very thin film of tin (10^{-7} cm) is plated onto the steel by the rapid passage of a continuous steel strip through the electrolysis bath (see illustration below).

Summary

1. Electrolysis is used in industry as a means of extracting, purifying and plating metals.
2. Aluminium is extracted electrolytically by the Hall–Heroult process.
3. Industrial electrolysis is used to produce highly refined copper.
4. Electroplating of metals helps to cut down corrosion and can make them more attractive.
5. Nickel, chromium and tin are good examples of important electroplating metals.

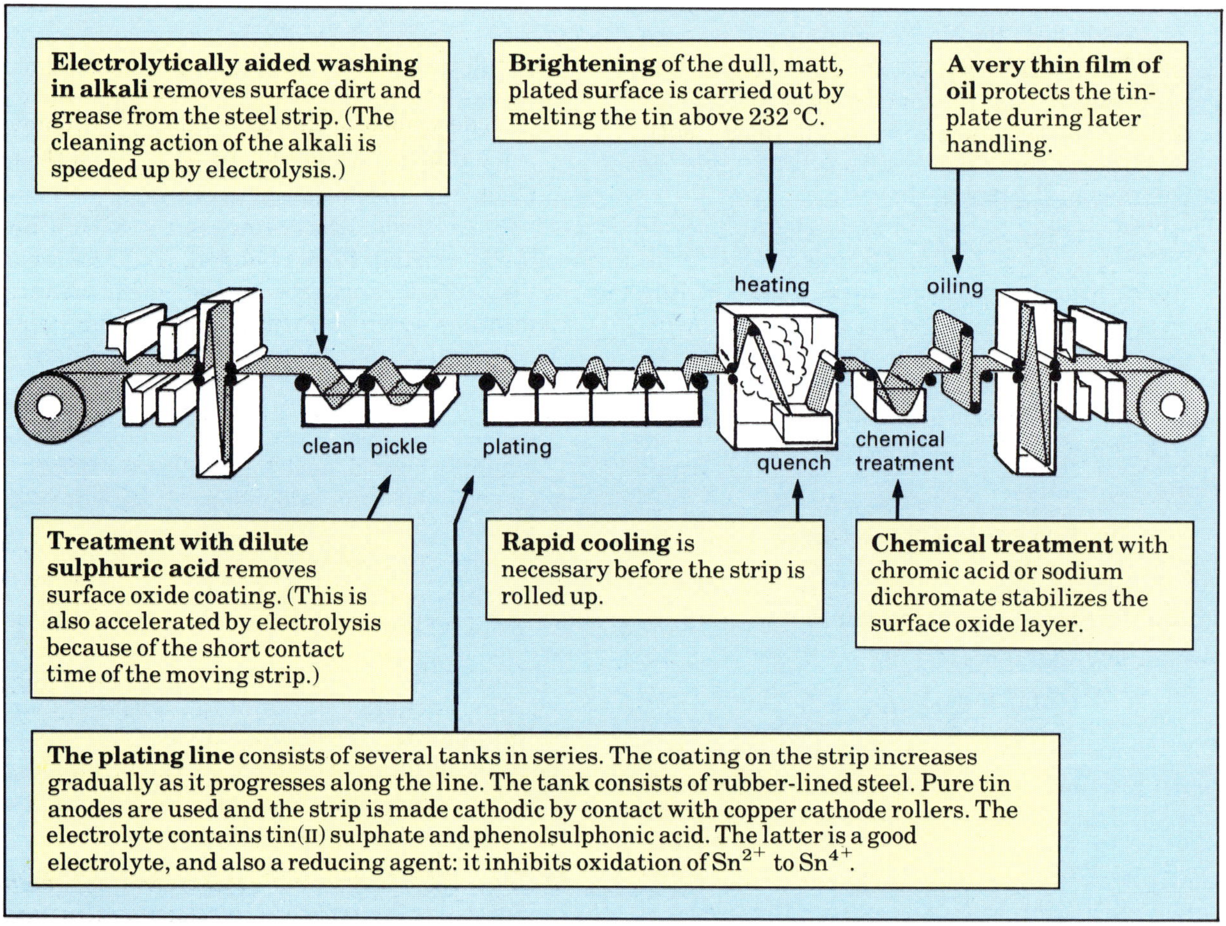

Electrolytic tinning

Extension

1. During the electrolysis stage of aluminium manufacture, small additions of certain electrolytes are made to the cryolite/alumina solution. These include AlF_3 and CaF_2. They help to keep the working temperature of the electrolysis cell down.
   - i Why is it important to keep the working temperature down?
   - ii If the Al_2O_3 concentration in the cell gets too low during the electrolysis, fluorine and sodium may be formed at the electrodes. At which electrode would fluorine be formed?
   - iii Write an equation to show the formation of sodium at an electrode.
   - iv What problems would result from the formation of sodium and fluorine?
   - v Why is sodium not normally formed during the electrolysis of cryolite/alumina solutions?
2. In the Hall–Heroult cell, some of the aluminium that is formed at the cathode diffuses to the anode, where it reacts with CO_2(g) to form CO(g).
   - i What does 'diffuses' mean?
   - ii Write an equation to account for the formation of CO(g) as described above.
   - iii What problems could arise from the process described above?
3. This Unit has been concerned with metals such as Al, Cu, Ni, Cr and Sn. These metals are examples of *non-ferrous* metals, that is, they are not iron. Similarly, alloys other than steels (i.e. those with no iron content) are sometimes called *non-ferrous alloys*. This extension is about some non-ferrous alloys.

   As you know, the properties of the constituent metals are modified considerably by alloying; for example an alloy may be much harder, or may have a lower melting temperature, than its constituents.

   The next table gives some data about a few alloys.

Alloy	*Composition (%)*		*Notable properties*
A	Cu Ni	75 25	hardwearing and resists tarnishing
B	Sn Pb	60 40	relatively low-melting (but weak and soft)
C	Al Cu Mg Mn	94.0 4.0 1.5 0.5	nearly as strong as mild steel but only one-third as dense
D	Cu Sn Pb Zn P	87.5 7.5 3.5 1.0 0.5	tough and springy
E	Cu Zn	70 30	very ductile, easily worked and yellow

Non-ferrous alloys

   - i Which alloy is:
     - *a* brass
     - *b* coinage alloy
     - *c* duralumin
     - *d* phosphor-bronze
     - *e* solder
   - ii Suggest one use for each of the alloys A–E described in the table and explain how the use is related to the properties described.
5. Potassium was first isolated in 1807 by the English scientist Humphry Davy. He also suggested the existence of a then unknown element 'aluminium' in alumina, but he was unable to isolate it. It was not until 1825 that aluminium was isolated for the first time by the Danish scientist Hans Christian Oersted.
   - i Davy used electricity to obtain samples of potassium. Suggest a method for the process that he might have used.
   - ii Why do you think he was unable to obtain aluminium by a similar method?
   - iii Oersted's method for obtaining aluminium did not involve electrolysis. Instead he used potassium as a reducing agent. Suggest a method for obtaining aluminium by a reaction of potassium. Write an equation for the suggested reaction and show how it is a redox process.
   - iv Find out more about Humphry Davy and Hans Christian Oersted.

Revision

1. What are the reasons for electroplating objects? Give examples to illustrate your answer.
2. The flow chart and illustrations show the step-by-step conversion of crude bauxite into pure aluminium oxide.
   i Draw an outline of the flow chart (not the illustrations) and insert labels to show the *processes* 1–7. (Match them up with *a* – *j* below.)
      a cooling and seeding of sodium aluminate liquor to precipitate $Al(OH)_3(s)$
      b crushing bauxite ore
      c filtration of precipitated $Al(OH)_3(s)$
      d grinding ore with $NaOH(aq)$ in a ball-mill
      e heating the precipitated $Al(OH)_3$ (s) in a rotary kiln at 1200 °C
      f heating alkaline bauxite slurry at 140–250 °C (under pressure) to 'digest' (dissolve) the alumina
      g separation of undissolved impurities from 'digested' bauxite
   ii Three of the *stages* A–F in the process correspond to:
      h crushed bauxite
      i hot sodium aluminate 'liquor' (filtrate)
      j hot sodium aluminate(aq) with undissolved impurity solids

      Put these in their correct places on the diagram.
   iii Insert captions for the remaining stages in the process.

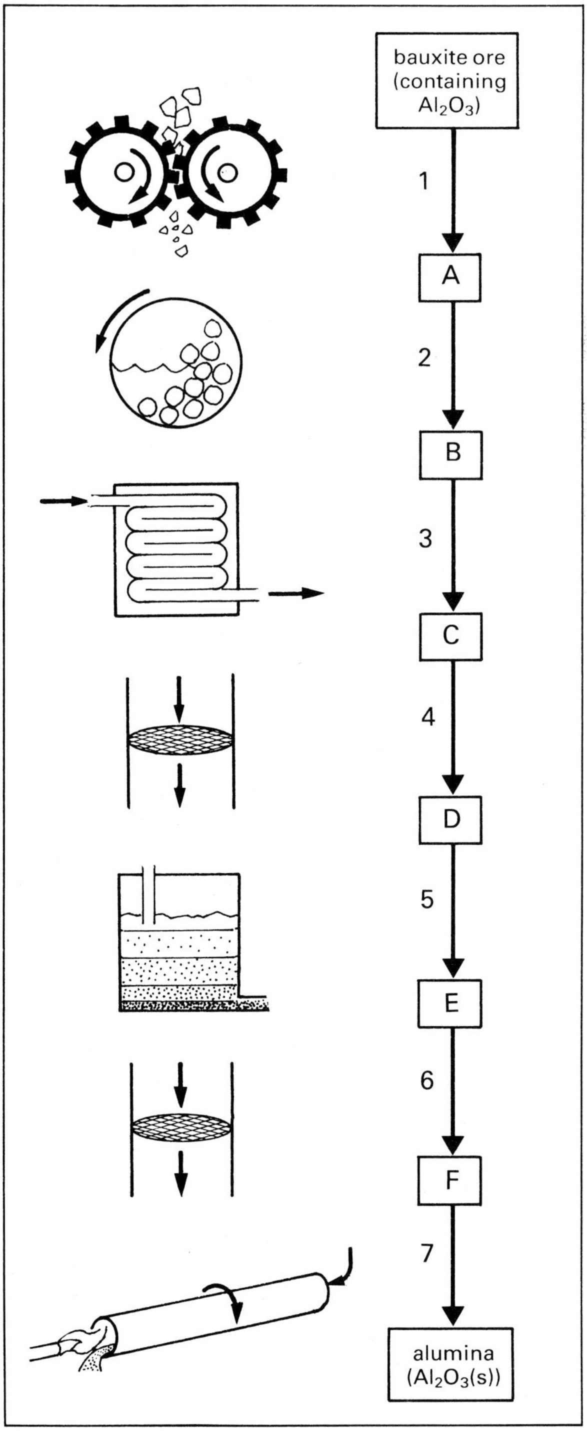

Flow-chart to show the conversion of bauxite to alumina

Unit 45
Nuclear power

Energy and civilization

A plentiful supply of energy is needed to keep up the present standard of living in developed countries. The many poor countries in the world need more energy to improve the lives of their people. Where will all the energy come from?

At present in the UK we get more than 80 per cent of our electrical energy from 'fossil fuels', that is, coal and oil. These fuels will not meet the demand for energy in the future. Stocks will begin to run out in the next century, if we continue to use them at the present rate. Already, the world's population is increasing faster than the oil supply. This is a good reason for looking for alternative energy sources now. (There is another argument against using coal and oil as fuels: they are precious raw materials for chemical products, and too valuable for burning.)

Alternative energy sources include solar energy, wind, wave and tidal power, and *nuclear power*. This Unit is about nuclear power, that is, about getting energy from the atomic nucleus, mainly by nuclear fission.

- *Using nuclear power for generating electricity is an alternative to burning fossil fuels.*

At present, about 14 per cent of our electricity is generated in nuclear power stations.

Nuclear fission

When a piece of uranium metal is bombarded with low-energy neutrons, it gets hot. The large amounts of energy that are given out may be put to use for generating electricity. Where does the energy come from? The answer has to do with the *splitting* of atomic nuclei.

Experiments have shown that very large nuclei, like those of uranium atoms, may split into two roughly equal fragments under suitable conditions. Each fragment is the nucleus of a lighter element. Uranium contains the isotopes $^{235}_{92}U$ and $^{238}_{92}U$. Bombardment of uranium with slow-moving neutrons causes the $^{235}_{92}U$ nuclei to split (figure below). Fast (higher energy) neutrons are absorbed less efficiently.

The splitting of $^{235}_{92}U$ nuclei is an example of *nuclear fission*. When fission happens, a very great deal of energy is released, together with a few 'spare' neutrons. Nuclei that can undergo fission are said to be *fissile*. Only about 0.7 per cent of uranium nuclei are of the fissile $^{235}_{92}U$ isotope. Most of the rest is $^{238}_{92}U$, which cannot be split by low-energy neutrons.

- *Uranium gets hot when it absorbs slow neutrons because of energy released by the fission of $^{235}_{92}U$.*

Chain reaction

Fission of one nucleus may produce two or three neutrons as well as the main 'fragments' (the new nuclei). The neutrons released by the fission of one nucleus can go on to cause the fission of other nuclei. If things are arranged so that sufficient neutrons collide with nearby nuclei, then the process of fission may keep itself going. This is called a nuclear *chain reaction* (figure p.230 left).

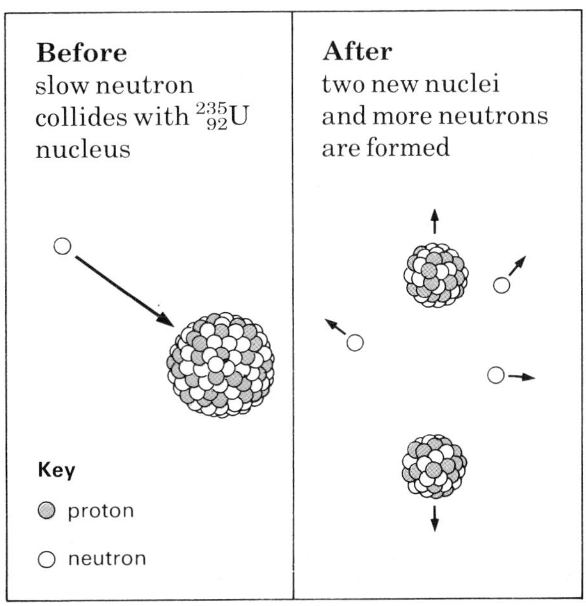

Splitting a nucleus

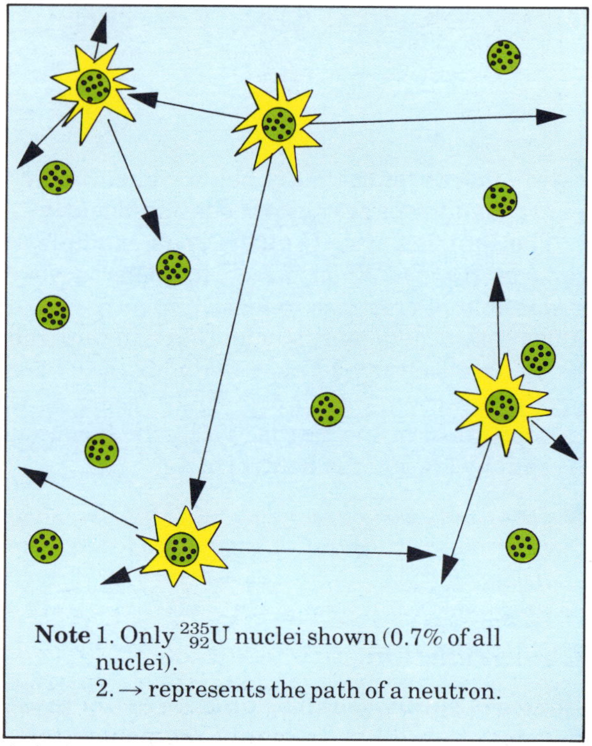

A chain reaction in uranium

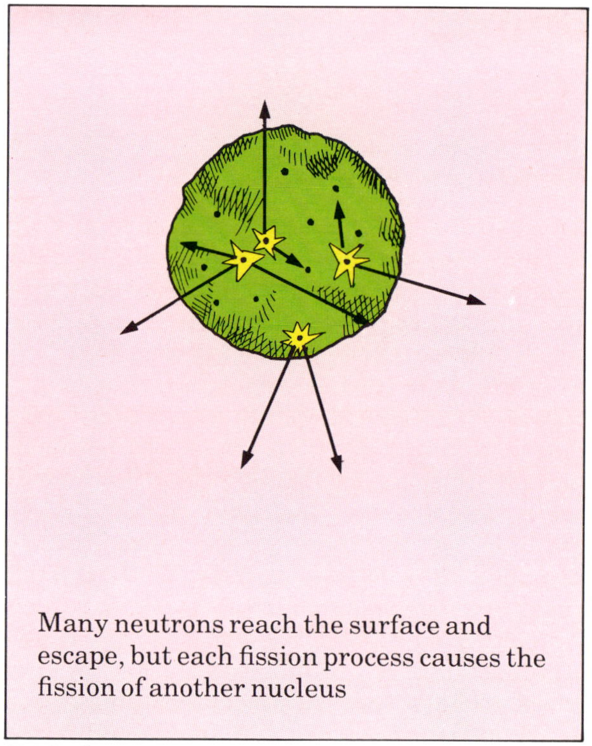

Critical mass

If every neutron formed in the chain reaction causes the fission of a nucleus, the increasing amount of heat released results in an explosion. However, if the piece of fissile material is small, many of the neutrons escape to the outside and the chain reaction hardly gets started. The larger the mass, the more neutrons are absorbed before they can escape. A piece of fissile material that is just the right size to absorb enough neutrons to keep the chain reaction going is said to have *critical mass* (see figure above right). (So, only masses larger than the critical mass can be turned into bombs.)

However, masses that are larger than the critical mass are used safely in nuclear reactors. This is done by the use of 'control rods' made of boron. The rods are inserted into holes in the block of fissile material, and the boron nuclei absorb the excess neutrons. Enough neutrons are left over to keep the fission process going at a steady rate.

● *A steady chain reaction occurs when only one neutron from each fission proceeds to cause another nucleus to split.*

Nuclear fuel supplies

Uranium ores are found in many parts of the world, although none is mined in Britain. The world has reserves of natural uranium amounting to about two million tonnes. Even though only 0.7 per cent is fissile, we would need a mass of coal thousands of times greater to get an equivalent energy source.

After mining, the metal must be extracted from the ore. For some types of reactor, the concentration of $^{235}_{92}U$ in the metal must be increased. This concentration (or 'enrichment') can be achieved by making uranium hexafluoride, UF_6, which is volatile. As a gas it will undergo gaseous diffusion. The UF_6 containing the $^{235}_{92}U$ isotope diffuses faster than the UF_6 containing $^{238}_{92}U$, and this allows partial separation of the two types of UF_6. The enriched UF_6 is usually converted into uranium(IV) oxide, UO_2, before being manufactured into 'fuel rods' suitable for use in a nuclear reactor.

An alternative fuel for nuclear reactors is the artificial element, *plutonium*. This is produced in small amounts as a by-product in uranium-powered nuclear reactors. While the ${}^{235}_{92}U$ is undergoing fission, some of the ${}^{238}_{92}U$ is converted into the plutonium isotope, ${}^{239}_{94}Pu$. The plutonium nuclei are fissile like ${}^{235}_{92}U$. They can be used to generate more energy if the plutonium is extracted from the uranium. Specially designed reactors (called 'fast reactors') are being developed to use plutonium instead of uranium. This development means that all the nuclei in natural uranium are potential sources of nuclear energy.

- *Nuclear fuels include natural ${}^{235}_{92}U$ and artificial ${}^{239}_{94}Pu$.*

(It is often convenient to call the isotopes uranium–235 and plutonium–239.)

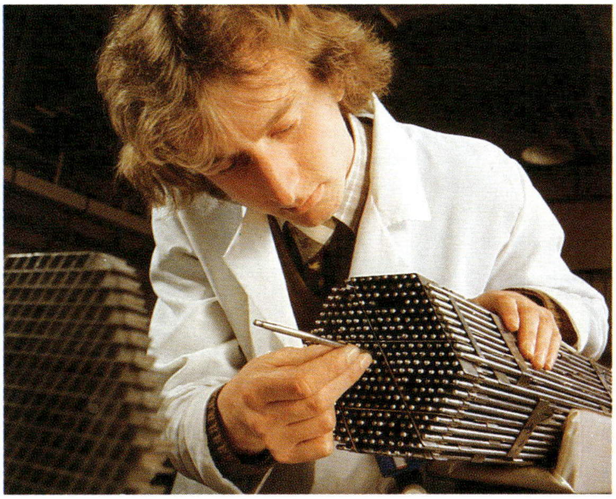

Uranium fuel rods being assembled

Nuclear reactors

The basic principle of a power station, whether it has a nuclear reactor or a coal-fired furnace, is the same. Energy is generated in the reactor or furnace, and is transferred to a water boiler. The transfer is carried out by the flow of a fluid that circulates (in a closed circuit) from the reactor (or furnace) to a heat exchanger in the boiler. The steam from the boiler is used to drive a turbine and generate electricity (see below).

At present, most nuclear reactors still rely on uranium–235 to produce energy. These so-called 'thermal' reactors all use a *moderator* in the core of the reactor. A moderator is a material that slows down high-energy neutrons. The use of a moderator allows the uranium–235 nuclei to capture the neutrons more efficiently. Graphite is used as a moderator in many thermal reactors, although water is used in others.

An important consideration in the design of a nuclear reactor is the choice of coolant. This is the fluid used to transfer heat from the reactor to the boiler. Two important types of thermal reactor used in the UK are the Magnox type and the Advanced Gas-cooled Reactor (AGR). Both use CO_2 gas as the coolant. The main difference between them is that the AGR uses enriched uranium containing about 2.3 per cent uranium–235, while the Magnox reactor uses uranium with the natural proportion of 0.7 per cent uranium–235 (figure p.232).

The development of experimental 'fast' reactors started in 1954. These reactors use the fission of plutonium nuclei, which can be brought about by high-energy (fast) nuclei. Moderators are not needed in fast reactors. They also differ from thermal reactors in another way: liquid sodium (instead of CO_2 gas or water) is used as the coolant. In the future, more of our energy may be generated in fast

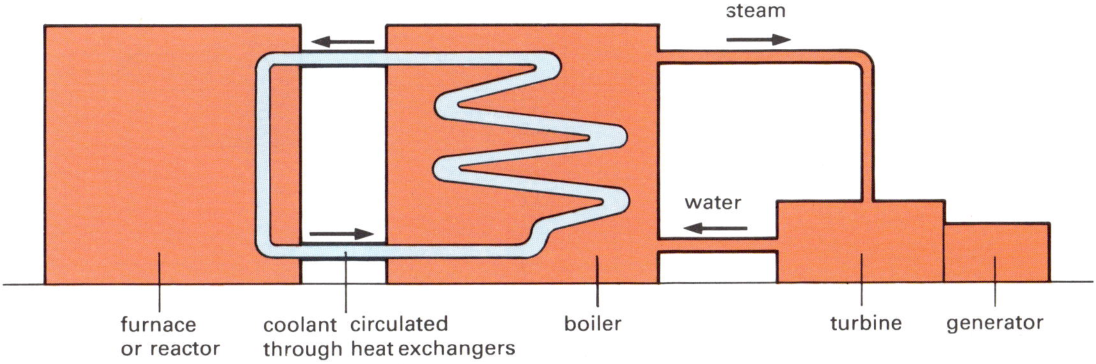

Basic principles of a power station

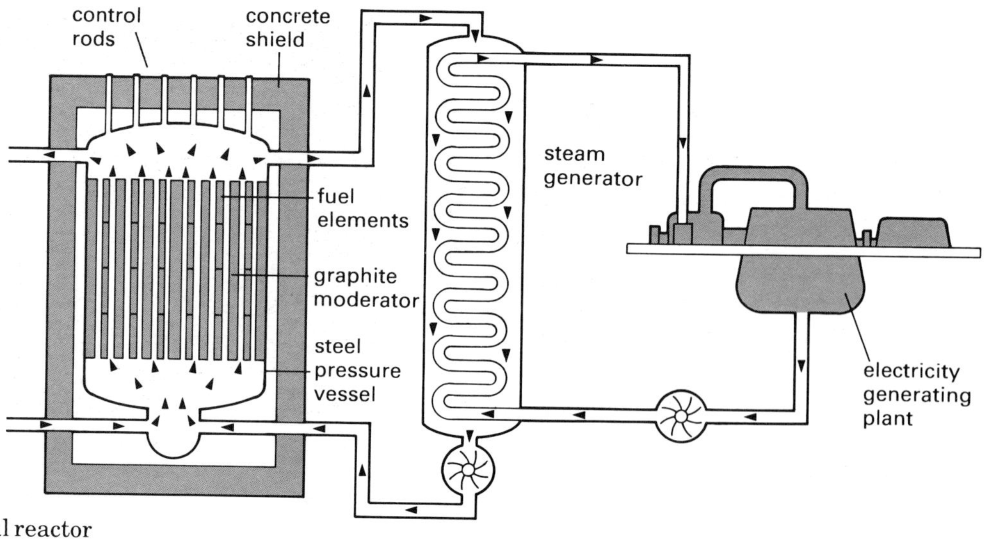

Magnox thermal reactor

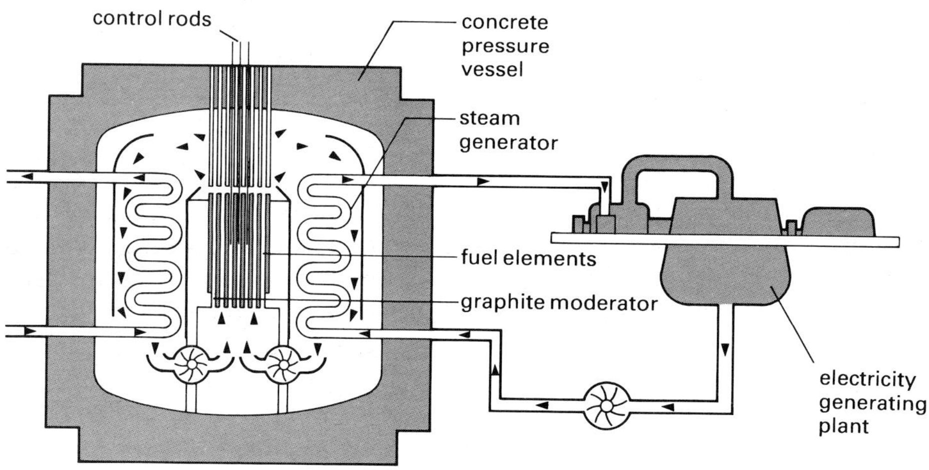

AGR

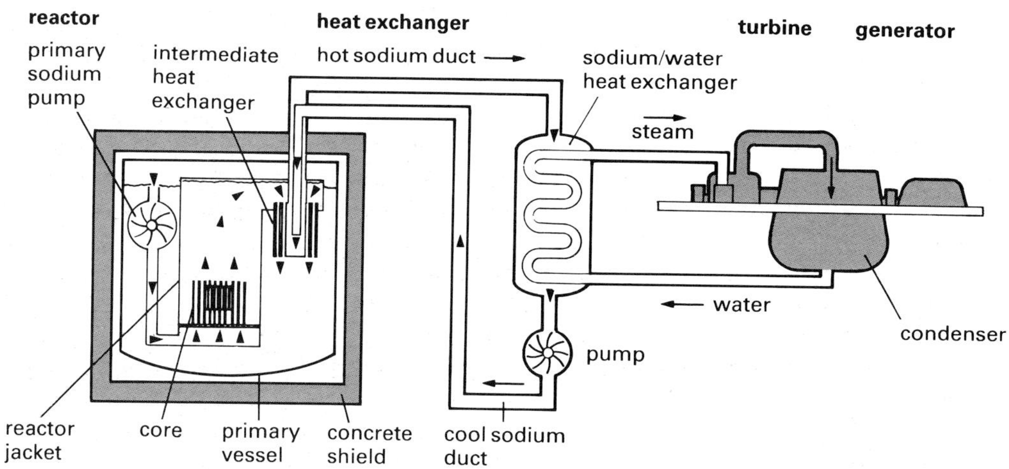

A fast reactor

The UKAEA fast reactor at Dounreay in Scotland; the new prototype fast reactor is shown in the foreground, with an earlier fast reactor on the right

A storage tank for highly radioactive fission product waste; the tanks are double walled and put into concrete vaults lined with stainless steel

reactors, but at present thermal reactors are still the main source of nuclear power.

● *Most nuclear power is generated in thermal reactors like AGR and Magnox reactors.*

A 'breeder' reactor is one in which the core is surrounded by a blanket of natural uranium. Escaping neutrons convert the uranium–238 into plutonium–239. After many years of use, a breeder reactor should produce enough plutonium to set up a second 'fast' reactor.

Nuclear problems

A major problem that the atomic energy authority has to deal with is the disposal of nuclear waste. What can you do with radioactive materials that you don't want?

There are two approaches to this problem. One is to store the waste, either on the surface or underground. If the waste is kept for long enough, the radioactivity drops to safe levels. In some cases, however, it would have to be stored for tens of thousands of years. The problems of handling and storing highly radioactive waste can be reduced if it is sealed in concrete or glass blocks before storage. Over long periods, materials such as glass or concrete may deteriorate because of weathering or corrosion. This problem would have to be guarded against and solved if it arose.

Another approach to the problem is to release the waste to the environment so that it gets diluted in the sea or in the air. This is only done in the case of low-activity waste that will not significantly affect the environment. Some low-activity waste is sealed in drums, which are set in concrete and dumped in the deep ocean.

Another major problem facing a society with nuclear power is the problem of security from terrorist activity. Plutonium is one of the most dangerous poisons that man uses; and it can be used to make nuclear weapons. The safe transport and storage of nuclear fuel, and the protection of nuclear reactors, are very important to all of us.

● *The use of nuclear fuels could lead to pollution of the environment or a dangerous terrorist threat.*

Summary

1. Uranium–235 undergoes fission by the absorption of slow neutrons.
2. A nuclear chain reaction can result if neutrons from each fission cause more nuclei to split.
3. The main nuclear fuel is uranium–235, and most nuclear power is generated in thermal reactors such as AGR and Magnox.
4. In the future most of our energy may be produced in fast reactors, which use plutonium–239 as nuclear fuel.
5. A society based on nuclear energy must learn to cope with the problems of pollution and terrorist activity.

Extension

1. **Renewable energy sources**
Fossil fuels will not last forever. Even uranium will eventually run out. Other sources of energy are everlasting. One example is wind power. Everlasting sources of energy such as wind power are sometimes called 'renewable' energy sources.
   i List some 'renewable' energy sources.
   ii What are the advantages and disadvantages of wind power and other renewable sources compared with nuclear power?

2. **The nuclear fuel cycle**
Write an account of the processes involved in the manufacture and recovery of nuclear fuels. Use the illustration below as a source of information.

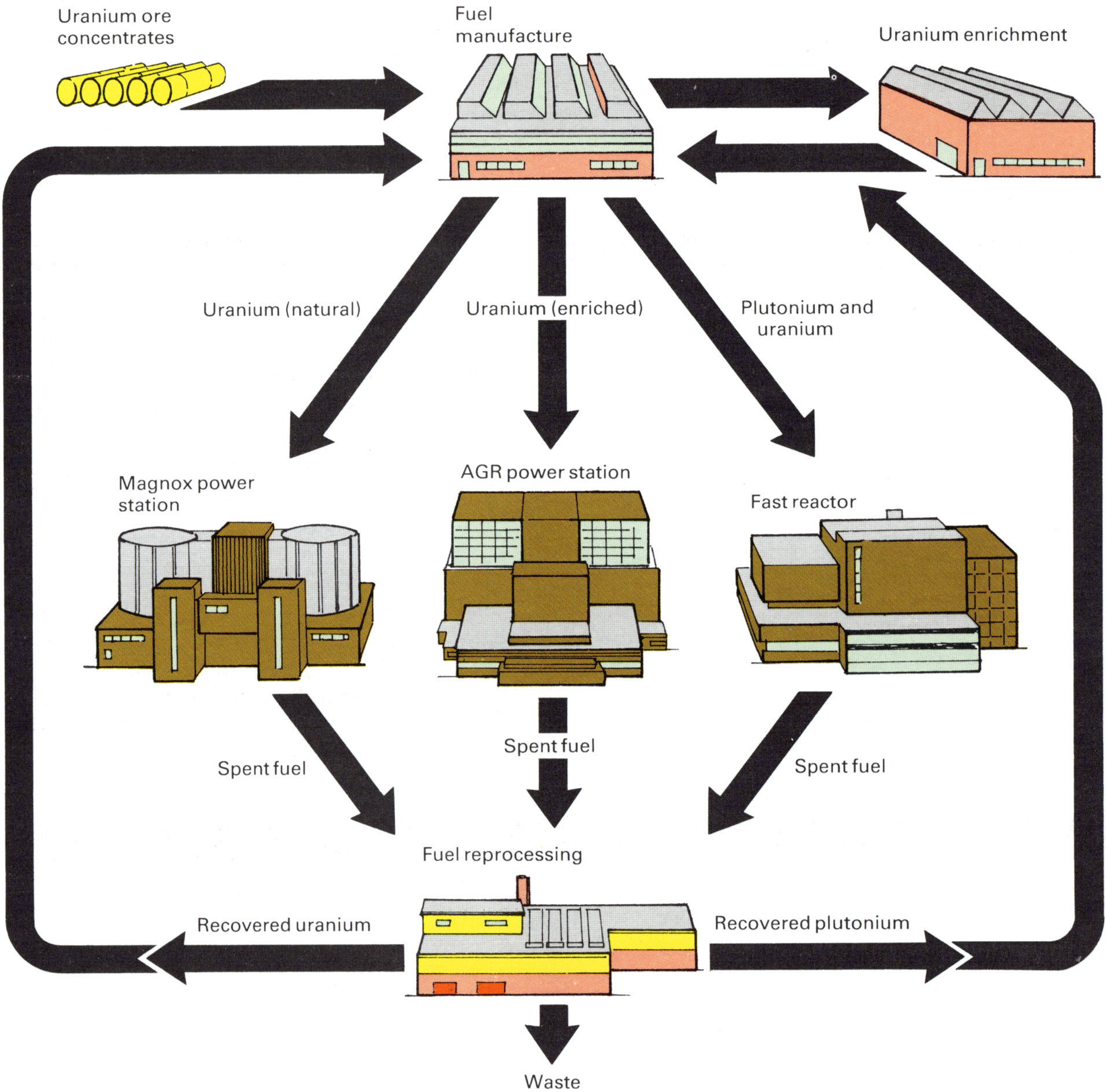

Nuclear fuel cycle

3. **Nuclear fusion**

As we have learned, energy is released when large ('heavy') nuclei are split during fission. Energy is also released when small ('light') nuclei are joined together. For example, two atoms of a hydrogen isotope (called deuterium) can be joined together to form a helium isotope. This joining of nuclei is a process that happens naturally in the sun and other stars. It is called *nuclear fusion*. Research is going on to develop fusion reactors. An important experimental fusion project, the Joint European Torus, is based at Culham in Oxfordshire.

Find out more about fusion and write an account of it, describing its possible advantages and disadvantages compared with fission.

A fusion chamber at Culham; the fusing atoms circulate in the chamber and the doughnut-shaped 'torus' produces a very strong magnetic field that keeps them from escaping

Revision

1. Explain the meaning of each of the following terms:
   - i nuclear fission
   - ii nuclear chain reaction
   - iii critical mass
2. In a nuclear reactor, what is the job of the:
   - i coolant
   - ii moderator
   - iii control rods
3. i What are the main differences between 'thermal' reactors and 'fast' reactors?
   - ii Explain what is meant by a 'breeder' reactor.
4. There are good reasons for not using coal and oil as fuels: they are useful sources of raw materials for chemicals. Future generations may regret the fact that a precious commodity like petroleum was 'wasted' in the internal combustion engine.
   - i Petroleum is converted into petrochemicals (like ethene) by the processes of *fractionation* and *cracking*. What do each of the words in italics mean?
   - ii Explain how ethene is important in the chemical industry.
   - iii If there were no fossil fuels left, what alternative raw materials would there be for making organic chemicals?
   - iv If we decided to stop burning fossil fuels to save them for future use, how could the internal combustion engine be replaced?

Unit 46
Using radioactivity

Radioactive isotopes are sometimes called *radioisotopes*. Chemicals containing radioactive isotopes may be called *radiochemicals*.

Many radioisotopes and radiochemicals are available commercially. Artificial radioactive isotopes of an element can be manufactured in nuclear reactors by exposing the element to neutron bombardment. Radiochemicals are manufactured by Amersham International for use throughout the UK and for export to all parts of the world.

Why are radioisotopes and radiochemicals important? How do we make use of them?

Energy from radioactivity

Huge amounts of energy are released by fission of U–235 and Pu–239 nuclei. This has been dealt with in the previous Unit. Energy is also released by the decay of radioisotopes. This energy can be used to power machines or instruments in remote or inaccessible places; for example, transmitters in space satellites, or heart pacemakers, may be powered by radioisotopes.

- *Radiation from radioisotopes may supply the energy for isolated electrical instruments.*

Measuring time

The radioactivity of a material containing a radioisotope gets less and less as time goes by. Measuring the radioactivity of a material may allow its age to be worked out. The most familiar example is the carbon–14 method for estimating the age of ancient remains. This is done by measuring the radioactivity from carbon–14 in a sample of the material. C–14 is chosen because it has a suitable half-life period (5570 years) and because carbon is a constituent of most ancient remains of interest (e.g. bone, wood). The method is called *carbon dating* and gives reasonably accurate values for the age of samples that are tens of thousands of years old (see Extension).

The proportion of a particular radioisotope decreases as time passes. For example, uranium-bearing rocks can be dated by measuring the proportions of U–238 and Pb–206. Very old rocks contain less U–238 and more Pb–206 because the uranium isotope slowly turns into lead. Geologists can date rocks that are thousands of millions of years old by measuring the uranium : lead ratio.

- *Geologists and archeologists use knowledge of radioisotopes to estimate the ages of rocks and ancient remains.*

Carbon dating of 'King Arthur's table' from Winchester Castle Hall; this table was formerly believed to be the famous table of the legendary King Arthur, for which an appropriate date might have been 5th century AD. The study showed that the table, although ancient, was not King Arthur's. It had been made in the 13th century AD.

Scientists analysing the movement of china clay off the Cornish coast by using isotopic tracers

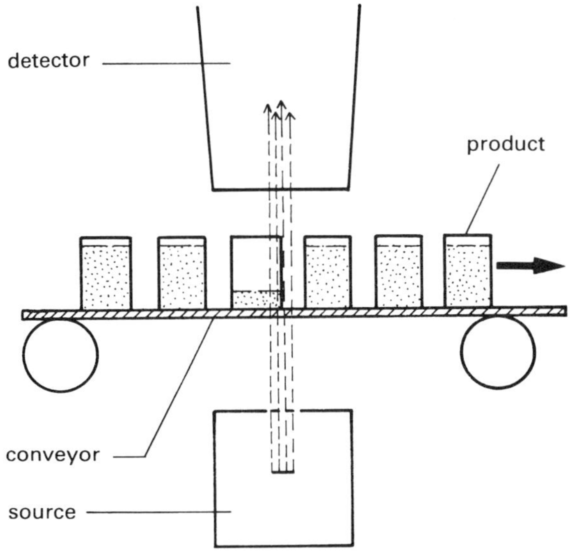

A beta-ray gauge

Tracers

We have instruments that can detect very low levels of radioactivity. If the source of radiation is moving, it can be followed by picking up the radiation on a detector. For example, the movement of a substance round the body can be traced if the substance has been 'labelled' with radioactive atoms in some of its molecules. Radiochemicals used to follow movement in this way are called *tracers*. Tracers are used for experiments in chemistry and biology, for example to investigate the transfer of atoms between molecules, or the transfer of substances in food chains. Tracers may also be used to detect leaks in industrial pipe-work (e.g. underground) and may be used to monitor pollution of the environment (e.g. movement of waste in rivers).

● *Tracers are used to follow the movement of substances, for example round the body or in the environment.*

Industrial gauges

Modern industries are automated. Cans of food, sheets of paper or strips of steel roll off production lines in fast processes. How can these processes be checked as they are working? How do you spot an empty can, or a sheet that is too thick or too thin? Sometimes, the answer to this kind of 'quality control' problem is to use a *beta-ray gauge*. The principle of these gauges is illustrated above.

The advantages of beta-ray gauges for quality control are that the checking can be done quickly, and it doesn't involve damage to the items being checked. The radiation detector can be connected to a device that causes the automatic removal of the defective item from the production line, or causes an alarm signal to go off.

● *Industrial gauges containing radioisotopes are used on industrial production lines.*

Radiation in medicine

Radiation is damaging to life. Very large doses of radiation kill living cells. This has its uses in medicine. For example, cancer cells deep inside the body may be killed off by treatment with gamma rays. This is especially useful when surgery is impossible, but is also often used after surgery to get rid of lingering cancer cells. Fortunately, cancer cells are more sensitive than normal cells to the effects of radiation.

Surgical instruments may be sterilized by exposure to gamma rays. If this is done after

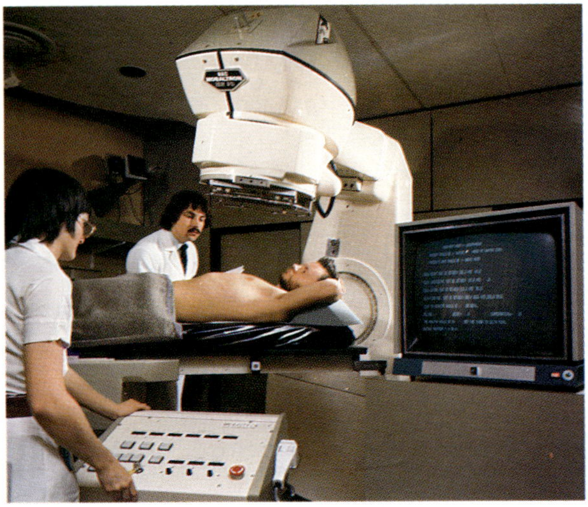

A 3-D radiation therapy unit; the machine contains cobalt–60

packaging, the instruments will remain sterile during storage or transportation.

- *Radiation is useful in medicine for fighting cancer and for sterilizing equipment.*

Extension

Carbon dating

Carbon–14 nuclei are formed in the upper atmosphere from nitrogen–14 nuclei. The carbon–14 nuclei decay by β-emission, and this keeps the proportion of carbon–14 in the environment constant.

All living things have a proportion of carbon–14 in their tissues. The proportion of carbon–14 remains constant until death, but then begins to drop.

1. What substance found in air is likely to contain most of the carbon–14?
2. How does carbon from the atmosphere find its way into plant and animal tissue?
3. Why does the proportion of carbon–14 in living tissue not increase during the lifetime of the organism?
4. Why does the proportion of carbon–14 begin to fall after death?
5. If the half-life of carbon–14 is 5570 years, how long would it take the rate of β-emission from a sample of dead wood to drop to one quarter of its original value?

Summary

1. Radioactive decay may be a source of energy for inaccessible places, for example heart pacemakers.
2. Knowledge about the rate of radioactive decay can be used for dating ancient objects.
3. Radiochemicals may be used as tracers to follow the movement of substances, for example round the body, or in the environment.
4. Beta-ray gauges are used on industrial production lines for quality control of the product.
5. Radiation is useful for medicine because it kills cancer cells and sterilizes instruments.

Revision

1. Explain what is meant by the following terms:
   i radioactivity
   ii radiochemical
   iii tracer
   iv sterilization
   v carbon dating
2. Describe how knowledge of radioisotopes could be used to:
   i work out the age of a rock
   ii investigate a food chain
   iii monitor pollution
3. How can radiation be used:
   i on industrial production lines
   ii in scientific research
   iii in medicine

Unit 47
Development and control of the chemical industry

Economic forces and the siting of industries

The following map shows that the chemical industry is concentrated in a few areas of Britain.

Why has the chemical industry been concentrated into particular places? A major consideration in siting is to put it where industry is likely to be most profitable.

- *Economic forces are very important in deciding where industry develops.*

In the past, chemical industry started close to raw materials, and also near to where there was a demand for chemical products. The difficulties of transporting bulk materials, especially bulk chemicals, meant that distances had to be reasonably short. The influence of these supply and demand factors can best be illustrated by considering a particular industry as an example.

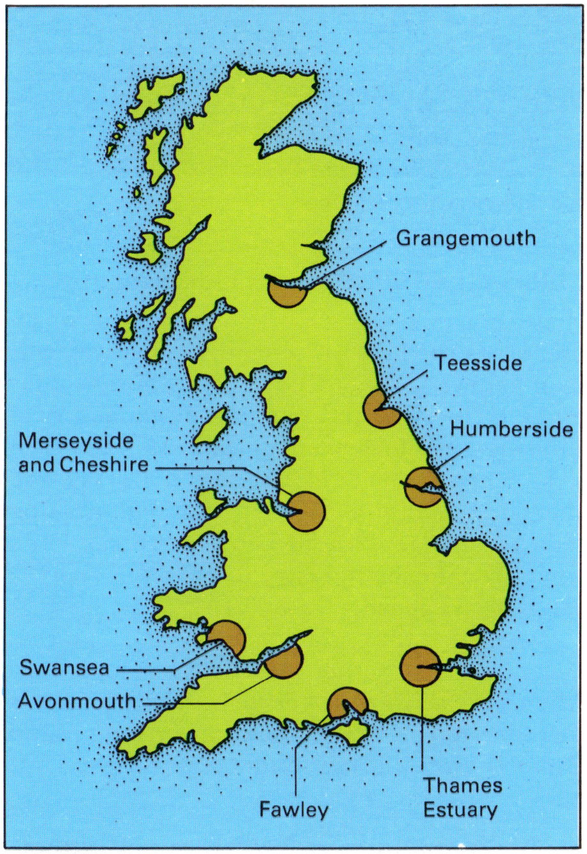

Where is the chemical industry situated in Britain?

A historical case study: the chlor-alkali industry in NW England

The production of chlorine and alkalis grew up in Cheshire and on Merseyside at the beginning of the nineteenth century. Developments from 1800 onwards marked the beginning of the chemical industry in Britain. Why did it take place then, and why in that particular region?

The textile industry

Both chlorine and the alkali sodium carbonate have connections with the cotton industry. This was flourishing in Lancashire at that time, close to the cotton trading port of Liverpool. The textile manufacturers needed both bleach (chlorine) and washing soda (sodium carbonate) for their manufacturing processes. The development of chlorine as a fast, effective bleach played a part in the expansion of textile production. In turn, this expansion of the cotton industry increased the demand for soda. Thus, chlorine and soda, manufactured by separate processes at first, grew up side by side as the cotton industry expanded.

- *The manufacture of both chlorine and alkalis increased as the cotton industry expanded.*

Raw materials

Early supplies of chlorine were obtained from salt by oxidation (using manganese(IV) oxide). Salt was also the raw material for soda manufacture in the *Leblanc process*. This method for converting a cheap, readily available raw material into a valuable industrial commodity was developed by the French chemist Nicolas Leblanc (1742–1806). It played an important part in the industrial revolution and is a landmark in the

Nineteenth-century industry in NW England

A Lancashire textile mill

A chemical plant producing sodium carbonate by the Leblanc process

Liverpool docks

A Staffordshire coal mine

development of industrial chemistry. The steps in the Leblanc process were as follows:

$$\mathbf{NaCl} \xrightarrow{\text{concentrated } H_2SO_4} \mathbf{Na_2SO_4 + HCl}$$

$$\mathbf{Na_2SO_4} \xrightarrow[\text{(heat)}]{\text{limestone, coal}} \mathbf{Na_2CO_3 + CaS}$$

For centuries, underground deposits in Cheshire have been the main source of *salt* in Britain. Other raw materials needed for the new industry were close at hand. *Coal* was available in Lancashire and Staffordshire. *Limestone* was quarried in Derbyshire. Thus, Cheshire and Merseyside were ideal locations for the development of the chlorine and alkali industries (figure p. 241).

● *Chlorine and soda were manufactured where there was local demand and where supplies of the necessary raw materials were close at hand.*

Chlorine and alkalis grow closer together

Hydrogen chloride was produced as a waste product in the Leblanc soda process. A way was soon found to exploit this as a raw material for making chlorine, and thus the manufacture of chlorine came to depend on the manufacture of soda. Then, from 1874, the less polluting and cheaper *Solvay process* (see Unit 38) for making soda began to replace the Leblanc process. For a time the chlorine industry found itself short of the NaCl it needed.

However, the problem of one process depending on another eventually disappeared when the *electrolysis of brine* (salt solution) was introduced as a way of making a strong alkali (NaOH) and chlorine in one process (see Unit 38).

$$\mathbf{NaCl(aq)} \xrightarrow{\text{electrolysis}} \mathbf{NaOH(aq) + Cl_2(g)}$$

This was successfully introduced in Runcorn in 1897 when the Castner–Kellner Co. began production. By this time, both chlorine and alkalis were finding uses as chemical raw materials in an expanding network of industries.

- *The final merging of the chlorine and alkali industries was brought about by the introduction of industrial electrolysis.*

The history of the development of the chlorine, sodium carbonate and sodium hydroxide industries, and their dependence on salt, are summarized in the figure on p.242, which shows how one process leads to another and how developments can eventually make an older process redundant.

Social and environmental factors are important

In the last century, the time and the place of developments in the chemical industry were determined by the economic laws of supply and demand. The effects that industry had on the population and the countryside were not taken into account. The Leblanc process alone was a most destructive influence as far as the environment was concerned. The huge amounts of waste HCl gas that were produced caused appalling pollution of the atmosphere close to chemical works. It damaged lungs, rotted clothing and blackened stone. The same process produced spoil heaps containing calcium sulphide, which generated another poisonous and evil-smelling gas, H_2S (see below under 'Alkali Act').

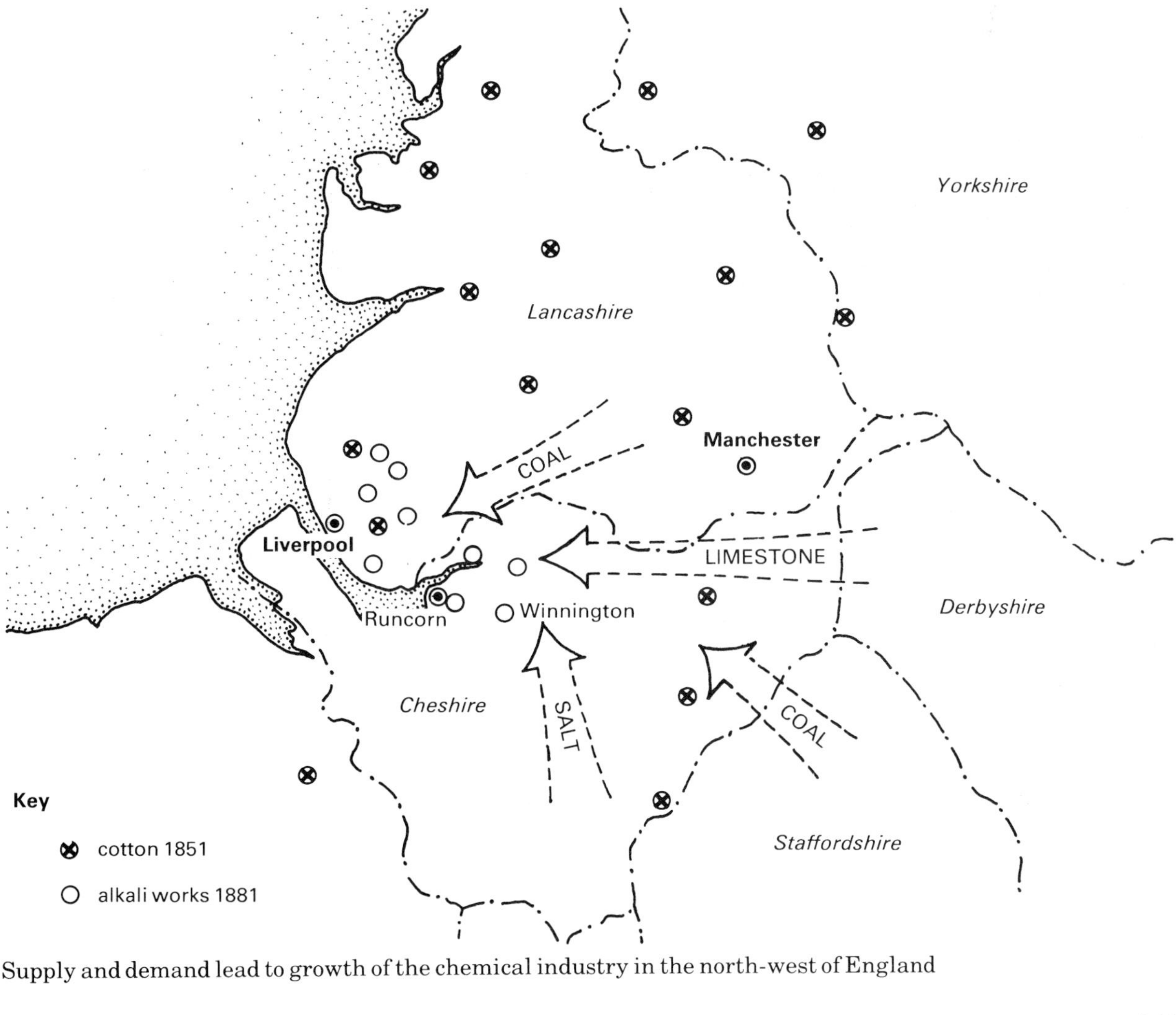

Supply and demand lead to growth of the chemical industry in the north-west of England

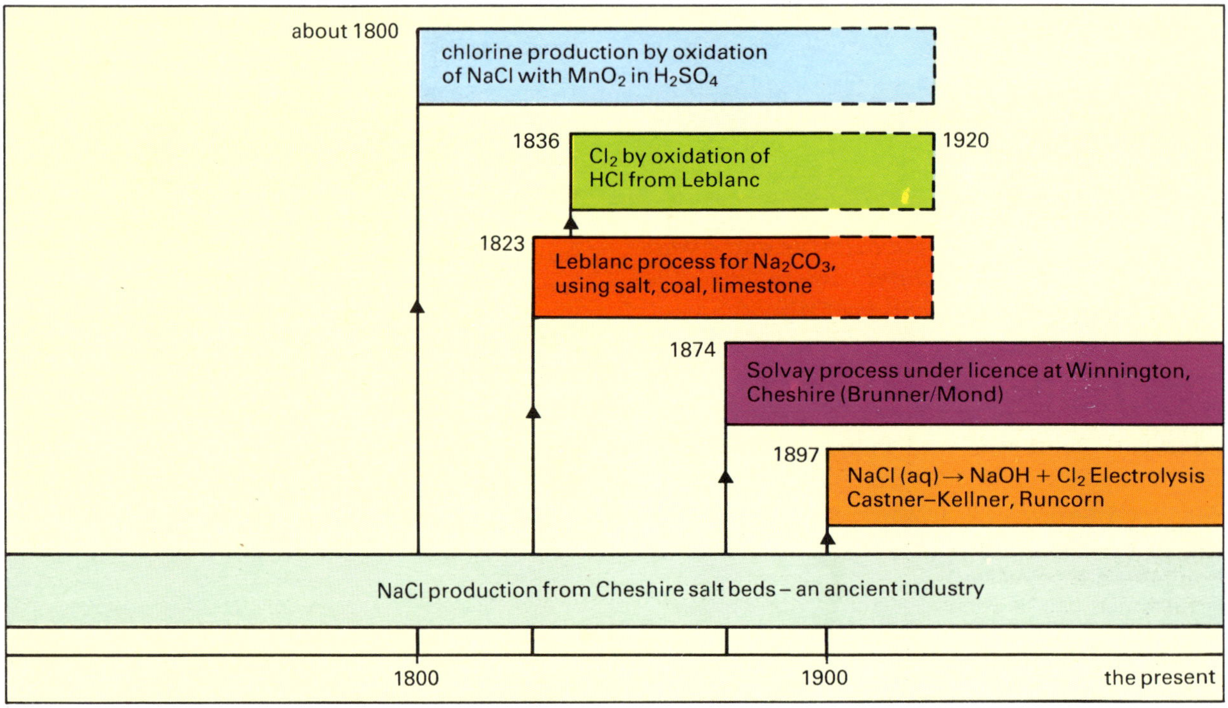

A century of industrial progress

In more recent times, it has been realized that economic factors, although important, are not the only ones to be taken into account when planning for the future.

● *It is important to take social and environmental effects into account when planning developments in the chemical industry.*

Local and national government controls and incentives nowadays have done much to direct the activities of the chemical industry into areas where the environmental effects are less harmful. The chemical industry's growing awareness of public concern about the environment has also contributed to changes in practice. A more recent case history helps to illustrate this.

An example of planned development: the south Humber bank development

Since the late 1940s, a variety of chemical works have been set up along the strip of south Humberside coastline stretching from Grimsby northwards to beyond Immingham, as shown in the figure on p.244.

Products manufactured include refined petroleum oil and associated products, agricultural fertilizers, ammonia, titanium oxide for pigments, synthetic fibres and chemical intermediates (i.e. chemicals used to make other chemicals, e.g. drugs, adhesives).

What advantages has this location in south Humberside got? Consider these factors:

1. All of the industries depend on imported raw materials, much of them in bulk, for example:

   petroleum from the North Sea and elsewhere; natural gas for ammonia manufacture; ilmenite ore from Australia and India for TiO_2 production; phosphate rock (from N. Africa and N. America) and potash (from Germany and USSR) for fertilizer manufacture.

   Immingham provides deep-water docking facilities for these imports, and the finished products mainly leave by the same route.
2. Huge quantities of water are required for large-scale chemical processes. There is sufficient water available, either from the water authority or bore holes. More importantly, the water must be discharged

Metals are added to estuaries from several sources, including industrial discharges; techniques such as sediment sampling (left) and grab sampling (right) allow the environmental effect of industrial discharges to be monitored and pollution to be kept under control. From these samples, the metal levels in the Humber estuary, for instance, can be compared with metal levels from other estuaries (below)

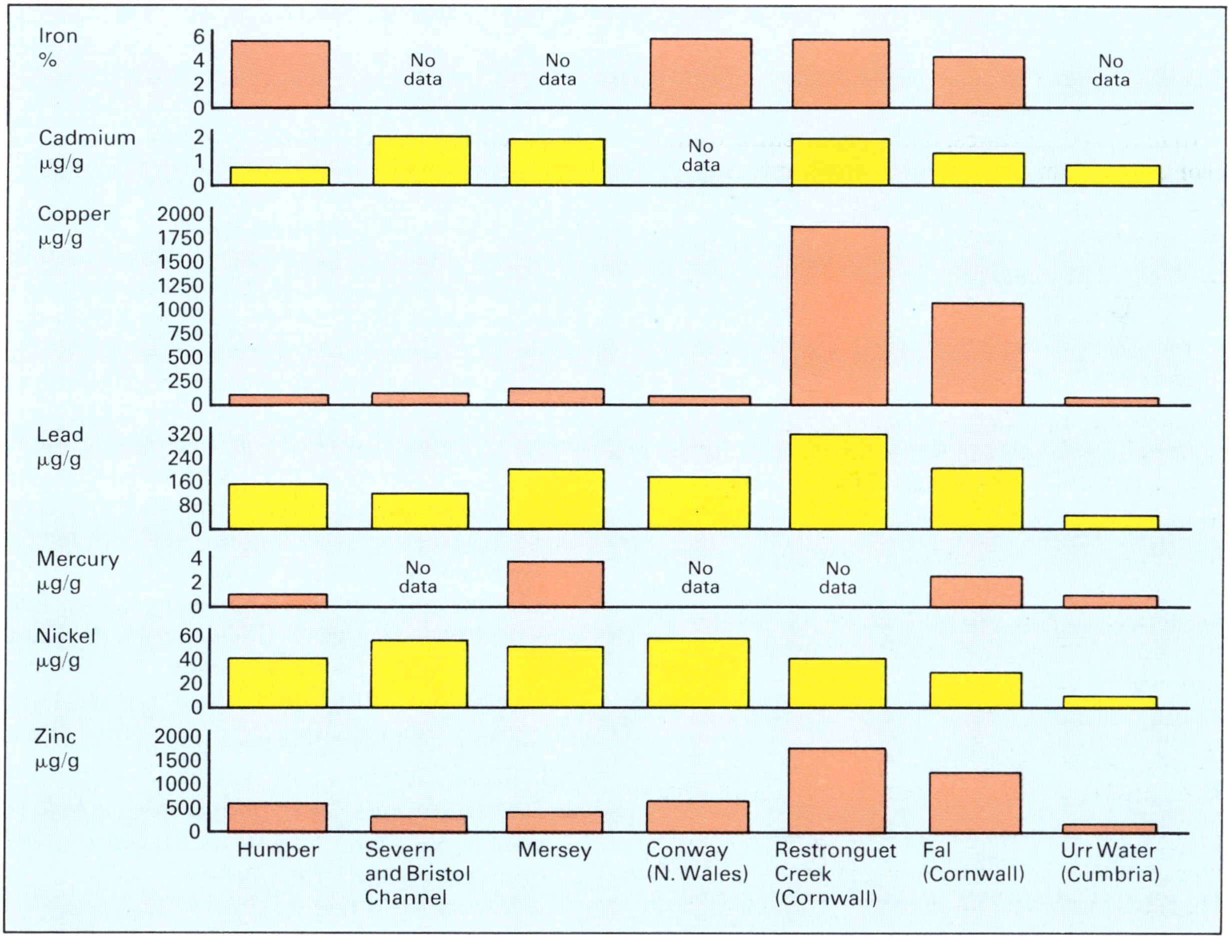

Metal levels in the Humber estuary sediment compared with those in other estuaries

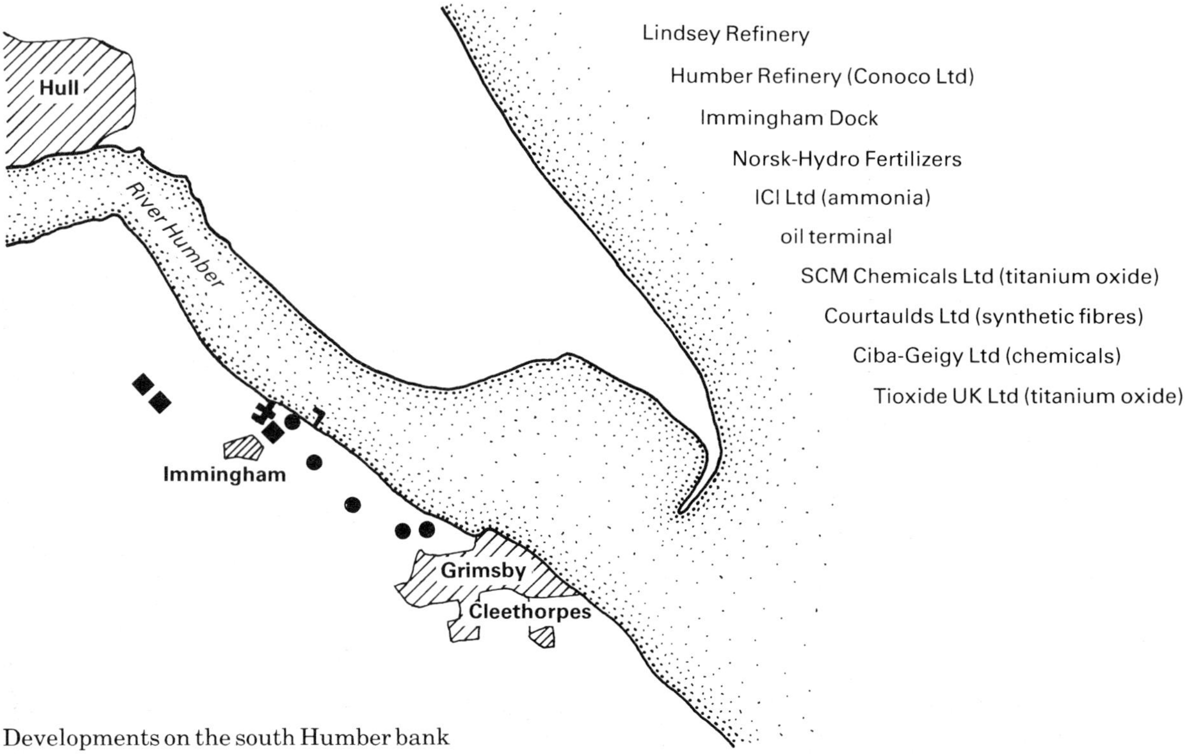

Developments on the south Humber bank

after use and the enormous volume of the Humber estuary absorbs all this used water (and other effluents) directly.

3. Chemical factories and refineries cover large areas. On the south Humber bank, the land on which they have been developed was formerly low-grade farming land and was relatively cheap.

● *Docking facilities, water supplies and cheap land were factors in the decision to develop the south Humber bank as an industrial area.*

These factors are mainly economic ones. However, social and environmental factors have also been taken into account in deciding on this site, for example:

1. Effluent discharge into the estuary (mentioned above) is better than inland pollution.
2. The area was not previously densely populated (traditional industrial areas of Britain are now densely populated).
3. Prevailing winds are from the south-west and normally carry gaseous discharges out to sea and away from nearby towns and villages.

Environmental damage: an inheritance

During the industrial revolution, the rapid growth of new industries was accompanied by the uncontrolled expansion of towns and cities. Here, the environment was attacked from two sides: by domestic pollutants such as smoke and sewage, and by industry's emission of gases into the air and effluents into the waterways. Spoil heaps of industrial solid waste were allowed to build up and, in time, the dissolving (leaching) effect of rain and the oxidizing effect of air on these heaps often produced further pollution of the environment.

Elsewhere the extraction of minerals such as clay and limestone from the surface of the land also affected the landscape. Similarly, extraction of salt or coal from underground frequently caused subsidence (sinking) of the land's surface.

● *Domestic pollution, industrial emissions, spoil heaps and land subsidence have caused damage to the environment.*

Effects of industry on the environment in Sheffield

A spoil heap from coal mining

Treatment of industrial effluent: settling tanks at the ICI chemical works

Rehabilitation of the environment

Today, in parts of Britain, people still have to live with the effects of that early uncontrolled development of industrial chemistry. However, attempts to undo the damage and prevent further damage have been gathering momentum. For instance, we no longer find it acceptable to pour untreated waste into the rivers or the sea. Water used by the chemical industry may be processed in various ways to avoid the worst pollution, for example:

recycling allows the same water to be used over and over again and reduces the amount that gets discharged;
settling tanks in some cases allow the bulk of solid matter to be removed by sedimentation before the water is discharged from the plant;
chemical treatment of effluents by processes such as precipitation can remove dangerous pollutants from waste water.

Other measures can lead to reduced atmospheric pollution. For example, removal of H_2S from fuel gas before combustion results in less SO_2 pollution. Other gaseous emissions can be treated by 'scrubbing' before discharge, for example acidic gases are neutralized by reaction with alkaline solutions.

Spoiled land can sometimes be successfully reclaimed. Gravel pits may be turned into water amenities or nature reserves; waste heaps can be removed or landscaped and planted.

Note: All the above measures are expensive and they limit the manufacturers' freedom of action. Thus, either directly or indirectly, they add to the cost of manufactured products.

● *Damage to the environment is nowadays limited by efforts to control chemical pollution. Damage from earlier times can be reversed, at a cost.*

Land reclamation: open-cast coal mining at Shipley Park, Derbyshire (left); after mining had finished the land was restored to parkland and a fresh-water lake to be used for recreation and wildlife (right)

Control agencies

Who checks and controls the activities of the chemical industry? Nowadays, these *control agencies* include the government (both national and local), voluntary conservation organizations, international bodies and the chemical industry itself.

Government controls

The first official attempts to protect the environment were made as early as 1863. In that year, the Alkali Act was passed through Parliament and the Alkali Inspectorate was set up to enforce it. This development was largely the result of the disastrous effects of the Leblanc process (see p. 241) on the environment. The original Act was aimed at cutting down emissions of hydrogen chloride into the atmosphere. Other gaseous emissions from industrial works were included later. More recently, the Clean Air Acts (1956, 1968) have had dramatic effects on atmospheric pollution. Under these Acts, *smokeless zones* were established, and new controls were imposed on the chemical industry. The aim of these Acts was the control of a much wider range of pollutants, for example dust from furnaces and smoke from domestic chimneys as well as chemical pollutants. The latest legislation continues to be enforced by the Alkali Inspectorate (now part of the Health and Safety Executive: see p.247).

Various Acts of Parliament also limit water pollution. Regional water authorities have the power to grant (or refuse) licences for the discharge of wastes to rivers, and they check (monitor) the discharges by sampling and chemical analysis.

Eventually all these Acts will be replaced by the Control of Pollution Act (1974), which is gradually being brought into effect.

Nowadays, possible environmental effects are taken into account when new industrial developments are planned. Government permission to allow development may only be granted on condition that the environment is protected.

Voluntary organizations

Voluntary conservation organizations such as Greenpeace and Friends of the Earth act as public watchdogs and seek publicity for the conservation movement. They have done much to increase public awareness and concern over the pollution problem.

International bodies

International bodies with an interest in pollution include the World Health Organization (WHO) and the European Community. WHO is a United Nations agency that is funded by its 158 member states. One of its main concerns is the improvement of drinking water supplies, especially in underdeveloped parts of the world. Both the European Community and WHO influence attitudes in the UK and thus may indirectly bring about change here.

Controls within the chemical industry

The chemical industry today is very much aware of public concern about pollution and in general makes every effort to limit any damaging effects its activities might have. However, its efforts will always be restricted by economic considerations.

● *Control agencies that limit the freedom of the chemical industry include the government, voluntary bodies and international organizations.*

Health and safety within the chemical industry

Workers in the chemical industry must be protected from the dangerous or harmful effects of the materials they may have to work with. These may include *toxic*, *corrosive* or *flammable* substances.

The Health and Safety at Work Act (1974), together with other legislation, has led to regulations and codes of practice being set up. These govern various aspects of industrial chemistry, for example:

a safe storage of highly flammable or explosive materials, such as petroleum spirit, liquified petroleum gas (LPG) and sodium chlorate weed killers;

b recommended occupational exposure limits for workers dealing with toxic substances, such as pesticides, mercury, degreasing solvents and lead. These limits take into account the possible *short-term effects* of acutely poisonous substances and also the possible *long-term effects* of cumulative poisons.

c control of other occupational hazards such as lung damage through exposure to asbestos, or dermatitis through exposure to skin irritants.

The regulations and codes of practice relating to health and safety at work are enforced by the Health and Safety Executive (HSE). Inspectors representing the HSE have the power to enter premises, take measurements and samples, ask questions and carry out investigations. They also have a duty to inform and educate employers and workers about the requirements of the Health and Safety at Work Act. If an Inspector discovers that the laws relating to health and safety are being broken he can take steps to bring about improvements, confiscate dangerous substances or equipment, or prosecute the offenders.

Summary

1. The siting of industry is mainly decided by economic considerations.
2. The early developments of the chlorine and alkali industries were linked with the textiles industry and took place close to supplies of raw materials.
3. The introduction of industrial electrolysis at Runcorn brought about the final merging of the chlorine and alkali industries in the north west.
4. Social and environmental effects of industry should be taken into account, as well as economic factors, when planning modern developments.
5. Favourable economic and environmental factors contributed to the suitability of the south Humber bank as an industrial site.
6. Domestic pollution, industrial emissions, spoil heaps and land subsidence have all caused damage to the environment.
7. Nowadays efforts are made to limit pollution and to reverse damage caused in earlier times.
8. The activities of the chemical industry are limited by various control agencies such as the Health and Safety Executive.

Extension

1. **Workers in the chemical industry**
These workers may be exposed to toxic materials that could be absorbed into the body. Employers and workers both have responsibilities to take precautions against

the risk of poisoning. Precautions might include: using protective clothing; providing a ventilation system; having regular medical inspections; providing facilities for proper hygiene; monitoring the environment at work; reducing emissions to the atmosphere.

i Toxic substances may be absorbed through the skin in some cases. Give two other ways in which absorption into the body may occur.

ii Describe measures that could be taken by *employers* to keep up high standards of safety in the environment of a chemical plant.

iii What measures might be taken by *workers* to reduce their personal risk of poisoning? Explain how the measures you have mentioned would help.

2\. i Read the following statement about the siting of oil refineries:

Factors affecting the siting of oil refineries in recent times are different from those that determined the siting of the chlor-alkali industry in the past. Thus, refineries are close to markets, not necessarily close to raw material supplies; refineries are close to deep-water harbours; refineries are sited away from densely populated areas.

Find out the locations of the major centres of oil refining in Britain and list them. Comment on the locations in the light of the statement above.

ii In many cases, centres of the chemical industry are close to major oil refineries. Compare your list from (i) with the map on p.239 and pick out any exceptions.

iii What possible reasons are there for an association between oil refineries and chemical manufacturing?

Revision

1\. i How was the early development of the chemical industry in NW England linked to the cotton industry?

ii Describe how the location of the alkali industry was governed by the availability of raw materials.

iii How were the chlorine and alkali industries finally merged?

2\. i Briefly describe:

a the Leblanc process
b the Solvay process
c the electrolysis of brine

ii How are the three processes connected historically?

3\. i Write a sentence about the aims of

a the Clean Air Acts, 1956 and 1968
b the Alkali Act, 1863

ii Briefly describe the activities of the following organizations:

a WHO
b HSE

4\. i What were the effects of the Leblanc process on the environment in the early part of the nineteenth century?

ii In what other ways was the growth of the chemical industry damaging to the environment?

iii What is meant by:

a recycling
b settling tank

iv Explain how the use of recycling, settling tanks and other measures contribute to a reduction in environmental damage nowadays.

5\. What factors favoured the siting of chemical factories on the south Humber bank?

Unit 48
Examination questions

1. This question refers to the following account of some industrial processes used to produce the raw materials nitrogen and hydrogen for the synthesis of ammonia.

   'Bosch had to devise cheap ways of getting nitrogen and hydrogen. At first hydrogen came from the electrolysis of water, and nitrogen from the liquefaction of air.

   To make hydrogen, Bosch invented a process in which steam was blown over coke at a high temperature and the resulting mixture *water gas* was catalytically converted into hydrogen and carbon dioxide. To make nitrogen, air was blown over the coke and the nitrogen-rich gas was freed from carbon dioxide'.

   a The account suggests that hydrogen was made by the electrolysis of water, but pure water is a very poor conductor of electricity and so cannot be electrolysed.
      i Give ONE reason why pure water is a poor conductor of electricity.
      ii How can the electrolysis of water be made to take place?

   b i What must be done to liquid air to obtain nitrogen?
      ii Name ONE gas, apart from oxygen, which can also be obtained in the process involved in (b)(i).

   c The water gas referred to is a mixture of equal volumes of carbon monoxide (CO) and hydrogen.
      i Write a balanced equation for the reaction producing water gas, including state symbols.
      ii The heat of the reaction of carbon with steam, $\Delta H = +132$ kJ mol^{-1}. Draw an energy level diagram to illustrate the reaction.
      iii Assuming that coke is pure carbon, what volume of water gas (measured at room temperature and pressure) could be produced from 12 kg of coke? (Relative atomic mass: C = 12; 1 mole of gas molecules occupies approximately 24 dm^3 at room temperature and atmospheric pressure.)

   d i Suggest a reason why the production of water gas is best carried out at high temperatures.
      ii Why is the conversion of water gas to hydrogen and carbon dioxide carried out catalytically?
      iii Explain briefly how the carbon dioxide may be removed from the carbon dioxide/nitrogen mixture.

   (LOND JAN. 1984)

2. The elements sodium to argon form a period in the Periodic Table.

   Describe how you would perform experiments and indicate the results you would expect to obtain for electrical conductivity of the elements and the acid-base properties of the oxides of the elements of the period.

   Explain how these and other tests might help you to classify the elements according to *type* and *structure*.

   (LOND JAN. 1984)

3. What is meant by the statement 'the properties of the elements and their compounds are said to show a periodic variation with atomic number'?

   Illustrate your answer by referring to the main physical properties and the chemical character of the elements of the third period (Na, Mg, Al, Si, P, S, Cl, Ar) and their oxides and chlorides.

   Use your knowledge of the Periodic Table to predict the properties of the element strontium, which is below magnesium and calcium in Group 2.

   You should emphasize the likely differences as well as the similarities.

   (LOND 1983)

4. Glucose, water and yeast were placed in a flask and kept at room temperature (20 °C) for several days. A froth appeared on the

surface of the mixture and a gas was given off. A dilute aqueous solution of ethanol remained in the flask.

a i Give the name of the process by which glucose is converted into ethanol.

ii Give the name of the gas produced during the reaction.

iii Describe a chemical test for this gas.

b What would be the effect of carrying out the reaction at 30 °C?

c How could a more concentrated solution of ethanol be obtained?

d i Ethanol may be converted into ethene by the action of concentrated sulphuric acid.

$$C_2H_5OH \rightarrow C_2H_4 + H_2O$$

What type of reaction is this?

ii Ethene undergoes polymerization to form polyethene. State the conditions for this reaction and write a suitable equation.

e Ethanol burns in oxygen to form carbon dioxide and water.

i Write an equation for this reaction.

ii What is the minimum volume of oxygen, measured at room temperature and atmospheric pressure, that would be required for 0.5 mole of ethanol to burn completely?

(LOND 1984)

5. The element rubidium, symbol Rb, is the element immediately below potassium in Group I of the Periodic Table.

a Give the name of a compound of rubidium you would expect to occur naturally.

b i Write an equation for the reaction of rubidium with water.

ii State TWO changes you would expect to SEE when rubidium is added to water.

iii Suggest a possible value for the pH of the solution at the end of the reaction.

c Write formulae for rubidium nitrate and rubidium sulphate.

d Give the names of the products that you would expect to be formed when rubidium nitrate is heated.

e i How many electrons are present in the outer shell of the rubidium atom?

ii How many other shells of electrons are present in the rubidium atom?

iii Give the formula of the rubidium ion.

(LOND 1984)

6. This question is about an experiment to find the equation for the reaction between a colourless solution containing carbonate ions, $CO_3^{2-}(aq)$, and a green solution containing nickel ions, $Ni^{2+}(aq)$, to form a precipitate of green nickel carbonate. 5 cm^3 of 1.0 M sodium carbonate solution, $Na_2CO_3(aq)$, was measured into a test tube, 1 cm^3 of 1.0 M nickel chloride solution, $NiCl_2(aq)$, was measured into the same test tube, the tube was shaken to mix the reagents, and the precipitate formed was allowed to settle evenly. The height of the precipitate was measured.

A second 1 cm^3 portion of the nickel chloride solution was measured into the same tube and, after shaking to mix and allowing the precipitate to settle evenly, the height of the precipitate was measured.

This was repeated for successive additions of 1 cm^3 of the 1.0 M nickel chloride solution. A graph of the results is given below.

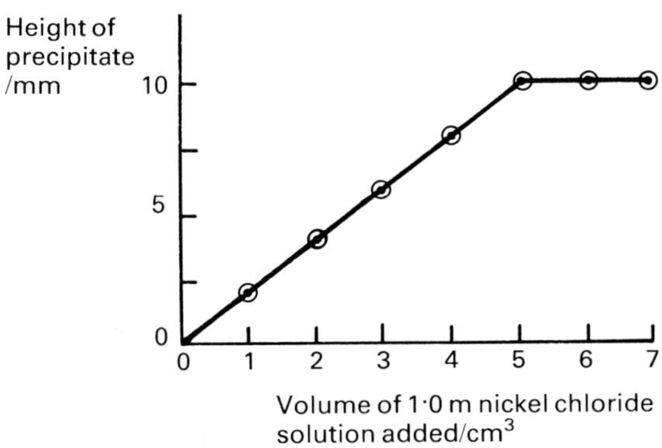

a Why did the height of the precipitate not rise after 5 cm^3 of nickel chloride solution had been added?

b What would be another observable difference (other than the height of the precipitate) in the contents of the test tube before and after the fifth 1 cm^3 portion had been added?

c In what ratio of moles of ions did the reagents react?

$$\frac{\text{Moles of } CO_3^{2-}(aq)}{\text{Moles of } Ni^{2+}(aq)} = \_\_\_\_\_\_\_\_$$

d Using the information given above, write an ionic equation for the reaction.

e If 0.5 M sodium carbonate solution were used, what volume of it would be required to produce the same mass of nickel carbonate as formed in the experiment?

(LOND 1982)

7. The reaction between zinc and copper sulphate solution is shown in the following equation:

$$Zn_{(s)} + Cu^{2+}{}_{(aq)} = Cu_{(s)} + Zn^{2+}{}_{(aq)}.$$

a Explain the reaction in terms of oxidation and reduction.

b The reaction is exothermic. What observations would you make to confirm this?

c What mass of copper would be precipitated by the addition of excess zinc to 500 cm^3 of 0.1 M copper sulphate solution?

d When the reaction in (c) had finished there was a mixture of zinc, copper, and zinc sulphate. How would you recover from the mixture a pure, dry sample of copper?

e Write an equation for a similar displacement reaction using a different metal and aqueous solution.

(SUJB 1983)

8. The diagram represents, in schematic form, the liquid streams normally produced by the fractional distillation of petroleum (crude oil).

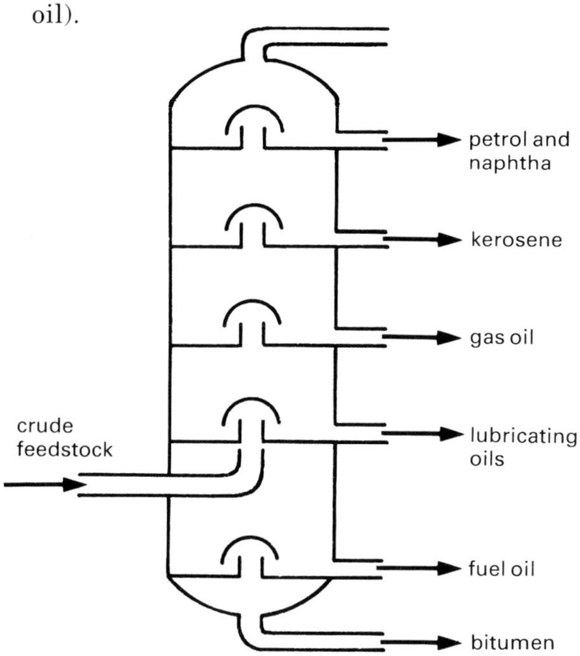

a Which of the streams has the lowest boiling range?

b To what class of organic compound do the principal components of petroleum belong?

c Outline one *chemical* use of the naphtha fraction other than as a fuel.

d Give *one* use of bitumen.

The distillation of crude oil does not produce enough petrol to meet current demand. Other liquid streams can, however, be converted into petroleum, at the same time yielding important reactive gases.

e Name the process used to form petrol from other liquid fractions.

f Name *one* reactive carbon containing gas produced in this way.

g Describe briefly the industrial importance of the gas you have named above.

h What other source of petrol could be developed as the World's petroleum supplies dwindle?

(AEB 1981)

9. a Name *three* naturally occurring forms of calcium carbonate.

b How is calcium carbonate converted into
 i calcium oxide
 ii calcium hydroxide?

Give the equations for the reactions involved.

c Discuss the part that calcium compounds play in
 i the extraction of iron,
 ii agriculture,
 iii the building industry.

(AEB 1981)

10. a Lithium, sodium and potassium have atomic numbers 3, 11 and 19 respectively.
 i Write down the electronic configurations of the three elements. What common feature of these configurations is responsible for the similar chemical behaviour of these elements?
 ii State, with a reason, which element would be expected to have the largest atoms.

iii Name the element which would be the best reducing agent and give a brief explanation in support of your answer.

iv Which halogen (chlorine, bromine or iodine) would be expected to react most vigorously with the element named in (iii)? What type of bonding would be present in the compound formed?

b Briefly explain why sodium metal conducts electricity when solid and when molten, but sodium chloride conducts in the molten state only.

(AEB NOV. 1982)

11. Sodium hydroxide is produced on a large scale from rock salt, an impure form of sodium chloride. If electricity is passed through a cell containing salt solution, hydrogen and chlorine are given off and sodium hydroxide is formed. Since chlorine and sodium hydroxide readily react together, cells are designed to prevent them mixing. Details of two cells used for the large scale production of sodium hydroxide are given below.

a Explain, with an example in each case, what is meant by (i) an *ion*; (ii) a *solution*.

b Why does only the sodium chloride crystallise out when the solution formed in cell X is evaporated?

c Which two processes in cell X require the largest amounts of energy?

d i Why is it possible to recycle mercury in cell Y?

ii State two advantages of recycling this mercury.

e 1.775 kg of chlorine is produced by cell X from 23.4 kg of saturated salt solution. The saturated salt solution contains 25% by weight of sodium chloride.

i What mass of sodium chloride is dissolved in 23.4 kg of the saturated solution?

ii How many moles of sodium chloride is this? (Relative atomic masses, Na = 23, Cl = 35.5).

iii How many moles of chlorine atoms are formed from 23.4 kg of the saturated solution?

iv What fraction of the chloride ions in this solution were discharged?

	Cell X	*Cell Y*
Method of preventing the chlorine reacting with the sodium hydroxide.	An asbestos diaphragm separates the positive and negative electrodes.	During electrolysis sodium is formed at a **moving** mercury electrode. The sodium dissolves in the mercury to form a *solution* which passes out of the cell.
Electrodes positive negative	Titanium Steel	Titanium Mercury
The effect of electrolysis	**Positive electrode** – chloride *ions* discharged and chlorine formed **Negative electrode** – hydrogen ions discharged and hydrogen formed **Salt solution** – becomes a mixture of sodium hydroxide and sodium chloride, and passes out of the cell.	**Positive electrode** – chloride *ions* discharged and chlorine formed **Negative electrode** – sodium ions discharged and sodium formed **Salt solution** – becomes diluted.
Method of isolating the sodium hydroxide.	The solution is evaporated. *The sodium chloride crystallises out.* The remaining solution contains 50% sodium hydroxide and less than 1% sodium chloride.	The solution of sodium in mercury is reacted with water. Hydrogen is given off and mercury is left behind. The remaining solution is very pure 50% sodium hydroxide.

f State, giving your reasons, *two* factors that the designers of these cells would have taken into account when choosing the material for the positive electrodes.

g State *six* factors, *in order of importance*, that would be taken into account when deciding on a suitable site to build and operate a new sodium hydroxide plant. Give reasons to justify the order of importance you have stated.

(AEB 1980)

12. When a piece of tin is placed in aqueous lead(II) nitrate, it becomes coated with a black deposit, but when tin is placed in aqueous zinc sulphate, no change is observed. (The symbol for tin is Sn and it can form the ion Sn^{2+}.)

a Predict what would be observed when tin is placed in
  i aqueous copper(II) sulphate
  ii aqueous magnesium sulphate.

b i Write an ionic equation for one of the reactions which occurs.
  ii State, with a reason, which reactant in the equation is being reduced.

c Arrange the metals copper, lead, magnesium, tin and zinc in order of increasing reactivity.

(AEB 1984)

13. The diagram below represents a cell in which electrolysis can take place.

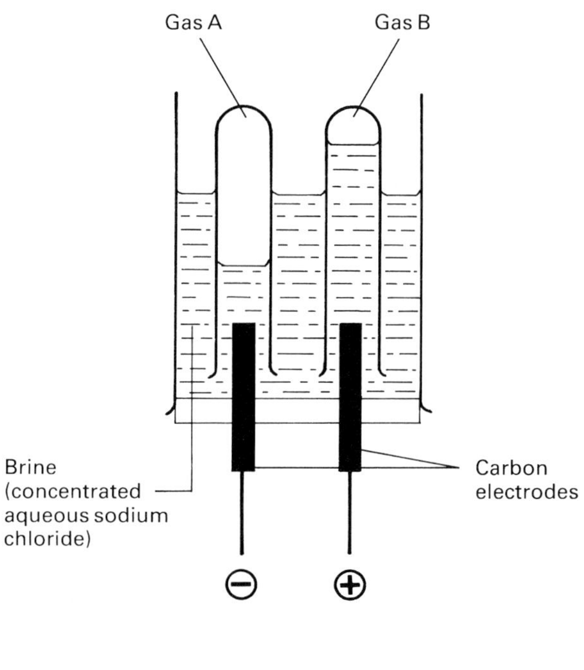

a Name the gases **A** and **B**, and write ionic equations for the reactions by which they are formed. Explain briefly why initially very little gas is collected at the anode.

b A piece of red litmus paper placed near the cathode turned blue; give a brief explanation for this observation and also state what change would occur in litmus paper placed near the anode.

c State **one** condition required in order that gas **A** will react with gas **B** on mixing at room temperature. Name the product and write the equation for the reaction.

d An iron cathode could be used in the cell, but this metal would not be suitable for the anode; why is this so?

e Name the compound which is produced on an industrial scale by the electrolysis of brine.

(AEB 1984)

14. a A site in the U.K. has to be chosen for a chemical plant capable of producing a high tonnage of product annually. The process to be carried out at the plant has the following requirements.
  i One important raw material not found in the U.K.
  ii The overall process is exothermic.
  iii The plant requires only a few people to operate and maintain it.
  iv The plant requires water in the processing, only some of which is actually consumed in the process.
  v The product is used by many U.K. based industries.
  vi The annual production will leave a surplus of the product for export.

  Discuss the features that you would expect an ideal site to have, explaining carefully why you feel these features are necessary. Name one location in the U.K. which possesses these features.

b Write an account of the commercial manufacture of sulphuric acid. Your account should include:
  i the nature and source of the raw materials;
  ii the chemical processes involved, including equations;

iii reference to an industry which needs a constant supply of sulphuric acid and the purpose for which it is needed.

(AEB 1984)

15. a When two gases **A** and **B** react together, there is partial conversion to product **X**. The following tables provide information about the percentage composition of gaseous mixtures which had reached equilibrium under various conditions.

At constant pressure:

Temperature (°C)	100	200	300	400	500
Percentage of product **X**	50	35	23	14	8

At constant temperature:

Pressure (MPa)	5	10	15	20	25
Percentage of product **X**	12	18	25	34	44

i Use the above data to decide whether the reaction which produces **X** is exothermic or endothermic. Briefly explain your answer.

ii State whether the volume increases, decreases or remains constant when **A** and **B** are converted to **X**.

iii What would be the best combination of temperature and pressure to use in order to obtain the highest equilibrium percentage of **X**?
Explain why one of the conditions you have suggested might have to be modified if **X** were to be produced in an industrial plant at a reasonable rate.
State another way by which the rate of production of **X** could be increased.

b i Name **one** industrial process to which the data given in (a) might apply.

ii Write an equation for the reaction.

iii List the conditions which are normally employed in the process.

c Explain briefly the expected difference in rate of reaction of a solid in a finely divided state and the same solid in the form of large lumps when each is mixed with a suitable reagent.

(AEB 1983)

16. Consider the following information about an imaginary new element named bodium, symbol Bo, which has recently been discovered.

Bodium is a solid at room temperature but is easily cut with a knife to reveal a shiny surface which rapidly tarnishes. It reacts vigorously with water liberating a flammable gas and forming a solution with a high pH value. When bodium reacts with chlorine, it forms a white solid containing 29.5% by mass of chlorine.

A_r(Bo) = 85.

a Calculate the empirical formula of bodium chloride.

b To which group in the Periodic Table should bodium be assigned?

c What type of bonding is likely to be present in bodium chloride?

d If concentrated aqueous bodium chloride was electrolysed, what would be the main products discharged at carbon electrodes? Write equations for the reactions which take place.

e Write an equation and name the products for the reaction between bodium and water.

f Write the formula for (i) bodium nitrate and (ii) bodium carbonate. For each of these compounds, state whether it would be expected to decompose at Bunsen burner temperature. Name any product(s) and write an equation for any reaction which occurs.

(AEB 1983)

17. a The pig iron obtained from the blast furnace contains carbon, as does steel. Explain why **all** the carbon is removed from the pig iron in the first part of the steelmaking process.

b Name **one** process for making steel and describe how the carbon is removed in this process.

c The physical properties of a pure metal

are altered by the addition of other metals.

i What is the general name given to such mixtures of metals?

ii Name **one** metal that is added to iron in steelmaking and describe the special property that this metal gives to the steel.

(AEB 1983)

18. Ammonia is synthesised in a reaction summarized by the equation

$$N_2(g) + 3H_2(g) \rightleftharpoons 2NH_3(g);$$
$$\Delta H = -92.1 \text{ kJ/mol.}$$

a What is the effect of raising the pressure on

i the percentage of ammonia formed at equilibrium?

ii the rate of synthesis of ammonia from its elements?

b What is the effect of raising the temperature on

i the percentage of ammonia formed at equilibrium?

ii the rate of synthesis of ammonia?

c What is the effect of using a catalyst on

i the percentage of ammonia formed at equilibrium?

ii the rate of formation of ammonia?

iii the rate of decomposition of ammonia?

(AEB 1981)

19. a Complete the following table concerning radioactive emissions.

Property of emitted particle	*Alpha(α) radiation*	*Beta(β) radiation*
Relative atomic mass		
Charge		
Symbol		

b In the event of a leakage containing an alpha emitter, the radiation is unlikely to be harmful unless samples of the material are inhaled or swallowed. Explain why this is so.

(AEB 1981)

20. a Dehydration of an alcohol *C* gives a hydrocarbon *D* which decolourizes bromine water. 1 dm^3 of *D* reacts with 1 dm^3 of hydrogen under suitable conditions to give 1 dm^3 of another hydrocarbon *E* only. *E* has empirical formula CH_3 and relative molar mass 30.

i Identify by name *C*, *D* and *E*.

ii Write the structural formulae for *D* and *E*.

iii Write equations for the reactions mentioned.

b What type of bonding is there between the atoms in a molecule of methane? Make a simple diagram to show the arrangement of the outer electrons.

c Explain why

i molten sodium chloride conducts electricity whereas liquid methane does not;

ii sodium chloride is a solid and methane is normally a gas.

(SUJB 1981)

21. a The diagram shows a process for the extraction of aluminium by electrolysis.

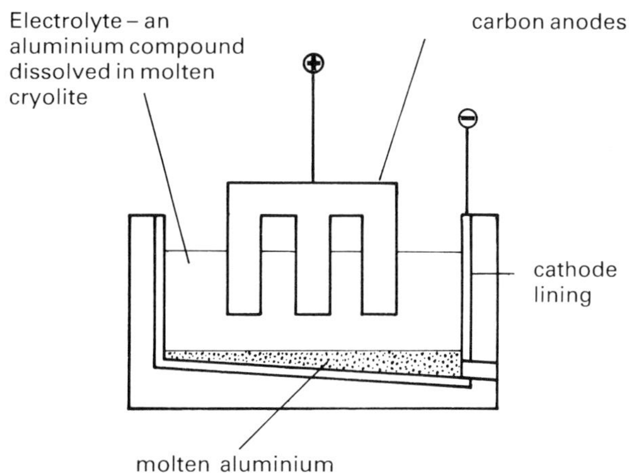

i Give the chemical name of the aluminium compound which is dissolved in cryolite to form the electrolyte.

ii Why is cryolite mixed with the aluminium compound?

iii Explain why it is not possible to obtain aluminium by the electrolysis of a solution of an aluminium compound in water.

iv Name the material used for the cathode of the cell.

v Write an ionic equation for the reaction at the cathode.

vi Name the product formed at the anode.

vii Explain why it is necessary to replace the anodes frequently.

b Aluminium is a typical metal in that it is ductile, conducts electricity and forms alloys with other metals.

i Explain what is meant by 'ductile'.

ii Explain in terms of the structure of the metal why aluminium conducts electricity.

iii Give two reasons for the fact that aluminium is used in overhead power cables in preference to copper, even though aluminium is the poorer conductor of electricity.

iv Name an alloy of aluminium.

v State one use of the alloy named in (iv) and give one advantage the alloy has over pure aluminium.

c When aluminium is warmed with excess dilute hydrochloric acid, a colourless solution (A) is formed and a colourless gas (B) is given off. The gas (B) produces a small explosion when mixed with air and ignited.

When sodium hydroxide solution is added, a little at a time, to solution (A) a white precipitate (C) is formed. If more sodium hydroxide is added, the white precipitate disappears leaving another colourless solution (D).

i Name solution (A).
Name gas (B).
Name precipitate (C).
Name solution (D).

ii Write a symbol equation for the reaction of aluminium with dilute hydrochloric acid.

iii Name one other metal which, if substituted for aluminium in the experiment described, would result in the same observations.

(JMB 1981)

22. a Study the following reaction scheme (below).

i Give the name of
gas (A).
gas (B).
substance (C).
gas (D).
acid (E).

ii Give **two** important uses of gas (B).

iii In the electrolysis of sodium chloride solution and in the conversion of acid (E) to gas (B), the same type of ion is oxidised to gas (B). Write an equation which explains why the ion is said to be oxidised.

iv The following are equations for two reactions of chlorine.

$$Cl_2 + 2KI \rightarrow 2KCl + I_2$$
$$Cl_2 + 2FeCl_2 \rightarrow 2FeCl_3$$

Choose from the two equations when answering the following.

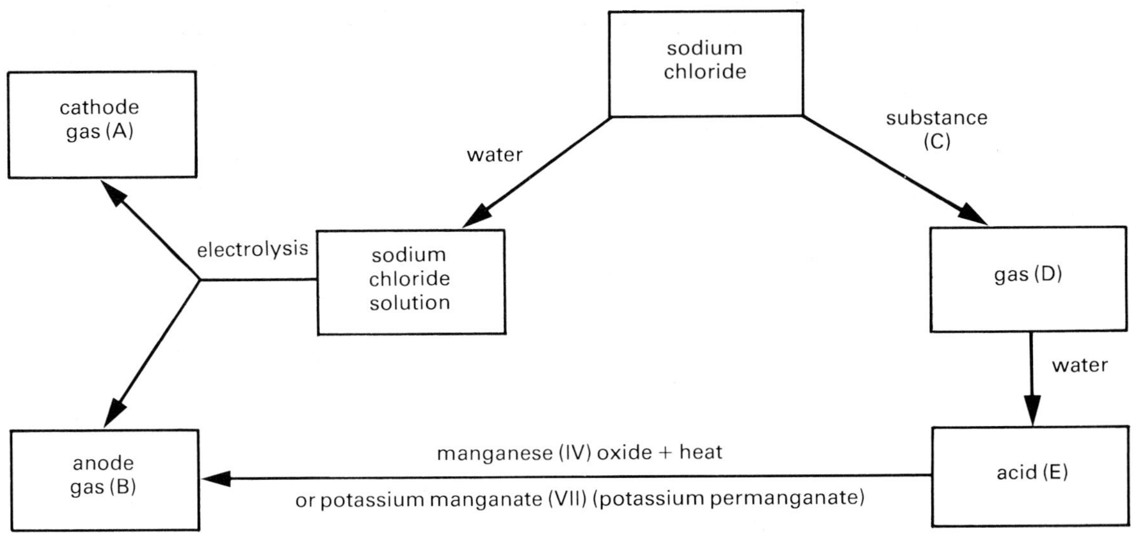

Name an oxidising agent.
Write the formula for a negative ion which is oxidised.
Write the formula for a positive ion which is oxidised.

b i Which one of the following substances is a good dehydrating agent?
concentrated nitric acid, chlorine, sulphur, concentrated sulphuric acid, nitrogen, concentrated hydrochloric acid

ii Describe and explain an experiment which shows the dehydrating property of the substance you have named.

c When chlorine is passed over heated iron, the reaction can be represented by the following equation.

$$2Fe + 3Cl_2 \rightarrow 2FeCl_3$$

(Relative atomic masses: Cl = 35.5 Fe = 56)
What mass of anhydrous iron (III) chloride would be obtained by heating 7 g of iron in excess chlorine? (Give your answer to the nearest 0.1 g.)

(JMB 1981)

23. a Give **two** sources of energy which do **NOT** depend directly or indirectly on solar energy.

b A 2.0 cm length of magnesium ribbon was added to 100 cm^3 of 2.0 M hydrochloric acid. All the magnesium reacted and the temperature of the acid increased by 20 °C.

i If a 1.0 cm length of magnesium ribbon had been used in 100 cm^3 of 2.0 M hydrochloric acid what would the temperature rise have been?

ii What volume of 2.0 M hydrochloric acid would produce a temperature rise of 20 °C with 1 cm length of magnesium ribbon?

c i Calculate the quantity of energy released when 4.0 g of calcium is burnt in excess chlorine.

$$Ca(s) + Cl_2(g) \rightarrow CaCl_2(s);$$
$$\Delta H = -800 \text{ kJ mol}^{-1}$$

(Relative atomic mass Ca = 40)

ii For the reaction in c(i) complete the following energy level diagram. Indicate clearly on the diagram the value for the heat of reaction (ΔH).

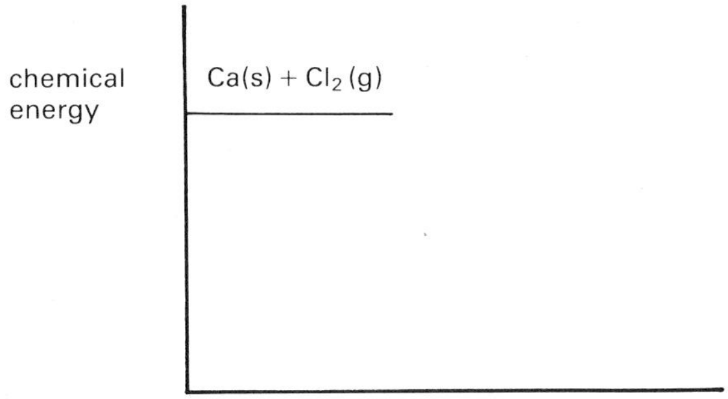

d Give an example of:

i a fast reaction, one which is completed in a few seconds.

ii a slow reaction, one which takes days or weeks.

(JMB 1984)

24. a Complete the following paragraph by filling in the three spaces.
Carbon exhibits allotropy because it is an ________ which exists in more than one ________ in the same physical ________.

b Most compounds containing only covalent bonding have low melting and low boiling points. They usually exist as gases (e.g. methane) or liquids (e.g. ethanol) at room temperature and pressure.
Diamond, an allotrope of carbon, has a very high melting point even though it contains only covalent bonding.

i Explain why most covalent compounds have low melting and low boiling points.

ii Explain why diamond has a very high melting point.

iii The five circles represent atoms of carbon. Draw lines to show the position of the bonds between these atoms in the diamond structure.

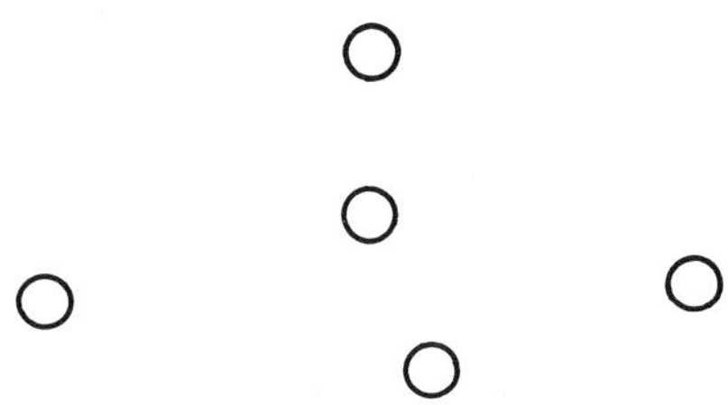

iv Another allotrope of carbon, is graphite. Give two properties which show that it must have a structure different from that of diamond.

c Crude oil is a mixture of hydrocarbons. The mixture is separated into fractions by the process of fractional distillation. One of the fractions is naphtha. This contains molecules which have from four up to ten carbon atoms. Ethene can be obtained from this fraction.

i Explain why crude oil can be separated into different fractions by distillation.

ii Name the process by which ethene is obtained from the naphtha fraction.

iii State the most efficient conditions under which this process could be carried out.

d Plastics are polymers which are formed from monomers by the process of polymerisation.

i Complete the following table.

Plastic	*Name of monomer*	*Structural formula of the monomer*
PVC (polychloroethene)	chloroethene	
polystyrene (polyphenylethene)		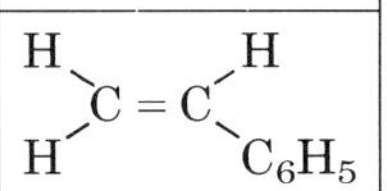

ii Draw a diagram to show the structural formula of the polymer, polystyrene.

e Some polymers (e.g. PVC) are described as thermoplastic or thermosoftening, whilst others (e.g. polyurethane) are described as thermosetting. Explain the meaning of: (i) thermoplastic; (ii) thermosetting.

(JMB 1984)

25. Nickel, a transition element, reacts with dilute hydrochloric acid to form a green solution (A) and hydrogen. When sodium carbonate solution is added to solution (A) a green precipitate of nickel carbonate ($NiCO_3$) and a colourless solution (B) are formed.
Heating nickel carbonate produces a solid (C) and carbon dioxide is given off. When solid (C) is mixed with a black solid (D) and the mixture is heated, nickel is reformed and a gas is given off.

i Give the name or formula of:
Solution (A). Solid (C).
Solution (B). Solid (D).

ii State **two** physical properties of the element nickel.

iii State **one** property of nickel compounds which is characteristic of transition element compounds.

iv Write the formula for the nickel ions present in nickel carbonate.

(JMB 1984)

26. The element gallium is in group III of the Periodic Table and exists as two isotopes $^{69}_{31}Ga$ and $^{71}_{31}Ga$.

i Complete the following table

	$^{69}_{31}Ga$	$^{71}_{31}Ga$
Number of protons		
Number of neutrons		
Number of electrons		

ii State the number of electrons in the outer energy level of a gallium atom.

iii Write the formula for an ion of gallium.

iv Write the formula for
gallium chloride.
gallium sulphate.

v A sample of gallium contains 60% of atoms of $^{69}_{31}Ga$ and 40% of atoms of $^{71}_{31}Ga$. Which one of the following is the relative atomic mass of this sample of gallium?
69.2 69.8 70.2 70.8

(JMB 1984)

27. In an experiment, 1.12 g of iron filings were added to a beaker containing an excess of copper(II) sulphate solution. An exothermic reaction occurred in which the heat change was 4 kJ. As a result of this reaction, 1.28 g of pure, dry copper were obtained.
(Relative atomic masses: Fe = 56; Cu = 64.)

a Calculate the number of moles of iron used in the experiment.

b Calculate the number of moles of copper formed.

c State the number of moles of copper

which would be formed if 1 mole of iron were used.

d Write an equation for the reaction of 1 mole of iron with copper(II) ions in solution. Calculate the heat change, ΔH, in kJ per mole, for this reaction.

e State why an excess of copper(II) sulphate was used in the experiment.

f Pure solids are often obtained by filtering and washing, and then drying the residue by heating strongly to remove all the water. Explain why the copper could not be heated strongly and how the pure, dry copper could be obtained.

(JMB 1984)

28. a Representing each covalent bond by a single line between two atoms, use diagrams to show the bonding in one molecule of
(i) methane, (ii) ammonia, (iii) water.
Beneath each structure, give the physical state of each compound at room temperature and pressure.

b Account for the ionic bonding between sodium and chlorine in sodium chloride and for its physical state at room temperature and pressure.

c Give three **general** properties in which simple ionic and covalent compounds differ, and state how they differ in each case.

d Magnesium oxide is an ionic compound. Explain why the melting point of magnesium oxide is much greater than that of sodium chloride.

e Explain why the melting point of diamond is greater than 3000 °C.

(JMB 1984)

29. a Give the *structural* formulae of ethane and ethene and explain how they could be distinguished from each other by a single chemical test.

b i How is ethene prepared on an industrial scale by the process of cracking?

ii State and explain **one** large-scale use of ethene.

c State **one** natural source of methane and explain why methane is an important fuel.

d i Write an equation for the complete oxidation of methane.

ii If 50 cm^3 of methane measured at room temperature and pressure were completely oxidised by air, what volume of air containing 20% by volume of oxygen would be required?

(WJEC 1982)

30. The following symbols and atomic numbers refer to the elements lithium, oxygen and fluorine.

a Give the electronic structure of: (i) $_3Li$; (ii) $_8O$; (iii) $_9F$.

b Fluorine forms

i a crystalline compound with lithium, LiF; and

ii a gaseous compound with oxygen, F_2O.

By means of a diagram or otherwise, show the electronic changes that occur in the formation of these compounds and state the type of bonding involved in each case.

i LiF ii F_2O

c State how you account for the fact that the compound LiF is a solid of high melting point whereas the compound F_2O is a gas.

d Fluorine is the first element in a group known as the halogens, the other elements in the group being chlorine, bromine and iodine.

i State what is the similarity in the electronic structures of these elements.

ii The halogens tend to undergo the general reaction

$$X_2 + 2e \rightleftharpoons 2X^-$$

Name this type of reaction.
State how it could be shown that chlorine undergoes this reaction more easily than bromine.

(WJEC 1983)

31. a Describe the industrial production of sulphuric acid from sulphur or iron pyrites by the Contact Process.

b Give an account of the laboratory preparation of magnesium sulphate crystals ($MgSO_4.7H_2O$) from magnesium.

c How and under what conditions does sulphuric acid react with (i) sodium nitrate, (ii) sulphur, (iii) aqueous ammonia?

(WJEC 1983)

32. Explain the difference between the following pairs of terms giving examples with formulae or equations where appropriate:
 a exothermic reaction and endothermic reaction;
 b electrolyte and non-electrolyte;
 c normal salt and acid salt;
 d oxidising agent and reducing agent;
 e basic oxide and acidic oxide.

(WJEC 1983)

33. Use your Periodic Table, when necessary, to help you with this question.
 a Write chemical symbols of
  i a metal
  ii a non-metal
 from the third period of the Periodic Table.
 b Write chemical symbols of
  i a metal
  ii a non metal
 from Group IV of the Periodic Table.
 c i Give electronic structures for magnesium and oxygen.
  ii Show diagrammatically the electronic structure of magnesium oxide.
 d i How many electrons has the rubidium atom? (Atomic number of rubidium = 37)
  ii How many of these electrons are in the outermost shell?
  iii How many neutrons are there in the isotope of rubidium with mass number 85?
  iv There is another fairly common isotope of rubidium. Would you expect its mass number to be greater or less than 85? Give a reason for your answer.
 e Describe the crystal structure of caesium chloride. You may use a diagram to assist you in your description if you wish.

(NI 1983)

34. Study a copy of the Periodic Table and answer the following questions:
 a Explain, giving one example in each case, what you understand by
  i a group,
  ii a period,
  iii a transition metal.
 b What determines the position of an element in the Periodic Table?
 c Note the position of indium, atomic number 49, in the Table.
  i Would you expect indium to be a metal or a non-metal?
  ii Give the formula of the compound formed between indium and chlorine.
  iii Give the formula of the compound formed between indium and oxygen.
  iv Would you expect the oxide in (iii) to be acidic, basic or amphoteric?
 d Construct a table listing four differences in the properties of the metals as compared with the non-metals. Indicate which one of the four properties you consider to be the most reliable in classifying an element as a metal or a non-metal.

(CAMB NOV. 1982)

35.

highly flammable — A; oxidising — B; corrosive — C

Which one of the labels, A, B or C, would you expect to find on bottles of the following chemicals? If no warning label is required write 'none'.
 i ethanol,
 ii concentrated hydrochloric acid,
 iii sodium hydroxide pellets,
 iv sodium chloride crystals,
 v potassium manganate(VII) crystals,
 vi sugar (sucrose).

(CAMB 1983)

36. Silica (SiO_2) is a white solid and has a structure similar to that of diamond. Sand is an impure form of silica. Silicon can be obtained from silica by reduction with carbon; the other product of the reaction is

carbon monoxide. Silicon does not react with hydrochloric acid.

a Draw a diagram to show the structure of diamond.

b The similarity of structure between silica and diamond leads to similar physical properties. Illustrate this statement by reference to two properties.

c Sand often contains small amounts of metal oxides. When a sample of sand is treated with hydrochloric acid and the mixture filtered, the filtrate gives a brown precipitate with aqueous sodium hydroxide. Name the metal oxide present in this sample.

d In the manufacture of iron in the blast furnace, how is silica removed from the iron ore?

e Construct the equation for the formation of silicon from silica and carbon.

f Explain why iron from the blast furnace always contains silicon.

g 0.500 g of an alloy of iron, carbon and silicon (silicon steel) when reacted with an excess of hydrochloric acid gave 192 cm^3 of hydrogen at room temperature and pressure. Calculate the percentage of iron in silicon steel.

h Comment on the following statement found in an old chemistry text-book. "Silicon and its compounds are of little economic importance."

(CAMB 1983)

37. The following list consists of raw materials that are used in industrial processes.

air	iron ore
bauxite	limestone
coke	water
cryolite	

Using only the raw materials from this list, name four important substances that could be obtained by four different processes. In each case give the name or names of all the essential raw materials and give **one** use for each substance.

Each raw material may be used once, more than once or not at all.

(CAMB 1982)

38. One of the hydrocarbons in petrol has the molecular formula C_8H_{18}. When petrol is burned in a motor car engine the exhaust fumes contain approximately 9% carbon dioxide, 5% carbon monoxide, 4% oxygen, 2% hydrogen, 0.2% hydrocarbons and 0.2% oxides of nitrogen.

a What is meant by the term "hydrocarbon"?

b The gases listed above make up 20.4% of the composition of the exhaust fumes. What gas makes up the greater percentage of the remaining gases?

c Suggest a reason for the presence of (i) carbon dioxide, (ii) carbon monoxide, (iii) oxides of nitrogen, in the exhaust fumes.

d Butene and butane can be formed by a process known as cracking, whereby a larger hydrocarbon molecule is broken down by high temperature,

e.g. $C_8H_{18}(g) \rightarrow C_4H_8(g) + C_4H_{10}(g)$.

i Is C_8H_{18} an alkane or an alkene? Explain your answer. Give one chemical test by which you could distinguish between an alkene and an alkane.

ii Write an equation to show how hydrogen could be formed from C_4H_{10} by cracking.

e Give **two** reasons why car exhaust pipes tend to rust more quickly than the bodywork although both are made of steel.

f Assuming that air contains one-fifth of oxygen by volume, calculate the minimum volume of air at room temperature and pressure needed for the complete combustion of 57 g of the hydrocarbon of molecular formula C_8H_{18}.

(CAMB 1982)

39. The following table summarises the reaction between 0.004 moles of various metals and 50 cm^3 (an excess) of dilute hydrochloric acid at room temperature and pressure. Use this information to answer the questions (a) to (e).

a Place these five metals in order of reactivity putting the most reactive metal first.

b Explain the observation in experiment **B** (ii).

Experiment	*Metal added*	*Rise in temperature/°C*	*Total volume of hydrogen given off/cm³*	*Observations*
A	Aluminium powder	15	144	Reaction very slow at first. Sudden rise and violent reaction after 20 minutes
B *i*	Copper turnings	0	0	No reaction
ii	Copper powder	1	0	Dark powder, changes to a pink powder. Solution goes very pale blue.
C	Iron filings	5	96	Slow reaction at first, then fairly rapid
D	Chromium powder	6	144	Fairly rapid reaction
E	Zinc powder	9	96	Moderately rapid reaction

c Draw a diagram of the apparatus you would use to obtain the two numerical results quoted in experiment **E**.

d What is the charge on the chromium ion formed in experiment **D**? Give reasons for your answer.

e Chromium is added to steel to make it rust-proof; state two other methods of preventing rusting.

(CAMB 1982)

40. Use the following information to answer the questions below about the elements **A, B, C, D** and **E**.

element	*atomic number*	*mass number*	*electronic structure*
A	3	7	2, 1
B	18	40	2, 8, 8
C	8	16	2, 6
D	12	24	2, 8, 2
E	19	39	2, 8, 8, 1

a Which element has 22 neutrons in each atom?

b Is the bonding between **C** and **E** ionic or covalent?

c Which element is a noble gas?

d Which two elements form ions with the same electronic structure as neon?

e Which two elements are in the same Group of the Periodic Table?

(CAMB 1984)

41. Suggest explanations for the following observations, and write equations for the reactions described.

a i When manganese(IV) oxide is added to aqueous hydrogen peroxide, a colourless gas is given off. The gas relights a glowing splint. The mass of manganese(IV) oxide remains unchanged throughout the experiment.

ii When manganese(IV) oxide is heated with concentrated hydrochloric acid, a green gas is given off. The gas bleaches damp litmus paper. The manganese(IV) oxide reacts forming manganese(II) chloride.

b i When dilute sulphuric acid is exactly neutralised by aqueous sodium hydroxide the resulting mixture is a very good conductor of electricity.

ii When dilute sulphuric acid is exactly neutralised by aqueous barium hydroxide the resulting mixture is a very poor conductor of electricity.

c i When iron is added to aqueous copper(II) sulphate, the colour of the solution changes from blue to pale green and a pink precipitate is formed.

ii When iron is added to aqueous iron(III) chloride, the colour of the solution changes from yellow to pale green, but no precipitate is formed.

(CAMB 1984)

42. Explain **each** of the following observations.

a Magnesium metal will conduct an electric current both as a solid and when it is molten but compounds of magnesium will conduct when molten but not as solids. The current causes no change in the metal but brings about decomposition of the compounds.

b i When iron reacts with dilute sulphuric acid, a pale green solution is formed and a colourless gas is evolved. (Write an equation for this reaction.)

ii When this green solution is warmed with dilute nitric acid the colour changes to yellow and a brown gas is evolved.

c i When aqueous silver nitrate is added to hydrochloric acid a white precipitate forms. (Write an equation for this reaction.)

ii On exposure to light the white precipitate darkens.

(CAMB NOV. 1984)

43. Nickel (Ni) is a transition metal which is placed between zinc and copper in the metal reactivity (electrochemical) series. Nickel reacts with dilute hydrochloric acid to form a green solution of nickel(II) chloride. Addition of aqueous sodium hydroxide to the green solution gives a precipitate which is not soluble in an excess of sodium hydroxide.

a You are provided with samples of the three metals copper, nickel and zinc and with solutions of their sulphates. Using only these materials, describe the experiments you would carry out to confirm the statement that nickel lies between zinc and copper in the reactivity series.

b With the aid of a diagram showing the complete electrical circuit, explain how you would electroplate a copper ring with nickel.

c Write the equations, including the state symbols, for the reactions between nickel and hydrochloric acid and between nickel(II) chloride and sodium hydroxide. State clearly what you would expect to observe during each of these reactions.

(CAMB NOV. 1984)

44. The table below summarises some of the properties of Group II elements (the Alkaline Earth Metals). The Periodic Table is shown in Appendix IV.

a Name the one other member (X) of the family of Alkaline Earth Metals.

b Arrange the four metals in bold type in order of reactivity, putting the most reactive first.

c Predict what would be observed when Beryllium is added to cold water.

d What precaution needs to be taken for the storage of Barium?

e When Barium is heated in dry chlorine gas it reacts to form a white solid. Name and give the formula for the compound formed.

f Magnesium can be made to react with steam in the apparatus shown. During the reaction magnesium oxide and hydrogen are produced.

i What is produced in the flask?

ii What is the purpose of Tube A.

iii Why must the delivery tube be removed from beneath the water in the dish **before** the heat is removed?

iv Describe how you would show the gas collected is hydrogen.

g In a similar experiment with Beryllium it was found that 0.9 g Beryllium, when

Element	*Symbol*	*Addition of metal to water*	*Formula of compound with chlorine*
Beryllium	Be		$BeCl_2$
Magnesium	Mg	Reacts slowly with water but vigorously with steam	$MgCl_2$
X		Reacts briskly with cold water	
Strontium	Sr	Reacts vigorously with cold water	$SrCl_2$
Barium	Ba	Reacts very vigorously with cold water	

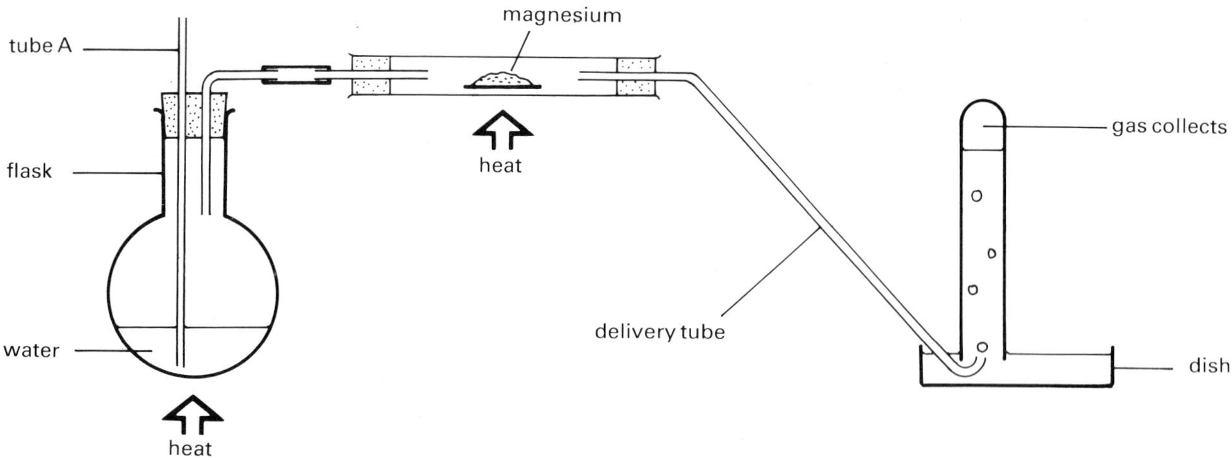

completely reacted, produced 2.5 g Beryllium oxide [Be = 9, O = 16].

i How many moles of Beryllium atoms are present in 0.9 g Beryllium?

ii What mass of oxygen combined with 0.9 g Beryllium?

iii How many moles of oxygen atoms combined with 0.9 g Beryllium?

iv What is the formula of Beryllium oxide from these results?

(SREB 1982)

45. The table below gives some properties of the elements R, S, T, W, X, Y, Z (these are not their chemical symbols). Use the table and your data sheet to answer these questions. Each element may be used once, more than once or not at all.

a From the list select an element which

i is a gas at room temperature

ii could be calcium

iii is a transition metal

iv is in Group 0 of the Periodic Table of Elements

v has a covalent chloride

vi probably has an atomic number of 6

vii forms ions with a charge of + 1

b Select an element with an oxide which will react with

i sodium hydroxide solution to form a salt

ii dilute sulphuric acid to form a salt

c Which two elements could be in the same group of the Periodic Table?

(SREB 1983)

Element	*Melting point °C*	*Boiling point °C*	*Oxide of element*		*Chloride of element appearance*
			Appearance	*Effect of water*	
R	3550	4200	colourless gas	slightly soluble pH 5.5	colourless liquid
S	29	690	white solid	soluble pH 14	white solid
T	1535	3000	red solid	insoluble	yellow solid
W	–189	–186	none	—	none
X	120	445	colourless gas	very soluble pH 2	yellow oily liquid
Y	845	1490	white solid	slightly soluble pH 11	white solid
Z	217	685	white solid	soluble pH 2	red oily liquid

46. This question concerns some elements in the periodic table. They are shown by a letter which is NOT their chemical symbol.

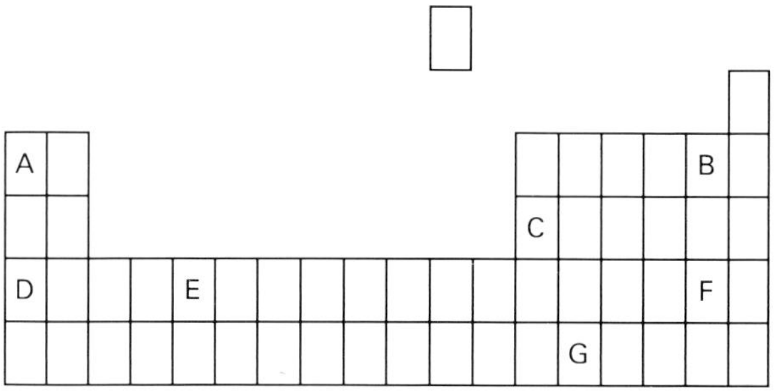

a i Which of the elements shown in the table is the most reactive non-metal?
ii Give the letter of one element which will have an alkaline oxide.
iii Give the letter of one element which will have coloured compounds.
iv On the periodic table shade a group which contains both metals and non-metals.
v Which element will be a gas at room temperature and pressure?
vi Give the letter of an element which will conduct electricity.

b Elements B and C have atoms with relatively similar masses (19 and 27) but their densities are very different. What is responsible for the difference in densities?

c Many elements are radioactive. One of these is the element with atomic number 91. One of its radioactive isotopes has an atomic mass of 234.
From this data, give the structure of an atom of this isotope.
i Protons = __________
Neutrons = __________
Electrons = __________
ii Which two particles will you find together and where will you find them?

If the activity of a sample of this element is studied in a liquid-counting Geiger–Muller tube, the following results may be obtained.

Count rate ($sec.^{-1}$)	*Time from start of experiment (secs)*
40	0
32	15
25	30
18	60
13	90
10	120

d Plot the results on graph paper.
e What is the half life of this isotope?
f Briefly describe one way in which a radioactive substance may be used.

(TWYLREB 1981)

47. a Iron is manufactured by reducing iron ore in a blast furnace. Explain, with the help of equations, how
i the energy for this process is produced,
ii the ore is reduced,
iii a slag is formed and removed.
b State two differences in composition between pig iron and steel.
c Explain how the fitting of blocks of magnesium to underground steel pipes prevents corrosion of the pipes.
d Name a metal used in a different way to magnesium in the prevention of rusting and explain how it works on an article of your choice.

(JMB 1984)

48. a Give an account of the manufacture of ammonia by the Haber process.
b Outline the reactions by means of which nitric acid is manufactured from ammonia.
c Describe an experiment to show that nitric acid can act as an oxidising agent.
d Ammonium nitrate (NH_4NO_3) and urea (NH_2CONH_2) are both important fertilizers containing nitrogen. Calculate which of these would give the most nitrogen in a 100 g of each compound.

$[A_r(H) = 1; A_r(C) = 12; A_r(N) = 14; A_r(O) = 16.]$

(WJEC 1981)

49. a Explain briefly, giving examples, how the method used for the extraction of a metal from its ore is related to its position in the electrochemical series.

b Describe the industrial preparation of aluminium from purified aluminium oxide.

c Explain the following:

i When aqueous sodium hydroxide is added slowly to aqueous aluminium sulphate whilst stirring, a gelatinous precipitate is formed which disappears when the sodium hydroxide is in excess.

ii When aluminium (from which the surface oxide layer has been removed) is added to aqueous copper(II) sulphate, the blue solution turns colourless and a brown deposit appears.

(WJEC 1982)

50. The table below shows the atomic numbers and mass numbers of atoms labelled A to F.

Element	*Atomic number*	*Mass number*
A	2	4
B	4	9
C	6	12
D	6	14
E	7	14
F	8	18

a How many protons are there in an atom of F?

b How many neutrons are there in an atom of D?

c Which atom has six electrons in its outer energy level?

d Select an element which is in Group IV of the Periodic Table.

e Which element is a noble gas?

f Which atoms are isotopes of the same element?

(AEB 1982)

Appendix I
Electron arrangements of the first 20 elements in the periodic table

			H 1				
							He 2
Li 2.1	Be 2.2	B 2.3	C 2.4	N 2.5	O 2.6	F 2.7	Ne 2.8
Na 2.8.1	Mg 2.8.2	Al 2.8.3	Si 2.8.4	P 2.8.5	S 2.8.6	Cl 2.8.7	Ar 2.8.8
K 2.8.8.1	Ca 2.8.8.2						

Appendix II
Alphabetical list of the elements

Name	*Symbol for one atom*	*Z* *Atomic number*	A_r *Relative atomic mass*
actinium	Ac	89	227
aluminium	Al	13	27
antimony	Sb	51	122
argon	Ar	18	40
arsenic	As	33	75
astatine	At	85	210
barium	Ba	56	137
beryllium	Be	4	9
bismuth	Bi	83	209
boron	B	5	11
bromine	Br	35	80
cadmium	Cd	48	112
caesium	Cs	55	133
calcium	Ca	20	40
carbon	C	6	12
cerium	Ce	58	140
chlorine	Cl	17	35
chromium	Cr	24	52
cobalt	Co	27	59
copper	Cu	29	64
dysprosium	Dy	66	163
erbium	Er	68	167
europium	Eu	63	152
fluorine	F	9	19
francium	Fr	87	223
gadolinium	Gd	64	157
gallium	Ga	31	70
germanium	Ge	32	73
gold	Au	79	197
hafnium	Hf	72	178
helium	He	2	4
holmium	Ho	67	165
hydrogen	H	1	1
indium	In	49	115
iodine	I	53	127
iridium	Ir	77	192
iron	Fe	26	56
krypton	Kr	36	84
lanthanum	La	57	139
lead	Pb	82	207
lithium	Li	3	7
lutetium	Lu	71	175
magnesium	Mg	12	24
manganese	Mn	25	55
mercury	Hg	80	201
molybdenum	Mo	42	96
neodymium	Nd	60	144

Name	*Symbol for one atom*	*Z* *Atomic number*	A_r *Relative atomic mass*
neon	Ne	10	20
nickel	Ni	28	59
niobium	Nb	41	93
nitrogen	N	7	14
osmium	Os	76	190
oxygen	O	8	16
palladium	Pd	46	106
phosphorus	P	15	31
platinum	Pt	78	195
polonium	Po	84	210
potassium	K	19	39
praseodymium	Pr	59	141
protactinium	Pa	91	231
radium	Ra	88	226
radon	Rn	86	222
rhenium	Re	75	186
rhodium	Rh	45	103
rubidium	Rb	37	85
ruthenium	Ru	44	101
samarium	Sm	62	150
scandium	Sc	21	45
selenium	Se	34	79
silicon	Si	14	28
silver	Ag	47	108
sodium	Na	11	23
strontium	Sr	38	88
sulphur	S	16	32
tantalum	Ta	73	181
tellurium	Te	52	128
terbium	Tb	65	159
thallium	Tl	81	204
thorium	Th	90	232
thulium	Tm	69	169
tin	Sn	50	119
titanium	Ti	22	48
tungsten	W	74	184
uranium	U	92	238
vanadium	V	23	51
xenon	Xe	54	131
ytterbium	Yb	70	173
yttrium	Y	39	89
zinc	Zn	30	65
zirconium	Zr	40	91

Two of the 92 elements are not found naturally in the Earth: promethium (Pm, $Z = 61$) and technetium (Tc, $Z = 43$).

Appendix III
Tests for anions and cations

Tests for the anions $Cl^-(aq)$, $SO_4^{2-}(aq)$ and $NO_3^-(aq)$

Chloride ion: The solution containing the suspected $Cl^-(aq)$ is acidified with dilute nitric acid. Silver nitrate solution is then added to the mixture. The following precipitation reaction takes place if $Cl^-(aq)$ is present:

$$Ag^+(aq) + Cl^-(aq) \rightarrow AgCl(s)$$

The precipitate is *white* at first but darkens on standing, especially in strong sunlight.

Sulphate ion: The solution containing the suspected $SO_4^{2-}(aq)$ is acidified with dilute hydrochloric acid. Barium chloride (or barium nitrate) solution is then added to the mixture. The following precipitation reaction takes place if $SO_4^{2-}(aq)$ is present:

$$Ba^{2+}(aq) + SO_4^{2-}(aq) \rightarrow BaSO_4(s)$$

The precipitate is *white*.

Nitrate ion: The solution containing the suspected $NO_3^-(aq)$ is made alkaline with dilute sodium hydroxide solution. Powdered Devarda's Alloy (a powdered mixture of Cu, Al and Zn) is added and the mixture is warmed. The following change takes place if $NO_3^-(aq)$ is present:

$$NO_3^-(aq) \rightarrow NH_3(g)$$

The ammonia gas that is evolved from the solution can be identified by its smell and its effect on moist litmus paper.

Tests for cations

(i) Addition of NaOH(aq)

(a) **Ammonium salt solutions** release ammonia gas on warming with NaOH(aq):

$$NH_4^+(aq) + OH^-(aq) \rightarrow NH_3(g) + H_2O(l)$$

(The ammonia is easily recognized by its smell and alkaline properties.)

(b) **Most other salt solutions** give precipitates of insoluble hydroxides on mixing with NaOH(aq), for example:

$$Cu^{2+}(aq) + 2OH^-(aq) \rightarrow Cu(OH)_2(s)$$

Exceptions include solutions of salts of alkali metals, barium and ammonium. Their hydroxides are soluble and no precipitation occurs.

The precipitates can be distinguished by their colour and by the effect of excess NaOH(aq). Amphoteric hydroxides dissolve in excess alkali:

Cation in solution	*Action of NaOH(aq)*	
	A few drops	*Excess*
$Mg^{2+}(aq)$	white precipitate of $Mg(OH)_2(s)$	no effect
$Ca^{2+}(aq)$	white precipitate of $Ca(OH)_2(s)$*	no effect
$Zn^{2+}(aq)$	white precipitate of $Zn(OH)_2(s)$	precipitate dissolves
$Pb^{2+}(aq)$	white precipitate of $Pb(OH)_2(s)$	precipitate dissolves
$Al^{3+}(aq)$	white precipitate of $Al(OH)_3(s)$	precipitate dissolves
$Fe^{3+}(aq)$	brown precipitate of $Fe(OH)_3(s)$	no effect
$Fe^{2+}(aq)$	green precipitate of $Fe(OH)_2(s)$	no effect
$Cu^{2+}(aq)$	blue precipitate of $Cu(OH)_2(s)$	no effect

*$Ca(OH)_2(s)$ is sparingly soluble.

(ii) Flame tests

Several metals produce colours in flames. The colour can be produced by putting a compound of the metal into a non-luminous bunsen burner flame. The colour for a particular metal is always the same whatever compound of the metal is chosen.

The usual method is as follows:

1. Mix some of the compound with a little concentrated hydrochloric acid. (Take care!)
2. Use a *clean* stainless alloy (e.g. 'nichrome') wire to pick up some of the mixture.
3. Hold the wire to the edge of a non-luminous (blue) bunsen burner flame.

Metal in compound	*Flame colour*
Li	bright red
Na	yellow-orange
K	pale purplish pink
Ca	orange-red
Ba	yellowish green
Cu	green (bluish)
Pb	white-grey

Appendix IV
Periodic table of the elements

						$_{1}$H											$_{2}$He
$_{3}$Li	$_{4}$Be											$_{5}$B	$_{6}$C	$_{7}$N	$_{8}$O	$_{9}$F	$_{10}$Ne
$_{11}$Na	$_{12}$Mg											$_{13}$Al	$_{14}$Si	$_{15}$P	$_{16}$S	$_{17}$Cl	$_{18}$Ar
$_{19}$K	$_{20}$Ca	$_{21}$Sc	$_{22}$Ti	$_{23}$V	$_{24}$ Ch	$_{25}$Mn	$_{26}$Fe	$_{27}$Co	$_{28}$Ni	$_{29}$Cu	$_{30}$Zn	$_{31}$Ga	$_{32}$Ge	$_{33}$As	$_{34}$Se	$_{35}$Br	$_{36}$Kr
$_{37}$Rb	$_{38}$Sr	$_{39}$Y	$_{40}$Zr	$_{41}$Nb	$_{42}$Mo	$_{43}$Tc	$_{44}$Ru	$_{45}$Rh	$_{46}$Pd	$_{47}$Ag	$_{48}$Cd	$_{49}$In	$_{50}$Sn	$_{51}$Sb	$_{52}$Te	$_{53}$I	$_{54}$Xe
$_{55}$Cs	$_{56}$Ba	$_{57}$La	$_{72}$Hf	$_{73}$Ta	$_{74}$W	$_{75}$Re	$_{76}$Os	$_{77}$Ir	$_{78}$Pt	$_{79}$Au	$_{80}$Hg	$_{81}$Tl	$_{82}$Pb	$_{83}$Bi	$_{84}$Po	$_{85}$At	$_{86}$Rn
$_{87}$Fr	$_{88}$Ra	$_{89}$Ac															

$_{58}$Ce	$_{59}$Pr	$_{60}$Nd	$_{61}$Pm	$_{62}$Sm	$_{63}$Eu	$_{64}$Gd	$_{65}$Tb	$_{66}$Dy	$_{67}$Ho	$_{68}$Er	$_{69}$Tm	$_{70}$Yb	$_{71}$Lu
$_{90}$Th	$_{91}$Pa	$_{92}$U											

Note: Man-made elements after uranium not included

Index

Note: numbers in **bold face** type refer to complete chapters: those in *italic* refer to illustrations.